Marriage and the Family
in the Middle Ages

Marriage and the Family in the Middle Ages

Frances and Joseph Gies

HARPER PERENNIAL

NEW YORK • LONDON • TORONTO • SYDNEY • NEW DELHI • AUCKLAND

HARPER ● PERENNIAL

Copyright acknowledgments follow the index.

A hardcover edition of this book was published in 1987 by Harper & Row, Publishers.

P.S.™ is a trademark of HarperCollins Publishers.

FIRST PERENNIAL LIBRARY EDITION PUBLISHED 1989.
SECOND HARPER PERENNIAL EDITION PUBLISHED 2019.

The Library of Congress has catalogued the hardcover edition as follows:

Gies, Frances.
    Marriage and the family in the middle ages

    1. Marriage—History. 2. Family—History. 3. Social history—Medieval, 500-1500. I. Gies, Joseph.
II. Title.
HQ513.G53   1989 306'.8'91'09   87-45048
ISBN 0-06-091468-8

ISBN 978-0-06-296681-0 (pbk.)

19 20 21 22 23 LSC 10 9 8 7 6 5 4 3 2 1

In memory of Tom

Contents

This book was researched at the Harlan Hatcher Graduate Library of the University of Michigan.

The authors once again owe thanks to Professor David Herlihy of Brown University for reading their manuscript and making valuable suggestions.

I.

Origins

I.

Historians Discover the Family

No element in social history is more pervasive than the family, the universal environment where human beings learn to eat, walk, and speak, and acquire their sense of identity and modes of behavior. Every culture that we know of, past or present, has included the institution of the family, a necessity for survival and common denominator of the society.

The family today, changing even as we write, is the product of human history, its evolutions and revolutions. Some of the events that have made their mark on the family have been relatively swift and dramatic, such as the Industrial Revolution, whose effects have been repeatedly catalogued and analyzed. Others have been slow and obscure, like the massive changes that occurred during the thousand years of the Middle Ages. These have received less attention, yet in sum they transformed the family in significant and enduring ways.

In investigating the history of the family, a problem is encountered at the outset: the ambiguity of the very term "family." In modern usage, the word has three meanings: a lineage or line of descent; a given person's living biological relations, including parents, siblings, grandparents, aunts, uncles, and cousins, whether co-resident or not; and finally, most commonly, a parent or parents and children living together—the nuclear, conjugal, or simple family, constituting a household. We habitually identify the conjugal family with the household because in modern society they typically coincide, but the two are not necessarily the same. Anthropologists and historians have had difficulty in developing a consistent definition of either to cover the numerous permutations that have flourished.[1] Does the household include all unrelated persons living under the same roof, or all related persons living on the same property but in separate dwellings?

The word "family" in the sense of residential and biological unit is relatively new. Before the eighteenth century no European language had a term for the mother-father-children grouping. The meaning of the Latin cognate, *familia,* from a common Indo-European word signifying "house," persisted from Roman times throughout the Middle Ages into the early modern period: the people who lived in a house, including servants and slaves.[2] Usually the *familia* was large, and sometimes the majority of members were biologically unrelated, as for example, in the *familia* of a king, a great lord, or a bishop. Relationships of consanguinity played an important part in the society of the past, a more important part than they do today, but family boundaries were more blurred. The conjugal unit did not exist in isolation as it does today; therefore it did not need a name.

Neither historians nor anthropologists have ever developed a general term for the family outside the conjugal unit. "Extended family," sometimes incorrectly used, properly refers to a kind of household, that is, to related persons living under the same roof, including brothers, widowed parents, nephews, nieces, or others outside the parent-child relationship. For the broader family group, composed of a variety of relatives not sharing a residence, no general term exists, though anthropology has provided terms for certain specific forms of it. This larger family group, an entity very important in pre-industrial society, might be called the supra-family.

The study of kinship and the family was initiated barely a century ago by a trio of brilliant amateur anthropologists, J. F. McClennan and Sir Henry Maine of England, and Lewis Henry Morgan of the United States. They were followed by sociologists, of whom one of the earliest, Frédéric Le Play of France, an engineer by profession, was also an amateur. In 1871 Le Play published a study of the European family of the recent past that extolled the "stem family," in which three generations lived together, parents, eldest son and his family, and younger unmarried brothers and sisters. Stable, moral, authoritarian, responsible, sacrificing the interests of the individual to the welfare of the larger group, Le Play's idealized "traditional" family contrasted with the small post-industrial family consisting only of parents and children. He characterized the latter as unstable and selfishly individualistic. He found it guilty of substituting impersonal external relationships for intimate kinship feelings, and sexual gratification for self-sacrifice (that is, late marriage or nonmarriage) practiced in the interest of the family.[3] A conservative social reformer, Le Play recommended a return to the old ways for the good of society, morality, and the family. Much of the study of the family in subsequent years has been concerned with correcting Le Play's picture of the pre-industrial family.

Nearly a century after Le Play, Philippe Ariès, another amateur—a French "Sunday historian" *(historien de dimanche)* in his own words—stimulated wide interest among both historians and the lay public by the publication of *Centuries of Childhood,* subtitled *A Social History of Family Life* (1960). Relying on iconographic and literary sources, Ariès presented the thesis that the concept of childhood as a distinct phase of life did not develop until the sixteenth and seventeenth centuries, when the child became the center of the new, close-knit nuclear family. His evaluation of the modern family was not far removed from Le Play's: what the family had gained in privacy and intimacy was outweighed by what it had lost in "sociability" and community feeling. Ariès parted company with Le Play by arguing that the nuclear family enforced conformity and so curbed rather than fostered individualism, and by viewing individualism as a desirable quality.[4]

Ariès's book proved a stimulus to academic historians. It was followed by three influential studies relating to the family. All dealt with the early modern pre-industrial period, two limited to England, the other to Western Europe, but all in some measure echoing Ariès's thesis: Peter Laslett's *The World We Have Lost: England Before the Industrial Age* (1965), Edward Shorter's *The Making of the Modern Family* (1975), and Lawrence Stone's *The Family, Sex, and Marriage in England 1500–1800* (1977). In the early 1970s Laslett's Cambridge Group for the Study of Population and Social Structure published a book, *Household and Family in Past Time,* and a series of articles, announcing the results of a comparative study of the family and household from the sixteenth century to the present.[5] Other studies, providing a variety of national perspectives, continue to appear.[6]

Thus the history of the family is a very new subdiscipline. Within it the early modern period (from 1500 to 1750) first received the lion's share of scholarly attention. Since 1970, however, a number of able medieval historians have engaged in research on the family and related subjects in a variety of specific regions, social classes, and time frames. One general survey covers the entire medieval period: American scholar David Herlihy's *Medieval Households* (1985).[7] A conference in Paris in 1974 entitled "Famille et parenté dans l'Occident médiéval" (Family and Kinship in the Medieval West) published papers by historians from all over Western Europe focusing on the aristocratic family.[8] Georges Duby has written two books on medieval marriage.[9] Several works on medieval women have cast valuable light.[10] Late medieval Italy has been the subject of demographic studies, notably those of David Herlihy and Christiane Klapisch-Zuber[11]; David Nicholas has produced a study of the family in fourteenth-century Ghent[12]; Barbara Hanawalt, a book on the English peasant family in the late Middle Ages.[13] Numerous scholarly articles have dealt with special aspects or areas of the subject. We now know, if far less than we wish to know about the medieval family, far more than we did a generation ago.

A general approach to the subject of marriage and the family in the Middle Ages poses fundamental questions that may be summarized under ten somewhat arbitrary headings. These will supply the basic lines of inquiry for the present book.

First, concept: What was the contemporary perception of the family? How was it viewed and defined? Outside forces such as economic pressures and mortality rates might govern the actual size and shape of the family, but the "ideal" type, expressed in custom and inheritance law, exerted crucial influence on attitudes and relationships, as well as on actions: who married and at what age, who stayed home, who held a position of authority in the family.

Second, function: Sociologists define the function of the modern family as twofold: the "socialization" of the child, and the channeling of the adult's sexual and emotional needs. In the past, however, the family had other very important roles. It functioned as a defense organization, a political unit, a school, a judicial system, a church, and a factory. Over the centuries these functions have been surrendered one by one to the great external institutions of modern society, the State, the Church, and industry.

Third, kind of kinship system: to which the family belongs. In Western society today the larger kinship groups—the ancestral lineage and the network of living relatives—are of limited importance. In the Middle Ages, as in most societies of the past, they loomed large. The kinship vocabulary adapted by historians from anthropology is not yet entirely fixed or entirely satisfactory, but a large descent group that claims a common ancestor is generally called a clan; a smaller descent group in which ancestry can actually be traced, a lineage. The network of an individual's relatives is called a kindred. A clan exists independently of its members and can own land and exert political power. A kindred, in contrast, has no existence as a separate body. It exists and acts only in relation to the individual. Kindred and clan (or lineage) can, and in the Middle Ages often did, co-exist.

Clans or lineages are patrilineal if descent is traced through the male line, matrilineal if through the female. The network of kindred is said to be "ego-centered," since its composition differs for all individuals except siblings. The kindreds existing in a given community form a series of overlapping circles. Kindreds may for certain purposes be defined as bilateral or cognatic if they include relatives on both father's and mother's sides, or as patrilateral (father's side) or matrilateral (mother's side).

In pre-industrial society, the two kinds of kinship groups played important, often determinative roles in the transmission of property, the choice of marriage partners, the protection of the individual and the family, legal disputes, and many other aspects of daily life.

Fourth, size and structure: This is a subject to which historians have devoted a great deal of attention, making attempts to classify principal types. At one time it was assumed that the family had undergone a "progressive nuclearization" from the early Middle Ages to the present, a straight-line evolution from the clan to the extended family to the nuclear family. Recent studies have shown quite a different picture.

Lawrence Stone in 1977 posited three historical family types: the large "open lineage family," which he thought prevailed throughout the Middle Ages; the smaller "restricted patriarchal nuclear family" (sixteenth through eighteenth centuries); and the "closed domesticated nuclear family" of the modern era.[14]

Peter Laslett's Cambridge Group took another tack, dividing households in the early modern era into three categories: simple (nuclear or conjugal); extended (a conjugal unit plus widowed parent, brothers, sisters, nephews, nieces, or cousins); and multiple (two or more related conjugal units). By far the commonest form, at least as far back as the sixteenth century, Laslett found to be the nuclear family. It was the form in which most people were "socialized" as children and which they were thereby led to reproduce as adults; thus Laslett saw the continuing prevalence of the nuclear family household as the result of learned behavior on the part of its members.[15]

Family historian Robert Wheaton rejected Laslett's categorization of household types as too static and quantitative, preferring Frédéric Le Play's hundred-year-old classification of household *systems:* the nuclear system, in which the children left home when they married; the stem system, in which one married child remained at home; and the joint system, in which several married children remained. This classification took into account the developmental cycle of the family, in which family size and structure change as parents age and children grow up and marry.[16]

American sociologist Marion Levy introduced a provocative hypothesis. The prevalence of the conjugal family (married couple, or parents and children) "in all known societies in world history" may be the result not of social psychology, that is, learned behavior, but simply of material factors. The high mortality rate in pre-industrial society made any alternative, larger family structure impossible to achieve. In transitional societies with some improved sanitation, medicine, and general technology, the actual structure of the family may approach the ideal, but it may simultaneously produce economic and psychological stresses that work in the opposite sense. Finally, societies equipped with modern technology that makes the large-family ideal fully realizable have paradoxically abandoned it in favor of the nuclear family, which they have elevated to the ideal type.[17]

Fifth, economic basis of the family: In the pre-industrial world, the family was the principal production unit, in agriculture, manufacture, and commerce. At the pinnacle of ancient, medieval, and early modern society, the wealthy aristocratic landholding family functioned as a managerial unit, and its control and exploitation of property were related to its household structure and inheritance customs. The peasant family assigned its labors according to age and sex and, like the nobles, controlled and passed on its property in established ways. In the towns, families performed the various tasks of the clothmaking trade—spinning, weaving, finishing—, made leather, wood, and metal goods, and manufactured a variety of handicraft products, with husband and wife usually acting as partners.

Sixth, marriage: The process that forms the family has changed in ways that are visible and reasonably well understood. In the developed countries today only two parties are closely concerned in the marriage process: the bride and groom. Parental consent, though desirable, is not required. The Church may or may not play a part. The state licenses the marriage and imposes conditions of property ownership and inheritance. Private arrangements for the disposal of property, such as marriage contracts, are the exception even among the wealthy.

In the past a very different situation obtained. The bridal couple were likely to be the least active elements in the forming of the marriage, with parents and other kin, Church, and community (through local customs and sentiments) all playing roles, often in competition with one another. The importance of the marriage ceremony itself varied with time, property arrangements between the two families commonly taking precedence over the actual rite.

In the past, as in the present, marriage has nearly always been exogamous: individuals have "married out," that is, outside some established degree of relationship. In many societies studied by anthropologists—African, Pacific Island, American Indian—exogamy has actually prescribed the choice of a marriage partner from a certain descent group or a specific category of cousin. In historic

Europe and America, exogamy has been passive, merely stating the relationships within which the individual was forbidden to marry.

Exogamy is commonly confused with the incest taboo, but the two are distinct if overlapping concepts. Exogamy relates strictly to marriage, incest to sex either in or out of marriage. Exogamy prescribes marriage outside one's own group, in contrast to endogamy, which encourages marriage within the group. Incest signifies sex within a forbidden category of relationship—parent, sibling, cousin, in-law, or other. Exogamy and endogamy often have discernible rationales in the need for alliances between families and the orderly distribution of marriage partners within a community. The incest taboo has so far resisted attempts by psychologists, anthropologists, and sociologists to develop a really convincing and generally accepted explanation. (Even if valid, modern rationales based on alleged genetic outcomes would have no application for earlier societies.)[18]

The degrees of kinship within which marriage is permitted have fluctuated erratically in history; so have the ideas of the nature of kinship. Theoretically kinship equates with blood relationship, yet many of its concepts are culturally determined. Some societies do not consider illegitimate children as kin of their parents' families; others do. In some cultures, adoption creates legal, or artificial, kinship. Other kinds of nonblood relationships, spiritual or ritual, such as the tie with godparents or that with sworn members of a brotherhood, may be treated as kinship, creating the same taboos.

Throughout history, marriage has involved transfers of money and property between families and individuals. These transfers fall into three rough categories:

1. "Brideprice" or "bridewealth," money paid by a suitor to the father of the bride to compensate him for surrendering his authority over the bride.
2. Dowry, money or property given to the groom by the bride's family, sometimes consisting of her share of the inheritance.
3. Endowment of the bride by the groom or his family, including payments immediately available to the bride and also her dower, a specified portion of the groom's estate to provide support in widowhood.

The conditions accompanying these transfers have fluctuated, brideprice sometimes being given to the bride rather than to her father, and dowry and dower assuming varying importance in relation to each other. The shifting weight of these "marriage assigns" remains one of the incompletely understood elements of the history of marriage.[19]

Though to modern perceptions the economic concerns that preoccupied parties to a marriage in former times seem discordantly mercenary, to families entirely dependent on land for their livelihood such concerns were inevitable and primary. Modern industrial society provides a multitude of options for young people contemplating marriage, but traditional land-based society did not. Inheritance of land and the contributions of families to marriage were indispensable basics.

Divorce rules also have varied over history. Divorce might be at the initiative of the husband alone, of either husband or wife, or both, or under conditions imposed by Church or State, or marriage might be considered indissoluble under virtually any conditions.

Seventh, relationships within the family: authority, age roles, sentiment or attachment, and sexuality. The egalitarian family, in which husband and wife share authority and in which democracy extends in some degree to the children, is a modern invention. In the past fathers had unquestioned authority, sometimes even the power of life and death. Wealthy families tended to be more authoritarian, poor ones, in which the economic contributions of the wife were indispensable, less so. Age differentials between husband and wife were also significant, husbands who were several years older than their wives tending to enjoy more authority.

The quality of emotional relationships within the historic family, like its structure and size, has created controversy among historians and sociologists. When Philippe Ariès made his challenging assertion that "in medieval society childhood did not exist" he added an immediate qualification: "This is not to suggest that children were neglected, forsaken, or despised." He nevertheless maintained on the basis of limited data from the seventeenth century that infant mortality was a standing bar to strong parental affection: "People could not allow themselves to become too attached to something that was regarded as a probable loss."[20]

Edward Shorter carried Ariès's negative picture of medieval childhood to the point of a blunt declaration that "maternal indifference to infants characterized traditional society." In Shorter's extreme view, "Good mothering is an invention of modernization," and among the lower classes a parental "pattern of indifference" extended well into the nineteenth century.[21] The idea that children were systematically maltreated in the past was given even more lurid expression by psychologist Lloyd DeMause in the introduction to a collection of essays edited by him, *The History of Childhood* (1976): "The history of childhood is a nightmare from which we have only recently begun to awaken. The further back in history one goes, the lower the level of child care, and the more likely children are to be killed, abandoned, beaten, terrorized, and sexually abused."[22] If DeMause is right, it is surprising that the human race has survived.

Surveying the recent flood of literature about childhood, much of it echoing DeMause's dark view, historian Linda Pollock discovered an interesting quirk. Each writer reported that, toward the end of the (usually lengthy) time period he had studied, the situation took a turn for the better. Sometimes the improvement came in the seventeenth century, sometimes in the eighteenth, the nineteenth, or even the twentieth. She then made another, even more telling discovery: whenever a researcher confined himself to a reasonably brief time period and used primary sources, the attitudes toward children that were uncovered proved distinctly different from those pictured by DeMause: children were valued and well treated.[23]

The denial of family sentiment in the past has also been extended to other relationships besides parent–child. Edward Shorter and Lawrence Stone have disputed the existence of affection and love between husband and wife before the onset of the industrial age. This hypothesis too has been attacked by other scholars' work, but manages to retain popularity with part of the lay public.

That the study of the emotions of the past is a difficult and complex matter is evident. American social historians Peter and Carol Stearns, in an article in the *American Historical Review* (1985), proposed a new subdiscipline, "emotionology," pointing out that on the one hand we cannot "assume without proof . . . that people in the past shared our emotional experience," but on the other that "affection in premodern society may not have been as different as vocabulary and child-rearing and courtship behaviors suggest to the modern researcher. . . . Or affection may have been more dispersed . . . but no less real. . . ." The historians' debate of a few decades ago on "past-mindedness" versus "present-mindedness" gains new relevance as late twentieth-century observers try to penetrate the emotional life of nobles, peasants, and craftsmen of distant times.[24]

Sexuality, in all ages an important dimension of family life, is at least as difficult to recover and analyze as parental affection, despite scatterings of data on a number of factors: age at marriage, courtship customs, means of contraception, and attitudes toward masturbation, prostitution, and extramarital sex. Such nineteenth-century thinkers as Freud and Engels believed that the period from the Middle Ages to the present was marked by increasingly effective sexual repression. Edward Shorter, on the other hand, postulates a late eighteenth-century sexual revolution.[25] Jean-Louis Flandrin has traced a more complex history: postponed marriage for young men in the sixteenth century caused tensions which found relief in the towns in prostitution and rape, and in the countryside in formalized premarital sex-play; suppression of these outlets in the seventeenth century, Flandrin believes, led to an "internalization" of sexual feelings.[26]

Eighth, control of family size: In modern times, this has come to be a widely accepted imperative. In the past, limited economic resources often made it necessary for the mass of people, while inheritance problems sometimes suggested it for the wealthy. Late marriage was a means of shortening reproductive years. Abortion has been widely practiced in past centuries, and infanticide was legal in some societies and practiced in most. Contraception has been practiced or attempted by a variety of means. Finally, continence has been adopted or imposed.

Ninth, attitudes toward aging and death: At the other end of the life cycle, the family's response in this regard has varied over the centuries. In some cultures, youth has reigned supreme, in others age has been accorded authority and dignity. The disabilities of age have been dealt with in different ways. Outlooks on death have changed radically, from the "tamed death" of traditional society described by Philippe Ariès in his little book *Western Attitudes Toward Death*—death openly anticipated and prepared for—to the "forbidden death" of modern times, unmentioned and unmentionable.[27]

Tenth, physical environment: Here the family has passed through historic changes: domestic architecture has affected the amount of privacy and comfort, the family's space in its community, and relations with other families. Houses gradually differentiated among living, sleeping, and eating rooms. Dwellings came to provide separate accommodations for parents, children, servants, and animals. Houses of rich and poor, in city as in countryside, sought to integrate work space into living space. How family members interacted was affected by developments in furnishing, heating, and illumination: the bed, the dining table, and other furniture, the fireplace (a notable medieval invention), windows, candles, and oil lamps.

Most research into the historic family has focused naturally on early modern and modern times because of the wealth of documentation available: letters, diaries, and memoirs, biography, fiction, sermons and moral treatises, portraits, illustrations, caricatures; artifacts and domestic architecture; legal documents, court records, and census data.

In contrast, source material for the Middle Ages is far less abundant and also less intelligible. For the early Middle Ages it shrinks to a few chronicles, scraps of hagiography, widely scattered legal and tax records, archeological remains, sculptures in churches, and inscriptions on tombstones. Medieval art is predominantly religious and symbolic, from the stylized though expressive sculpture of the Romanesque period to the more representational art of the Gothic. After the year 1000, written evidence, including record-keeping, slowly multiplies. For the later Middle Ages, particularly in Italy, most of the modern types of sources become available, though in limited volume. One source that is not found until nearly the end of the Middle Ages is the portrait. Philippe Ariès attached significance to the absence of medieval portraits of children; in fact, there were no medieval portraits of anyone, apart from the conventionalized effigies on tombstones. The first portraits, of kings and magnates, begin to appear in the fifteenth century; the family portrait does not emerge until the seventeenth.

With the aid of recent scholarly exploration of available sources, this book will attempt to show the main lines of development of marriage and the family through the thousand years of the Middle Ages (A.D. 500 to 1500), among the aristocracy, the middle class, the peasants and artisans. Beginning with the dual heritage of the Roman and Germanic worlds and the influence of the early Christian Church, we will follow the family through the first five centuries of the Middle Ages, up to the year 1000, when important changes began to take place in its shape and organization, through the high Middle Ages up to the catastrophe of the Black Death, and finally into the fifteenth century and the beginning of the modern era. We will trace changes in the concept of the family, in its role in society, in the composition of the household and its relation to larger kinship groups, in the effects of the Church's perception of marriage, in the authority structure of the family, in the disposition of its property, and in its physical environment. At the same time we will examine family sentiment and attitudes toward sex.

What follows represents a distillation and interpretation of the best and most useful information that medieval scholars in the field of marriage and the family have gathered. Our intention as far as possible is to let the people of the Middle Ages, through the documentary evidence they have left us, speak for themselves.

2.

Roots: Roman, German, Christian

The family of modern times is a historic product of the European Middle Ages, but it had its beginnings in a still earlier period. The final stage of the Roman Empire witnessed a gradual fusion of Roman civilization and Germanic or barbarian society while simultaneously a third element, the Christian religion, imposed its influence. The contributions of other civilizations and religions were relayed almost entirely through these three. From their interaction the early medieval family, and the marriage institution from which it sprang, emerged with certain attributes in law and custom and with a recognized set of roles for its members.

The main outlines of this important early chapter in the history of the family may be discerned from a brief retrospective look at its three elements as they clashed and mingled in the pre-medieval centuries. Commencing as an agrarian republic (after the overthrow of the ancient monarchy), the Roman state spread by conquest first over the Italian peninsula and then throughout the Mediterranean littoral. By the time of Christ it had grown into a multinational military empire, underpinned by a slave labor economy and embracing a sophisticated urban culture, a flourishing long-distance commerce, and an advanced technology in civil engineering. Its spectacular political adventures were accompanied by an accumulation of wealth by the upper class but little change in the daily life of the mass of the population. The conquests provided the wherewithal for the famous free grain distributions that sustained and augmented the idle proletariat of the city of Rome but had little effect on the countryside. Subsistence farming with hand implements, low-yield crops, and a few animals supplied the basis of work and life. Orchards and vineyards supplemented crop farming, in which wheat remained the staple.

The classical period of Rome, the one most commonly thought of as "Roman" in its literature, arts, and customs, was the age of Augustus, politically the "principate" that acted as the hinge between the Republic and the Empire. By coincidence it includes the birth of Christ and so bridges the Western dating system from B.C. to A.D. It was also a period of momentous reform in Roman law and government, including legislation that had far-reaching effects on the European family.

More than two hundred years after Augustus (reigned 27 B.C.–A.D. 14), the Empire he founded began to experience the Great Migrations that over its long twilight brought the Germanic peoples into Western and Southern Europe. Despite the turmoil of the barbarian centuries (not all caused by the barbarians), most of the Germanic peoples settled down in Gaul, Italy, and Spain in a peaceable, side-by-side association with the native inhabitants, melding gradually into new social, cultural, and political combinations.

Aside from meager archeological evidence, our principal sources of information about the barbarians come from before and after the Great Migrations. In the earlier period two Romans, Julius Caesar (c. 100–44 B.C.) and Tacitus (c. A.D. 56–c.120) wrote accounts based on their observations; in the later one, the law codes of the Franks, Burgundians, Lombards, and others sketch a picture of a farmer-warrior society much like that of early Rome.

Coincident with the Great Migrations was the rise of the Christian Church from powerless, persecuted splinter sect to state religion of the Roman Empire. It enjoyed extraordinary success with the barbarians. Where the Roman proletariat came over gradually and the Roman elite tardily and reluctantly, the Germanic invaders of all national persuasions embraced Christianity with innocent enthusiasm, even though some of its doctrine promised serious conflict with barbarian custom, as it did with Roman law.

The Roman Family

Like the Greeks, the Romans gave a name not to the parent-child unit but to the larger group contained in the household (Latin *familia*, Greek *oikos*). A poor household might comprise parents, children, and other relatives such as a brother's widow or a grandmother. A middling household might also include three or four servants, whether free or slave. A wealthy household numbered scores of persons, mostly slaves; a very wealthy one, hundreds. Under the Republic the small farm had predominated, deliberately encouraged by the system of rewarding army veterans with land on which the soldier typically settled with wife and children. Under the Empire, however, large plantations, or latifundia, grew steadily in size and number.

Originally the Roman *familia*, like its counterpart in other civilizations, was the fundamental economic, the fundamental social, the fundamental legal, the fundamental educational, and the fundamental religious unit of society. The economic role comes first, because the family's function as chief producing unit was the basis for all the other roles, which flowed naturally from this one. Property was held jointly by the family. Individual members, blood-related or not, slave or free, owned little property and had few rights as individuals. Crime was punished within the family or settled between families, public law only rarely intervening on occasions when the security of the state was affected or public order threatened.[1]

Religious worship was so strictly centered in home and hearth that a modern writer has described Roman religion as "hardly more than a spiritualization of family life."[2] The "high gods" of the Olympic pantheon were more literary symbols than objects of worship. The function of the temples of Rome was largely restricted to requests for special favors. In contrast, every household had its private altar, whose sacred flame was kept perpetually burning by the vigilant devotion of the women. There the entire household gathered to worship the Lares or Penates, a miniature pantheon of images associated with ancestors, "human souls deified by death."[3] Statues of Lares were used in early days to mark boundaries between properties, and later their shrines were erected at crossroads, much in the fashion of the roadside calvaries of latter-day Europe. When Augustus was deified by the Senate, his apotheosis was signaled by the addition of his image to the Lares of all Roman households.

Though of paramount importance, the *familia* was not the sole kinship unit. The ancestors who figured so prominently in religious observance were those not only of the household but of the *gens,* or clan, the large kinship group described as consisting of all the persons descended from a founding ancestor, real or mythical.[4] The distinctive Roman system of nomenclature was based on it. Caius Julius Caesar belonged to the *gens* Julius, his father's name was Caesar, and his own individual name *(praenomen)* was Caius. Women were given the clan name as their own: Caesar's sister was named Julia, and a younger sister would have been called Julia Minor.[5]

Families belonging to the *gens* were divided into two classes, the patricians, or true members, and the clients, who formed an auxiliary underclass.[6] In structure every Roman family was autocratic. The head of the household, whether father, grandfather, uncle, or slaveowner in relation to its other members, under the title of *paterfamilias* occupied the position of petty absolute monarch. The word *pater,* in fact, like the word *mater,* had in its origins no biological significance, but simply described the person in command, the head of the household. His authority, designated the *patria potestas,* extended to life-and-death decisions. A new recruit to the household, whether a newborn infant, a bride, or a new servant or slave, had to gain the formal acceptance of the *paterfamilias.*[7] The newborn was laid before him; if he picked it up it was admitted into the family and given a name; if not, it was "exposed," that is, abandoned with the chance that it might be rescued. In a society never far beyond subsistence, a new mouth to feed might represent a threat to family survival. Romulus himself, legendary founder of Rome, had been exposed with his twin brother Remus and only rescued by a she-wolf.

The *paterfamilias* also presided over religious observances, meted out justice, and directed the family work. On his death the land belonging to the *familia* was divided, an equal share going to each adult male, providing the basis for establishment of new households. This system of partible inheritance was made possible by two factors, the availability of land and the high rate of mortality that kept the number of heirs low. New households formed from an old one continued membership in the same *gens*.[8]

Throughout the early Republic the *paterfamilias* exercised his unchallenged authority, but as time passed the steadily growing power of the Roman state began to impinge on it. A significant change in family relationships came about through the wars that formed so conspicuous a feature of the national history. A soldier's booty had always been treated as the legal property of his *familia*, controlled by his *paterfamilias*, but as conquests extended and booty grew richer, dissatisfaction inevitably also grew until the government intervened. Henceforth the veteran soldier retained his plunder, which he might use to equip his own estate. For the first time, individual property rights were recognized as opposed to family or clan property rights.[9]

The wars also brought a degree of de facto liberation to Roman women by freeing them from the surveillance of absent male relatives and awarding them masculine responsibilities such as running the farm or estate. By the time of Augustus, Greek observers were struck by the freedom of upper-class Roman women; where the ladies of Athens remained secluded at home while their husbands socialized, those of Rome accompanied the men to dinner parties, creating a small but noteworthy revolution, the world's first elegant mixed society.[10]

The increasingly spacious dwellings of the Roman upper class added another element to social life, hitherto at least rare: a degree of privacy. The richest Romans built themselves masonry villas, often in both town and country. Cicero (106–43 B.C.) was reputed to own eight villas besides smaller houses along main roads for convenience in travel. Among the common people, change was less discernible. In the countryside, parents, children, relations, servants, and slaves crowded together in a house that ranged from a hovel shared with animals to a timber farmhouse with outbuildings. In the city the family of a craftsman or petty merchant occupied an apartment that doubled as shop—bakery, fish market, tannery—in which the whole family turned a hand.[11]

From a modern perspective, the distinctive feature of Roman marriage was its private, familial character. In the time of Augustus nearly all Romans married without benefit of clergy, and at no time was an official of the state involved. Nevertheless, Roman marriage had both a strongly religious and a strongly legal significance. The principal element in early Roman marriage, the bride purchase *(coemptio)*, by historic times had diminished to a token payment. Simultaneously there appeared the dowry *(dos)*, a payment in the opposite sense, a contribution from the bride's family, seeming to imply a shift in the marriage market from demand for brides to demand for husbands. The dowry differs from the bride purchase in another way. Where the purchase price went to the bride's family or kinsmen, the dowry went to the bridegroom, to help support the marriage.[12]

Bride purchase signified the transfer of legal authority over the bride from her father or guardian to her husband, a woman not being recognized as a legal personage and so constrained to living her life under the power *(manus,* "hand") of a man—father, brother, guardian, or husband. Despite the subordinate position of the bride, Roman marriage custom was in advance of many of its contemporaries in requiring the consent of both principals as a condition of valid marriage, a rule expressed in the legal formula *Nuptias consensus non concubitus facit* (consent, not intercourse, makes marriage). And in the third century B.C. a new form of marriage was introduced that wrought a decisive change in favor of women. Known as marriage *sine manu* (without power transferred), the new form permitted the bride to retain membership in her father's *familia* despite moving into the home of her husband. By so doing she kept her inheritance rights as a daughter, assuring a considerable degree of independence from her husband. The husband in the marriage *sine manu* received only the bride's dowry, and even that conditionally. Under the Empire, marriage *sine manu* became overwhelmingly the more popular form. By the time of Hadrian (reigned A.D. 117–138), says a modern historian, a father "dreamed neither of forcing a daughter's marriage nor opposing her determined choice."[13]

In the marriages of wealthy Romans, sustaining the "burden of matrimony" was perceived as requiring the assignment of an appropriate amount of income-producing property to the young couple. Under the Republic and early Empire, the bride's dowry remained the most important instrument for this intergenerational

A Roman wedding: detail of relief on a Roman sarcophagus, Palazzo Ducale, Mantua. (Alinari)

transfer of wealth, but under the mature Empire the pendulum swung. The custom of a substantial marriage gift *(donatio)* from the groom's family to the bride was introduced and by the third century A.D. came to exceed the dowry. By mid-fifth century the *donatio,* pledged and delivered before the marriage ceremony could take place, had grown so large as to constitute an obstacle to marriage for many young men, who as a result tended to delay marriage plans, whereas young women (and their families) sought to arrange as early a match as possible.[14]

Most forms of interclass marriage were forbidden or hindered by legal obstacle or social disapprobation. Even when sanctioned, such a *matrimonium non justum* was long handicapped by assignment to the children of the status of the lower-ranking parent.[15] Nevertheless, interclass marriage persisted, as indicated by repeated legislation. Slave marriage was not recognized by law, which did not prevent slaves from marrying and treating their marriages as serious.

Even stronger than the bar to interclass marriage was the proscription against incest or marrying "in." Early Rome forbade marriage between second cousins, but over time the rule was relaxed, and even first cousins were allowed to marry. When the Emperor Claudius (reigned A.D. 41–54) chose for his fourth wife his niece Agrippina, the public was shocked, but the Senate obligingly revised the legal definition of incest, and (according to

Suetonius) at least two other uncle-niece marriages were re-corded.[16] This was an exceptional case, but in revealing the flexible nature of exogamy rules it foreshadowed much medieval controversy.

Betrothal and wedding, private in the sense of not involving officialdom, were public in the sense of overt. It was important for the community at large to be informed. Besides the exchange of pledges *(dos* and *donatio)* the betrothal ceremony involved the exchange of promises between groom-to-be and father of the bride-to-be: "Do you promise to give your daughter to me to be my wedded wife?" "The gods bring luck! I betroth her." The couple kissed and the young man placed an iron ring on the third finger of his fiancée's left hand.[17] A Roman conviction that a vein ran from this finger straight to the heart was passed on by Macrobius (c. A.D. 400) to the Middle Ages, whose bridal couples transmitted the tradition of ring and ring finger to modern times. The wedding ceremony a few days later was also marked by long-lasting symbols: white bridal gown and veil, a best man *(auspex)* who pronounced a legal formula, a shower from the wedding guests not of rice but of walnuts, a wedding feast, and carriage of the bride over the threshold of the bridal chamber.[18]

Once it had achieved its *sine manu* state, Roman marriage changed little over a period of centuries. Not so its dissolution, which underwent extensive modification under Augustus, not all in accordance with the government's intentions.

Termination of a Roman marriage had always been possible, and even quite easy for a Roman husband. This legal expression of the inferior status of women was a logical inference from the old marriage *cum manu*. The *cum manu* husband who wished to rid himself of his wife summoned a council of his family, to which the wife now belonged, and cited his reasons, among which the custom-honored were adultery, poison concoction, excessive drinking, and counterfeiting household keys. Yet though the husband's right to repudiate his wife was inherent in his legal power over her, the family's approval was evidently more than a formality, and the act of repudiation in the absence of convincing reasons socially deprecated.[19]

Only over time, and with the increasing wealth brought to Rome by wars of conquest, did upper-class husbands gradually succeed in appropriating the right to divorce at will. The prerogative may be seen as a substitute for the institutions of polygamy and concubinage, both practiced by the men of contemporary elites. In Rome concubinage was legal, but two principles of the law deprived it of much of its potential value in Roman eyes: a man could not keep both a wife and a concubine, and children of the latter were ineligible to inherit. Thus concubinage did not do what easy divorce could do.[20]

But Roman men did not monopolize the new freedom. At the very time they began practicing divorce at will, Roman women obtained virtually equivalent license via marriage *sine manu.* Since the *sine manu* wife still belonged to her father's family, her male guardians could repossess her *(abducere uxorem)* or, even without their intervention, she could exercise her own legal right *(sui juris)* and recover her own liberty.[21]

By the close of the Republic a wife could even secure a divorce under marriage *cum manu* if her husband deserted her, if he was convicted of certain crimes, or if he was made prisoner of war. The paramount consideration was the wife's property. The husband repudiating his wife pronounced the formula *"Tuas res tibi agito"* ("Take back what is yours"). The repudiating wife's formula ran *"Tuas res tibi habeto"* ("Keep what is yours").[22]

Thus, in the time of Augustus, divorce by mutual consent or at the unilateral wish of either party was an old Roman custom, at least among the upper classes. Multiple marriages were common for both sexes. Sulla (138–78 B.C.) had set an example by taking a young divorcée as his fifth wife. Julius Caesar had contributed a metaphor to the language by repudiating Pompeia because though innocent she had not remained "above suspicion." Cato of Utica (95–46 B.C.), famed for his virtue, divorced his wife and then repossessed her when she inherited a fortune from her second husband. Cicero divorced the mother of his children, Terentia, to wed his rich seventeen-year-old ward, while Terentia herself remarried twice. According to Seneca (c. 4 B.C.–A.D. 65), wealthy women recollected dates not by the name of the incumbent consul but by that of a first, second, or succeeding husband.[23]

Augustus himself was a divorcé, a detail that had no bearing on the history-making legislation he inaugurated in respect to Roman domestic life. Apart from the moral issue involved in frivolous divorce, Augustus perceived a threat to the state: a census revealing that the men of the senatorial and knightly classes, forming the Roman aristocracy, were predominantly bachelors. Augustus recommended to the Senate a series of laws penalizing the childless and unmarried in respect to inheritance, limiting betrothals to two years, and requiring fathers to provide dowries. Motherhood was correspondingly rewarded, the mother of three being freed from male guardianship.

This last provision alone amounted to a dramatic intrusion into the sanctity of the male-dominated home. In sum, the Augustan legislation completed the shift away from the ancient concept of the family as an integral and autonomous mini-state, and toward that of the family as a subordinate social unit, its members individually answerable to the authority of history's rising power, the large national state.

Since it was desirable to facilitate remarriage of divorced couples, a need was felt for a greater formalization of divorce. Henceforth seven witnesses were required to attest to the dissolution of a marriage.[24] The procedure among the upper classes was for the divorcing partner to send a freedman bearing the message to the other spouse. Juvenal (c. A.D. 55–127) pictures an unfortunate wife: "Let three wrinkles show themselves on Bibula's face" and her husband's servant will call to "give her the order, 'Pack your traps and be off! You've become a nuisance.' "[25] Wives, however, were equally capable of breaking off the union. Martial (c. A.D. 40–103) composed a pithy epigram: "Who weds often does not wed but commits legal adultery."[*26]

As in all ages, the conspicuous marital adventures of celebrities may be an imperfect mirror for the behavior of society at large. Most Roman couples did not divorce, and marital fidelity did not go unhonored. A popular heroine was Turia, a noble lady who saved her husband's life during the civil wars of Marius and Sulla and who after years of childless marriage offered to step aside in favor of a younger wife, to whose children she promised to be a second mother. Turia's husband indignantly refused, with the words, recorded in an inscription to her memory: "How could having children matter to that degree?"[27] Many other inscriptions

*Even pithier in Latin: *"Quae nubit totiens, non nubit; adultera lege est.*

A fifth-century mother and her son and daughter: Galla Placidia and her children, Museo Civico Cristiano, Brescia. (Alinari)

bear similar messages: "She was dearer to me than life. . . ." "For love of her I have sworn never to remarry. . . ." "Never have I endured aught from her of evil save her death." Similar sentiments were expressed by widows.[28]

The opinion of Turia's husband notwithstanding, children were nearly universally perceived as the most important outcome of marriage. In early times the cult of ancestor worship conferred a mystic value on childbirth, which did not however prevent the practice of abortion, socially frowned on and vainly prohibited by the Imperial government in the second century A.D. Previously it had been illegal only if performed without the permission of the *paterfamilias*. Contraception was likewise widely practiced, though with only mediocre success. Preparations to insert in the vagina to block or kill semen had a long history antedating Rome, as did the rhythm method. Hippocrates, whose oath contains an explicit condemnation of abortion but not of contraception, erroneously specified that the most fertile period was that immediately following menstruation. The abundance of patently quack remedies and superstitious nostrums indicates both the interest in contraception and the absence of reliable techniques.[29]

Childbirth was supervised by midwives, often credited with great skill. Among upper-class families, the midwife was succeeded by a wet nurse, about whose selection a second-century A.D. treatise on gynecology advised, "One should choose a wet-nurse . . . of good constitution, of large frame, and of a good color. Her breasts should be of medium size, lax, soft, and unwrinkled, the nipples neither too big nor too small and neither too compact nor too porous. . . . She should be self-controlled, sympathetic and not ill-tempered, a Greek, and tidy."[30]

Despite such solicitude for the infant born to affluence, infanticide remained an accepted practice, widespread among the poor, occasional among their betters. Roman law also sanctioned the ancient custom of selling surplus children, limiting it (second century B.C.) to very young children for whom the parents were unable to provide support. In the second and third centuries A.D., emperors further restricted the power of fathers by barring the sale of children except in cases of extreme poverty.[31] In A.D. 318 Constantine, acting under the humanitarian influence of the Christian Church, and also out of a concern for population decline, made infanticide a capital crime.

Infanticide and the sale of children notwithstanding, Latin literature abounds with expressions of parental devotion to children. "Our parents are dear, dear are our children," wrote Cicero, because "nature implants in man above all a strong and tender love for his children."[32] Lucretius (98–53 B.C.) lamented death when "Now no more shall your glad home welcome you, nor your good wife and sweet children rush to snatch the first kisses and to touch your heart with a silent thrill of joy."[33] Tibullus (c. 54–c. 19 B.C.) pictures a child seizing his father's ears to give a kiss and an old grandfather making himself ever available for a child's prattle.[34] In the typical Roman household children were decently fed and decently dressed (in small versions of adult costume, tunic, cloak, toga, stola). On the farm they were perforce put to work as soon as they were old enough to contribute. Among upper- and middle-class city families they were given systematic training for their future (sex-determined) roles as adults. By Augustan times education had moved outside the home for upper-class Roman children, especially boys, who went to school in the Forum to train for future service to the state.

The male bias in Roman attitude and custom had always been conspicuous in respect to sexual activity. Throughout pagan Roman history adultery was a crime only for women. Under the Republic a husband had the right to kill an adulterous wife caught in the act, together with her lover, if he was a freedman or slave. Augustus's legislation substituted a more humane and more worldly penalty in the shape of a fine based on the size of the woman's dowry. The law also touched on husbands' conduct. A little later the wronged wife was given the valuable right of recovering her dowry, but not until Constantine three centuries later did Roman adultery become an equal crime for either sex. Augustus in fact was mainly concerned with husbandly complacence and the thrust of his law was to compel divorce proceedings. In a sensational invasion of traditional privacy, a corps of paid informers was authorized to provide testimony against erring wives of forgiving husbands.[35]

Neither custom, law, nor informers prevented wives from continuing to stray into other arms, as is indicated by reenactments of legislation by later emperors, and by a wealth of satiric literature. "Pure," wrote Ovid, "are only those women who are unsolicited, and a husband who is angry at his wife's amours is a mere rustic."[36] Juvenal pictures the contrasting attitudes toward a sea voyage of women journeying with their husbands and those going off with their lovers: "If it's their husband who wants them to go, then it's a problem to get on board ship. They can't stand the bilgewater; the skies spin around them. The woman who goes off with her lover of course has no qualms. She eats dinner with the sailors, walks the quarter-deck, and enjoys hauling rough ropes. Meanwhile the first woman gets sick all over her husband."[37]

The practice of homosexuality, especially male, was evidently widespread, at least among the Roman upper classes. Slave boys like slave girls were made to serve their masters' pleasure (and on occasion also that of their mistresses, who by a law of Constantine were threatened with the death penalty for such fornication).[38] Oddly rare in both Roman history and Latin literature are references to illegitimacy, apparently because little stigma was attached. Derogatory imputations on the part of political or other enemies dwelt instead on base parental or ancestral status. A related puzzle is the scarcity of spinsters. The convent did not yet exist as an alternative to marriage, yet the unmarried woman hardly makes an appearance in literature or law.

Death came to a Roman without fanfare. As medicine provided no palliative for the dying, pagan religion provided no comfort. A Roman died at home, commonly alone, according to Seneca's dry observation: "No one sits with a dying friend. None can bring himself to witness the death of his father, however much he wishes for it."[39]

Obsequies were private, death remaining one of the few events in life untouched by the Roman state that had intruded on so many others—marriage, divorce, sexual conduct—always for its own perceived paramount interest, but with far-reaching and long-lasting effects on family and society.

The Barbarian Family

The second great source from which the medieval family derived was the barbarian. Despite its formerly pejorative meaning, modern historians still find the word "barbarian" convenient for designating the Germanic newcomers who, in an overall sense, lagged behind the Romans in the arts of civilization, but who readily acquired many Roman techniques and who brought with them certain capabilities of their own.

The Great Migrations, beginning roughly in the middle of the third century A.D., coincided and interacted with the onset of economic decline and social and political difficulties in the western Roman Empire. Contact between Romans and Germans, however, went back much further, to the incursion of the Cimbri and Teutones, late in the second century B.C. These two bellicose tribes penetrated northern Italy and Roman Gaul (Provence) and were expelled only after several hard campaigns. Thenceforward the "barbarians" remained much in the Roman consciousness. Caesar in his memoirs included a description of the Germans he observed in two brief invasions of the Rhineland (55 and 53 B.C.) and Tacitus devoted a book (A.D. 98) to "Germania." In Tacitus's day the barbarians represented no threat, but rather in the historian's eyes an example of simplicity and good morals that he felt might provide a healthful model for the Roman aristocracy: "No one in Germany finds vice amusing, or calls it 'up-to-date' to seduce or be seduced."[40]

For the next century the Germans hovered on the fringes of the Roman world, raiding, trading, occasionally mounting a threat of invasion. Then, impelled from their homes by cataclysms still shrouded in mystery, they began pressing westward and southward in a series of waves climaxing in the fifth and sixth centuries. In addition to feeling pressures from behind—famine, drought, Huns—they were drawn into the Roman Empire by the magnet of an economically and technically advanced region, with its cities and villas, granaries and warehouses, shops, tools, coins, and ornaments, in a species of "gold rush" (in the phrase of a modern historian).[41] Columns of thousands or tens of thousands of Goths, Gepids, Alemanni, and other peoples from the north and east, men, women, children, and animals, filtered or flooded through the Roman frontier defenses, sometimes peacefully and by permission, sometimes violently or by taking advantage of the moments when the legions were absent contesting the Imperial succession on behalf of their generals.

The legions themselves became barbarianized by numerous individual enlistments; indeed many Germans rose to high rank. In the later stage of the Migrations, large numbers of several major groupings—Burgundians, Ostrogoths, Visigoths, Franks—entered Gaul and Italy as *foederati*, or allies, by a negotiated arrangement that settled barbarian families on arable land in much the same fashion that Roman veterans had been settled in the earlier period. This episode in the Great Migrations apparently took place with little friction between newcomers and old inhabitants.*

Half soldiers of fortune, half migrant farmer-herdsmen, lacking the polish of Roman society and the virtuosity of Roman engineering, the barbarians appeared to nineteenth-century historians as an unrelieved calamity, their arrival inaugurating a "Dark Age" out of which Western Europe only slowly emerged into a new light. Modern scholarship, assisted by archeology, has provided a corrective. While the barbarians lacked a written language and therefore possessed neither history nor literature, and were incapable of the mathematical and organizational feats embodied in the bridges, aqueducts, roads, temples, arches, arenas, and public baths with which Roman technology strewed the Mediterranean littoral, the newcomers brought capabilities and innovations of their own. To European dress they made the valuable addition of trousers. Their steel weapons were the equal if not the superior of the best of Roman fabrication. Though they preferred fighting on foot, they were expert horsemen and introduced at least two major improvements in equipment, the saddle and (later) the stirrup. A recent discovery of archeology is the evidence of economic and cultural links between the pre-Migration Germans and the indigenous Celts of Northern and Western Europe.[42]

Nor was barbarian society so different from Roman as was once supposed. Rather, it resembled that of Rome at an earlier stage. Among the Germans as among the early Romans the family was the basic unit, economic, social, legal, and religious. Families were aggregated into kin groups for which the German term was *Sippe*, and whose structure, character, and exact functions have been the subject of extensive controversy and conjecture among modern

*Walter Goffart (*Barbarians and Romans, A.D. 418–584*) postulates that instead of being given lands expropriated from Roman and Gallo-Roman proprietors, many of the Germans were assigned revenues from normal taxation in the provinces in which they were settled, in return for which they garrisoned the frontiers against later arrivals.

historians. At one time the "retinue," a voluntary military cohort owing allegiance to a chosen leader, was thought to be synonymous with the *Sippe,* but this now seems dubious. The *Sippe* appears to have been a descent group, perhaps founded by a distinguished individual, lasting a few generations and then dissipating. Before the Migrations, each *Sippe* is believed to have occupied its own territory, with recognized boundaries, and to have held seigneurial rights in the lands of its member families, among whom it made allocations, adjudicated disputes, and executed certain other supra-family functions, such as organizing hunts or moves to new territories. According to David Herlihy *(Medieval Households),* the German *Sippe* rarely numbered more than about fifty families.[43]

Caesar, writing in the first century B.C., reported that the Germans worked the land in common, though he also mentions the existence of isolated homesteads. Tacitus, who had contact with them as an official in the provinces a century and a half later, reported private (individual family) ownership of cropland, along with common (evidently *Sippe*) ownership of pasture. By the time of the Migrations, the German family typically raised wheat or barley, and sometimes flax, peas, and beans, and herded a few sheep or cattle. In their new homes inside the Roman Empire they adapted quickly to the more advanced Roman techniques. The Lombard law code, written down in the sixth century but largely reflecting earlier conditions, mentions vines, fences, mills, animal pastures, fruit and olive trees, domesticated fowl, beekeeping, pigs, and swineherds.[44]

In addition to farming, Germans engaged in both manufacture and trade. Ironwork, including fabrication of weapons, was a male vocation, pottery making, both by wheel and by hand, largely female. Among products long imported into the Roman Empire from the Germanic lands outside it were slaves, furs, skins, and amber. In the Migration period the moving bands often combined looting with trade.[45]

The barbarian equivalent of the Roman father's *patria potestas,* sometimes called the *mundium,* awarded very similar authority with only one important subtraction: barbarian sons attaining majority (the age varying among different peoples) acquired legal independence.[46] Family solidarity was assumed as the basis of law and order, with crime treated as tort and the family and clan given the responsibility for translating individual grievance into resolution by collective action. The injured individual solicited his family's support and the opposing party's family undertook to defend him or to make suitable amends. To facilitate the process, the Germans had developed an ingenious legal instrument, the wergeld, or "man-worth," a value attached to every individual on the basis of sex, age, and status. Payment of compensation for a crime against the person was assessed as a fraction or multiple of the victim's wergeld. Thus for the crime of rape the Burgundian law code exacted nine times the wergeld of the victim. Tacitus reported compensation in kind—cattle, sheep, or chattels—but as the barbarians settled down in the money economy of the Roman empire, gold solidi and silver denarii were substituted.[47]

Barbarian marriage was even more family-governed and male-dominated than was Roman. (Tacitus approved: "No feature of their morality deserves higher praise.")[48] Betrothal was arranged by the male relatives of the bride, whose consent was not required. Bride and groom were probably slightly older than their Roman counterparts. Betrothal consisted of the promise of marriage and the agreement on its terms. It was followed by a feast of the two families at which the actual payment of the brideprice by the groom's family took place. The bride, according to Tacitus, completed the marriage by a gift of arms to the groom, but it is clear that the main direction of endowment was from the groom. The significant difference between barbarian and Roman practice was the source of the endowment: the barbarian paid for his wife, the Roman contributed for his daughter. Again, the implication is of a shortage of women among the barbarians, a supposition strengthened by the prevalence of abduction. Speculation has centered on sexually biased infanticide and on the practice of polygamy and concubinage by the elite, but in the absence of evidence neither explanation can be called thoroughly convincing.[49]

Dissolution of a barbarian marriage, like that of an early Roman marriage, was impossible for the wife, easy for the husband, whose only obligation was a financial amend to the family into which the discarded wife was forced to return.[50] If we believe Tacitus, adultery by German women was very rare, and was punished on the spot by the husband, who "cuts off her hair, strips her naked, and in the presence of her kinsmen turns her out of his house and flogs her all through the village." Once dishonored, she could never return. "Neither beauty, youth, nor wealth can find her another husband."[51] According to the law codes, a husband had the right to kill an adulterous wife and the option of killing her lover or demanding compensation, set by Salic Frankish law at two hundred solidi. Lombard law permitted appeal by the accused lover to trial by combat, provided he was not a slave or caught in the act.[52]

The double standard was even more manifest in German than in Roman attitudes. Tacitus justified the nobility's polygamy on the grounds of the need for matrimonial alliances, but offered no excuse for the equally wide practice of concubinage. Ordinary prostitution, on the other hand, was much rarer than in Rome. Libertinage among German men was, in a word, less democratic than among the Romans.

Despite their subordinate status, barbarian women were valued, and not only for sex and procreation. They possessed particular skills, passed from mother to daughter: besides making pottery, they spun and wove with a skill attested by garments recovered by archeologists from peat bogs. They also did the food processing and preparation, performed the healing, and brewed the beer that was already the staple German beverage. Legal texts reveal another value: descent was commonly reckoned in the female line for the good reason that female descent could be more reliably determined than male.[53]

Tacitus pictures child-rearing among the Germans in the same rosy light in which he depicts marriage. "In every home the children go naked and dirty, and develop the strength of limb and tall stature which excite our admiration. Every mother feeds her child at the breast and does not depute the task to maids or nurses. The young master is not distinguished from the slave by any pampering in his upbringing. They live together among the same flocks and on the same earthen floor, until maturity sets apart the free, and the spirit of valor claims them as her own."[54]

The admiring Roman goes so far as to assert that "to restrict the number of children, or to kill any of those . . . after the [firstborn], is considered wicked," and credits German morality in this regard with greater effectiveness than Roman laws.[55] Tacitus was mistaken. The Germans practiced infanticide on into the medieval period, in a fashion very similar to the Roman. The infant was placed before the father immediately upon birth; if he took it in his arms, sprinkled water on it, and gave it a name, it was accepted and allowed to live. Not till the seventh century was the ancient custom modified, and then only in the regions where the powerful voice of the Christian Church could make itself heard.

Yet there was a measure of justice in Tacitus's view of the Germans, which bears a resemblance to the "noble savage" depiction of American Indians by eighteenth-century European writers. The normal situation of a barbarian family was stable and rural. They worked their plot of land, herded their animals, spun and wove their cloth, and fashioned their garments, which in addition to the revolutionary trousers included short wool tunics or cloaks and in cold weather animal skins, usually of domestic animals but sometimes of wolf, deer, or even bear.[56] Game, including birds and fish, supplemented the family's grain-based diet.[57]

The family typically lived in a house of either of two forms. The "long house" or "aisled house" was a long rectangle divided in three: a central aisle flanked by side aisles created by two parallel rows of timber uprights. At one end the aisles were subdivided into stalls for the cows or other animals, which faced inward toward a fodder rack. At the other end a single large room served as family quarters. Foundations of long houses that have been excavated vary from about eight meters to nearly thirty meters in length. The earliest of these date from the Bronze Age (about 3000 to 1000 B.C.), but the long house was still widely built long after the Migration period.[58]

The second type of house was the sunken hut or *Grubenhaus*, a simple timber structure erected over a shallow excavation with either a gabled framework of slanting poles tied to a ridgepole, supported by two to six posts, or a series of poles or branches sloping to the edge of the hollow. Walls were sometimes plank, sometimes wattle and daub, a timber frame supporting interlaced oak or willow wands (the wattle) plastered with clay mixed with straw (the daub). Carpentry was of a respectable order, executed with a variety of tools, including the lathe.[59]

Barbarian furniture is known to have included tables, benches, beds, and chairs, but since the only pieces that have survived are from the burial sites of the elite (and Tacitus is silent), our knowledge of the interiors of ordinary homes is conjectural. Certainly furnishings were of the simplest. Clay and metal surviving better than wood, we are better informed of the ordinary family's household utensils, which included buckets, platters, dishes, sieves, and pots and pans. Tools were sometimes iron or iron-tipped, though plows with iron shares were probably not used till after the Migrations.[60]

Thus in the parallel worlds of Romans and barbarians, the institutions of marriage and the family show many similarities and some differences. In both worlds the family was the basic unit of society. The larger kinship grouping (supra-family), much weakened in Rome by the power of the state, remained strong among the barbarians. In both worlds, transfer of property was a major legal and social element in marriage. In both, divorce was easy for husbands; in Rome it was possible for wives, especially rich wives. Infanticide was practiced, mainly by the poorer classes, and was probably biased against female children. Abortion was also practiced, as was contraception, the latter with largely ineffective techniques. Training of children was based mainly on sex distinctions deriving from adult roles. The male head of the household was accorded autocratic power, a part of which, however, the Roman state had usurped. Slavery was practiced by both societies, with slave labor a major element in the Roman economy. Slaves were subject to oppressive discrimination in respect to sex and marriage as in other areas, while at the top of the social pyramid the elite class enjoyed extensive special privileges, among the barbarian men those of polygamy and concubinage.

The Impact of Christianity

In the fourth century, as the Great Migrations swelled toward their climax and the vast military-administrative apparatus of the Roman Empire strained and cracked under their pressure, a new force entered into the turbulent European scene. After struggling through three centuries of persecution and indifference, the Christian religion matured into a position of status and authority, routing the gods from the Pantheon and the Lares from the hearths. Among the Romans it won its converts more rapidly in the cities than in the countryside, where pockets of paganism and remnants of pagan practices survived for centuries, or even permanently, without preventing the triumph of the cult throughout Europe. It gained first official toleration (A.D. 313) and then elevation to state religion (c. A.D. 380), while simultaneously and even more dramatically it captured virtually the entire mass of barbarian invaders as they crossed the frontiers. The first great barbarian intellectual, Ulfilas (c. A.D. 311–383), devised a written Gothic language in order to translate the Bible.

As the barbarian and Roman peoples and institutions collided, mingled, and adapted to each other, the Christian community aligned itself, within the fragmenting Empire, into history's first great Church organization. Inevitably it was confronted with a classic problem of revolutionary success, that of doctrinal divergency. To combat a variety of heresies—Gnosticism, Manicheism, Arianism—the "orthodox" Church intellectuals formulated a body of doctrine designed both to answer esoteric theological questions and to provide rules of conduct for everyday Christian life. In this latter area St. Augustine (354–430) and his fellow Church Fathers were at once confronted by the marriage and family customs of the Roman and barbarian worlds. In several significant respects the Fathers brought a new perspective to bear. In others, their Christian teaching proved congenial to existing custom or law. In still others, the Church ranged itself on one side of an ongoing controversy. In all cases Christian doctrine as expounded by the Fathers, especially Augustine, was explicit and categorical. Even when not uniformly adhered to by the faithful, it exercised a profound influence.

In searching the Old and New Testaments for guidance, St. Augustine found a number of recurring tenets but not a completely harmonious consistency. The Old Testament pictured marriage as good, and the normal state in which man and woman were sexually related.[61] The New Testament on the other hand, while affirming the goodness of marriage, attached a superior value to virginity.[62] The Old Testament pronounced human fecundity good, in fact mandatory; the New Testament echoed the command only perfunctorily. The Song of Songs proclaimed the independent value of human sexual love, while the Psalms associated sexuality with sin. The New Testament was eloquent in recommending the value of love without making very clear what love was, except for Christ's example. The Old Testament formally barred adultery and incest, yet some Old Testament figures practiced concubinage and polygamy. Divorce in the Old Testament was obtainable by men, whereas the New Testament not only endorsed monogamy but pronounced marriage indissoluble with one exception: "Whosoever shall put away his wife, except it be for fornication, and shall marry another, committeth adultery" (Matthew 19:9). In contrast to the Old Testament, the New carried implications of equality of the sexes: Jesus and St. Paul condemn with an even hand dereliction by either spouse (Mark 10:11, 12; I Cor. 7:11).

In addition to the Christian scriptures, Augustine and the Fathers were influenced by contemporary pagan and Jewish thought. There was the Stoic ideal of the subordination of sex to reason, including the pronouncement by Pliny the Younger (c. A.D. 61–113) and others that intercourse even in marriage was morally acceptable only if its purpose was procreative (thus implicitly excluding contraception). Philo, the Jewish philosopher of the first-century Diaspora, condemned sexual passion and husbands who behaved unchastely with their wives.[63]

Studying the doctrines of his predecessors in the social and legal context and moral atmosphere of the Roman Empire, where adultery, prostitution, and sexual choice had wide license, St. Augustine set himself firmly against the current with a sweeping condemnation of prevalent immorality. Theologically, that was the easy part. Less readily dealt with was the question of sex in marriage. Genesis expansively recommended, "Go forth and multiply." But times had changed since Genesis, whose author had perceived a young world, just getting started, awaiting its population. Augustine in the fifth century perceived an old, dying world, awaiting Judgment Day. He concluded: "There is not the need for procreation that there once was."[64]

Yet Augustine refused to go along with the dissident Manicheans who flatly denied that procreation was a worthy goal of marriage. By such a denial, he felt, they "make the bridal chamber a brothel."[65] More appealing was the moderation-in-all-things approach of the Stoic philosophers, which found an echo in St. Paul: "The wife hath not power of her own body, but the husband: and likewise also the husband hath not power of his own body, but the wife. Defraud ye not one the other, except it be with [mutual] consent for a time, that ye may give yourselves to fasting and prayer and come together again, that Satan tempt you not for your incontinency" (I Cor. 7:4–5). Marital sex thus found a second justification, to avert sin. If the unmarried· or widowed "cannot contain," said Paul, "let them marry; for it is better to marry than to burn" (I Cor. 7:9).

In developing the theme of moderation, the Church Fathers recommended small families over large ones, the practice of continence for Lent and religious holidays, and, insofar as possible, virginity for both sexes. One Father, St. Jerome, borrowed a scale of values from Jesus's parable of the seed to rate virginity at 100, widowhood at 60, and the married state at 30.[66]

Nevertheless, the Bible unquestionably endorsed marriage, and St. Paul seemed to go beyond the Roman insistence on mutual consent in calling for a degree of enthusiasm (Ephesians 5:24–33): "As the Church is subject unto Christ, so let the wives be to their own husbands," "Husbands, love your wives, even as Christ also loved the Church," and "Let every one of you in particular so love his wife even as himself, and the wife see that she reverence her husband." Such sentiments, in contrast to the cool sex-and-property perceptions of the Romans and barbarians, introduced a higher imperative, idealistic, even mystical. Augustine concluded that marriage for Christians must be regarded as a sacrament (sacramentum), a permanent union. It contained three discernible goods: fides, faith; proles, offspring; and sacramentum, a sacred bonding not merely of two persons, but of whole lines of descent, a principle by no means foreign to pagan thought, either Roman or German.[67] As with Romans and Germans, Christian doctrine held that the two relationships of blood and marriage must be kept distinct through the incest taboo and the rules of exogamy. In this direction the Church reinforced the law of Moses (Leviticus 18:6–21, 20:11–12).

With marriage accorded the status of sacrament, a nuptial blessing by the priest seemed no more than logical. Yet the priest's participation long remained more incidental than central, and not essential for a valid union. Among the Visigoths, who established themselves in Gaul and Spain in the fifth and sixth centuries, the priest's role was enforced by the threat of a fine of one hundred solidi or one hundred lashes, but elsewhere the Church's presence only very slowly insinuated itself into the wedding ceremony.[68]

From the sacramental character of marriage several conclusions followed. Polygamy and concubinage were impermissible to Christian men. Finally, in accord with Matthew (19:6), divorce was discountenanced: "What God hath joined together, let not man put asunder." Here the Church came into sharp collision with Roman law, which, encoded in the sixth century in the Corpus Iuris Civilis of Justinian, long remained operative in most of its territory. Constantine and succeeding Christian emperors had acted to restrict the old freedom of divorce, but they had made no attempt to abolish it. Yet the legal atmosphere was affected by the Church's attitude, and especially by its inclination toward equality of the sexes, in jurisprudence a "fertile novelty."[69]

Augustine rejected all the grounds for divorce allowed by existing secular law, such as prolonged absence or captivity. He was "the workman who put the final hand to the theory of indissolubility," according to canon-law authority Adhémar Esmein,[70] although it was his fellow Church Father, St. Ambrose (340–397), archbishop of Milan, who perhaps stated the Church's view most bluntly to Christian men: "Do not seek a divorce, because you are not allowed to marry another while your wife is living. . . . It is the crime of adultery. . . . And it is more serious that you think you should seek the authority of the law for your sin."[71] Yet the Church labeled it only a venial, not a mortal sin. In short, neither the Church nor Roman law found a satisfactory solution for the problem of remarriage by the victim of adultery. Only barbarian law did, by never mentioning male adultery while prescribing death for the adulterous wife.[72]

Further radical breaks with pagan custom and belief derived inescapably from the identification of procreation as the only justification for marital sex. The Church roundly condemned both abortion and infanticide, and, by further logical extension, opposed contraception, including the rhythm method advocated by Hippocrates and the Manicheans.

The Church undertook not only to shield fetuses and infants from abortion and exposure but also to protect children from mistreatment. It condemned the practice of selling children and drew the attention of the faithful to biblical examples of kindly

Early Christian depiction of the Holy Family: Adoration of the Magi, fourth century, Musée de l'Art Chrétien, Arles. (Authors' photograph)

and loving parental attitudes in the examples of young Samuel, Daniel, the Holy Innocents, and the Christ child. While Augustine taught that children needed firm discipline such as he himself had received in a Roman school, Leo the Great (pope 440–461) declared that "Christ loved childhood, teacher of humility, rule of innocence, model of sweetness."[73] Parental love like conjugal love was a significant part of the Church's teaching.

Thus as political unity dissolved in the Roman world, religious unity appeared in its place. In respect to marriage and the family, Romans, barbarians, and Christians saw eye to eye on several important premises: the primacy of the family unit, the sacredness of the incest taboo, and the necessity of exogamy. Romans and barbarians were in harmony on the superior status of men and the authority of the male head of the household; Christianity demurred mildly on both. Roman law insisted on mutual consent by a marrying couple; the Church concurred. Romans and barbarians shared many details of betrothal and marriage ritual as well as a history of gradual shift from bride purchase to bride profit. The

Church confirmed two major aspects of the ceremony, its public character and the endowment of the bride. To these it added a spiritual imperative by conferring the blessing of the sacrament.

Romans and barbarians gave husbands generous latitude in the dissolution of marriage, and the Romans had come to accord some liberty to wives as well. The Church stoutly contradicted both and insisted on the permanence of marriage. The Romans attached great importance to procreation in the interest of population growth; the barbarians had little if any such interest; the Church had none, but for its own humane and theological reasons opposed infanticide, abortion, and contraception. Barbarians and Romans gave men sexual freedom; the Church refused it to them. All in unison denied it to women.

In the history textbooks of the nineteenth century, the "fall of Rome" was categorically dated at A.D. 476, the year the last Roman emperor to reign in the West abdicated his insubstantial throne. Modern historians prefer the round, half-millenary date of A.D. 500 as the commencement of the Middle Ages. No particular event has significance, though many are associated with the shift from the ancient to the medieval time period. From the point of view of marriage and the family, the transition is from living under Roman, barbarian, and mixed political, economic, and social orders to inaugurating a new system that preserved some of the old elements, discarded others, and invented some new ones. For the next thousand years European society evolved toward the modern era, taking the individual and the family through a series of adventures in historic development that we are only beginning to see clearly.

II.

The Early Middle Ages

3.

The European Family: 500-700

One of the most momentous social and economic transformations experienced by Western society, with critical consequences
for the history of the family, occurred at the very outset of the
Middle Ages. Yet it took place inconspicuously, virtually offstage,
and remains almost undocumented. In the late Roman Empire, the
cultivated part of the European countryside was dominated by
great slave-manned plantations (latifundia). By the 700s, when, in
Georges Duby's words, the rural landscape becomes for historians
"suddenly flooded with light,"[1] the giant plantations had vanished, replaced everywhere by clusters and scatterings of small
farms.

This vast transformation marked the beginning of a long evolution that occupied the entire course of the Middle Ages, in which
the individual peasant and the peasant family passed from slavery
through an intermediate serfdom to freedom, and a slave society
metamorphosed into a free society. The emancipated peasant class
formed the basic human material of European civilization.[2]

Exactly how the transformation took place remains obscure.
Even the meaning of the terms by which the peasants' status came
to be designated, and which might explain their origin, is unclear.
One important lever of change seems to have been a revolution in
the organization of work. Where formerly the broad fields of the
great plantations were cultivated by slaves working in gangs, separate small fields or strips came to be worked by individual families

paying landowners rent in the form of labor services and part of the crop. A major factor in the revolution may well have been the increasing cost of slaves in the late Empire and an awakening recognition of the inefficiency of slave labor. Improved efficiency came not only from the better motivation of people working for their own benefit but also from the inherently superior organization of the peasant family over the slave gang. Gradually the industrious peasant families acquired a moral, in medieval terms a "customary," right to their use of the land, a right they passed on to their children.

A second instrument of change was colonization, the settlement of men, free or slave, on wilderness land. The colonizers cleared, improved, and cultivated in return for permanent use of the land by their families. Again, there was an obligation to pay rents and services to the entrepreneur who organized the settlement, and again an understanding that use of the land was inheritable in the settler's family.[3]

The varying origins and status of the peasants working the new small farms are indicated by the variety of Latin terms used to designate them. The *liber* was a free man. The *servus* or *mancipium* was descended from slaves. The *colonus,* a new invention of Roman law, was a "free" man but bound for life to an estate. The *lidus,* a person of intermediate status, may have descended from a barbarian warrior settled on land by the Roman government. The status of the nonfree peasant was a new social rank, not previously known to Romans or barbarians. Even though the same Latin term, *servus,* continued in use in documents for several centuries, the person to whom it came to be attached was no longer a slave but a "serf." Chief among rights a slave never possessed was the serf's right to cultivate land for his own needs, including the time to do the cultivating and the right to organize his own labor and that of his family.[4]

No records exist to tell us the size and structure of the families that worked the small farms of the sixth and seventh centuries. The only certainty is that the family-household was in the process of becoming the basic economic unit in agriculture. Other sources of information about these first critical centuries of the Middle Ages do, however, exist, and illuminate many aspects of family life. These sources fall into five categories:

First, rulings of Church councils that record the development of the Church's standards for family behavior and by implication the conditions with which it had to deal.

Second, an extraordinary body of moral guidelines known as the penitentials, which emerged in the sixth century, flourished in the early Middle Ages, and declined after the year 1000. Produced by monks to guide priest-confessors in assessing penances, the penitentials lacked canonical authority but were tremendously popular and have consequently survived. Often they incorporated existing barbarian law and custom. Like the records of the Church councils, the penitentials are at once descriptive and prescriptive; they indicate conditions that the monks believed needed correction and define desirable behavior. The penalties prescribed are categorical: for such a sin, such a penance, typically fasting or abstention from sex. Following Germanic law, the penitentials often prescribed fines for personal injury.[5]

Third, the Germanic law codes, most of which were written down for the first time during this period.

Fourth, the lives of saints (hagiography), a literature that flourished from the fourth century on.

Finally, the chronicles, most notably that of Gregory, the bishop of Tours (538–594) whose *History of the Franks* provides an often piquant, often lurid trove of information about the family life of the barbarian aristocracy.[6]

In sixth-century Western Europe, Germanic and Roman cultures existed side by side, slowly melding through association and intermarriage. In Gregory's *History*, Gallo-Roman notables, members of the old Roman senatorial class, take their place separate but coequal with the conquering Frankish nobility.

The new Frankish state founded by Clovis (reigned 481–511) early usurped some of the functions of the Germanic *Sippe*, which nevertheless retained substantial authority, especially in the realm of justice. Crime—murder, assault, rape—might be pursued by the victim's *Sippe* in the form of either blood vengeance or wergeld, compensation in money. The *Sippe* of the accused criminal had corresponding obligations to defend him, creating a feud, or to pay the compensation due his victim. First in line of responsibility for payment were the guilty person's father and brothers, next his six closest relatives, three on the paternal side and three on the maternal side. The relatives of the victim shared in the proceeds. Under Salic law, the wergeld of a murder victim was divided into two equal parts, the first going to his descendants, the second to his collaterals on both paternal and maternal sides.

The Frankish kings sought to outlaw blood vengeance in the interest of public order, and to make the author of the crime pay the wergeld personally, but the old customs were hard to suppress.[7] Many violent examples of the blood feud color Gregory of Tours's *History*. Often these were provoked by concern for the honor of the family's women. In Tournai late in the sixth century a man rebuked his brother-in-law for neglecting his wife in favor of loose women, and when the husband did not mend his ways, attacked and killed him "and some of his relations." The killer was slain in turn by relatives of the husband and "in the end," reports Gregory of Tours, "not a single member of either family remained alive, except one survivor for whom there was no opponent left." At this point more distant relatives entered the quarrel. The Frankish queen Fredegund ordered a cessation before the feud became "a public nuisance" and, when her command was not heeded, dealt with it herself. Inviting to a dinner party the three principal survivors of the two feuding families, she plied them and their servants with wine till the men were drunk and the servants drowsing, then signaled three of her own men, armed with axes, who "swung their weapons and decapitated them."[8]

Another illustration from Gregory of family solidarity barbarian style: A Parisian wife was rumored to be living in adultery with another man. The husband's relations demanded that her father swear his daughter's innocence "or else let her die, for we cannot permit her adultery to bring disgrace upon our family." The father swore her innocence on the altar of St. Denis, but an argument got started, the men drew their swords, and the church was spattered with blood. The bishop exacted a fine, and the woman, according to Gregory, hanged herself.[9]

In another case, a priest of Le Mans, given to gluttony, fornication, and other sins, took for his mistress "a woman of free birth . . . from a good family," had her hair cut short, dressed her as a man, and took her to another city. When her relatives found out, "they hastened to avenge the dishonor done to their family." The priest they took prisoner but allowed the bishop of Le Mans to purchase his freedom. "The woman they burned alive."[10]

Gregory himself relied on the support of his family. When a priest of his church tried to undermine his authority, Gregory commented: "The poor fool seems not to have realized that, except for five, all the other bishops who held their appointment in the [archdiocese] of Tours were blood-relations of my family." Gregory had the troublemaker imprisoned in a monastery "under close surveillance."[11]

While the family presented a united front against outsiders, violence within it was far from rare. Rivalry among heirs, whose numbers were multiplied by polygamy and concubinage, was a fruitful source of intrafamily conflict. According to Gregory, Clovis ensured his grip on his kingdom by killing brothers, nephews, and cousins and confiscating their lands and treasure. He then summoned a general assembly of Franks to which he lamented: "How sad a thing it is that I live among strangers like some solitary pilgrim, and that I have none of my relations left to help me if disaster should threaten!" His lament was disingenuous, according to Gregory: "He said this not because he grieved for their deaths, but because in his cunning way he hoped to find some relative still in the land of the living whom he could kill."[12]

Unlike the Roman kinship system, which was patrilineal, the system that dominated medieval society until about the year 1000 was cognatic (bilateral): descent was traced (though only a short distance) through both men and women. The family's social status derived equally from both sides, and the obligations and rights of kinship, such as wergeld, operated bilaterally. The system was ego-centered, that is, a network focused on a single person with links that implied obligations and regulated relationships and attitudes.[13]

As bilateral kinship implies, and as Gregory of Tours's chronicle illustrates, Frankish brothers and sisters maintained close adult relationships. King Childebert I (reigned 511–558) journeyed to

Baptism of Clovis, founder of the Frankish state (upper panel), from **Vie de Saint Denis.** (Bibliothèque Nationale, MS Nouvelle Acq. Fr. 1098, f. 50)

Spain to rescue his sister Clotild from her husband, Amalric, an Arian Christian who was mistreating her because of her Catholic faith. Clotild had sent her brother "a towel stained with her own blood" shed when her husband had struck her.[14] Bertram, bishop of Bordeaux, protected his sister Berthegund, who had left her husband and entered her mother's convent, even circumventing the order of King Guntram (d. 593) that she return to her husband and children.[15]

Marriage alliances played an important role in the politics of the Frankish kingdom, notably in the unions between the barbarian nobility and the old Gallo-Roman senatorial class. Women seem to have actively participated in the game of marriage strategy.

The names that fill Gregory's pages are a mixture of Germanic and Roman. Since Caesar's time Roman nomenclature had undergone a revolution reflecting the decay of the ancient *gens* and a heightened genealogical respect for women. Gregory himself, a Roman who traced his ancestry to a senator of the second century, bore the names of his father, paternal grandfather, and maternal great-grandfather—Gregorius Florentius Georgius. But his great-uncle, equally Roman in origin, was named simply Gundulfus, in accordance with Germanic custom, which gradually prevailed. The single name borne by Germans was drawn from a collection that was part of the family's legal property and could be repeated from generation to generation, or given variations from one generation to the next (Theuderic, Theudebald; Sigibert, Dagobert, Charibert).[16]

Sixth-century women shared equally in inheritance of money and movable property, but not usually in land. Most of the Germanic codes provided for sons to divide land equally (partible inheritance), with no advantage for the eldest. In the absence of sons, the codes either awarded the inheritance to daughters or made daughters secondary heirs behind close male collaterals. A lack of male heirs, however, was seldom a problem, at least at the aristocratic level. Thanks to polygamy, concubinage, and easy divorce, the problem was rather the reverse. A number of sons, dissatisfied with their shares, and failing to negotiate a settlement, fought it out to the death.[17]

Partible inheritance applied to kingdoms as well as to estates, with similar results. Clovis's kingdom was divided among his four sons, who plotted, murdered, and battled until only one line survived. Gregory's *History* records many such bloody struggles.

Throughout the early Middle Ages, the old Germanic concepts of marriage contended with the new teachings of the Church. At first the debate was muted, as the Church slowly defined and enlarged its ideas while augmenting its power to impose them. Exogamy and the incest taboo provided one area of conflict whose opening skirmishes were fought in this period. The Church began by a series of strictures against marriages contracted with affines (in-laws), which council after council labeled "incestuous." The penitentials spelled out the biblical justification (for example, the Canons of St. Patrick): "For the Lord saith, 'and they shall be two in one flesh [Matthew 19:5]: therefore, the wife of thy brother is thy sister." The third synod of Paris (c. 557) ruled: "Incestuous marriages are forbidden, that is, with the widow of one's brother, with the mother-in-law, with the widow of an uncle, with the sister of his own wife, with the daughter-in-law, with the aunt."[18] Gregory I, the Great (pope 590–604), answering a series of questions posed to him by St. Augustine of Canterbury (d. c. 604), labeled marriage to one's stepmother or sister-in-law "a heinous crime," because marriage makes two people one flesh and "Thou shalt not uncover the nakedness of thy father." John the Baptist, he declared, was martyred for defending this truth when he denounced Herod's incestuous marriage to his brother's wife.[19]

Unfortunately, such marriages were often highly convenient. One Frankish king, Chlotar I, married his brother's widow and later his wife's sister. Another, Merovech, married his uncle's widow. A Visigothic king, Leuvigild (d. 586), married his brother's widow.[20] On the other hand, individuals or families sometimes found the Church's position useful, as for example when two matrimonial projects came into conflict and one ambitious family could accuse another of contemplating or committing incest. In the course of the sixth century, the Church's laws slowly came to prevail, and were incorporated one by one into the secular law codes. In 596 Childebert II enacted legislation providing the death penalty for a man who married his father's widow or his wife's sister, or for a widow who married her husband's brother. Early in the seventh century Chlotar II, whose own grandfather had married his living wife's sister, pronounced the death penalty against a noble who had married his stepmother.[21]

Roman law prohibited marriage between partners closer than the fourth degree of relationship, meaning aunts, uncles, nephews, and nieces, leaving first cousins free to marry. The Church at first agreed, but at the Council of Agde (506) it forbade marriage between first cousins or even their children (second cousins).[22] Pope Gregory offered a rationale on eugenic grounds: "We have found by experience that no offspring can come of such [cousinly] wed-lock."[23] The Penitential of Theodore (late seventh century) distin-guished three categories: second cousins, whom it pronounced free to marry; first cousins, who were forbidden to marry but tolerated if already married; and closer relations, who if married should be separated.[24]

For the time being, the incest-and-exogamy issue remained cloudy. With polygamy and concubinage, the Church articulated clear enough principles, but made only slow headway. Kings and nobles of the sixth and seventh centuries kept concubines, main-tained multiple wives, and repudiated one wife to take another with no more formality than a word and a gesture.[25] A common practice was for a young man to take a concubine before he mar-ried. When Childebert II married at the age of fifteen, he already had a concubine and a son. Clovis II took an English slave girl, Balthild, as his concubine before he was fifteen and later married her.[26]

Chlotar I had at least two concurrent wives, probably four. His son Charibert, captivated by a pair of sisters among his wife's retinue, repudiated the wife and married the sisters sequentially, sandwiching still another wife, the daughter of a shepherd, in between. St. Germain, bishop of Paris (d. 576), excommunicated the amorous king, who refused to be coerced, but whose latest wife's death was recorded with satisfaction by Gregory of Tours as "a judgment of God."[27] Charibert's brother Chilperic married the Visigothic princess Galswinth "although he already had a number of wives."[28] Dagobert I repudiated one wife and married three others simultaneously while maintaining so many concu-bines that the chronicler Fredegar declared that he could not spare space to name them all.[29]

Yet by the eighth century the principle of one wife at a time had gained substantial acceptance, even though royalty and nobility were still far from setting an example of marital decorum.

Another contentious problem lay in consent to marriage. Of the two kinds of consent involved, only that of the parties to the marriage was controversial. That of their parents and relatives was a long-established tradition. The only relevant biblical pro-nouncement was St. Paul's injunction, "Let a widow marry whom she wills, only in the Lord" (I Cor. 7:39), but the Church Fathers had adopted consent of the bride and groom from Roman law, and Isaac, a fourth-century commentator on Paul, had noted pragmatically, "Unwilling marriages usually have bad results."[30] The Church gradually imposed its doctrine, though in light of early marriage and intense parental interest, truly free consent of the parties remained questionable. Young men were theoretically free to choose their marriage partners once they had attained majority—at ages twelve to fifteen in the various law codes—but nearly always needed parental approval for economic reasons, while young women were not given equivalent freedom even on reaching their much later majorities (at twenty to twenty-five). The Lombard code, written down in the seventh century, allowed a father or brother to choose a girl's husband without her consent.[31] Yet as early as the mid-fifth century the Canons of St. Patrick, while conceding that "what the father wishes the maiden shall do, since the head of the woman is the man," insisted that "the will of the maiden be inquired after by the father."[32] The later Penitential of Theodore went further: "A girl of seventeen has the power of her own body. . . . After that age a father may not bestow his daughter in marriage against her will."[33]

But even if parental coercion was not accepted, parental approval was. The barbarian codes unanimously assessed heavy wergeld on the man who married a woman without obtaining the consent of her father, and the Church reinforced secular with canon law. The fourth synod of Orléans (541) pronounced: "No one may marry a girl against her parents' will under threat of excommunication."[34]

One means of circumventing parental consent was abduction, still commonplace in the early Middle Ages, carried out with or without the complicity of the woman. In the early sixth century the laws were chiefly concerned with compensating the family and the injured man—fiancé or husband—to head off a blood feud. A marriage formula was composed for rapists and abductors in which the criminal turned bridegroom made public apology: "Dear and beloved wife, as it is publicly known that I seized you contrary to your will and that of your parents, and that by the crime of abduction I have associated you with my lot, which might have put my life in danger if the priests and distinguished persons had not restored understanding and peace, it has been agreed that

I give you what I should in the way of [endowment]. That is why by this act of recompense I give you [a list of properties]. . . ."[35]

Not all law codes allowed marriage, even if the abducted woman had consented. Some levied stiff fines or declared the union invalid. A Church synod (557) prescribed excommunication for abduction against parental will. King Childebert in 596 decreed the death penalty for abduction by force, and, even if the woman agreed to marriage, in the absence of parental approval sentenced the guilty pair to exile or death.[36]

The normal Germanic marriage ceremony consisted of three elements, just as in Tacitus's day: betrothal, agreement on terms, and the marriage celebration. Gregory of Tours describes a betrothal ceremony completed by the young man's bestowal of a ring, a kiss, and a pair of slippers. To the bride's family he gave the *arrha*, a token remnant of the old brideprice, its name the Latin for any payment made to guarantee delivery of goods. The engagement could now be broken only by mutual consent, with the penalty for rupture heavier for the woman than for the man.[37]

The *arrha*, however, was by no means the bridegroom's sole obligation. In the course of the sixth and seventh centuries the economic direction of Germanic marriage shifted significantly. Where the old brideprice payment had gone entirely to the bride's family, now a bridegift was paid to the bride, and was supplemented by the *Morgengabe*, paid the day after the marriage in recognition of the bride's surrender of virginity and the groom's acquisition of sexual rights. Both bridegift and *Morgengabe* were usually defined in monetary value in the discussion of terms, but were increasingly made in land, thus amounting to an endowment not only of the bride but of the new conjugal household. The Code of the Ripuarian Franks set the customary morning gift at fifty solidi, a quarter of the wergeld of a freeman, or the value of twenty-five oxen.[38]

Thus marriage was no longer seen as created by mutual consent, as among the Romans, or by bride purchase, as formerly among the Germans, but by consummation and payments to the bride. "In the early Middle Ages," says Diane Hughes, "formal consummation made a marriage, and *Morgengabe* was its sign." The Church bestowed its sanction on the new arrangement, popes and councils declaring that the legality of marriage required the endowment of the bride by the bridegroom.[39] At the same time the old *mundium,* or formal authority over the bride, lost some of its importance. The Lombard Edict of Rothari (643) recognized marriages in which the husband failed to acquire it.[40]

To the marriage the bride brought no land or money but a trousseau, among the poorer classes bedding and utensils to set up housekeeping, among the aristocracy jewels, clothes, and furnishings. Fifty wagonloads accompanied the Frankish princess Rigunth on her journey to marry the son of the Visigothic king of Spain. Unfortunately the princess's guards stole much of the treasure and the duke of Toulouse the rest. Brought home in humiliation, according to Gregory of Tours, Rigunth developed the "habit of sleeping with all and sundry."[41]

Little information has survived about the sixth-century wedding ceremony. Publicity was the essential factor; the Council of Arles which had made endowment of the bride a requirement also stated, "Nor may anyone marry without publishing the nuptials."[42] The benediction of a priest was now in many places a customary but not indispensable accompaniment.

Though the Church's doctrine of indissolubility remained in clear conflict with both Roman and Germanic divorce law, Church councils of the first two centuries of the Middle Ages made little effort to combat divorce, and what effort they made was largely ineffective. A contemporary legal formula began frankly: "As between so-and-so and so-and-so his wife there is no charity according to God, but discord which reigns, and consequently they cannot agree at all, both desire to separate, which they have done. . . . They have decided that each of them should be free to enter into the service of God in a monastery or to contract a new marriage."[43]

Under Germanic law, a man could still repudiate his wife for a variety of reasons—barrenness, adultery (for which crime he could also kill her and her lover), or illness that prevented her from fulfilling her conjugal duty. If he was willing to relinquish control over her property and pay her compensation, he needed no justification at all. Wives, on the other hand, could not initiate divorce even from adulterous husbands. The law codes were not concerned with moral issues, only with protecting family interests and apportioning property.

The Church, in contrast, was interested first and foremost in moral issues, but it proceeded with circumspection. The Council of Agde (506) ruled that a man could not repudiate his wife without submitting the case to the bishop's court. The canon went largely ignored.[44] Later councils (Compiègne in 757, Verberie in 758 or 768) mentioned a number of valid divorce grounds: leprosy, plotting a spouse's murder, entry of a spouse into religious orders, enslavement of one spouse. The statute of Verberie noted a special, and touching, exception in the case of enslavement: if one spouse sold himself into slavery to save his family from starvation, the surviving spouse was forbidden to remarry.[45]

The penitentials cautiously recommended patience to warring spouses, but stopped short of forbidding separation. That of Finnian warned that a man must not divorce his barren wife, since God might still deal with them as with Abraham and Sarah, that is, give them children. Even if a wife committed adultery, the husband "ought not to take another wife while she is alive"; in fact, if she did penance, he should take her back "as a slave, in all piety and subjection." A repudiated wife, similarly, must not remarry but wait "in all patient chastity" for her husband to take her back. Either partner guilty of adultery should do penance for a year, living on bread and water and sleeping alone.[46]

The Penitential of Theodore explicitly ruled that a woman could not divorce her husband even for adultery except to permit him to enter a monastery; a legal marriage, in fact, could not be broken without the consent of both parties. Still, in a first marriage either partner might give the other permission to enter a monastery, and a man who repudiated his wife and remarried was subject only to a lengthy penance.[47] If a woman could prove that her husband was impotent, the marriage was dissolved and she could remarry.[48] If a wife left her husband "despising him" and refused to return, the husband should extend his patience to five years but then might remarry "with the bishop's consent."[49] Theodore was hopeful that even an adulteress might be reconciled with her husband, in which case "her punishment does not concern the clergy, it belongs to her husband."[50]

In discouraging second marriages, the Church found itself more or less in harmony with German law and custom, concerned about protection of property and of the children of the first marriage. The Penitential of Theodore assessed penalties: for a second marriage, a year of fasting on Wednesdays and Fridays and during three 40-day periods; for a third, seven years of fasting. Yet only moderate waiting periods were prescribed: a month for a widower, a year for a widow.[51]

A more delicate problem for the Church arose in clerical marriage. In accordance with St. Paul's prejudice in favor of chastity, priests had been forbidden to marry as early as the third century. This did not prevent many men already married from taking orders, including a number eminent in the lay world as governors, senators, and military officers who had converted to Christianity and become bishops. A provincial council at Elvira, Spain, in 306 had declared that priests and bishops, married or not, should refrain from sex, but the larger ecumenical Council of Nicaea in 325 had debated the question and declined to insist.[52] The issue did not become troublesome until the sixth century, when synods first barred from the priesthood men married more than once or married to widows, while permitting consecration of other married men. A question was raised: could priests and prelates sleep with their wives, or were they obliged to avoid the contamination of sex? Provincial councils began to assert that they were. "The bishop must treat his wife as his sister," pronounced the fourth synod of Orléans (541). Recognizing the difficulty of enforcement, the synod commanded that every married archpriest, deacon, or subdeacon "must have constantly with him a cleric who follows him everywhere and who has his bed in the same room as he. Seven subdeacons or lectors or laypersons must alternate in exercising this surveillance" because "the people must not respect but scorn the priest who cohabits with his wife, for in place of being a doctor of penitence he is a doctor of libertinage."[53]

Gregory of Tours tells several stories about married bishops. When a Breton noble named Macliaw became bishop of Vannes, he put aside his wife, but on inheriting the family estates, he renounced his vows and retrieved his wife. Macliaw was excommunicated.[54] Bishop Urbicus of Clermont-Ferrand, a convert from a senatorial family, arranged for his wife to live separately from him, as a nun. But the woman was "driven by the Devil's own malice" which "inflamed her with desire for her husband and turned her into a second Eve," so that she made her way to the bishop's palace in the night and, finding everything locked up, beat on the doors, shouting, "Bishop! Why do you scorn your lawful wife? Why do you shut your ears and refuse to listen to the words of Paul, who wrote: 'Come together again, that Satan tempt you not' [I Cor. 7:5]. I am here! I am returning to you, not as to a stranger but to one who belongs to me." The bishop "forgot his religious scruples and ordered her to be admitted to his bedroom, where he had intercourse with her and then said that it was time for her to go." Later, full of remorse, he went off to a monastery in his diocese to do penance "with lamentation and tears," returning after a time to his own city. The encounter had made the wife pregnant, and she bore him a daughter who became a nun. Bishop and wife never again lived together, but wife and child were later buried at his side.[55]

Most of the bishops seem to have solved the problem either by separating completely from their wives or by continuing to live under the same roof but officially abstaining from sexual relations. It came to be accepted that bishops must be celibate, but lower (and younger) clergy, if already married when they were ordained, could continue normal married lives. At the end of the seventh century, the rule was spelled out by the Council of Trullo, in Constantinople, and for well over three hundred years married priests were accepted throughout Catholic Europe.

The early medieval centuries saw no change in the authority over the family vested in the husband and father. Roman marriage *sine manu*, in which women retained membership in their fathers' families, had disappeared and was never recognized by German law, which had always made wives strictly subject to their husbands' *mundium*. Yet the medieval husband's power was less absolute than that of the old Roman *paterfamilias* over wife, minor sons, and unmarried daughters. The German law codes varied in their restrictions on paternal authority, but most provided that sons reaching majority became independent of their fathers, that wives had to be consulted in important matters, that husbands could not sell wives' property without their consent, and that widows controlled their inheritances and had custody of their minor children.

Church canons, penitentials, and German law were alike silent on abuses of paternal or parental power. Fathers still had the right to disavow infants and sell children, practices that the Frankish kings joined the Church in attempting to suppress.

On sentiment within the family, the sources cast little light. Many of the marriages of the Frankish kings described by Gregory of Tours seem to have been motivated by sentiment as well as reasons of policy. Chlotar I loved his wife Ingund "with all his heart," and also married her sister Aregund because "he was filled with desire for her."[56] King Charibert "fell violently in love" with the two sisters who were his wife's servants.[57] Gregory's use of the word "love," however, is ambiguous. King Chilperic "loved" the Visigothic princess Galswinth "very dearly, for she had brought a large dowry with her." And "he also loved Fredegund, whom he had married before Galswinth." He reconciled his divided affections by having Galswinth garrotted and seizing her dowry.[58]

No diaries, personal memoirs, or moral tracts exist to illuminate sixth- and seventh-century attitudes toward children, but Gregory again supplies a gleam of light, one that indicates that even in this brutal age children were not regarded with indifference. Gregory describes an epidemic of dysentery that "attacked young children first of all and to them it was fatal: and so we lost our little ones, who were so dear to us and sweet, whom we had cherished in our bosoms and dandled in our arms, whom we had fed and nurtured with such loving care. As I write I wipe away my tears and I repeat once more the words of Job the blessed: 'The Lord gave, and the Lord hath taken away. . . .'"[59] Even Chilperic, "the Nero and Herod of our time," and his redoubtable queen, Fredegund, on losing two young sons in the epidemic, expressed profound grief. Fredegund "beat her breast with her fists," declaring that as punishment for their greed she and Chilperic had lost "the most beautiful of our possessions," and went so far in atonement as to order the tax books burned. Then "with broken hearts" they buried the children.[60] A few years later the couple were "prostrate with grief" when a third son died of dysentery at the age of two. Queen Fredegund gathered "all his clothes, some of them silk and others of fur," and all his other possessions, and burned them, even melting down the gold and silver objects "so that nothing whatsoever remained intact to remind her of how she had mourned for her boy."[61]

The desperation of ordinary parents in the face of such epidemics may be read in the penitentials, which reveal mothers resorting to magic to save their children. One extreme practice, punished by a severe penance, was for the mother to place an ailing child either on the roof of the house or in the oven "to cure it of fever sickness."[62]

Children's gravestones furnish further evidence of parental feelings. Among sixth-century inscriptions collected in the church of St. André-le-Bas in Vienne are more than two dozen epitaphs of children from two to sixteen years old. Most, such as those of seven-year-old Dulcitius and three-year-old Valeria, couple a conventional "Rest in Peace" with the hope of resurrection. Some, like that of Marucius, whose age is painstakingly recorded as three years, six months, and eight days, give the names of the parents (Elcentianus and Palesta) who "placed him here for love."

The penitentials assessed harsh penalties for infanticide but treated it as a recognized alternative to abortion and contraception. Penalties were progressively more severe for three stages: killing an embryo before it showed signs of life (before "the soul entered the body"); after "animation"; and after actual birth. The Penitential of Theodore assessed a year's penance if a woman committed abortion before the fetus showed life; three years if more than forty days had passed since conception; and ten years if she killed the child after it was born. Allowance was made for economic motivation: "If a poor woman slays her child, she shall do penance for seven years" rather than ten.[63] The Penitential of Columban (c. 600) punished a "layman or woman" with a year on bread and water and two years' abstinence from wine and meat for "overlaying" a child, that is, killing him by inadvertently rolling over on him in bed, an accident frequently mentioned in later penitentials and in legal records up to modern times.[64]

Defective children, their deformities usually ascribed by parents to their own sinfulness, were often sold or killed. Gregory of Tours tells of a woman who attributed the deformity of her child to its sinful conception on Sunday and who sold the child to wipe out the memory. Similarly, St. Odilia's father, seeing her blindness as a punishment for his sins, ordered her killed. Her mother intervened to save her life.[65]

Sexuality occupied a large place in the penitentials, whose view was consistently Pauline and Augustinian. "We advise and exhort that there be continence in marriage," declared that of Finnian, "since marriage without continence is not lawful, but sin, and [marriage] is permitted by the authority of God not for lust but for the sake of children."[66] Pope Gregory I attributed the spread of the practice of wet nursing to women's desire for sex, normally forgone until the child had been weaned. "A bad custom is sprung up . . . that women disdain to suckle [their children] . . . and give them to other women to suckle."[67]

A union entirely on the spiritual plane was the ideal. Gregory of Tours tells the edifying story of Injuriosus, a wealthy young man from a senatorial family in Clermont-Ferrand, who married a girl from the same social class. When following the wedding ceremony the couple were led to their bedroom, the bride wept bitterly because "I had determined to preserve my poor body for Christ, untouched by intercourse with man. . . . At the moment when . . . I should have put on the stole of purity, this wedding gown brings me shame instead of honor. . . . I have nothing but scorn for your vast estates and your lands which spread so far and wide, for it is the joys of Paradise for which I yearn." The young man was moved to compassion by her tears, but protested that their parents were the most nobly born in Clermont and that they were their only children; the marriage had been planned to produce children "so that when they are dead no heir from outside our families may claim the inheritance." But eventually he was persuaded: "If you are determined to abstain from intercourse with me, then I will agree to what you want to do." Gregory concludes, "Hand in hand they went to sleep, and for many years after this they lay each night in one bed, but they remained chaste in a way which we can only admire." After their death, they were buried in separate tombs, but, according to Gregory, the next morning the tombs were found side by side—"a miracle that proved their chastity."[68]

At the same time that the Church praised continence, it attached great importance to the other Pauline thesis: conjugal duty, the obligation of the partners to satisfy each other's passions as a remedy against concupiscence. Husband and wife could decide between themselves to take a vow of continence, but such a decision could not be unilateral; so ruled the Church councils of the sixth century.

Most penitentials prescribed abstinence from sex during Lent. That of Finnian recommended continence for three 40-day periods as well as Saturday or Sunday. Sex was also to be shunned during a wife's pregnancy, or at least for the last three months, and for forty days after birth.[69] The Penitential of Theodore went so far as to declare that "a husband ought not to see his wife nude."[70] Generally forbidden was "unnatural" intercourse, meaning any deviation from the position of the woman supine and the man on top, which was believed to be the most favorable for conception. If a man entered his wife from behind, the penance was comparatively light, especially for the first offense. But for anal intercourse

Illustration for Psalm 113: "He maketh the barren woman to keep house, and to be a joyful mother of children." (British Library, Harley MS 603, f. 58r)

"he ought to do penance as one who offends with animals." Oral intercourse was "the worst of evils."[71] Not only were these practices considered unnatural, but they were contraceptive. Contraception itself is oddly not mentioned in the early penitentials.

A whole spectrum of penalties was applied to "fornication," more severe for a cleric than for a layman, and taking account of other circumstances: Was the woman a virgin? Was she a neighbor's wife? The Penitential of Columban ruled that a layman who begot a child with another man's wife should do penance for three years, "abstaining from juicy foods and from his own wife" and paying a fine to the wronged husband. Fornication with a widow drew a one-year penance; with a girl, two years, plus "the price of her humiliation" to her parents, but if the man chose to marry her, both partners were let off with a year's penance.[72]

Masturbation, homosexuality, and bestiality were severely penalized, with harsher punishment for clerics than laymen and for men than boys. The clergy were subject to a complicated gradation of penances for sins that ranged from "libidinous imagination" or "evil thoughts," through nocturnal emissions, "familiarity" with a woman, "touching or kissing" her, attempts to seduce a woman, sex with a woman, masturbation, and sex with men or boys, up to "fornication with beasts." Intention of sin was penalized, though not as heavily as actual commission: while the Penitential of Finnian assessed a heavy penance on the priest or monk who had "given himself to association with [many women] and to their lascivious embraces," it inflicted a lighter punishment on the cleric who "lusts after a virgin or any woman in his heart but does not utter [his wish] with the lips," a slightly heavier one on such a man who "continually lusts and is unable to indulge his desire" and who has therefore "committed adultery with her in his heart."[73] The sin of a man who took advantage of his age and rank—particularly if he was a clergyman—was considered most grave, whether a confessor with a female penitent or a prelate with a young boy. Penalties for a man who had a wife and yet committed sins of masturbation or bestiality were harsher than those for a single man.

Most of the sexual provisions in the penitentials referred to men, but the Penitential of Theodore also listed a penalty for female homosexuality: "If a woman practices vice with a woman, she shall do penance for three years." If she had a husband, she incurred a severer penalty.[74]

Prostitution, like contraception, is never mentioned in the early penitentials and apparently was little practiced in the largely rural environment of the early Middle Ages.

Incest received curious treatment in the penitentials. Penances were assessed for relations between mother and son, described by anthropologist Robin Fox as "rare or non-existent" in modern society, and between brother and sister, which he classifies as uncommon.[75] "He who defiles his mother shall do penance for three years with perpetual pilgrimage," declared the seventh-century Penitential of Cummean,[76] while the Penitential of Theodore assessed either fifteen years or seven years "with perpetual pilgrimage." Theodore stipulated a like penance for brother-sister incest. And "if a mother imitates acts of fornication with her little son, she shall abstain from flesh for three years and fast one day in the week, that is, until vespers."[77] No mention is made of relations between father and daughter, categorized by Robin Fox as "easily the most common type." Although Gregory's *History* is a veritable catalogue of crimes, mostly sanguinary, only on one occasion does it seem to refer to incest: A certain petty Frankish king "was so sunk in debauchery that he could not even keep his hands off the women of his own family. He had an adviser called Farro who was given to the same filthy habits." Gregory does not specify whether the women were daughters or daughters-in-law.[78]

Little information survives about the physical environment of the family in the sixth and seventh centuries. In post-Roman Europe masonry construction was rare, and few traces remain. Even the houses of the rich were usually of wood. Gregory describes how a well-to-do man in Le Velay trapped a drunken enemy in his house, locked the doors "which were made of wooden planks," piled sheaves of wheat around and on top of the house so that it "was completely covered and you could not have told that it was there," and then set it ablaze.[79] When the citizens of Châteaudun retaliated against an attack by those of Orléans and Blois, "they left nothing inside the houses and nothing outside

. . . and then they knocked the houses down."[80] A Frankish captain, marching on Tours, "pulled to pieces the church-house," which was "nailed together," the army pocketing the nails as valuable loot.[81] Much construction was of wattle-work, like the chapel outside one of the gates of Paris described by Gregory, whose history is full of burning cities.[82]

Gregory also gives an occasional glimpse of an interior: The house in which Fredegund entertained the feuding families was furnished with benches and a dining table that was removable "as is the Frankish custom," and as became the universal medieval custom; the guests' manservants dined in the same room as their masters.[83] The majordomo of Fredegund's daughter Rigunth killed his bailiff (and was killed by the bailiff's son) because the officer had ignored his orders to "sweep the house and to put covers on the benches."[84] The wealthy served their guests on gold and silver, but some of their dishes were made of wood. Feasting with Gregory in Orléans, King Guntram boasted that he had a plate weighing 170 pounds.[85] Queen Brunhilde sent "a great salver of incredible size made out of gold and precious gems" to the king of Spain, "together with a pair of wooden . . . basins, which were also decorated with gold and jewels."[86]

Archeological evidence shows that the first two centuries of the Middle Ages witnessed the beginnings of the European village. In place of the isolated farms of antiquity, small clusters of dwellings appeared, still lacking the most salient features of later medieval villages: the church or castle around which settlement formed an orderly pattern.[87] The peasant farm usually consisted of several buildings. Houses ranged from large byre-houses sheltering men and animals under one roof to smaller houses for human beings alone. Sunken huts were used to house animals and for storage.[88]

Thus in the first two centuries of the Middle Ages, as a rural revolution took place, silent and unrecorded, the family and the *Sippe* continued to dominate society, Church and State merely impinging on their ancient authority. Land inheritance remained partible among males, and women remained under the guardianship of their fathers and husbands. Yet relationships through the female side played an important role, and strong links existed between brother and sister.

The Church's concepts of exogamy were still forming. By the seventh century it had imposed its prohibition of marriage to affines (in-laws) and had made some progress against polygamy, but its fundamental doctrine of indissoluble monogamy was far from being accepted by the new European elite.

4.

The Carolingian Age

In the eighth and ninth centuries the agricultural revolution combined with other forces to shape European society into its medieval pattern. For a moment Charlemagne's vast French-German-Italian empire, founded in 800, seemed about to revive that of Rome in a new geography, but Europe quickly fragmented again and fell prey to the raids of Vikings and Saracens. The prolonged period of petty but destructive invasions that followed forged the landowning class into a distinctive castle-dwelling, armor-wearing warrior elite, supported by the peasant families who looked to it for protection.

The late eighth and early ninth centuries provide the first evidence of the social change that had taken place. One major class of documents is the estate surveys, called polyptychs because of their many folds, which listed tenants and assessed rents and services on the basis of the single-family farm, the manse *(mansus)*. This term and its regional variants gradually accumulated other associated meanings, but the basic sense was that of a tenure: a house, garden, and fields, property that however burdened with seigneurial dues was fully inheritable in the peasant family that worked it.[1]

Information about the lives of the nobility is as scarce as that about the peasantry. A unique if enigmatic document called *Dhuoda's Book* or *Dhuoda's Manual (Liber Manualis)* gives us a glimpse—hardly more—of the attitudes and the family consciousness of the Carolingian upper aristocracy.[2]

The third great element of society, the Church, left extensive documentation of its theories and policies in reference to marriage and the family.

Peasants and Polyptychs

The polyptychs present their data in varying forms, each, from the modern scholar's viewpoint, with its own advantages and deficiencies. All are incomplete, and in none is it certain that the entire population is represented. Unlike the records of manorial courts of later centuries, they tell us little about personal lives. From scanty literary and archeological sources we know that peasant men dressed in coarse linen shirts topped with loose hooded tunics and wore leggings and heavy shoes, and that they worked with crude tools, mostly wooden. Peasants lived in one-room houses, usually of timber and clay, furnished with a table, a bench or two, and straw pallets on which the family slept on the earthen floor.

The polyptychs supply significant information on family size and structure, and permit some tentative conclusions about the peasant way of life. A survey made in about 820 of the property of the rich abbey of Santa Maria di Farfa,[3] in the foothills of the Apennines east of Rome, lists dependent tenants in a uniform way ideal for demographic analysis: for each household, the head, his wife, and his unmarried children; his married sons, if any, and their wives and children; and finally, "houses and holdings" (casae et substantiae) and animals, most commonly a donkey and sometimes cows, calves, oxen, or horses. Poultry are not listed, although peasants evidently kept them, since one group owed, among other items, a rent in kind of one chicken (unfortunately the only case in which rents are given).[4]

The first name cited in the household listing is always that of the person who assumed the burden of responsibility on the farm. The survey does not record the ages of the tenants or the extent of their holdings, but the economic status of each household can be estimated from the number of animals it owned and its order in the village listing, the better-off peasants always preceding the poorer.

Historian Richard Ring,[5] seeking to identify the family system that predominated in Farfa, first analyzed the survey using Peter Laslett's classification of households into five groups:

1. solitaries;
2. unmarried siblings living together;
3. simple (conjugal) families;
4. extended families; and
5. multiple families.

He found that of the 244 classifiable households in the survey comprising 1,147 persons, only eleven were composed of solitaries, and only three of unmarried siblings. The great majority (194, or 72 percent) were made up of simple families: married couples with or without children, or widows or widowers with children. Only eighteen (6 percent) were "extended," that is, contained a single conjugal family unit plus one or more people related to its adult male head. Forty-six of the households (17 percent) were "multiple"; that is, they included two or more married couples.[6]

Of the 194 simple family households, twenty-seven were married couples without children: "Autari with his wife," "Sabinianus with his wife Maria";[7] 154 were couples with children: "Petrus with his wife Rosa, his children Fusulus, Ado, Simpula, Adileupa."[8] Ten were headed by widows, three by widowers.[9]

The majority of the eighteen extended households were extended upward, by the presence of the husband's widowed father or mother. Four of the families were extended laterally, three including married brothers of the head of the family and one an unmarried sister. Two were extended downward by the inclusion of nieces or nephews: "Palumbus with his wife Teuda and his nieces Sindula, Rattula."[10]

Of the forty-six multiple households of Farfa, half consisted of a married couple and one married son. Among the many other permutations were seven that included a couple and their two married sons, and sometimes also their unmarried children, and three pairs of married brothers, possibly living in a *frérèche* or *fraternitas*, an arrangement in which property was held jointly by brothers.[11]

Several facts emerge from the analysis. First, in all the households, the father of the family typically remained head until he died. When a widowed father lived with his son's family, he was head: "Antoninus, Teudimundus his son with his wife Gutta," "Fredo, Sindolfus his son with his wife Rodeldi, one male son."[12] In only two of the forty-six multiple households was a living father supplanted by his son, and in both cases the father was apparently very old.[13] At the same time, the sons who inherited after their fathers' deaths were either married or widowed. Only one household is headed by a man not specifically so described.[14]

Second, while multiple households included one or more married sons, married daughters or sisters were conspicuously absent. When a daughter married, she left the household and only rarely returned as a widow. A marrying son, on the other hand, either set up his own household or brought his wife home to his father's household. In only one case, however, were there possibly more than two married sons.[15]

Women shearing wool and weaving in a gynaeceum, from the Utrecht Psalter. (Trinity College, Cambridge, MS R. 17, 1, f. 263)

Third, while a few households contained stepchildren or adopted children, only one contained members unrelated to the family: that of a childless couple at Saxa who had two female slaves.[16] The only other slaves listed in the survey were a group of almost a hundred on the monastic farm at Forcone. Three quarters of these were women, who "worked well" (bene) or "fairly well" (mediocriter), probably in a gynaeceum or female cloth workshop. The remaining (male) slaves at Forcone included a groom, a blacksmith, a cook, millers, and gardeners.[17]

The scarcity of stepchildren (five) in the survey seems to indicate that widows with children were seldom able to remarry. Most of the ten widows in simple households seem to have been poor. Only two owned animals: Aidelinda and her four sons had a calf and a donkey; Auderada and her three sons and two daughters, a donkey.[18]

Fourth, the mean household size of the survey was 4.7, a figure that conceals a significant fact: although half of the households (122) contained four or fewer members, more than half the population of 1,147 people lived in households that contained six or more members.[19]

Fifth, economic or psychological pressures, typically acting to split apart the multiple households, are evident in Ring's analysis. Unmarried sons and daughters might remain after one of their brothers married, but when he began to have children they were likely to leave. When two of the brothers married, unmarried siblings often left, particularly if their parents had died. When the older of two married brothers had children, the younger tended to leave.[20]

Ring argues that the overwhelming predominance of conjugal family households in the survey is misleading in respect to what people really wanted, that the ideal family of the peasants was probably something else: the joint family, in which more than one married son remained at home. The small size of the family farm, high infant mortality, and low life expectancy operated to prevent most families from attaining it.

Almost every family passed through stages in its cycle in which it was conjugal. A household began with a conjugal couple, who presently had children. When the children reached adulthood, they left to form new conjugal units, or the sons brought their wives home to live under the paternal roof, creating a multiple household. After the death of the father this multiple household usually broke up, creating two or more new conjugal households, which then might progress through the same cycle. The household might never achieve the multiple stage, however, if no sons survived to adulthood, if the father died before sons reached marriageable age, or if the family land was insufficient to feed additional mouths.

Joint families are theoretically found in peasant societies where, as in the early Middle Ages, the custom is to divide land equally among male heirs. Instead of partitioning an already small holding, the heirs might choose to work it in common. A comparison of Farfa with a statistical model of a society with a joint family system leads Ring to conclude: "It can be assumed that a sizeable minority of the [Farfa] population at one time or another . . . lived in a joint household and that perhaps a majority passed part of their lives in households consisting of a married couple, their unmarried children, and one married son."[21]

How the peasant family of Farfa in the early ninth century compared with families in other parts of Europe is difficult to determine. At least two other surveys seem to give credence to the theory that there was a preference for large family groupings. The most famous and extensive of the estate surveys, that of the monastery of St. Germain-des-Prés near Paris (801–820),[22] suffers considerable defects. It probably does not list all tenants (there is a mysteriously large number of solitaries), lists others more than once in different capacities, and does not spell out the relationships between conjugal units on the same manse. So divergent are the possible interpretations that Emily Coleman, assuming that the conjugal units were unrelated, concludes that the nuclear family not only predominated but was the only type found on the estates,[23] while David Herlihy, assuming that they are related, estimates that a very large 43 percent of the households were multiple but that few three-generational families existed. He also reaches the conclusion that the children, particularly girls, of peasants of the lowest status were often absorbed as servants into the richer households and returned to their parents when they reached the age of marriage, a pattern that later became common.[24]

A fragmentary survey of thirteen villages belonging to the

abbey of St. Victor of Marseilles in 813–814,[25] a time when the Saracens were invading Provence, shows a high proportion—35 percent—of the inhabited farms supporting multiple households, usually with two but sometimes three, four, or even five conjugal units. A more striking feature of this survey is the fact that in only four of the thirteen villages were all the farms occupied; in two all were vacant; and in seven 30 percent were unoccupied. Furthermore, although there were an unusually large number of adult unmarried children (127 men and 120 women specified as "bachelor son" or "bachelor daughter"), 60 men and women were specified as having "foreign" spouses *(maritus extraneus, uxor extranea)*, that is, taken from outside the villages belonging to the abbey; the "foreign" spouse came to live with the family of his or her native wife or husband. Stephen Weinberger, analyzing this survey, suggests that the peasants of St. Victor, chronically threatened by the Saracens, formed a society in which the most important consideration was "maximizing security and stability." Families clung to their members, brought in outsiders to augment their numbers, and crowded into overburdened land resources.[26]

Certainly the St. Victor survey seems to present a picture of families huddled together for protection. Chroniclers tell us that later in the century the population entirely abandoned their farms and fled to the mountains. Later documents show that when the peasants returned in the following (tenth) century, the patterns of habitation, social status, family organization, and the previously stagnant economy all were revolutionized as the farms became totally occupied, serfdom disappeared in favor of sharecropping, and a looser and more flexible family structure appeared amid an expanding economy. The multiple or extended family household at St. Victor, in other words, was a function of protection in a threatening environment, the conjugal family household a product of stability and freedom.[27]

A Bavarian survey of the same period, a rare record of a lay seigneury, Lauterbach, has led Carl Hammer, Jr., to interesting conclusions about how seigneurial management distributed personnel and arranged marriages of serfs for efficient agricultural operation. While peasants seem usually to have chosen marriage partners from within the community, if suitable candidates were not available they married serfs from another estate and the transaction was balanced by an exchange of serfs between the two estates. Similarly, the overwhelming predominance of simple family households and their uniformity of size may reflect active administrative manipulation. Childless tenants or older couples whose children had left home may have been given additional manpower by the delegation of servants to live with them, thus ensuring that every holding would be fully exploited but that none would have too many mouths to feed, and at the same time finding work for children and help for the aged. Thus the entire seigneury rather than the individual family went through a life cycle and was, in Hammer's words, "literally one big family."[28]

From the sex ratios in the St. Germain-des-Prés and Farfa surveys, some scholars have hypothesized a policy of infanticide. The sex ratio among children was 143 boys to 100 girls at St. Germain and 136 to 100 at Farfa, figures that have been used to argue the killing of female infants.[29] But, although infanticide may indeed have been practiced, in the eyes of most scholars the evidence of the two surveys is inconclusive (for adults at Farfa the ratio inexplicably becomes 103 to 100)[30] and may better be attributed to other factors, including idiosyncrasies of reporting. Furthermore, the third survey, that of St. Victor, shows girls outnumbering boys by a ratio of 100 to 93.[31]

The polyptychs are the main source that documents the emergence of the family farm and with it the peasant family, to which the accidents of birth, death, and economics gave a variety of shapes and sizes, perhaps only rarely the configuration its members would have preferred. The fact that such information as we possess, including even the names—Fredo, Ado, Autari, Adileupa, Gutta, Saxula—of these obscure people, has been preserved for more than a thousand years is a minor miracle, one that discloses the shadowy beginnings of the European family.

A Noble Family of the Ninth Century

Dhuoda's Manual, a book of advice, was composed in the years 841–843 by a noble Frankish lady for her fifteen-year-old son William. Although many of the male members of Dhuoda's family are known historical figures, only the *Manual* testifies to her own

Louis the Pious, whom Dhuoda's husband, Bernard, served and in whose palace Dhuoda and Bernard were married. From Hrabanus Maurus, De **Laudibus S. Crucis** *(831–840).* (Nationalbibliothek, Vienna, Cod. 652, f. 3)

existence; no other documents mention her, nor does she appear in contemporary chronicles.[32]

Dhuoda's father-in-law, William of Gellone, was a hero of Charlemagne's wars against the Moors of Spain who was later celebrated in epic poetry as "William of Orange." A first cousin of Charlemagne, who appointed him count of Toulouse, William founded a monastery at Gellone, whither he retired to die in 812; he was canonized as St. William (St. Guillaume-du-Désert). Dhuoda's husband, Bernard of Septimania (the Mediterranean province bordering Spain), was an official at the court of Charlemagne's son Louis the Pious. Louis had sponsored Bernard at his baptism, and Bernard had served as tutor to Louis's youngest son.

In the preface to her book, Dhuoda tells her son that she and Bernard were married in the emperor's palace at Aachen on June 29, 824, ten years after the death of Charlemagne. From chronicles and archeology we can construct a description of the palace built by Charlemagne beginning in 794. Inside a four-gated wall, four clusters of buildings were arranged in a square: the great hall, with an adjacent tower containing archives and treasury; the king's residence, with his chamber on the second floor; a combined barracks and court of justice, connected to the great hall by a gallery; and a complex of religious buildings in the shape of a cross, at its center the octagonal chapel where Dhuoda was married.[33] The chapel, wrote chronicler Einhard, was "decorated with gold and silver, with lamps, and with lattices and doors of solid bronze" and marble columns brought from Rome and Ravenna.[34] Charlemagne's biographer Notker reports that the emperor, "shrewd as he was," arranged to have the houses of his nobles built around the palace in such a way that "through the windows of his private apartment he could see everything they were doing, and all their comings and goings, without their realizing it."[35] The palace compound also had a cemetery, a hunting park, and a menagerie.

Chronicles, manuscript illuminations, and statues provide a picture of the way the courtiers dressed. Charlemagne and his successors wore "the national dress of the Franks" (Einhard): a linen shirt and linen drawers next to the skin, over that long hose and a tunic edged with silk, shoes on the feet and bands of cloth wrapped around the legs, in winter a fur vest topped by a great cloak.[36] The women wore a wide-sleeved tunic cinched in at the waist by a jeweled belt, a mantle over the tunic, and a veil attached by a gold headband.[37]

Soon after the marriage of Dhuoda and Bernard, he was entrusted with the task of defending the Spanish frontier against the Saracens. On November 29, 826, Dhuoda gave birth, she does not say where, to William, named for his grandfather. "You were born of me into this world, you, my so longed-for first-born son," she writes.[38] The following year, after a victory in Spain, Bernard was named Louis's chamberlain at the court of Aachen, "second man in the empire," according to the chronicler Nithard,[39] and the emperor's lieutenant in wars against his rebellious sons.

Dhuoda evidently followed Bernard in the shiftings of his political and military career. In the last chapter of her book she tells William that she borrowed heavily to aid her husband's projects "and so that he would not separate himself from you and me, as one sees so many others do."[40] She does not mention the fact that in 830 Bernard was accused by political enemies of having an affair with Louis the Pious's second wife, Judith, who "established her innocence by an oath taken with her kinsmen before the people" (Nithard).[41] Nor does she refer to the multiple disasters that the family experienced in the 830s during warfare between the emperor and his sons: the drowning of Bernard's sister Gerberga, who was sealed in a cask and thrown into the Saone "like a witch" (Nithard), the beheading of his brother Gaucelm,[42] and the blinding of his brother Heribert, all at the orders of Louis the Pious's eldest son, Lothair I.[43]

No sooner had one bloody familial war ended than a fresh one began, this time with Bernard enlisted in the cause of Louis's grandson Pepin II of Aquitaine. At this juncture (March 841), after fifteen childless years, Dhuoda bore another son, at Uzès, near Nîmes. She was now in her late thirties or early forties. Before the child was baptized, while he was, in her own words, "still very little," Bernard requested from Aquitaine that the bishop of Uzès bring the baby (later named Bernard) to him,[44] perhaps to protect him from Bernard's enemies. William was apparently with his father; Dhuoda says that she had been for a long time far from their presence, remaining at Uzès "by the order of my lord [Bernard], rejoicing in his successes," but alone, her baby taken from her, her other son absent.[45]

When the war of fraternal succession ended in the defeat of Bernard's side, he sent William to the court of Charles the Bald, one of the victors, to do homage in return for confirmation of William's lands and titles.[46] It was at this moment that Dhuoda undertook to compose her manual. Her intention was not, as one might expect, to instruct the young man in court etiquette or political tactics, but to ensure his moral and spiritual welfare. "You will find in my book a mirror," she told him, "in which you can contemplate the salvation of your soul."[47] Written in Latin, and like most medieval compositions stuffed with biblical references and quotations, the book nevertheless manages to express much real feeling. An autobiographical preface explains Dhuoda's motive in "having this little volume transcribed" (doubtless by a cleric) for her son.[48]

The first section is concerned with the young man's religious instruction: the love of God, the search for God, the greatness of God, the mystery of the Trinity, the virtues, especially charity, and how to pray. The next deals with William's social debts, toward his father, toward his lord (Charles the Bald), and toward bishops and priests. Next the manual discusses the vices, advising him to convert pride into courage and arrogance into gentleness; the Holy Spirit will help him to resist other vices, principally that of fornication, and to practice the continence that conquers concupiscence—"And how great the strength and splendor of a continual chastity which makes a mortal man the compatriot and equal of the angels!" Man was threatened by tribulations—despair, false riches, persecution, temptation, poverty, suffering, danger, illness—which nevertheless could not keep him from glorifying God.

Dhuoda then outlines the steps to human perfection; touches upon the double nature of birth (carnal and spiritual) and of death (temporal and eternal); and advises William on the prayers he should offer for clergy, kings, his lord, his father, the family forebears, and especially for his uncle and godfather, Thierry, count of Autun. Following this is a curious section devoted to a favorite medieval subject: numerology, the symbolic significance of the letters of Adam's name, the religious importance of the number seven (the seven gifts of the Holy Spirit), the number six (the six ages of the world), the number eight (the eight souls saved from the flood in Noah's Ark), the number nine (the nine orders of angels). Finally she gives a list of the dead of the family for whom William must pray, and the epitaph she wants engraved on her tomb, an inscription of eight verses asking God to forgive her sins and "you, of all ages and sexes, who pass by" to pray for her.

The manual was begun in November 841 and completed the following year for William's sixteenth birthday, with a few reflections added the subsequent winter. We know no more of its author. A chronicler reports the marriage of a sister of William, leading one scholar to suggest that Bernard visited Uzès in the summer of 843 and that from this meeting a daughter was born to Dhuoda in 844. That year Bernard was accused of treason by Charles the Bald and executed in Toulouse. Nineteen-year-old William joined Charles's cousin and rival Pepin II, who made him count of Bordeaux in 845, but four years later William in turn was executed. The younger Bernard seems to have survived until 872, and may have been the Bernard Plantevelue whose son, Duke William the Pious of Aquitaine, founded the great abbey of Cluny.[49]

Beyond its uniqueness as an early medieval book of advice written not only by a lay person but by a woman, the enduring value of *Dhuoda's Manual* is the insight it gives into three aspects of the family: feelings within the family circle, authority in the family, and the family consciousness of the ninth-century European aristocracy.

Dhuoda describes herself as grieving at the absence of husband and son. "In spite of the many concerns which preoccupy me, that of seeing you again one day with my own eyes is the greatest. . . . My heart languishes with this desire. . . ."[50] She charges William with the responsibility for seeing that her book is later read to his younger brother, and reminds him of the affectionate bond that should unite the two boys: "When your little brother, whose name I still do not know, has been baptized in Christ, do not fail to instruct him, to educate him, to love him . . . for he is 'your flesh and your brother' [from the Old Testament Joseph story]."[51]

But most important is the authority of William's father, to whom she invariably refers as her lord. "Above all to your lord and progenitor Bernard, in his presence as in his absence, you owe fear,

Charles the Bald, from Charles the Bald's Psalter, *ninth century.*
(Bibliothèque Nationale, MS lat. 1152, f. 3v)

love, and loyalty. . . . Obey him in every important matter, listen
to his advice."[52] In a possible reference to the unruly sons of Louis
the Pious, Dhuoda reminds William that when he reaches the age
of maturity he himself might have children and that he would not
want them to be "rebellious, proud, and greedy," but "modest,
peaceful, and obedient"; a man who had such children would

"rejoice in having himself been a dutiful son." William might owe homage to kings and emperors, but his loyalty throughout life is first and foremost "to the man whose son you are," who merits his "special homage, loyal and sure." He must never forget that to his father he owes his situation in the world.[53]

The list of dead relatives for whom William is to pray includes eight names without title or explanation of relationship: William, Cunegonde, Gerberga, Guiborg, Theodoric, Gaucelm, Guarnarius, and Rodlinda. Most possibly all, seem to be members of Bernard's immediate family. Six of the eight have been tentatively identified: William and Cunegonde as Bernard's parents, Gerberga as his sister, Guiborg as his stepmother, and Theodoric and Gaucelm as his brothers. "Some other members of this kindred," Dhuoda writes, "are still alive with God's aid," and she advises William that if any of them die while he survives, he should add their names to the list and pray for them.[54] No other members of Bernard's or Dhuoda's family are mentioned, nor is there any hint of knowledge of ancestors beyond grandparents.

Although Dhuoda composes her own epitaph, she does not say where she will be buried, nor does she mention William's birthplace; she and Bernard were married, not on an estate of her own family or Bernard's, but at the emperor's palace. A noble family of the ninth century owned land, even many estates, but had no central residence, no "family seat" where members were born, married, and buried, no core property to provide identity to family and lineage. The titles and offices they held were not hereditary. William's grandfather was "count of Toulouse," but the title was not passed on to William's father, whose descendants had to win their own titles and offices, and the benefices that went with them. Most important to the ninth-century noble family was what German scholars have called "king's nearness" (Königsnähe), its relation to the ruler who bestowed benefices and titles. Instead of clustering around a principal landholding, families attached themselves to relatives who held important offices. In the words of one historian, "The noble kins of the Carolingian and post-Carolingian world . . . had a fluidity, and present to the historian an oddly horizontal rather than a vertical aspect. . . . The center of gravity and even the sense of identity of these large families could shift, sometimes within very few generations."[55] Maternal as well as paternal relatives were important, but (as in Dhuoda's list) the emphasis was on the paternal. The contemporary *Libri memoriales*, monastic registers of living and dead members of the family used at nobles' funerals, give a similar picture comprising two or three generations, perceived as on a single level: not a lineage, but a kindred.[56]

Dhuoda's Manual puts forward the current aristocratic ideal of the family: parents and children, grandparents, uncles and aunts on both sides living in close association. Reality fell short of the ideal. "Most women have the joy of living in this world with their children," she wrote, "and I, Dhuoda, oh my son William, am separated and far from you."[57] Her children taken from her, her husband absent and in danger, members of the larger family dispersed or dead, Dhuoda presents the picture of a family divided and buffeted by the external forces of a violent age.

Marriage and the Carolingian Church

Until the Carolingian era, the impact of Christianity on Germanic marriage customs was modest. The Church's attitude remained lukewarm toward the institution of marriage. It officially accepted the necessity of sex for procreation and even grudgingly admitted St. Paul's view of sex as a need that sometimes had to be satisfied, but its preference lay with the severe views of St. Jerome. Sex for pleasure alone, even for married couples, was catalogued as a mortal sin.

By the end of the seventh century the Church had achieved a measure of victory in its war against polygamy. It had also succeeded in banning marriage between first cousins and between in-laws. But nothing in its earlier pronouncements seems to point to the aggressive new extension of the ban on consanguineous marriage that it now put forward. The new rule was twofold. First, the definition of consanguinity was broadened to include not only blood relations and in-laws but "spiritual kin," that is, godparents and godchildren. Second, the forbidden degree of kinship was radically increased.

What motivated the Church to multiply the impediments to marriage is a mystery to which scholars have not found a satisfactory solution. British anthropologist Jack Goody in 1983 advanced a bold suggestion: that the Church's extension of exogamy, together with its opposition to polygamy, concubinage, and divorce-remarriage, constituted a deliberate strategy designed to limit the aristocracy's ability to produce heirs so that its estates might more easily fall into the hands of the Church through bequests.[58] Any such Machiavellian policy presupposes a wholly undemonstrable capacity for secret, concerted action on the part of the medieval Church. It ignores the way Church policy was actually formed, openly, and typically with two steps forward and one back: the debate of a council, the declaration of a synod, the decision of a pope.

David Herlihy, the leading contemporary historian of the medieval family, suggests another reason for the Church's attitude: a wish "to prevent rich and powerful males from collecting or retaining more than their share of women."[59] Though more believable than Jack Goody's thesis, this explanation too lacks documentary confirmation. In fact, the Church's insistence may require a kind of psychological detective work for which historians do not yet possess the capability.

The author of the extension of degrees of kinship was the English missionary St. Boniface (c. 672–754), acting as papal legate to the Frankish church. As late as the first half of the eighth century, canon law employed the Roman method of computing relationships, counting back from one of the two spouses to their common ancestor, then forward to the other spouse, and limiting its definition of consanguineous marriage to four degrees (father or mother, grandfather or grandmother, uncle or aunt, first cousin).

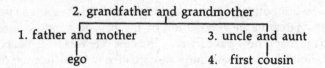

2. grandfather and grandmother

1. father and mother   3. uncle and aunt

ego   4. first cousin

Councils held in Rome in 721 and 743 ruled that a man could not marry his niece or first cousin, relations in the third and fourth degree Roman style. In 747 Boniface undertook to reform the marriage customs by which the great Frankish nobles had created a network of alliances among related families. King Pepin (reigned

*Table of consanguinity, using the Roman system of calculating relationship.
Ego is face at center; father and mother (circle above) and son and daughter
(circle below) are related to him in the first degree; brother and sister (circles
on either side) in the second; nephew and niece in the third, and so on. From
a thirteenth-century manuscript, Atelier of Gautier Lebaude, Paris.* (The
Pierpont Morgan Library)

751–768), who saw these alliances as a threat to royal power, backed Boniface, who, after consulting the pope, recommended that consanguinity be defined as extending to seven degrees. The new prescription became part of Frankish law. Thus the extended prohibitions were, in their origin, not solely the invention of the Church, but the product of a convergence of religious ideology and royal self-interest.

Boniface also extended the incest prohibition in another direction. If a man had had sex with a woman, he was forbidden to marry her relative; if he disregarded the prohibition, his marriage was invalidated, he was forbidden to marry at all, and he had to perform lifelong penance. This novel taboo surprisingly took hold and operated throughout European society for several centuries.[60]

At the same time, breaking ground untouched by Roman law, the Church in the mid-eighth century began to confer the force of blood relationship on the Christian spiritual kinship created by both the rite of baptism and that of confirmation. The child and his family were henceforth regarded as related to the godparents or sponsors and their families. The new concept derived a certain social sanction from the fact that godparents were deliberately chosen to create family alliances. Yet Boniface himself expressed doubts. In a letter to the archbishop of Canterbury commenting on a marriage that he himself had approved, that of a man who had been godfather to another man's child and on the father's death had married the mother, Boniface wrote: "The people in Rome say this is a sin, even a mortal sin, and state that in such cases divorce* is necessary . . . [but] I cannot understand how spiritual relationships in marriage can be so great a sin, since through baptism all Christians become sons and daughters of Christ, brothers and sisters in the Church."[61]

An even more bizarre innovation presently followed. The early ninth-century compilation of texts known as the Pseudo-Isidorian Decretals, often cited in later canon law, records a broad extension of Boniface's prohibitions, which had been instituted in the meantime almost by sleight of hand, simply through the substitution of one method of counting for another. The Roman method of com-

*Divortium. The same Latin word is translated as either divorce or annulment, two concepts which the medieval Church treated as synonymous.

puting kinship, heretofore invariably used by the Church, reckoned back from ego to the common ancestor and then forward to
the proposed spouse. The Germanic method, in contrast, counted
back only to the common ancestor. Thus where in Roman reckon-
ing first cousins were related in the fourth degree, in Germanic
they were related only in the second. The replacement of the
Roman method with the German, recorded in the Pseudo-
Isidorian Decretals, ruled it incestuous to marry a descendant of
one's great-great-great-great-great grandfather.[62]

The absurdity of the prohibition seems to defy explanation. On
the one hand, if it were actually adhered to, hardly anyone within
the narrow circle of the aristocracy could marry at all; on the other
hand, no one could by any stretch of the imagination identify
ancestors so far back (probably few members even of the aristocracy could identify all eight of their great-grandparents). Canon-
law historian Adhémar Esmein, noting that the Eastern Church
never adopted the seventh-degree rule, thought the Western
church might not have done so if it had continued to operate
entirely within the old Roman-law regions, but this hardly explains the aberration.[63]

In practice the rules seem to have acted mainly to deter the more
obviously endogamous unions. They rarely affected those involving more distant kinship except—an unforeseen effect—in cases
where kings and nobles wished to free themselves from inconven-
ient marriages. This legal stratagem, the expedient discovery of a
forbidden degree of kinship, first employed in the ninth century,
caused immediate concern among farsighted clerics. A distinguished scholar, the abbot of Fulda, Hrabanus Maurus (d. 856),
declared that incest was too broadly defined and that annulment
of marriage on the grounds of a previously undiscovered relationship circumvented the Church's stand on a more important matter:
divorce.[64]

The major issue in the Carolingian era respecting marriage was
in fact not exogamy but the Church's insistence that the bond was
monogamous and indissoluble, a lifelong commitment to one person. Whereas the kings and aristocrats of the Merovingian era had
been openly polygamous, the Carolingians married one wife at a
time, content to season their monogamy with concubinage. Young
nobles typically enjoyed a concubine or two before undertaking

marriage, and not all abandoned the habit. The Church's primary concern, however, was not with concubinage but with divorce. In the last half of the eighth century, Church councils retreated somewhat from earlier positions, acknowledging certain valid grounds for divorce and remarriage: adultery, servile status, leprosy, lack of consent, impotence, one partner's becoming a monk or nun. It still tenaciously resisted the divorce by mutual consent which contemporary legal formulas show was widely practiced.

In his early years, Charlemagne had dismissed a concubine in order to contract a political marriage with a Lombard princess; a year later he divorced the princess, apparently because she was barren. But in the 780s and 790s, under pressure from his bishops, he enacted rigorous legislation prohibiting divorce on any grounds. He then set the example, contracting three more marriages and living monogamously with each wife until her death (but comforting his old age with four concubines). His son Louis the Pious not only supported measures against divorce but refused to divorce his second wife, Judith, when she was accused of adultery with Dhuoda's husband, Bernard of Septimania. Church councils during his reign reinforced the new principle that adultery was insufficient grounds for divorce.[65]

In the second half of the ninth century, a royal divorce case occasioned the first great medieval confrontation of king and Church, which had repercussions for the institution of Christian marriage as well as for political history.[66]

In 858 Lothair II, king of Lotharingia (Lorraine), wanted to divorce his barren wife, Theutberga, in order to marry his former concubine, Waldrada, who had given him children that he now proposed to legitimize. As grounds for divorce, he accused Theutberga not merely of unchastity but of incest. Before their marriage, he claimed, she had had sexual relations with her brother Hubert, a prelate of dubious moral reputation. Lothair's allegation presented two obstacles to belief. He had waited two years before making the accusation, and he had officially confirmed his bride's virginity by bestowing the traditional *Morgengabe*. He offered an extraordinary explanation: Hubert, he said, had had anal intercourse with his sister and so left her maidenhead unimpaired. He carried his indictment a lurid step further. Despite the contraceptive character of her intercourse with Hubert, she had conceived a fetus by means of occult practices and had then aborted it. Why the king felt the need for such a multiplication of mutually contradictory slanders is a mystery.

Protesting her innocence, Theutberga successfully demanded a trial by ordeal in which her champion heroically immersed himself in boiling water and emerged unscalded. Refusing to accept defeat, Lothair imprisoned his wife until she agreed to a separation. Evidently under duress, Theutberga then made a secret confession to the king's chaplain, Gunther, archbishop of Cologne, a written record of which was submitted in January 860 to a synod of Lotharingian bishops at Aachen. Theutberga refused to repeat the confession publicly, but the bishops "authorized" her to retire to a convent preparatory to the annulment of her marriage. Lothair at once resumed living openly with Waldrada. In February 860 a second synod was called at which the queen, evidently threatened with torture, threw herself at the feet of the bishops and confessed: "My brother Hubert, a cleric, corrupted me when I was a girl; he several times practiced fornication against nature on my body."[67] She was sentenced to do public penance, but the Lotharingian bishops now hesitated. Refusing to give Lothair permission to remarry, they appealed to a distinguished authority on canon law, Hincmar, archbishop of Reims (c. 806–882).

In this first of the great royal divorce cases, the political issue, the need for an heir to the throne, was well understood to be paramount. In fact, the very existence of Lothair's kingdom of Lorraine was at stake. His uncles, Charles the Bald and Louis the German, rulers of the other two territories into which Charlemagne's empire had been split, were ready to partition Lorraine between them. Lothair obtained the support of Louis the German in the divorce question by promising to cede him territory. Theutberga then fled to the court of Charles the Bald, whose protégé Hincmar was.

Hincmar produced a treatise, On the Divorce of King Lothair and Queen Theutberga (De Divortio Lotharii Regis et Tetbergae Reginae), in the form of a series of responses to questions posed by the Lotharingian prelates.

He began by pointing out that although the case was of a very common type, Lothair was a king, a man chosen by God, with many more responsibilities than other men, one of which was to set an example.[68] The synod at Aachen, he continued, had acted arbitrarily. What pressures had been put on the queen to exact such an admission? She had successfully defended herself by ordeal. The Lotharingian bishops had suggested in explanation that "this woman thought of another name than that of her brother when she sent her substitute [vicarius] to the judgment, and that is why he was not cooked."[69] Hincmar rejected the argument and declared that the ordeal was a valid procedure justified by the Bible, a way in which God pronounced his judgment. The champion had emerged unharmed; therefore Theutberga was innocent.[70]

To the bishops' question as to whether the Scriptures and the Church Fathers confirmed that "a woman can conceive and remain a virgin after abortion" and whether a marriage undertaken after such a crime would be valid, Hincmar replied with a detailed description of how conception normally takes place, concluding with elaborate irony: "It has never been heard in this world, nor is it read under this sky in the Scripture of Truth, that the vulva of a woman has received semen without coitus, and that she has conceived, although her uterus was closed and her vulva unopened, so that she produced a living or aborted child, except for the uniquely happy and blessed Virgin Mary, whose conception was not by nature but by grace."[71] And he demanded, "If our lord king received this woman as a virgin, why does he now say she is defiled? But if she came to him not a virgin, why did he keep her so long?"[72] If the crime had indeed occurred, it could be atoned for in only two possible ways: vengeance or penitence. To discover the truth, Hubert himself must be called to witness, and if it could be shown that Theutberga was not a consenting party, Hubert must bear the burden of guilt and must be punished.[73] (On this point Hincmar parted from his patron Charles the Bald, whose ally Hubert was.)

In their action against the queen, Hincmar continued, the bishops had erred in four ways:

First, a secret confession must remain secret, even if it was made before several bishops.[74]

Second, the bishops were not empowered to pronounce a separation without a public trial and judgment, with competent witnesses, the chief of whom must be Hubert himself. The only grounds for separation was adultery (which still remained invalid as grounds for divorce). Any other complaint could be handled with penance and absolution.[75]

Third, the bishops were not qualified to judge Theutberga. Here Hincmar came to grips with a potentially dangerous problem. The Church's courts had slowly but surely gained popularity and influence in cases involving marriage and the family, and now were virtually equal rivals of the lay courts. Hincmar grasped the nettle. Marriage, he said, required two kinds of justice, that of the lay world for its social aspect and that of the Church for its moral and sacramental aspects. The lay world was concerned to avoid conflict between two families and their allies; the Church was concerned only with the indissolubility of marriage. Hincmar cited an example of collaboration between the two justices. In 822, during the reign of Louis the Pious, a lady named Northilda had complained before a synod that her husband Agembertus had forced her to have intercourse "in a shameful way." The synod refused to pronounce a separation, referring the case to a civil court of "lay people and married men," better able to judge such matters. If the civil court found the husband guilty, the Church would assess a penance. This kind of collaboration was not only possible but essential, said Hincmar: clerical justice must not compete with lay justice.

In Theutberga's case the procedure was clear: Lothair must bring her before a secular court. If it found her guilty, she could then appeal to the Church, which would commute the civil sentence—death—to ten years' penance and lifelong chastity. If it found her innocent—as Hincmar obviously believed her to be—Lothair must take her back.[76]

Fourth and finally, the bishops had been unreasonably severe with Theutberga and unwarrantably tolerant toward Lothair. Without waiting for further judgment, Lothair had openly resumed relations with his concubine. Incest might be worse than adultery, but that did not make adultery acceptable. The marriage of Theutberga and Lothair was valid and therefore indissoluble. The king had no right to marry Waldrada.[77]

Two years passed with Lothair not giving up but not daring to marry his concubine. At last he appealed "very mournfully" to another synod at Aachen and "in querulous tones" complained of

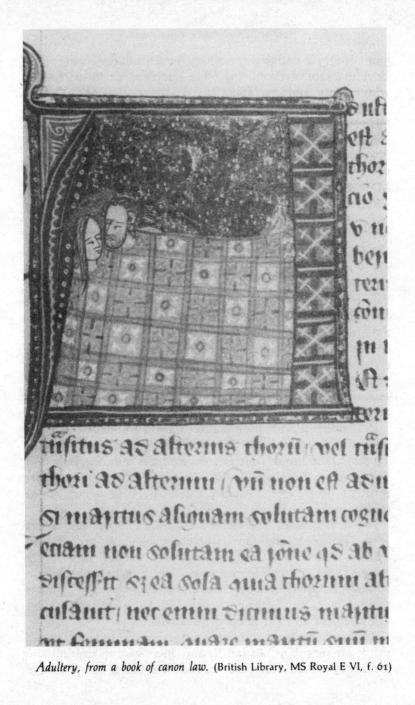

rusitus ad alternus thoru vel rusi
thor ad alternum / vn non est ad
Si majitus aliquam solutam cogne
ctiam non solutam ea jone q3 ab ...
discessit si ea sola aula thorum ab
culauit / nec enim dicimus majitu
...

Adultery, from a book of canon law. (British Library, MS Royal E VI, f. 61) his sexual needs and insisted that "if [Theutberga] had been worthy of the nuptial bed and were not contaminated by the deathly pollution of incest and publicly condemned by oral confession, he would willingly have kept her."[78] The synod annulled the marriage on the grounds of incest, and Lothair married and crowned Waldrada. Yet he evidently still felt uncomfortable with the legality of his situation because still another synod, in Metz in 863, found wholly new grounds for him. It ruled that Lothair's relationship with Waldrada had been a legal marriage all along, and that he had been bullied by Hubert into marrying Theutberga "though he didn't want to."[79]

Now Theutberga countersued. Appealing to Pope Nicholas I, she protested that she had been "forced by violence" into her confession and was still being subjected to coercive pressure. The pope sent an investigating team to Lorraine to examine the history of Lothair's relationship with Waldrada to see whether he had taken her "with prearranged dowries before witnesses according to law and ritual" and whether she had been "admitted by public manifestations to be his wife." If so, they must inquire why she had been repudiated and Lothair had married Theutberga; if not, he must be reconciled with Theutberga "if she is innocent."[80]

The findings of the papal investigation were decisive in support of Theutberga. Nicholas called a synod of his own, cancelled the decision of Metz, deposed the prelates who had pronounced it, and ordered Lothair to take Theutberga back. Charles the Bald and Louis the German added their advocacy, and in 865 Theutberga was formally reinstated as queen, with twelve of Lothair's chief noblemen taking oaths that he would treat her well. Bishop Adventius of Metz reported to the pope that Lothair and Theutberga attended mass and supped together at the royal table, and afterwards, "as rumor hints, [Lothair] undertook joyfully to discharge his conjugal duty." Adventius assured Nicholas that Lothair had not touched Waldrada since the pope ordered him to take back Theutberga. But a few months later he wrote a fellow bishop begging him to make Lothair stop sleeping with Waldrada before the pope found out and excommunicated them.[81]

Lothair in fact had not abandoned his intention. In 866 he forced Theutberga herself to plead with Pope Nicholas for the divorce on the basis of her sterility and the claimed prior marriage between Lothair and Waldrada, and to request permission to enter a convent. Nicholas replied sternly that sterility was no grounds for a divorce and that her sterility was caused not by her own body's infertility "but by your husband's iniquity." Even if she entered a convent, the pope declared, Lothair could not remarry.[82]

Early in 867 Nicholas warned Charles the Bald that he had heard that Lothair intended to murder Theutberga or to have her convicted in a trial by combat and executed. At the same time, Nicholas wrote Lothair threatening him with the full weight of God's retribution if he harmed her. Further, since he had committed adultery with Waldrada, he could never marry her, even if Theutberga were dead.[83]

But Theutberga was tiring of the struggle. In 868 she journeyed to Rome to interview Nicholas's successor, Hadrian II, but not in the interest of reconciliation. A bishop present at the council that heard her plea reported: "She swore that she would rather flee among the pagans than see again the face of the glorious king Lothair."[84]

The litigation had lasted eight years. As successive grounds for divorce Lothair had offered incest, previous marriage, absence of consent on his part, sterility on that of his wife, and her wish to enter a convent. Each had been categorically rejected by the Church. The stalemate ended only when both Waldrada and Theutberga entered convents.[85] In 869 Lothair traveled to Rome as a penitent, received absolution from Hadrian II, and died on the return journey, still without legal heirs—a judgment of Providence, according to his enemies.[86] The following year his kingdom was partitioned by his two uncles.

Two other divorce cases in which Hincmar also played a large role were contemporary with Lothair's and served to reinforce the Church's posture. One involved a north Italian count named Boso whose wife Ingiltrude had eloped in 856 with one of her husband's vassals. Following the Church's standard policy of recommending reconciliation, Popes Benedict III and Nicholas I ordered her to return to her husband, who accused her of adultery but declared himself willing to take her back. Ingiltrude, however, afraid that her husband would kill her, fled to Lothair's court. The pope then excommunicated her. The archbishop of Cologne, the same Gunther who had heard Theutberga's secret confession, consulted Hincmar: Should he exact a public penance from Ingiltrude but allow her to remain in Cologne separated from her husband? Or should he insist that she return?

Hincmar responded that it was not proper for Gunther to authorize the separation or to pronounce penance, but that he must confine himself to obtaining "security for her fair treatment by her husband." Then Ingiltrude must be returned to her husband, who if he mistreated her would be subject to canonical justice from the bishop of his own diocese. The couple must be reconciled, and the woman's safety must be guaranteed, but of the two reconciliation was the more important.

In 865, nine years after her elopement, Ingiltrude agreed to go to Rome escorted by a papal legate, but on the way changed her mind and fled. Pope Nicholas refused to allow Boso to remarry, upholding the principle that adultery was not grounds for divorce.[87]

A third case was that of Count Stephen of Auvergne, who in 860 explained to a synod that he had not consummated his marriage to the daughter of Count Raymond of Toulouse. Before his betrothal, Stephen had had an affair with a young woman who was a relative of his fiancée, thus violating St. Boniface's extension of the incest taboo. Tardily affected by scruples, Stephen tried to withdraw from his engagement, but Count Raymond insisted on the marriage being completed. Stephen allowed himself to be shepherded through the financial settlement and the ceremony, but balked at the marriage bed. He now declared himself ready to do whatever the Church advised "for my salvation before God, and for my reconciliation and pacification of Raymond, and for the safety and honor of the lady."

The case was treated in the dual manner Hincmar had recommended for Lothair and Theutberga, by a collaboration of ecclesiastical and lay justice, the simultaneous convocation of a synod of local bishops and a royal law court. The former was to deal with the moral question of whether the marriage could be dissolved; the latter would confront the possibility of politically dangerous violence between Raymond's and Stephen's families and their allies, and would assess what civil fines Stephen might owe. Hincmar stressed that it was important to ascertain whether the bride "said the same thing as Stephen put forth; because we have often heard that between men and women what one says the other denies." All the conditions necessary to marriage must be examined, the sacrament itself, the free status of the partners, and the sexual union. Hincmar announced his own conclusion: Stephen's marriage was not indissoluble; he had done well not to consummate it, and the union must be dissolved. The synod agreed. The bride was returned to her father's guardianship, free to marry or enter a convent. Hincmar recommended that Stephen "should accept regular penance from his own bishop . . . and after his absolution, if he cannot contain . . . he should seek to join with a legitimate wife lest he fall again into the crime of fornication." Whether he married again is unknown.[88]

Hincmar's views, expounded in his treatise, strengthened and clarified the Church's doctrines of marriage, chief among them indissolubility. In marriage "God joins a man and a woman, making them one flesh; man must not separate them; only God can separate them."[89] The Christian must accept this fact with all its consequences. Hincmar advised men to exercise caution in choosing their wives, because once they had taken them, their defects had to be borne, as vividly spelled out by St. Jerome (c.331–420): "If she guzzles, if she is bad-tempered, loose, lustful, gluttonous, frivolous, quarrelsome, scurrilous, must one keep such a wife? Want to or not, we must."[90]

Hincmar portrayed the men of his day as practicing all kinds of stratagems to get rid of their wives. They "accused them of adultery and killed them, without proof, without trial, without reason, but only out of hatred and cruelty or desire for another wife or concubine." Taking flight in hyperbole, he asserted that some men had their wives "led to the market to be butchered and thrown to the pigs," while others slew them with their own hands. They seized any pretext to suspend conjugal relations after a few years of married life, took mistresses, slandered their spouses to the clergy, forced them to tolerate concubines and to testify that their husbands were impotent or to pretend that they themselves longed to retire to a convent.[91]

If individuals were given license to separate at will and either to contract other unions or to pollute themselves with clandestine fornication, a numberless crowd of ex-partners would soon be violating God's law, which took immeasurable precedence over man's law. Both men and women were pictured among this wretched throng, but Hincmar's emphasis was upon men, whose selfish cruelty and libertinism principally threatened the institution of marriage.

Endorsing St. Paul's view that total chastity was best, Hincmar nevertheless declared that marriage created order and stability, freeing the individual to concentrate on his soul's salvation. Adultery and fornication overturned spiritual equilibrium.[92]

Legitimate marriage, said Hincmar, was defined by four great conditions: the parties must be equal, free, and consenting; the woman must be given by her father and properly endowed; the marriage must be publicly celebrated; and the marriage must be consummated.[93] The betrothal ceremony and nuptial blessing were important but belonged to the secondary plane of marriage's social and legal aspects.[94] What made marriage indissoluble was neither social nor legal, but consisted of three elements inextricably entwined in the four conditions: the sacrament, a mystical act analogous to the union of Christ and the Church; mutual consent; and the sexual union. In Stephen's marriage, the social and legal forms had been respected, but there had been no mutual consent and no sexual union. Therefore the sacrament had not taken place and the marriage could be dissolved. Lothair, on the other hand, had given consent and had consummated his marriage; therefore the marriage was legal.[95]

Hincmar cited the relevant passage of St. Paul about each marriage partner not having the "power of his own body" (I Cor. 7:4) and concluded explicitly: "Whereby, according to the authorities . . . is designated the use of the genitals, which spouses do not owe to others but nuptially between themselves."[96] In the eyes of Christ there was only "one law for man and woman."[97]

Equality of the sexes, however, was incidental to the main issue, which was monogamy. Hincmar rejected all excuses for divorce previously admitted by both lay and canon law: a wife's illness, her sterility, her practice of sorcery, the captivity of either partner, the entry of either into religious life, or adultery. Where many of his contemporaries believed that a man who was not himself an adulterer (like Boso) had the right to divorce an adulterous wife and to remarry, Hincmar said no: adultery did not break the sacrament. As an analogy he pointed to the sacrament of baptism, which was not cancelled by the sin its recipient might commit; proper penitence restored its benefits. The adulterous partner in a marriage could likewise do penance and be reconciled.[98]

The only basis for dissolving a marriage, then, was its illegitimacy: in other words, proof that it had never properly taken place.

In addition to its impact on divorce, Hincmar's work contributed to a gradual transformation in the concept of marriage, a shift in emphasis from the contractual—family alliance, property exchange—to the personal and sexual—mutual consent of bride and groom and their physical union. At the same time the social focus moved from the families and kin of bride and groom to the newly formed conjugal unit. The political and economic aspects of marriage were far from withering away, above all for the wealthy class, but in the eyes of the Church money, land, and power were now forced increasingly to share the stage with human feelings.

5.

Anglo-Saxon England

On the European continent during the first five centuries of the Middle Ages, barbarian and Roman cultures interacted with each other and with the Christian Church. In the British Isles a less extensive Roman presence, a tardier migration by the barbarians, and a degree of geographic isolation produced in these early centuries a somewhat different picture, one that shows Germanic society in a less diluted form. *The Anglo-Saxon Chronicle*, written four hundred years after the event, treats the arrival in England of the Anglo-Saxons in the late fifth and early sixth centuries as a strictly military invasion, but archeological and documentary evidence indicate that, as in the Continental migrations, whole peoples came to occupy the English countryside.[1] The Romans had already withdrawn (A.D. 410), making conquest easy for the newcomers, who mixed less readily with the native population than did their counterparts on the Continent. The systematic contracting of intercultural marriage alliances that occurred in Gaul was absent in Britain. The invaders retained their own language nearly intact, and their conversion to Christianity was slower. Much of it took place in the seventh century, with intermittent setbacks; the historian and cleric Bede (c. 673–735) reports a number of incidents of kingdoms temporarily backsliding into paganism.

Information about Anglo-Saxon England has been mined from chronicles (unfortunately none as rich as Gregory of Tours's *History of the Franks*), literature, archeology, and two other principal sources: the law codes of the various local kings, from Aethelbert of Kent (c. 560–616) to Alfred of Wessex (reigned 871–899); and a substantial collection of wills and charters, most dating from the ninth and tenth centuries. The sources are thus even sparser and more obscure than those for continental Europe, and they largely concern the upper classes.

Like the other Germanic peoples, the Anglo-Saxons brought with them a form of society in which the dominant element was the larger kinship group. This group was not the territorial clan (a corporate body with a territorial base, tracing its origin to a common ancestor) but the kindred (an ego-focused group consisting of each individual's close relatives).[2] This network of overlapping clusters of parents, grandparents, siblings, aunts, uncles, and cousins exercised important social, economic, and juridical functions. It determined the status of its members, negotiated marriages, and arbitrated inheritance. It exercised a degree of control over individual behavior, lent protection to its members, pursued vengeance for them, and paid or exacted compensation. As with the *Sippe* on the Continent, the Anglo-Saxon kindred's juridical authority was eroded by the rival power of lords and kings, who flourished in the prosperous agricultural environment of England.[3] Yet kinship retained social importance, determining a man's (or woman's) prestige and even identity. Beowulf introduces himself to King Hrothgar of the Danes as "Hygelac's kinsman and close retainer," before listing his own heroic accomplishments,[4] and he is identified again and again in the poem as "Ecgtheow's son." The eighth-century Anglo-Saxon poem *The Wanderer* expresses the feelings of the kinless and lordless exile, the "unfriended man":

> *So I in my grief driven from my homeland*
> *Far from my kinsmen have often to fetter*
> *The memories of the heart in heavy chains. . . .*
> *If only I could find whether far or near*
> *One to show favor to me in the mead-hall,*
> *One to give solace to me friendless,*
> *To treat me with kindness. . . .*[5]

Like the *Sippe*, the Anglo-Saxon kindred was bilateral, with emphasis on the father's side of the family. Its exact extent was indeterminate. The circle of relations who could be enlisted for such aid as payment of wergeld compensation probably depended on proximity and accessibility, but every individual could rely on a basic group of close kin that scholars have concluded from analysis of Old English terminology always included the conjugal family plus a few collaterals. Just as modern English adds "grand-" or "great-grand-" to "father," "mother," "son," and "daughter," Old English added "old," "third," "fourth": *faeder,* "father"; *ealda faeder,* "old father" or "grandfather"; *thridde faeder,* "third father" or "great-grandfather." Similarly, *sunu,* "son," *sunasunu,* "son's son" or "grandson." The most commonly used terms for uncles, aunts, nephews, and nieces specified the side of the family: father's sister was *fathu;* mother's sister, *moddrige;* father's brother, *faedera;* mother's brother, *eam.* Brothers' and sisters' sons and daughters were likewise distinguished. No specific terms existed, however, for different kinds of cousins, indicating that such distinctions were not significant.[6]

Despite the male bias of the kinship system, marriage did not change a woman's status. She retained the wergeld she was born with and did not take her husband's. Although her children assumed their father's status, she kept that of her own father.[7]

A prominent figure in Anglo-Saxon literature is the woman torn by conflicting loyalties, the "peace-weaver" whose marriage was contracted to implement an alliance between feuding families. At a banquet in *Beowulf,* a bard tells the story of the Danish princess Hildeburg, whose marriage to the Frisian king Finn was designed to reconcile hostile dynasties. In a Danish raid on Frisia, Hildeburg's brother Hnaef and her son are killed fighting on opposite sides. The "sad princess" orders her son placed on her brother's funeral pyre. After a truce, Hengest, Hnaef's successor, returns with reinforcements, kills King Finn, and, taking Hildeburg with him aboard a fleet laden with treasure looted from palace and countryside, he leads her "to her people."[8]

Bede tells a similar, real-life story: Osthryth, sister of Ecgfrith of Northumbria, married Aethelred of Mercia; in 670 the Northumbrians and Mercians fought the battle of Trent, in which her eighteen-year-old brother Aelfwine, "much beloved by both [Mercians and Northumbrians]" was killed; two decades later "Queen Osthryth was murdered by her own people, that is, the nobility of the Mercians."[9]

The law codes of the Anglo-Saxon kings yield a few clues about inheritance customs: that women shared in inheritance, along with children and close kin, and that some land could be freely disposed of by will, while other land, received from a kinsman, had to be handed down within the family.[10] A law of Aethelbert (sixth century) stated that a woman who had borne her husband a child could inherit half his goods.[11] A law of King Alfred (ninth century) limited a man's heirs to kinsmen in an unspecified range in the case of land that came to him from kinsmen.[12] An eleventh-century law of King Cnut ruled that if a man died intestate his property was to be divided "very justly among the wife, the children, and the close kinsmen, each in the proportion which belongs

Woman with spindle and distaff, symbols of her sex. (Bodleian Library, MS Ashmole 1504, f. 34)

to him," with no definition of "close kinsmen" or the proportion.[13]

Surviving Anglo-Saxon wills show no strong preference for sons over daughters or for elder over younger sons in the inheritance of land. Sometimes an estate was left to a wife with the provision that after her death it was to return to the husband's own kin or to the Church, and sometimes it was left to her unconditionally. Land was willed to a wide range of relatives, many of them female: mothers, fathers, sons, daughters and sons-in-law, brothers and sisters-in-law, grandsons and granddaughters on both the male and female side, nephews and nieces on both sides, even to stepchildren, godchildren, and foster relations.[14] King Alfred's own will explains that his grandfather had left his land in the male line, not the female—"on the spear side, not on the spindle side"—with the implication that the grandfather was free to decide in the matter but that perhaps his choice was the conventional one. Alfred himself chose to leave estates to all his children, male and female, with the only concession to male inheritance a provision that the males could buy back the land from the females.[15] A military leader, contemporary of Alfred, left more land to his daughter than to his son (who may have been illegitimate) and specified that some of his other property should go to kin on his own father's side, some to kin on his mother's.[16]

Royal succession, however, was limited to males, and the ancestry of kings was traced agnatically (through the male line). Royal dynasties listed their ancestors going back many generations, usually through historical grandfather and great-grandfather to mythical forebears. In early times the ultimate progenitor was the German chief god, Woden, who after the Anglo-Saxon conversion to Christianity was supplanted by Noah, Adam, and Christ. The *Anglo-Saxon Chronicle* recites the genealogy of King Aethelwulf, Alfred's father, back to "Sceaf, son of Noah," explaining, "he was born in Noah's ark," and thence, following the genealogy presented in chapter five of Genesis, through "Noah, Lamech, Methuselah, Enoch, Jared, Mahalaleel, Cainan, Enos, Seth, Adam the first man," and ending with "our father who is Christ."[17]

Until the late tenth century, the Anglo-Saxon kings commonly employed a unique form of succession. The kingdoms were neither divided among brothers nor passed from father to eldest son, but transmitted intact from brother to brother. King Alfred was preceded on the throne by his older brothers Aethelbald, Aethelbert, and Aethelred. Not surprisingly, the system led to trouble. When Alfred died in 899, descendants of his older brother King Aethelred unsuccessfully contested the throne with Alfred's son Edward. Edward's sons Athelstan, Edmund, and Eadred then reigned successively, but by the end of the tenth century succession from father to eldest son had triumphed.[18]

Clerical pronouncements against incest imply that Anglo-Saxon society permitted marriage within the degrees of relationship prohibited by the Church, whose opposition seems usually to have been limited to adverse comment. Popular attitudes toward incest are reflected in one of the Old English riddles composed in the eighth or ninth century and written down in the tenth-century compilation known as the *Exeter Book*. The riddle is based on Genesis 19:30–38, in which Lot's two daughters, taking refuge with their father in a cave in the mountains after the destruction of Sodom and Gomorrah, get him drunk and seduce him into fathering their sons. An Old English version of the biblical episode thus describes it:

> Each sister took to her drunk father's bed,
> And the wise old man whose heart and head
> Were bound with wine saw wives not daughters.
> His mind was locked—and they were pregnant
> With the proud sons of their own dear father.
> The elder's was Moab, the younger's Ben-ammi.
> Scriptures say the two princes fathered nations.[19]

The *Exeter Book* riddle reads:

> A man sat down to feast with two wives,
> Drank wine with two daughters, supped with two sons.
> The daughters were sisters with their own two sons,
> Each son a favored, first-born prince.
> The father of each prince sat with his son,
> Also the uncle and nephew of each.
> In the room's reach was a family of five.[20]

The riddle poet does not seem to take the problem very seriously; neither, in fact, does the author of the Genesis verse (or, for that matter, Genesis itself).

Pope Gregory I, in his response to St. Augustine of Canterbury condemning marriage to first cousins, stepmothers, and in-laws, took a more severe view, asserting that many of the English were "joined in this execrable matrimony" and must fear "the dreadful judgment of God."[21] Despite the pope's warning, Anglo-Saxon kings continued their incestuous ways. In the seventh century, King Oswiu of Northumbria married his first cousin Eanflaed; no evidence of Church opposition survives.[22] Alfred's son Edward, perceiving his succession threatened by his cousin Aethelwold, married the cousin's niece, a clearly incestuous match in the eyes of the Church, which nevertheless does not seem to have challenged it.

Aethelwulf (r. 839–858)

Aethelred I (r. 866–871)   Alfred (r. 871–899)

Aethelm   Aethelwold   Edward (r. 899–924)

Aelfflaed

Fifty years later, however, when Edward's grandson Eadwig married Aelgifu, another woman from the same line, the archbishop of Canterbury, spurred to action by Eadwig's brother and rival Edgar, annulled the marriage on the grounds that the couple shared a great-great-grandfather.[23]

Anglo-Saxon kings and nobles also married affines, just as did the Merovingians in France. In the seventh century, Eadbald of Kent married his own stepmother, his father's widow, provoking a shocked comment from Bede.[24] In 858 Aethelbald of Kent married his stepmother, the Frankish princess Judith. King Alfred's biographer, Asser, describes the union as "contrary to God's prohibition and Christian dignity . . . earning much infamy from all who heard about it." Yet the marriage was allowed to stand.[25]

Again like their Frankish contemporaries, the Anglo-Saxon kings drew censure from the Church for their polygamy and concubinage, with two differences. Their transgressions were less spectacular and the Church's strictures more muted. King Aethelbald of Mercia never contracted a lawful marriage, confining himself entirely to concubines, to the concern of St. Boniface, who joined in writing a remonstrance against the king's "sin of lasciviousness and adultery." Aethelbald's assassination in 757 by his own bodyguard, leaving no heirs, was seen as a vindication of Boniface's censure.[26] Edward the Elder had children by his concubine Ecgwyna and contracted a legitimate marriage only after the death of his father, King Alfred. He subsequently married twice, probably repudiating one wife; his grandson Edgar dismissed one wife and possibly two in the course of his three (serial) marriages.[27]

Marriage settlements followed a pattern similar to those of the Germanic peoples on the Continent. The laws of Aethelbert specified that the groom must pay a brideprice, which by the late Anglo-Saxon period seems to have gone to the bride;[28] the groom also presented the bride with a *morgengifu*, the Anglo-Saxon version of the *Morgengabe*, in England usually in the form of land.[29] According to a document probably dating from the late tenth century, betrothal required a promise from the groom to the bride's kinsmen to "maintain her according to God's law as a man should maintain his wife; and his friends are to stand surety for it." He was also required to give evidence of his ability to support her, and "afterwards . . . to announce what he grants her in return for acceptance of his suit, and what he grants her if she should live longer than he," that is, the dower. Agreement reached on all points, "the kinsmen are to set about betrothing their kinswoman as wife and in lawful matrimony to him who has asked for her."

The document specifies that a priest, though evidently not indispensable, should "by rights" be present to "unite them together with God's blessing," and that care should be taken that "they are not too closely related." Wedding arrangements must "please" not only the bride's kinsmen but the bride herself.[30] The law codes of Cnut indicate that at least by the early eleventh century consent was regarded by state and Church as necessary to marriage. "And neither a widow nor a maiden is ever to be forced to marry a man whom she herself dislikes, nor to be given for money, unless he chooses to give anything of his own free will."[31] Whether the families of prospective brides and grooms always obeyed the spirit of the law may be doubted.

The wills of three tenth-century women contain lists of bed-clothes, table linen, seat covers, and wall hangings that suggest a trousseau, enriched by their own handiwork, being passed on either to descendants or to the Church. A Somerset woman named Wulfwaru included a bequest to St. Peter's monastery at Bath of "a set of mass-vestments with everything that belongs to it, and the best dorsal [altar hanging] that I have, and a set of bed-clothing with tapestry and curtains and everything that belongs to it," while leaving tapestries, bed clothes, and table linen to her two sons.[32] Another lady, Wynflaed, left her grandson two chests containing "a set of bedclothes, all that is needed for one bed," and her granddaughter two other chests with her "best bed-curtain and a linen cover and all the bedclothes which belong in it." A third, Aethelgifu, left furnishings to be distributed among her relatives and the women of the household, including tapestries and seat covers.[33]

The sole marriage contracts that have survived, two Anglo-Saxon documents of the early eleventh century, illustrate the kind

Lady directs operations in the kitchen. (Trinity College, Cambridge, MS B 11.22, f. 37v)

of gifts an upper-class bride might anticipate and also show that these gifts went to her rather than to her kinsmen. In one a noble-man named Wulfric, contracting marriage with the archbishop's sister, "promised her the estates at Orleton and Ribbesford for her lifetime . . . and gave her the estate at Alton to grant and bestow upon whomsoever she pleased during her lifetime or at her death, as she preferred, and promised her 50 mancuses of gold and 30 men and 30 horses." The other identifies itself as "the agreement which Godwine made with Brihtric when he wooed his daughter. In the first place he gave her a pound's weight of gold, to induce her to accept his suit, and he granted her the estate at Street with all that belongs to it, and 150 acres at Burmarsh and in addition 30 oxen and 20 cows and 10 horses and 10 slaves."[34]

Like the Romans and Merovingians, the early Anglo-Saxons displayed a casual attitude toward divorce by men, but unlike them they extended some of the same attitude to divorce by women. The seventh-century laws of Aethelbert contain a clause

Folding linen. (Trinity College, Cambridge, MS B.11.22, f. 144v)

that carried permissiveness to an extreme not found elsewhere: "If [a wife] wishes to go away with the children, she is to have half the goods." The law goes on to state: "If the husband wishes to keep [the children], [she is to have the same share] as a child." In this early code, adultery was treated in the same nonjudgmental spirit. A wronged husband must be compensated with a wergeld payment by his wife's lover, who in addition must find the husband another wife "with his own money, and bring her to the other's house."[35] In the following century, King Ecgfryth of Northumbria divorced Aethelthryth because she refused to sleep with him. Bishop Wilfrid told Bede that Ecgfryth "had promised he would give many lands and much money if he could persuade the queen to consent to pay the marriage duty." The queen was consigned to a convent.[36] Other Anglo-Saxon kings succeeded in dismissing their wives on unknown grounds, apparently without the Church's intervention. English bishops created no *causes célèbres* analogous to Hincmar's prosecution of Lothair II.

Both law and literature depict the role of the wife in the Anglo-Saxon household. Mistress of the house, she was legally entrusted with the keys to "her storeroom, her chest, and her coffer."[37] Serving the drink was a woman's special office, whether as a cup-bearing slave or as a lady and hostess. A "gnomic verse" in the *Exeter Book* prescribes her function:

> . . . the woman shall prosper
> beloved among her people, shall be cheerful,
> shall keep a secret, shall be generous
> with horses and treasures. At the banquet
> she shall always everywhere before the band of comrades
> first of all greet the protector of the nobles,
> quickly offer the first cup
> to her lord's hand, and know good counsel
> for the two of them together in their household. . . .[38]

Bede tells how the wife of a thane, cured by Bishop John of Beverley of "an acute complaint," rose from her bed; "finding herself . . . restored to her former strength, she brought a cup to the bishop and us, and having performed this duty, continued to serve us with drink until the close of the meal."[39] In a feast in

Beowulf, the Danish queen Wealhtheow offers the mead cup to her husband, his men, and to Beowulf, who "partook of the cup at Wealhtheow's hands, that soldier fierce as death." At a later banquet, while "cup-boys" serve most of the guests, the queen herself serves the king and Beowulf.[40]

Another of the gnomic verses in the *Exeter Book* recommends a second special role for women:

> *A woman is in her fitting place at her embroidery;*
> *a gadding woman causes talk to spread, she is often accused of vices;*
> *men speak of her with contempt; often her beauty fades. . . .*[41]

From the codes of kings Wihtred of Kent and Ine of Wessex in the seventh century to that of King Cnut in the eleventh, Anglo-Saxon law repeatedly insisted that when a man committed a crime his wife and family were not to be automatically regarded as accomplices. The implication is that society had treated them as such in the past and that they were still so regarded by many. The laws of Ine specified different penalties for crimes committed with and without the knowledge of the family: "If anyone shall steal in such a way that his wife and children know nothing of it, he shall pay sixty shillings as fine: but if he steals with the knowledge of all his household they are all to go into slavery."

If the husband was convicted of stealing cattle, he forfeited his two thirds of the family property. The wife could clear herself by swearing that she had had no share in the crime and had not eaten the meat: "If she dares to declare on oath that she has not tasted the stolen food she shall retain her third" (of the family property, probably her dower portion).[42] Cnut's legislation acknowledged that a wife could not forbid her husband to bring anything that he pleased into their house, but that unless stolen property was placed "under her lock and key," in one of her three storage places, she was not responsible. Neither, evidently, were the children, for Cnut added: "Up till now it happened that the child which lay in the cradle, although it had never tasted food, was reckoned by avaricious folk as being as guilty as though it had had discretion. But I earnestly forbid this henceforth. . . ."[43]

The Anglo-Saxon codes allowed widows to raise their own children, but under the guardianship of their husbands' kinsmen. The laws of Ine of Wessex declared that a widow was to "have her child and rear it," with money provided for its maintenance and "a cow in summer, an ox in winter," and "the kinsmen are to take charge of the paternal home until the child is grown up."[44] The laws of Kings Hlothaere and Eadric of Kent had a similar provision, with one of the child's paternal kinsmen appointed as a protector, "to look after the property until he is ten years old."[45] Later legislation protecting widows indicates that they were under guardianship, but leaves details unclear.[46]

Despite the material considerations ever present in marriage arrangements, evidence of affectionate relationships between husbands and wives may be gleaned from the chronicles. Bede tells us that the mother of Hilda, the celebrated seventh-century abbess of Whitby, had a nightmare in which she "was seeking most carefully" for her banished husband "and could find no sign of him anywhere."[47] Another seventh-century personage described by Bede, Hildemer, friend of St. Cuthbert, took care of his insane wife and wept when he believed that she was dying.[48] Bede also describes the joy of King Edwin of Northumbria when his young wife was delivered of a child "in safety and without much pain." Edwin, Bede notes, "gave thanks to his [pagan] gods" but the child was baptized a Christian, the first Northumbrian to be christened.[49]

Among literary representations of married love is a passage from the same gnomic poem that described the wife as cup bearer:

> Dear is the welcome one
> to his Frisian wife, when his ship is at anchor;
> his boat has arrived and her man come home,
> her own husband; and she calls him in,
> washes his sea-stained raiment and gives him fresh clothes,
> grants him on the land what his love requires. . . .[50]

To define the relationship between husband and wife, literary sources often use the Anglo-Saxon term *freondscype*. It denotes something more than its modern cognate, "friendship," though less than passion; perhaps "affection."

*   *   *

Literature also yields glimpses of the feelings of parents for children. In *Beowulf* we see Hildeburg grieving for her dead son, and Beowulf's uncle, King Hrethel, "shaken with grief" when one of his sons kills the other. The father is unable to take vengeance on the killer since "so mournful a thing it is for an old man to live to see the time when his child swings young from the gallows." Finally, "driven by sorrow," Hrethel departs from life.[51]

A poem in the *Exeter Book*, "The Fates of Men," describes the raising of a child:

> It very often comes to pass by God's might
> that man and wife bring, by means of birth,
> a child into the world, and provide him with delights,
> cheer and cherish him, until the time comes,
> arrives in the course of years, that the young limbs,
> the living members, become grown.
> Thus father and mother carry him and walk with him,
> give and supply; God alone knows
> what the years will bring to the growing boy.

Among the fates that the years may bring are disasters:

> the gray prowler on the moor,
> the wolf, shall devour him, and his mother
> will mourn his death, which is beyond man's control.

Or when he is half grown

> Another the flame shall attack in a conflagration;
> the cruel fire, the red fierce blaze . . . the woman will wail
> who sees the flames envelop her son.[52]

Bede in his biography of St. Cuthbert gives a glimpse of a seventh-century childhood. Although Cuthbert's parents seem to have been peasants (he started life as a shepherd), he was "nursed in his infancy" by a woman whom he often visited in adult life, and whom "he was accustomed . . . to call his mother." Up to the age of eight, "the first year when boyhood succeeds to infancy," he "took delight . . . in mirth and clamor; and, as was natural at his age, rejoiced to attach himself to the company of other boys, and to share in their sports; and because he was agile by nature, and of a quick mind, he often prevailed over them in their boyish contests, and frequently when the rest were tired he alone would hold out, and look triumphantly around to see if any remained to contend with him for victory. For in jumping, running, wrestling, or any other bodily exercise, he boasted that he could surpass all those who were of the same age, and even some that were older than himself." One day, however, when "some customary games were going on in a field" among a group of boys that included Cuthbert, a younger boy ran up to him, weeping, and admonished him to put away these childish occupations. Cuthbert pacified him, "abandoned his vain sports," and devoted himself to prayer, meditation, and teaching.[53]

Sexuality is very much present in the Anglo-Saxon law codes, in provisions against sexual crimes, chiefly rape and seduction, with penalties graduated according to the rank of the woman. The laws of Aethelbert assessed a man who slept with a nobleman's serving woman ("female cupbearer") a penalty of twenty shillings; with the servant of a *ceorl* (free peasant), six shillings; there were lesser penalties for intercourse with slave women.[54] Alfred's laws contained a scale of payments to husbands with different wergelds for the seduction of their wives. If a man assaulted a woman of *ceorl* status, he had to compensate the woman herself according to the seriousness of the assault: five shillings for grasping her breast, ten for forcing her down but not raping her, sixty if he raped her. Rape of the slave woman of a *ceorl* imposed a fine of sixty shillings to the king and a payment of five shillings to the *ceorl* (nothing to the woman). But if the rapist was himself a slave, he was castrated. Sexual overtures to a nun—seizing her by her clothes or by her breast "without her leave"—brought double the regular fine. A man who found another man with his wife, sister, daughter, or mother "behind closed doors or under the same blanket" was entitled to punish him as he saw fit. A betrothed girl was also fined according to her wergeld for committing fornication. With girls of the *ceorl* class the fine was in cattle rather than money, the fines going to the "surety," the man's kin and friends who had guaranteed the betrothal agreement.[55]

By the eleventh century, however, a new harshness had set in. By the laws of Cnut, a woman who committed adultery became "a public disgrace, and her lawful husband is to have all that she owns, and she is to lose her nose and ears."[56]

A series of double-entendre riddles in the *Exeter Book* demonstrate a masculine kind of sexual humor, usually centering on phallic symbols. The sword, "a strange creature shaped for battle," brings death to men and sorrow to women; unlike its counterpart it is celibate and "must stroke in brideless play / Without the hope of child-treasure."[57] The key, the bellows, the gimlet, the shirt, even the onion ("I am a wonderful creature bringing joy to women")[58] take their place in this sexual wordplay. In one riddle a young man and a woman strive together:

> *Both swayed and shook.*
> *The young man hurried, was sometimes useful,*
> *Served well, but always tired*
> *Sooner than she, weary of the work.*
> *Under her girdle began to grow*
> *A hero's reward for laying on dough.*[59]

The answer: churn (Anglo-Saxon *cyren,* a feminine noun).

In another:

> *I heard of something rising in a corner,*
> *Swelling and standing up, lifting its cover.*
> *The proud-hearted bride grabbed at that boneless*
> *Wonder with her hands, the prince's daughter*
> *Covered that swelling thing with a swirl of cloth.*[60]

The answer: dough.

Such earthy pleasantries suggest the rough simplicity of the ninth-century physical environment. Like their contemporaries on the Continent, Anglo-Saxon peasant families sheltered themselves in straw-thatched houses of wattle and daub or turf. The same three types that prevailed on the Continent were built in Britain, with some variation in their use. The long byre-house enclosed numbers of animals along with the family. The smaller above-ground house contained people only. The sunken hut was used sometimes for storage or to protect animals, sometimes for weaving or other craft work—loom weights have been found in several—and sometimes for habitation by the poorest families.[61] Fire was a hazard for all types and, like the blaze that started at one end of the village where St. Cuthbert's nurse lived, might threaten the whole community.[62]

Early settlements were small and scattered. During the eighth and ninth centuries, the period of Viking raids, many were apparently abandoned in favor of new larger villages clustered around parish churches and surrounded by common fields.

No trace of the dwellings of noblemen and kings has been unearthed. The hall of King Hrothgar in *Beowulf* is described as a large oblong building that "soared upwards, noble and broad of gables," with wooden walls hung with tapestries that glittered with gold, a paved floor, benches along the walls where the warriors slept, and doors wide enough to admit horses. Separate quarters were allotted to married couples and to unmarried women.[63] However, the eighth-century *Beowulf* poet may have been describing his concept of a Danish palace of an earlier time rather than a contemporary Anglo-Saxon hall. Asser tells us that King Alfred built halls and chambers in both stone and wood.[64] The castle, or fortified residence, which began to dot the Continental landscape in the ninth century, scarcely made an appearance in England until 1066, though the walled town, or *burh,* offered protection against the Vikings.

Wills, manuscript illustrations, and the Bayeux tapestry supply more reliable information about furnishings. The houses of the wealthy, according to these sources, contained chests, curtained beds, tables, and seats that had covers and possibly cushions. Wall hangings were common, doubtless embroidered like the Bayeux tapestry rather than woven like the tapestries of the late Middle Ages. In a word, wealthy families enjoyed more commodious and luxuriously furnished quarters than the peasants, but little comfort or privacy.

Marriage and the Family
in the Year 1000

The world did not come to an end in the Christian millennial year of 1000 as some had anticipated. Instead it prepared to enter a new era. The "second period of invasions," by Scandinavians from the north and Saracens from the south, had stimulated construction of castles and town walls and thus contributed to a gradual improvement in public order. The old warrior nobility that had long ruled Europe's serf-peasant population began reluctantly to give up its violent habits and even offered intermittent observance to the Church's "Peace of God," which forbade plundering churches and monasteries and robbing the poor.

The Church had by now made some headway in its long battle against traditional male sexual freedom. Archbishop Hincmar and other strong-minded prelates and popes had forced kings and great nobles to swallow indissoluble monogamy as a principle, and had imposed a large extension of exogamy and the incest taboo. Repeated strictures against adultery and fornication did not succeed in putting a stop to these traditional practices, or even have much discernible effect. Yet in the course of the tenth century the Church's struggle to impose its ideals had won it ascendancy over secular law in matters pertaining to marriage and morals. In the year 500 the Church could only protest and admonish; in the year 1000 it could threaten and command.

Marriage at all levels had now undergone a significant shift in assigns, notably in the appearance of the morning gift to the bride from the bridegroom. Emphasis had moved away from the old contractual, family-alliance purpose of marriage toward financial support for the new conjugal household. Yet parents maintained control. Marriages were still rationally planned, among peasants as among their betters.

The larger kinship group—clan, kindred, *Sippe*—continued to play a social role, but the individual household gained in importance. Nearly every family, poor or rich, still lived on the land, whose transmission from generation to generation followed the ancient law of partible inheritance. In most of Europe the estate was divided among the male heirs; in Anglo-Saxon England women also shared. Here, both in England and on the Continent, a significant change lay in the offing.

III.

The High Middle Ages

6.

The Family Revolution
of the Eleventh Century

Garin le Loherain is one of numerous epic poems written in the twelfth and thirteenth centuries but set in a much earlier time, the eighth century, the heroic age of Charles Martel and Pepin.[1] It describes in its prologue a crisis of the family that actually occurred in history, but only two hundred years earlier instead of four hundred. In the poem, the aristocracy of France, including young Hervis, duke of Metz, who later fathers the hero of the epic, is pictured as reduced to poverty, unable to afford the arms needed to help Charles Martel drive the Vandals from the country. The reason is that in these times the head of a family, on his deathbed,

> . . . in great fear of death
> Disregards his brother and his son,
> His other relatives and his cousins german;
> To the black monks of St. Benedict
> He gives his land and rents and mills:
> His daughter and son have nothing.
> As he departs the world, the secular is impoverished
> And the clergy are enriched. . . .[2]

The desire for individual salvation has triumphed over the

"spirit of family"; individualistic inheritance practices have weakened the bonds of kinship.

The author of *Garin* blames the greed of the clergy for the calamitous new custom. He has Charles Martel take the problem to the pope, who is holding a council in Lyon, surrounded by three thousand prelates all richly appareled, who have arrived on excellent horses, in contrast to the twenty thousand knights who accompany Charles on foot and bearing no armor or arms except their naked swords. Charles tells the pope that his country has been overrun, his fields burned, his castles demolished. The enemy stables his horses in the churches and slaughters the priests, bishops, and archbishops, and Charles's knights have not the means to resist. The pope appeals to the assembled prelates. One, the archbishop of Reims, protests that if the Church yields some of its wealth to the knights, such a precedent will soon become custom. Hervis, duke of Metz, replies that the king's twenty thousand knights have lost the revenues of their bake-ovens and mills, which their fathers have given to the clergy.[3]

The abbot of Cluny throws in his support: "If we are rich (Lord be praised), it is because of the lands that their ancestors willed to us. Let each of us then contribute a little, lest by refusing anything we lose all." Finally, over the objections of the archbishop of Reims, who declares that rather than yield two *angevin* pennies to the knights he would have himself dragged at the tails of their horses, the pope promises Charles Martel *"vair* and *gris"* (luxury furs) and "all the gold and silver that the clergy possess, their palfreys and packhorses and mules" to defeat the enemy and save the country. For seven years the knights can collect tithes, but when the enemy is vanquished they must return the revenues. Accordingly the knights seize the clergy's *vair* and *gris*, silver and gold coins, cups of fine gold, and weapons, arm themselves, deliver Paris, Sens, Soissons, and Troyes, and drive the enemy out of France.[4]

Most historians agree that the "family revolution" brought on by the crisis pictured in the prologue of *Garin le Loherain* transpired in Europe sometime around the millennium.[5] If indeed donations to the Church played a role in causing the crisis, it should be noted that land transactions between Church and laity were by no means one-sided; the Church was often the loser as great nobles who controlled their own local monasteries caused property to pass back and forth as it suited them. Deathbed bequests to the Church were evidently one factor in the deterioration of the old order. Others included the fragmenting of patrimonies by partible inheritance and the weakening of the central monarchy and dispersion of its power.

In his study of the region of Mâcon, in Burgundy, Georges Duby describes the deepening crisis among the tenth-century aristocracy as brought on by increasing individualism at the expense of the family, including the deathbed donations to the Church by heads of families. Six great families dominated the Mâcon district at the beginning of the tenth century. All were direct beneficiaries of the generosity of king or Church. The bulk of their extensive lands were "allods," that is, they were not held by the conditional terms of feudal tenure but owned outright, to be disposed of as the owners chose. Minor aristocrats owned smaller allods: a rural church or two, a dozen manses, patches of wood and pasture.[6]

The result of allodial ownership under a system of partible inheritance was a rapid fragmentation of estates. By the year 1000 the property of the six great families was divided among twenty-four families. This proliferation was combined with a narrowly individual concept of ownership through which "every family event, marriage, birth, death, fragmented the allod."[7]

Nonallodial land was scarcely affected. At the bottom of the hierarchy, the peasant held most of his land from a lord whose consent was needed for him to divide or sell. Similarly, at the top, some parts of the great patrimonies were held as grants from a lord. In both cases, the lord's interest opposed division.[8]

In the case of subdivided allodial land, joint ownership was possible, and sometimes undertaken, usually by brothers who formed a temporary frérèche or joint holding, but only a very small number of these arrangements were in existence in the tenth century. The bulk of the land passed in ever-diminishing acreage to an ever-growing number of conjugal families. Even within this basic unit, the spirit of independence brought further fragmentation. Emancipated from their fathers' authority at an early age, sons could dispose at will of inherited property. Husbands and wives controlled their own estates, which they could sell without consulting each other; the wife's dower share of the husband's patrimony became her immediate possession to deal with as she chose. Kin outside the conjugal unit could do nothing to prevent either sales or bequests to the Church of lands that were the owners' "to hold, to sell, to give."[9]

Under these conditions, according to Duby, "enormous transfers of property" took place, a large share of which went to the Church, not only in death gifts but also to endow monks and nuns entering religious establishments. "The Church provoked and arranged these offerings, managing to obtain lands that would best complement their domains." Descendants of the great families, living on the scattered remnants of ancient patrimonies, sank in the social scale into the minor nobility.[10]

A few of the leading families held public office and with it benefices that they could not sell, divide, or give away. One such office was that of the count of Mâcon. The other officers were all "castellans," governors of the royal castles built in the ninth and tenth centuries. Some families, by contracting advantageous marriage alliances, managed to survive and even improve their positions.[11]

As for the lesser aristocracy of 950, many had so descended in the social scale by the year 1000 as to become indistinguishable from the peasantry. A few families disappeared completely. The four sons of Robert de Curtil divided his patrimony equally. Two died soon after, leaving most of their land to the abbey of Cluny. The other two then surrendered their share to the abbey in return for being maintained for life "in food and clothing." Robert's cousins sued, but the abbey succeeded in swallowing his entire estate.[12]

Around the millennium, by a mechanism that is not well understood, a profound change took place in family dynamics. In the Mâcon region, where during the tenth century the six noble families had split into twenty-four, in the course of the eleventh century the number stabilized, four more family branches appearing but four others disappearing. A rapid proliferation of noble families thus was followed by a phase in which the existing aristocracy solidified its position, while at the same time family bonds were strengthened.[13]

The most significant discernible element in the change was a shift from partible to impartible inheritance. Among the minor nobility in the Mâcon region, the *frérèche,* the association of brothers in joint ownership, previously limited to a few families, became the rule. One son, not necessarily the eldest, was designated to succeed the father in managing the family estates and representing the family in the outside world. Marriage was restricted to this son and at most one other. Households were large. The typical household of the minor aristocracy of the time, as described by Duby, contained perhaps a dozen family members: parents, one brother with his wife and children, and brothers and sisters who remained unmarried, with some of the unmarried brothers often groomed to follow in the footsteps of an uncle who was a church official. The young men lived under the control of their parents, or, when the parents died, of the brother who became head of the family. The share of each in the enterprise was modest, but together they could afford to equip and maintain one or two of the brothers as knights.[14]

At the top of the hierarchy, and moving steadily down the social ladder in the eleventh century, a different form of impartible inheritance made its appearance, the succession of a single son, usually the eldest: primogeniture. The most important factor behind the development was the breakdown of central public authority—the monarchy—and the consequent diffusion of power to regional authorities, such as the counts who had been the appointees and delegates of the Carolingian kings.

The Frankish monarchy had slowly decayed through the late ninth and early tenth centuries. As the king gradually lost touch with the counts, once merely his deputies, they became autonomous hereditary regional sovereigns. In 890 in the Mâconnais, the office of count was held jointly by two men, Letaud and Racoux, probably brothers, who passed it on to Racoux's brother-in-law, Aubry of Narbonne. Aubry was succeeded by his son Letaud in about 945, and his son's son Aubry in about 970. Thus the office was first made heritable, then heritable by primogeniture.[15]

An identical process took place one level down at a slightly later period. Under the count's authority, his representatives were the castellans, governors of the castles built amid the turbulence of the Viking and Saracen invasions to guard public order. The tenth-century "motte and bailey" castle consisted of a natural or artificial mound (motte) topped by a timber blockhouse and fronted by a ditch and palisade, the whole enclosed in a court (bailey) with its own palisade and ditch. By the end of the tenth century a few had been rebuilt in stone, and a few rectangular stone keeps had been constructed.[16] Crude as these early castles were by later standards, they conferred immense power on their commandants, who dominated the local populations, wielded their power unchallenged, and soon made their office of castellan hereditary.

In the Mâconnais, a certain Garoux was made governor of the castle of Brancion in the early 900s. At his death the office passed to his son Lebaud, then to Lebaud's son Garoux, and then to the younger Garoux's son-in-law Guinebaud. The fortress where the castellan's family had lived and commanded for generations, surrounded by the family's allodial lands, was first claimed and then accepted as the castellan's personal property. Around the year 1000 the castellans went a step further, withdrawing their obedience to the count and assuming autonomous lordship of their own areas.[17] Late in the eleventh century, the lesser aristocracy, the knights, also began to pass on family estates to a single heir, abandoning the *frérèche*.[18]

The change in the shape of the family was signaled by an element that made its historic first appearance in the documents of the time: the surname or patronymic, passed down in the paternal line. This development was entirely original, bearing little resemblance either to the complex Roman system of nomenclature or to the naming system of the early Middle Ages, in which the individual was designated only by a first name chosen from a short family list.[19] In accordance with that system, the early Capetian kings were for six generations either Hugh or Robert; the counts of Anjou were either Geoffrey or Fulk; the counts of Tonnerre were all Milo or Gui; the counts of Nevers, Landric or Bodo. The counts of Poitou were Rannulf or Eblo and abandoned those names for William, the ancestral name of the dukes of Aquitaine, when they took over that duchy.[20]

Deeds recorded in the Mâcon region before the year 1000 list no family surnames. In the next thirty-five years a few surnames appear, the number increasing throughout the eleventh century. These were taken from three different sources: descriptive nicknames or epithets originally bestowed on an individual and later attached to his family (the Gros family, for example, lords of the castle of Uxelles—*gros*, "big"); names of the castles themselves (Montmerle, Senneçé); and names of a family's principal estate (Merzé). In the long run this last source, the name of the principal estate, became universally the name and title of nobility. Not all noble families held castles, but all owned estates.[21]

At the same time the number of first names in use by the nobility shrank. A preponderance of Hughs, Bernards, Josserans, Geoffreys, and Humberts appeared in the Mâcon region, borrowed from powerful neighboring families and implying relationship. A few names were adopted from heroes of epics (Gerald, Roland, Oliver), and a few from the New Testament (Peter, Stephen).[22] In Germany, historian Karl Ferdinand Werner notes, variations of the prominent New Testament name John (Johannes, Hans, Ivan, Jean), almost unknown north of the Alps until the tenth century, became so prevalent in the late Middle Ages that hundreds of historical figures bore them. Similarly, the names Henry and Conrad, confined to two royal German dynasties in the ninth and tenth centuries, became so popular that their diminutives "Hinz und Kunz" were used in the sense of "Tom, Dick, and Harry."[23]

Constance Bouchard found a similar process taking place somewhat later in a castellan family from the region of Auxerre, southeast of Paris on the borders of Burgundy. In the tenth and eleventh centuries the lords of Seignelay identified themselves by their Christian names only, alternating two names, Aswalo and Daimbert, from father to son. Even when they began to be known as Aswalo de Seignelay or Daimbert de Seignelay, the surname was neither exclusive nor familial. Ordinary knights of the castle garrison identified themselves with the castle name, as shown by records citing a certain Salo de Seignelay, who when he inherited an estate of his own became Salo de Bouilly. Brothers of the castellans, like the garrison knights, might use the name "de Seignelay" while they lived in the castle, but when they changed their residence, they adopted the name of the new lordship; thus Stephen de Seignelay married the heiress of Pierre-Pertuis and thereafter was known as Stephen de Pierre-Pertuis. Not until the twelfth century did "de Seignelay" become a true surname.[24]

In most areas scholars trace the development of the patronymic from the top down: first the great magnates, next the castellans, and finally the lesser nobility. In Bavaria, Wilhelm Störmer found that it was the castellans who first adopted surnames and were copied by the lesser nobility, the great magnates feeling sufficiently well known to require no such added identification.[25]

The alteration in family dynamics was marked not only by new inheritance customs and patronymics but by a significant shift in the control of resources within the family. *Morgengabe,* the ancient Germanic morning gift from husband to bride, passed into disuse, and the dower, formerly an outright transfer of property from husband to wife, was restricted to a lifetime concession, received only when the husband died, and in the absence of children reverting to the husband's family. A wife could no longer bequeath to the children of a second marriage lands of her first husband received as dower. In contrast, her dowry, the gift of her own parents, now reappeared after an eclipse as part of the family estate, heritable by her husband and children. She retained some rights over lands she had inherited before marriage but could not sell even these without her husband's authorization. In a word, estates of husband and wife became common property, but under the husband's administration and to his advantage and that of the inheriting son.

The change in the wife's status accorded with the new ideology of the integrity of the estate, which was now transmitted from one generation to the next through the male line. Family property and male head were united by name and in function; other family members were auxiliary or subordinate. Thus noninheriting sons were victims of a second major change: instead of being emancipated at a youthful age by their portion of the patrimony, they were endowed only if they entered the Church. If they left for other reasons, they left empty-handed. A son who married during his parents' lifetime was unable to found a new household but forced to bring his wife to the paternal home. The dower he gave her remained part of the common property to which her dowry was added.[26]

Finally, a third change was the marked diminution of deathbed gifts to the Church. Even those that were made could remain part of the family patrimony, with the Church, like a widowed daughter-in-law, merely given a share of the income.[27]

The weakened authority of king and count returned to the family a function it had forfeited centuries earlier: that of a community of defense. As a consequence the bonds of blood outside the conjugal family regained importance. In the tenth-century documents of the Mâcon area, few family members are recorded as witnesses; in the first half of the eleventh, brothers, uncles, nephews, and cousins figure more and more in the deeds; after 1050 they are always present and include remote collaterals.[28] Duby pictures family councils meeting at intervals to consider actions, with geographically distant members sending representatives and even monks who had renounced the world attending. An injured member's relatives came to his aid, offering themselves as avengers, hostages in arbitration, or guarantors of a settlement.[29] In Constance Bouchard's words, the *consanguinei*, the blood relations in the male line, "fought together, made pious gifts together, assisted one another, whether in secular or ecclesiastical life, and were buried together."[30]

The progress of the family revolution varied from region to region with the political and economic situation. Local studies by different scholars disagree as to when it principally occurred, from the late ninth to the eleventh century. But an overwhelming consensus exists that sometime within this period a radical change took place in the structure and self-perception of noble families. Previously the fluid horizontal kindred was grouped around a member who held royal office. It practiced partible inheritance and gave equal weight to maternal and paternal forebears. It identified itself merely by distinctive family first names. Now the family assumed a vertical dimension, firmly seated on an estate, a patrimony which descended from father to one son and which gave the family its new, unique surname.

The rise of patrilineage paralleled that of feudalism, the social, economic, and political system by which a lord granted land to a vassal in return for military and other services, the act solemnized by exchange of oaths of protection and loyalty. The personal bonds of feudalism became a substitute for the old royal chain of command, from king to count to castellan to knight. The great noble families took on the character of ruling dynasties, and at every level of the aristocracy the family became a kind of little dynasty, with a single heir who succeeded to a domain. In Duby's words, "The significance of a family has become the significance of its heir."[31]

Two striking symbols of the new perception of the noble family made their appearance. One was the coat of arms, which gave rise to the arcane system of heraldry. The other was the genealogy. The Anglo-Saxon kings traced their ancestry in the male line back to Woden and Adam, but the practice was not general, even among kings. In the tenth and eleventh centuries, genealogies began to be composed for the great regional lords: the counts of Flanders, Vendôme, Boulogne, and Anjou. As time went on, genealogies were written for the lesser lords, and eventually for the knights. At first invariably the product of the abbeys belonging to the lords' estates, the genealogies gradually became secularized and, though still usually the work of clerics, were written in courts rather than monasteries.[32]

The earliest surviving noble genealogy was prepared in the 950s for Count Arnulf of Flanders by Witger, a monk of the abbey of St. Bertin, in St. Omer. Arnulf was descended from the Carolingian kings, whose own descent the document painstakingly traces to the Merovingian king Chlotar before carrying it forward to Count Arnulf. All the generations recorded are male with the exception of the two key connections: the Merovingian-Carolingian, through a daughter of King Chlotar, and the Carolingian-Flanders, through Arnulf's mother, a great-granddaughter of Charlemagne who married Count Baldwin I. Thus though agnatic (male) descent was the formal rule, where the greater status lay on the distaff side, the agnatic line was dropped with no ceremony. After praising Arnulf for his piety, wisdom, goodness, and assiduity as "consoler of widows and orphans," the document recounts his marriage to Adele, daughter of the count of Vermandois and niece of two French kings; the birth of their son Baldwin II; the younger Baldwin's marriage to Mathilda, daughter of "the most noble prince Heriman"; and closes with prayers for Arnulf and his son: "Amen. Amen. Amen. Amen. Amen. Amen. Amen."[33]

A series of genealogies drawn up at the monastery of St. Aubin, Angers, evidently with the purpose of establishing the status of a new line of counts of Anjou, similarly hews to the male line except for key connections with the Capetian dynasty and the counts of Mâcon and Besançon.[34] In a chronicle composed a few years later, Count Fulk Rechin himself gives a brief account of his genealogy, relying on his own memories and information from the uncle who preceded him, prefacing it with the explanation: "I, Fulk, count of Anjou . . . have wished to record how my ancestors acquired their honor [estate] and held it up till my own time, and how I myself have held it, by God's grace." He is "the son of Geoffrey of Château-Landon and Ermengarde, daughter of Fulk [Nerra], count of Anjou, and the nephew of Geoffrey Martel who was . . . the brother of my mother and count of Anjou for twenty-eight years."[35]

Thus patrilineage triumphed as a system but did not hesitate to emphasize the female line wherever advantage of either wealth or status lay. It preserved the family property intact as a patrimony by limiting the number and size of claims on it. The old bilateral kindred did not disappear, however, but was, in David Herlihy's words, "superimposed upon" the lineage, remaining not only to assure the family's survival by providing additional potential heirs, but also for its emotional value.[36]

After Garin de Loherain's prologue, with its picture of a land impoverished by selfish yearning for individual salvation and disregard for the communal needs of the family, the epic proceeds to its main theme: a feud between two great families, the Lorraines and the Bordelais, raging throughout France. The cast is almost exclusively male: Garin and his younger brother Begon and their sons and nephews and male cousins. Only one of Garin's seven sisters, the eldest, is even given a name; as for the others, we are told only of their marriage alliances with various counts and dukes and other nobles.[37] Their sons, however, Garin's nephews, play an important role and are considered members of Garin's family as well as that of their fathers. The central element of the story is the lineage, for which every man—father, son, uncle, nephew, or cousin—feels a responsibility that embraces mutual defense and vengeance, hospitality and asylum for fugitive kin, and standing guarantee or serving as hostage. The ground in which the lineage is rooted is the family property, to be defended against all comers, a symbol and focus of solidarity.

Such was the novel perception of the family on the part of the European elite in the wake of the transformations of the tenth and eleventh centuries. No longer were estates divided among sons.

Instead a single inheriting son assumed his father's lands and with them his castle and his name, creating a family dynasty planted firmly in a family seat and exercising nearly royal authority in its immediate region. Women's status diminished with the enthronement of male primogeniture, while castellans and knights as well as the great autonomous counts and barons amused themselves with their new coats-of-arms and genealogies.

7.

The Twelfth Century:
New Family Models

From the changes of the tenth and eleventh centuries new patterns of family structure and family life emerged. Besides the effects of feudalism and primogeniture, the family at all levels felt the impact of the great commercial revival of the high Middle Ages, the rapid growth of trade and manufacture and the generation of a money economy. One factor in the surge was the slow, steady growth of the agricultural segment. Another, more spectacular, was the rapid proliferation of long-distance commerce, as the Muslim domination of the Mediterranean was successfully disputed by the fleets of the Italian cities. Pack trains wound over the Alpine passes carrying wool cloth from the Flemish cities, and in the opposite direction, luxuries from Italy. Venice, Pisa, and Genoa launched argosies that ferried Europe's products to the Levant and brought back silks and spices.

In Italy an aristocracy rooted in the countryside adapted resourcefully to an urban setting and a commercial metier. Elsewhere in Europe the new merchant class was composed mostly of parvenus lifting themselves up by their bootstraps from beginnings as peddlers and craftsmen, a contingent that itself grew into a large European urban underclass. The most numerous craftsmen were those associated with the cloth industry, centered in Flanders and Italy, and comprising weavers, fullers, dyers, and finishers. Working in family units in their own homes, they constituted a primitive system of mass production and in many respects formed Europe's first proletariat.

The countryside as well as the city experienced the economic awakening. From the North Sea to the Mediterranean, forests were cleared, swamps drained, and villages founded, creating for many families a frontier environment. Especially noteworthy in this respect was the Iberian peninsula, where an advancing frontier developed in the wake of the Reconquest of the land from the Moors.

Improved cultivation, associated with technological innovations—horse traction, the wheeled plow, the three-field system—helped provide a more stable economic basis for the nobility, replacing the plunder no longer so readily available in a world growing more orderly. At the same time, the new inheritance policy of the nobility resulted in a strange new byproduct: the younger son. Hitherto scarcely differentiated from his siblings, the noble cadet was converted by disinheritance into a rootless adventurer, an upper-class social problem. His sisters constituted a second problem: marriageable young women marooned in a world where only a fraction of the marriageable men possessed a source of livelihood. The revival of the dowry, along with the surrender of some of their dower rights and of their morning gifts, were concessions made by daughters and their parents to the new state of things. Noble women found themselves returning to a greater dependency on their kin, especially their fathers, to find, or rather purchase, husbands, or, failing husbands, to procure them suitable positions in convents.

The Church simultaneously found itself pressed by problems respecting marriage law and custom. By 1100, the revolution had been completed whereby the Church courts and their canon law had, through popular preference, eclipsed secular jurisprudence on all matters relating to marriage. The jurisdictional shift came at the very moment when marriage questions were growing more numerous and more urgent.

One was an embarrassment within the Church's own ranks. Although marriage had long been abolished among the upper clergy and frowned on for the lower, many priests were married and many more openly kept concubines, generally with the approval of their parishioners. Pope Leo IX had condemned clerical marriage in 1049, and ecumenical councils at the Lateran in 1123 and 1139 pronounced priestly orders a fatal (diriment) impediment to marriage and vice versa.

A broader issue was the necessity of consent by parties to a marriage, a principle still only grudgingly accepted by upper-class parents. Still another was consanguinity, the Church's extreme seventh-degree taboo having opened the door to unforeseen troubles. Finally, there was indissolubility, a bedrock Church dictum on collision course with the fundamental requirement of royal and aristocratic marriage, the procreation of heirs. The battle that Hincmar of Reims had fought in the ninth century was far from won by the twelfth. Kings and great nobles were determined to manipulate marriage to suit their interests, material, familial, and sexual, as they had always done.

The Marriage Crisis: Gratian and Peter Lombard

Philip I of France (reigned 1060–1108) had been married for twenty years to his queen, Bertha of Friesland, when he fell in love with the wife of the count of Anjou, repudiated Bertha, shut her up in a castle, and either with or without the approval of the count of Anjou took the countess, a lady named Bertrade, as his second wife. He succeeded in assembling to bless his wedding most of the clergy of the realm, with one notable exception. Bishop Ivo of Chartres replied to the king's invitation with a blunt, even combative refusal: "You will not see me in Paris, with your wife of whom I know not if she may be your wife. . . . I shall not come until I know if a general council has found that you and your spouse are legitimately divorced and that you and the woman you wish to wed may legitimately be married." Ivo concluded with a brief homily on lust, reminding the king how Adam, Samson, and Solomon had all met disaster through women.[1]

Philip refused to be deterred, but Ivo successfully enlisted the support of Pope Urban II, who pronounced excommunication. Philip still refused to bow. When Bertha, the first wife, died, the controversy might have lapsed, but neither Ivo nor Urban was willing to leave it. The excommunication stood, and in the end Philip went through the motions of surrender. Barefoot and in penitential garb, like Henry IV at Canossa, he swore to abandon his "carnal and illicit copulation." Bertrade swore the same thing; however, the two continued to live together till Philip's death two years later.[2]

Thus the twelfth century opened with a sensational scandal that focused Europe's attention on the sharply divergent views held by the ruling laity on the one hand and by the Christian Church on the other on the most fundamental questions of marriage and divorce. Kings, nobles, and the public in general still felt that a husband could, if he wished, divorce his wife. The Church flatly disagreed.

It was simultaneously confronted with other marital issues. The daughter of Jourdain I, Norman prince of Capua, had objected strenuously to being married to the duke of Gaeta in the interest of her father's policy. Though favorably inclined toward Jourdain for his own reasons, Urban II courageously ruled in the girl's favor and annulled the marriage. The question persisted: how much pressure could a parent bring to bear to make a daughter (or son) see reason?[3]

Still another question nagged. Polygamy was gone, but concubinage lingered, and in a form at once less morally objectionable and more legally awkward. Nobody kept multiple concubines any more, and nobody openly kept both a wife and a concubine. But kings, nobles, and the general public felt it quite permissible for an unmarried man to keep a mistress. St. Jerome had called concubines "one-man harlots" but law and custom had always distinguished between the two professions. Justinian's Civil Code, which tardily reached the West in the eleventh century, followed Roman tradition in treating concubinage as a second-class marriage. To most, that seemed reasonable—if a sexual relationship was exclusive and durable, why not call it marriage? But in that case, could it be ended simply by one party's decision (the man's, of course)?

That brought up another question: Sex or no sex, what constituted a marriage contract? When could a woman, or for that matter a man, be confident that a marriage had taken place? Among the peasants informal, or clandestine, marriage, often without witnesses, was an old custom, and one that was coming to trouble Church courts more and more.[4]

At the upper social level Church authorities found themselves inheriting a new problem created by their predecessors' fixation on consanguinity rules. St. Boniface had extended the incest taboo in the eighth century, and it had been further extended in the ninth. Now Ivo of Chartres had inadvertently drawn attention to the potential for divorce in consanguinity by introducing it into the Philip-Bertha-Bertrade case by way of strengthening the argument against Philip's remarriage. There the incest factor was, incongruously enough, a kinship bond discovered between Philip and Bertrade's first husband, Count Fulk of Anjou.[5] For the Church to turn so illusive a bar (reminiscent, however, of the case of Stephen of Auvergne in the ninth century) into legal substance was an invitation to divorce seekers and their lawyers. A husband who wanted to get rid of a wife had only to locate some kind of distant, nearly imperceptible connection—a transitory affair, a godparent, an ancestor lost in the mists of antiquity—or to hire a clever fellow to concoct one.

Two of the greatest intellectual luminaries of the Middle Ages grappled with these problems, *inter alia,* in two of the masterworks of ecclesiastical literature. The first, Gratian, completed his vast *Concordia discordantium canonum,* which became known as Gratian's *Decretum,* in Bologna. Appearing about 1140, it consisted of a collection of nearly four thousand texts drawn from Church councils, papal pronouncements, and other sources in the matrix of a commentary designed to harmonize them into a coherent set of Christian legal principles.

At the heart of the marital problem, Gratian perceived the conundrum of what constituted a marriage. He found his answer in the mutual consent of the two parties. Consent was a requirement propounded equally by Roman law and the Church Fathers, but Gratian carried their principle a giant step forward by crossing the threshold from passive to active consent. Neither Roman law, the Church Fathers, or popular opinion regarded the need for consent as an obstacle to parental guidance. Children were taught to be obedient, and every young couple relied on their parents' cooperation in providing an economic basis for their union. Given the youth of nearly all women at first marriage, an arrangement totally free of family influence was unrealistic.

Nevertheless, commenting on the Jourdain case, Gratian gave the doctrine of consent a strong new coloration by declaring that even "a father's oath cannot compel a girl to marry one to whom she had never assented."[6] Consent, in Gratian's eyes, was not only indispensable to a valid marriage, it was the sole essential that could not be omitted.[7] To drive the point home, he cited the extreme hypothetical case of the couple who exchanged vows in absolute secrecy. Was their marriage valid? Yes, said Gratian, the two had conferred the sacrament on themselves. He added two qualifications. The act of physical union (copula carnalis) "perfected," that is, completed, the marriage. And the consenting couple must share "marital affection," because, Gratian reasoned, "where there is to be union of bodies there ought to be union of spirits."[8]

St. Augustine had considered the question of a marriage entered into only for the purpose of sex, and had decided that such a marriage was "perhaps" valid. Gratian did away with the "perhaps" but insisted that "marital affection" be present. A young couple lustful but maritally affectionate should be called "not fornicators but spouses."[9]

Thus according to Gratian two people sexually attracted who felt affection for each other could marry in total privacy without the assistance or permission of anyone—family, friends, feudal lord, or holy Church. This was radical doctrine, however logical to Gratian. Was concubinage a form of marriage? Gratian accepted the challenge and endorsed the judgment of Justinian's code. Provided that there was "marital affection," the concubine relationship amounted to an informal and imperfect but nevertheless valid marriage. As long as a man limited himself to one concubine, Gratian ruled, he should not be refused communion.[10]

Gratian's *Decretum* gained immediate wide influence, especially in moving the attitudes of clergy and public toward free consent as the basis of legal marriage. But while Gratian solved some problems for Church courts, he created others. The difference between an "informal" marriage and a casual sex relationship was not always readily discerned, and was difficult to articulate as an abstract principle that could be used to guide court judgments.

A dozen years after Gratian's *Decretum*, a rival compendium appeared. Its author was Peter Lombard (c. 1095–1160), like Gratian an alumnus of the University of Bologna and now bishop of Paris and doctor of theology at the school of Notre Dame. Peter's *Senten-*

tiarum Libri IV (Books of Sentences) became the standard textbook of theology in medieval universities. On the subject of marriage, Peter departed from Gratian's concept in two significant ways. Physical consummation could not be important to validity, he felt, because to make it so would cast a shadow on the marriage of Joseph and Mary (Gratian had drawn theological criticism on this score). On a practical level, if a man contracted marriage with one woman but left it unconsummated, and then contracted a second marriage and consummated it, the second was the valid one according to Gratian, a less than satisfactory solution in the eyes of much of the clergy and laity. Suppose, for example, a pair of noble minors were put through a marriage ceremony by their families in order to execute a mutually desirable transfer of property, and suppose the boy groom died and left the child bride a child widow. Was she entitled to her dower right of a third of her husband's property?[11]

For a decisive solution, Gratian's doctrine of consent alone seemed insufficient. What was needed was some more weighty form of affirmation. To supply the need, Peter Lombard advanced the theory of present consent. The consent recorded in the betrothal agreement he found too tentative, amounting only to "words of the future" *(verba de futuro)*. For a real marriage, legally uncontestable, the couple must pronounce "words of the present" *(verba de praesenti)*, words that stated explicitly that they took each other, starting at this moment, as man and wife.

That, however, sufficed. No ecclesiastical formality, no ritual act was necessary in Peter Lombard's eyes, only the unequivocal declaration. A benediction would be good, and dowries and endowments had value, but the couple's "words of the present" were alone indispensable.[12]

For several decades both Gratian and Peter Lombard had their adherents (Gratian's mostly in Italy, Peter's in France) without a final decision between them. At last Alexander III (pope 1159–1181) formulated a sort of delayed-action compromise. First, reaffirming indissolubility, he accepted Peter Lombard's "words of the present" as the essential of marriage, given at minimum ages of fourteen for the bridegroom, twelve for the bride. But a little later he in effect accepted most of Gratian's view by declaring that "words of the future," given as early as age seven, also created a

valid marriage bond when they were followed by physical consummation. Thus the Church officially endorsed two different
means of contracting marriage.[13]

More significant than the confusion, however, was the consensus. Of the marriage doctrines adopted by Gratian, Peter Lombard,
and the papacy, Michael M. Sheehan says: "It is unlikely that all
the consequences of those twelfth-century decisions have yet
been realized [in the twentieth]."[14]

Meantime another king and queen of France revived the consanguinity issue in a new royal divorce case. Louis VII (reigned
1137–1180) and Eleanor of Aquitaine, whose fifteen years of marriage had been blessed only with daughters and who were getting
tired of each other besides, uncovered a kinship of the fourth and
fifth degree that they had hitherto overlooked. Mutually recoiling,
they resisted a reconciliation attempted by Pope Eugenius III, and
through their own friendly archbishop of Sens got a Church council to sanction the divorce. Eleanor at once married Henry II of
England, taking Aquitaine with her as her own inherited estate
and creating the famous trans-Channel "Angevin empire." Thus
the exogamy rules so tirelessly pressed by the Church, and so
heedlessly extended to irrational limits, spawned a political event
that only two hundred years of warfare finally cancelled.[15]

Others were not slow to follow the example of Louis and Eleanor. The tracing, or creation, of genealogies, in which both witnesses and documents might be bought and paid for, supplied
employment for an army of lawyers and copyists. The case that
proved a last straw involved yet another king of France, the great
Philip Augustus (reigned 1180–1223), whose capricious dismissal
of his second wife, Ingeborg of Denmark, the morning after their
wedding night, brought conflict first with Pope Celestine III and
then with the formidable Innocent III.

A twenty-year wrangle followed, terminated only by the fortui-
tous death of Philip's third wife and the birth of an inheriting
grandson.[16] But everyone had had enough of the seventh degree
of consanguinity, which had caused trouble not only in high circles but in low ones. The Fourth Lateran Council, convened by
Innocent in 1215 to deal with a host of problems, summarily
reduced the forbidden degree from the seventh back to the fourth,
putting an end to one of the oddest chapters in the long history

of the incest taboo. It also called for endowment of brides and public weddings, in church, with declarations of consent by both parties, and publication of banns. This last was a custom already practiced in northern France and England. The priest read the announcement of the forthcoming marriage in church on successive Sundays or holy days, and parishioners were expected to report to him any known impediments, such as a prior contract by one of the parties. Such publicity made a clandestine union impossible, but the Council stopped short of actually nullifying clandestine marriage and remained silent on monogamous concubinage. That left moral and legal conundrums to vex canon lawyers and Church courts for another three hundred years.[17]

Younger Sons: Rogue Males of the Aristocracy

The clerks who composed the genealogies, and who themselves were often members of the family whose tree they were exploring, found their task sometimes fraught with difficulties and even embarrassments. If certain princes and lords wanted their genealogists to find consanguineous ties in order to justify divorce, most shrank from any such discovery. The genealogist of Siboto IV, count of Falkenstein (southern Bavaria), cited the count's parents' ancestry for two generations back in the male line, but discreetly omitted the fact that they were descended from a common great-grandfather.[18]

Yet, where some ancestors of twelfth-century aristocrats had to be suppressed from the record, others created a fundamental problem by their absence. The genealogist of a great ducal or comital family might be able to trace the male line back as far as the ninth century, while one employed by a castellan could get no farther back than the tenth, and by a mere knight seldom beyond the late eleventh or early twelfth, but no matter how far back the line could legitimately be pursued, at some point the researcher inevitably ran into a blank wall.[19] Modern scholars have filled in some of these blanks, often with a curious result: the twelfth-century lord proved to have had nobler ancestry than he himself suspected, typically as the result of a marriage between a successful adventurer and a princess or heiress of a great house blessed with an excess of daughters.[20] The information, however congenial it might have been to a twelfth-century clerk, could not have resolved his dilemma. What he needed was a means of terminating his genealogical construction in a male ancestor.[21]

He hit on a solution that was repeated over and over in genealogy after genealogy: invention. The counts of Flanders, creators of one of the first genealogies in the tenth century, had their family tree redrawn in the twelfth to supply the deficiency of early forebears on the male side. A complete set of new ancestors was created out of whole cloth. Other nobles received equally imaginative services from their scribes, above all in fabricating the original progenitor, the founding father of the noble line. Repeated over and over, this figure was ever the same, a successful adventurer, idealized and stylized to resemble the twelfth century's popular literary image: the heroic knight-errant.[22]

That image, fashioned and polished by troubadour poetry, the Arthurian cycle, and the *chansons de geste,* was derived by the poets from real-life models. Though the originals typically required some tidying up before being presented in ballads and epics, they possessed by right of birth the three essential qualities: they were brave, adventurous, and trained in arms. They were the younger sons of the nobility, disfranchised by primogeniture. In England they were not even classed as noble; on the Continent their technically noble status was an irony in light of their deprivation of land and revenue and consequent condemnation to bachelorhood. A twelfth-century moralist sympathized with their fate:

> Who made brothers unequal among the fraternal relationships of nature?
>
> Our sons have to yield their place to the isolated fortune of a single rich one. The first of them is overwhelmed with the whole paternal inheritance: the second deplores the exhaustion of a rich patrimony and laments his penniless dower. But did not nature divide equally among sons? Nature assigns equally to all. . . .
>
> [You ought not] to make unequal in their patrimony those whom you have made equal by the title of brotherhood, and whom, indeed, you have made to be both alike by the accident of birth. You ought not to grudge their having in common a thing to which they are common heirs.[23]

For these disinherited younger sons, the sought-for solution was to marry an heiress and thus to become what was otherwise denied them: the head of a family, no longer a *juvenis* (youth) but a true adult, a *senior*, entitled to occupy with his wife the great chamber that in the twelfth century usually contained the only real bed in the castle, reserved for the family's progenitors.[24]

The castle Lambert of Ardres describes in his *History of the Counts of Guines* was not one of the newer masonry structures but the old motte-and-bailey timber fort of the tenth century. It had its hall and attendant service rooms (larders, pantry, and buttery) on the second floor, above the ground-level storerooms with their boxes and barrels and utensils. Adjoining the hall were "the great chamber in which the lord and lady slept" and "the dormitory of the ladies-in-waiting and children," in other words, the nursery. The attic, designed mainly for the adolescents, was divided into two sections, evidently outfitted with pallets. On one side the sons of the lord stayed "when they so desired," and sometimes the watchmen and servants; on the other the daughters "because they were obliged"—where they could be watched over until they were suitably married.[25] There was only one "great chamber"; the castle was not designed for more than one married couple. The heir could not marry until his father died, unless he found an heiress and won a house and bedchamber of his own. Count Baldwin of Guines's eldest son, Arnoul of Ardres, did this in 1194 when, with his father still alive, he married the heiress of the castle of Bourbourg, whose brother had died.[26]

Finding an heiress was thus a convenience for older sons, an imperative for younger sons, who were otherwise lifelong bachelors. Everywhere they were numerous. Lambert de Wattrelos, whose memoir throws much light on the contemporary lesser nobility, mentions several families among his relations who had from five to eleven children.[27] Except for those who went into the Church, all young noblemen, heirs as well as cadets, underwent a period of vagabondage, often with a mentor chosen to initiate them into the game of knight-errantry—war, tournament, adventure. Traveling with bands of companions, the young knights led a life in which pleasure mingled with violence, death was a commonplace, and turbulence reigned.[28] The eldest sons among the knights-errant normally succeeded to their estates, though their accession was sometimes long delayed. Arnoul of Ardres was in his thirties when he married the heiress of Bourbourg.[29] For younger sons, "youth" was nearly always extended, often ending only in death.

The contemporary *History of William Marshal* gives a vivid insight into the career of such a younger son. Fourth son of an official of the English court, William was sent to Normandy to be trained as a squire in the household of a wealthy and powerful cousin. Knighted in anticipation of his first battle, William fought well, but made the blunder of neglecting to take any booty; his comrades gave him good-humored corrective counsel. Thereafter William took care to seize horses, armor, and prisoners for ransom, both in war and in tournaments. By the time he was twenty-six, he was a veteran knight-errant and was chosen by Henry II to act as mentor to the king's eldest son Henry, roving France and Flanders, taking part in tournament and battle, including a rebellion against young Henry's father. William teamed up with another knight to travel the tournament circuit; in ten months they took 102 knightly prisoners. By his exploits William won great prestige, but he remained a "youth," that is, landless and unmarried. He was in his forties before his services to the king at last brought him both a fief and a wealthy bride. By outliving his three elder brothers he also inherited the Marshal office and estates.[30]

Few of William's compeers among the army of younger sons were so fortunate. Most expended their green manhood "in tourneys and in war," in expeditions and Crusades, in hunting, carousing, and lechery, and died at a young age. Lambert de Wattrelos mentions several, including a brother of his own who died in battle and ten brothers of his maternal grandfather who were memorialized in verse for having all fallen on the same day in a single battle.[31] Whatever their fate, the younger sons of the nobility were the martyrs of the new system of primogeniture. At the same time, by a poetic irony, and at a second remove, they were the real-life models for their families' fictitious noble progenitors.

Many of their sisters were also martyrs, though less dramatically. As families sought to marry all their daughters but only one of their sons, the marriage ages of brides dropped while those of grooms rose, dowries inflated while spinsters multiplied. The convents were unable to accommodate the demand, and in Flanders a new social phenomenon, beguinage, made its appearance. A beguine (from Lambert Bègue, founder of the order) was a nun without a convent. Living a chaste, cheerless, and lonely life, she was a female counterpart of the knight-errant younger son.[32]

Genoa: Aristocrats and Artisans in the City

The central Middle Ages was a city-building era. The shrunken Roman cities of France and England were expanded and rebuilt, and new towns sprang up along trading routes and in market locations. The monastic movement created large, orderly nuclei around which craftsmen, merchants, and farmers could congregate. Even the Vikings, who sacked so many ninth-century cities, founded a few, such as Dublin, to use as trading depots for their plunder. They also stimulated their numerous victims to build city walls, an improvement in security that attracted business-minded immigrants. All over northwest Europe fresh clusters of houses, workshops, gardens, barns, and pigsties clung to monasteries and castles or crowded behind city ramparts. Enlightened rulers gave charters of freedom to settlements that proclaimed their origin in their names: Villeneuve, Neustadt, Villa Nova—"New City."

On the Italian peninsula, Venice, Amalfi, Genoa, Pisa, and other towns, nonexistent or insignificant in Roman times, were born or reborn at coastal points protected on their land side by marshes, lagoons, cliffs, or mountains. When Muslim corsairs raided the Ligurian coast, the Genoese aristocrats who lived in the hills above the city came down to spearhead the defense, and when resistance turned into counteroffensive, the nobles, headed by the Marquis Obertenghi, assumed military command. Since the profession of the aristocracy was arms, that seemed natural. What was less foreseeable was that the Genoese aristocrats, having descended to the city to fight, should remain there to do business, making a smooth transition from maritime warfare to maritime commerce, which they staked out as their legal monopoly. *Genuensis, ergo mercator,* ran a medieval proverb, "Genoese, therefore a merchant." Yet Genoa had no class of base-born merchants and bankers to correspond with those of the cities of northwest Europe. Instead it had its urban aristocracy, whose outlook, habits, and family life were shared in some degree with the wealthy classes of other Italian

Tower of the Embriaci family, Genoa. (Authors' photograph)

cities but were quite distinct from those of the rural aristocracy.[33]

Physically, the city was marked by a feature noted by all visitors, a skyline of conspicuous towers. Rising well above the limit of eighty feet that the city's own consuls tried to impose, the rugged square towers dominated neighborhoods that were fortified compounds, within which banded together the great aristocratic lineages. The core of each enclave was composed of a few wealthy families claiming relationship, around which were settled a number of lesser families, some of them poor relations, some dependent clients. Houses fronted on a square enclosing market, shops, loggias, ovens, gardens, baths, and church.[34]

The guardian towers were of rough-hewn masonry, but the houses were nearly all wooden, with narrow frontage extending back typically forty-eight feet from the street. The central room *(caminata),* the kitchen, and the arsenal filled the ground floor, with the family bedrooms and the servants' quarters above. Each floor had access to the tower, into which the entire household could retire for defense. The cramped, warlike house contrasted with the

Palazzi of the Doria family, one of Genoa's family enclaves. (Authors' photograph)

commodious, loggia-bordered compound of which the house was a part, just as the family occupying it was a part of the great lineage that populated the compound. "It was not within the walls of the house but within the shelter of the family enclave," says Diane Hughes, "that the aristocratic Genoese seem to have lived most fully. . . . Its bath became a center for family gossip while its loggias were a more public place for family meetings and festivities. Its church . . . like the loggia, which was often decorated with family emblems, provided a means of family identification through plaques inscribed to the ancestral dead, through ever more splendid tombs and monuments, and through a constant hum of masses sung to mark the anniversaries of the deaths of its members." The noble aggregations of Genoa were not unique. Such tower-guarded enclaves dominated the aristocratic quarters of other Italian cities, but in Genoa the tendency was earliest and most marked.[35]

The family unit within each house was large and patriarchal. Sons lived at home until their father's death, and sometimes more than one son stayed on after it. The physical limitations of the house rather than custom evidently determined the actual number of persons accommodated. A married son with children might have to move out; if so, he found a house nearby. Thus the Genoese "family" (as distinct from the lineage) was not the household contained under a single roof but rather a broad patriarchal kinship group, including daughters-in-law and children, clustered under roofs in close proximity.

The partible inheritance of the Roman, Lombard, and Frankish law codes remained in force, but in a strictly male sense. Estates always passed to sons, and in their absence to brothers, grandsons, or nephews. "Aristocratic property rarely left the lineage group."[36]

The lineage had commercial, social, political, and military dimensions, to meet whose requirements it expanded and contracted as necessary, encompassing more or fewer clients and poor relations. When in 1188 a thousand Genoese men affixed their signatures to a peace oath sworn with rival Pisa, a third of the names were grouped in lineage-residence blocs, those of the male leaders of the great families followed by the individuals linked not by kinship but by clientage.[37] The private wars that intermittently racked the city traced their beginnings, as did the lineages themselves, to the tenth century, when two of the city's founding fathers, Obertus Vicecomes (Visconti) and Obertus de Maneciano, fell out; two hundred years later their descendants, the descendants of collateral branches, and allied lineages still fought in the streets and besieged each others' compounds. The head of the Camilla family, entreating the pope for permission to build his own church, pleaded that his family could not risk the trip to the neighboring church of Santa Maria delle Vigne.[38]

Marriage arrangements had political and military as well as commercial aims. Rarely were marriages contracted between enemy lineages, nearly always with sought-after allies. An alliance once entered into was likely to be perpetually activated for commercial as well as military purposes, and to endure for generations and even centuries. As elsewhere, the exchange of the dowry and dower formed the cornerstone of the marriage, and as in many places, the twelfth century saw a significant shift in the weight of the two contributions. In Genoa the patrician bride originally received two endowments, an *antefactum* in money or valuables, plus a *tercia*, a vested interest in one third of her husband's total estates. In 1143 the *tercia* was abolished and the *antefactum* limited to one half the size of the dowry or one hundred Genoese pounds, whichever was less. Thus here too the nuptial scales were tilted to the advantage of the bridegroom, who was frequently still in his teens and under the tutelage of his father or older relative. Emancipation took place only at twenty-five. A young man's first voyages were made with his father, uncles, or older brothers. Attempts by the city government to give young people more voice in property settlements, together with individual responsibility for crimes committed, were successfully resisted; patrician Genoa remained a father-dominated society.[39]

Family life among the other major Genoese social class, that of the artisans—craftsmen, shopkeepers, petty merchants, laborers—differed markedly from that of the aristocrats. Among the artisans, lineage did not exist, and the extended family, so important to the aristocracy, was imperceptible. For the shoemaker, the cooper, and the fishmonger, the family was wife and children, clustered beneath his small roof. The wife was business partner, working by his side; the children also helped or were put out as apprentices in the same or another trade. If the family was extended, it was by the retention of an adult son to run the shop when the aged parents could no longer do so, or by the inclusion of a son-in-law for the same purpose.[40]

Yet the artisan belonged to a larger group than his immediate household. This larger group consisted not of kin but of professional associates. In the same way his church, on which he depended for salvation and other benefits exactly as did the aristocrats, was the parish church, devoid of any familial connection with him. Wills clearly show the sense of the artisan's loyalties. One shoemaker, dying in 1190, had two brothers living but bequeathed his house and most of his estate to his shoemaker partner and named the parish church as his residual heir—"something that no aristocrat would ever have done," says Diane Hughes, who found that of artisan wills made in the absence of direct heirs, 14 percent bequeathed the estate to nonrelatives. The kind of arrangement for old age that aristocrats made with relatives, artisans and their widows commonly made with associates or neighbors, trading house and property at death for bed and a place at table and at hearth. Again, 23 percent of extant artisan wills make wives principal heirs, sometimes even in the presence of children, "an award the aristocracy never contemplated."[41]

The bond between artisan husband and wife differed in kind from that uniting the aristocratic couple. The artisan wife contributed her labor, either in her husband's craft or another, while the two made equal or comparable contributions at the beginning of the marriage in dowry and *antefactum*. The median value of artisan *antefacta* (fourteen pounds) was 70 percent of that of the dowry (twenty pounds). More than 70 percent of artisan *antefacta* were one half or more the value of the corresponding dowry. Among aristocratic marriages the same was true of only 44 percent. Genoa's artisans, in other words, resisted the sense of the law limiting the husband's contribution. Among the aristocracy, the size of a daughter's dowry conferred status, a consideration little in the minds of working-class fathers, occupied with stretching all the available resources on both sides to provide a basis for the marriage.[42]

In child care also the two classes differed. Artisan mothers nursed their own infants; aristocratic mothers put them out to nurse or brought a wet nurse into their home. Many remembered both their own and their children's nurses in their wills.[43] Nursing doubtless helped bond artisan children to their mothers; a few years later, however, the same children were pushed out of the nest into an often harsh apprenticeship. From it the artisan son graduated to independence, marriage, and the foundation of his own family.[44] The artisan daughter often had to wait for the death of a parent to acquire the dowry needed for her own departure. Once married, she probably enjoyed a more nearly equal share of authority than did the aristocratic wife, thanks to her dowry contribution, her working partnership, and sometimes her identity as the master's daughter whom an aspiring apprentice had courted.

Widowhood added still another variant between the two Genoese classes. The working-class widow was strongly motivated to remarry and, unless she was too old, very likely to do so, either taking her children with her into the new household or bringing her new husband into the old one. Often a widow chose a practitioner of her former husband's (and her own) trade, occasionally even an ambitious apprentice. The aristocratic widow, in contrast, rarely remarried, because to do so obligated her to surrender her children to guardians appointed by her husband's lineage. In recompense, widowhood conferred on the noble wife and mother a degree of freedom she had never enjoyed before.[45] Most received a formal contract guaranteeing control of their homes and estates. Early thirteenth-century records show Drua Stregghiaporco investing over a thousand pounds in maritime ventures to Spain, Africa, and the East; Giardinia Boleto investing 615 pounds in similar overseas ventures; and Mavilia Lecavella selling wine to the king of France, dealing in land and commercial property, investing 325 pounds in four contracts to Africa and the East, and training her children in their father's business.[46] Aristocratic wives seldom appear in Genoese business records; aristocratic widows are conspicuous. A reasonable inference might be that such wives were more conversant with their husbands' affairs than appears in the record.

As for the orphaned children, to those of the working class the death of the father brought either the shock of moving into a new household under a stepfather or the struggle to survive in a family bereft of its head and with few resources. For the children of the nobility the tragedy was softened by the continuation of life in a home surrounded on all sides by protective uncles, aunts, and other kin.[47]

Thus twelfth-century Genoa, commercial city par excellence, shows two distinct family patterns. The aristocratic pattern may perhaps be seen as an urban version of the aristocratic pattern everywhere, with its self-conscious lineages and military demeanor, modified in many details of material and social environment, but profoundly in only one direction, the adoption of commerce as a profession. Similarly, as will be seen, the artisan pattern resembles the universal model of the peasant family, with its emphasis on the conjugal roof and the husband-wife partnership and its preference for neighbors and co-workers over more distant kin.

Reconquest Spain: Families on the Frontier

Frontier conditions in the form of new settlements in the wilderness were widespread in twelfth-century Europe, where an immense work of land clearance, comparable in many ways to that carried out in North America seven centuries later, was in progress. On the Iberian peninsula, the Reconquest, the recovery of the land from the Moors, created a genuine frontier. When a district was liberated, a fortified urban core was built around a castle and quickly encircled by farmlands, pastures, and dependent villages. Such new communities strove to replace the violent swirl of warfare with order and stability, and to substitute for the masculine military presence the normal compound of civil society. Newcomers were encouraged by a variety of incentives to "make smoke," that is, to bring wives to found hearths and households.

In the frontier settlements, the townswoman (muger villana) or village woman (muger aldeana) pursued much the same daily rounds as women in more peaceable regions, spinning, weaving, sewing, nursing babies, supervising children, carrying her bucket to the spring or fountain, queuing up at the community oven, visiting the bathhouse on women's day. There were differences, however. Notable ones in both legal status and economic role are pointed out by Heath Dillard in Daughters of the Reconquest. [48]

A maxim out of the old law code of Spain's earlier conquerors, the Visigoths, held that in all matters of inheritance the woman should be "recognized." In practice, the principle took the form of a sex-blind partible inheritance, in which all heirs and heiresses of the same degree of kinship shared equally. Frontier communities rigorously upheld the tradition. If a son or daughter died leaving children, the children shared in their grandparents' estate; if a married woman died before her parents, her share reverted to her siblings rather than passing to her husband. Finally, every child inherited separately from father and mother, so that property descended in independent, parallel streams. [49] Inheritable property in the wake of the Reconquest included war booty—livestock, slaves, captives held for ransom—all shared by a wife who helped pay for her husband's equipment. The horse and arms that gave him his status as a caballero villano (non-noble knight of the urban militia) were excepted from the shared-inheritance rule as strictly masculine chattels, but even these could be acquired by a woman as war booty and could be passed on to her sons or her second husband, on whom they could confer the *caballero* status.[50]

The effect of such legal assets was doubly to enhance a woman's value, first as heiress, second as transmitter of property. Where elsewhere in Europe women were losing many of their old property and inheritance rights to the new wave of male dominance, and marriage gifts to the bride were depreciating while her dower rights were curtailed, in Spain none of these things had yet happened. The new philosophy of primogeniture and male lineage that robbed women of both power and status had made no headway here. On the frontier especially, the wife enjoyed prestige and authority, owing to the husband's frequent absences on military expeditions, from which he often failed to return.

Involvement of the bride's family in marriage arrangements also received added emphasis here because of the inheritance system. Where every daughter inherited a significant share—a quarter, a third, a half—of all one owned, parents were bound to take a serious interest in her choice of a husband. Spanish custom went so far as to make a girl's marriage in the face of parental disapproval grounds for her disinheritance.[51]

Visigothic law, anticipating the Church by several centuries, required satisfactory endowment of the bride by the groom's marriage gift, in Spain called the *arras,* from the Latin *arrha,* meaning "earnest money." Endowment charters *(cartas de arras)* list land, houses, villages, livestock, slaves, saddles, mules, horses, clothing, hides, and tithes.[52] A Castilian noble typically added another gift, a tent made of fine leather, large enough to accommodate the entry of an armed *caballero.* Heath Dillard suggests that this unusual gift implies an itinerant domesticity imposed by scattered estates or by attendance on the king.[53]

The *arras* might be deferred and merely pledged, by a rule whose intent was to prevent wealthy suitors from gaining unfair advantage in courtship. The groom's family, however, had to pay for the wedding celebration, especially the generous feast. The bride's trousseau, which was subtracted from her future inheritance, included cooking utensils, quilts, linens, and other household furnishings. A wealthy bride might bring a vineyard, a garden, or a corral.[54]

Sunday was the traditional wedding day, and in Spain (as in parts of northern Europe) the priest now played a role. The bride rode on horseback to church, where the priest blessed the secular and liturgical symbols, the *arras* and the rings, said a mass, and enjoined the couple to observe the "night of Tobias" by refraining from sex until the next day, a recommendation drawn from Gratian. Feasting, dancing, jousts, and games followed, with the wedding guests' revelry often provoking fines.[55]

On the rough-and-ready frontier, marriage did not always remain decorously within the confines specified by law, custom, and the Church. Couples eloping by mutual agreement found havens in the towns, distance robbing parents of the community's sympathy. Even abduction, though theoretically treated as a crime, was subject to a wide latitude in judicial practice. What was relevant was the identity of the wronged woman as a local or an outsider. If she was a townswoman, penalties against her abductor ranged from a heavy fine (royal or seigneurial) to flogging, enslavement, or death. If, however, she was an outsider, the abductor might escape unscathed. He might even be welcomed. Some towns explicitly granted male colonists the privilege of bringing in abducted women. The act could be construed as a community benefit, since it added a new smoke-maker to the settlement and diverted the new male from the competition for local women. Further, an abductor might be perceived as just the sort of bold fellow needed on the frontier.[56]

In light of the number of armed, rootless men on the loose, fathers were well advised to keep a watchful eye on their daughters. Toward rape, local law took two opposed attitudes. In some places the rapist was obliged to marry his victim, in others he was forbidden to do so, a proviso designed to frustrate the adventurer or fortune hunter who hoped to force a marriage with a daughter of wealth.[57]

Ordinary sex outside marriage was constrained by rigid but liberal restrictions. For a young bachelor to keep a *barragana* (mistress) until he was ready for marriage was not only tolerated but expected. The privilege was extended to single men in general, and rather particularly to priests. Spanish priests scarcely differed from clergy elsewhere in their domestic arrangements. Several decades after two Lateran councils had prescribed celibacy, according to

Esmein, "everyone who entered the clergy made a vow of chastity but almost none observed it."[58]

The *barragana* privilege, however, was not passed on to married men, since if a married man kept a *barragana* he was not only committing adultery but was depriving another man of a possible partner. Flogging was the usual punishment. Adultery on the part of a wife was even more severely dealt with, expulsion from the town being added to the flogging.[59]

Sex between engaged couples was neither unknown nor unexpected. Spanish custom did not go as far as Pope Alexander III in regarding a promise followed by sex as constituting a marriage, but breach of the man's promise after engaging in sex was treated as a serious offense, penalized by a heavy fine. A woman so betrayed sometimes preferred to cover up her embarrassment. A certain Dona Elvira of Villa Armento was betrothed to a *caballero* who broke off the engagement and asked for return of his gifts. Dona Elvira refused. A judge ruled that she could keep them if her betrothed had "kissed and embraced" her; otherwise she must return them. She returned the gifts. The judge's ruling may have been inspired by the law respecting a bride-to-be whose fiancé died before the wedding: if they had had sex, she kept his gifts; if not, she had to return them to his family; and if they had only kissed, she was obligated to return half of them. If it was the bride-to-be who died before the wedding, the groom returned all gifts unless they had had sex, in which case he kept them all; in this instance at least, the embrace counted as marriage ceremony.[60]

Sexual harassment was also a punishable offense, and the fines levied for molesting women in two towns, Alcala de Henares and Sepulveda, throw further light on frontier attitudes. The scale of values taught by St. Jerome was turned upside down. Fondling a married woman cost the offender four marivales; the same act committed against a widow cost only three in Alcala, two in Sepulveda; against a virgin, two and one marivale, respectively.[61] A husband who imagined his wife to have encouraged an advance undoubtedly punished her himself, wife-beating receiving sanction from custom as well as canon law.

Those detected in sexual transgressions were not all caught and punished. Flight was easy and frequent, as indicated by the system of levying heavy fines on the family of a fugitive guilty of a serious crime. Even nonpayment of debts by a runaway husband brought a transfer of the burden to his family, though a husband's gambling debts and his loans from Jews could not be assessed against a wife's inheritance.[62] A fugitive husband had no difficulty in finding another community ready to welcome him, authorities insisting only that the newcomer make peace in advance with any enemies he might have in the town. Troubles left behind were freely cancelled out.[63]

On the moving frontier of the Reconquest, daily life differed from that in regions grown more peaceful. Spanish men were more lawless, more prone to violence, more perpetually armed, and more frequently engaged in war, in a word more like the men of France, England, and Germany in an earlier era. Women were more jealously guarded, more often abused, and simultaneously accorded more respect, more responsibility, and more share in family affairs. Alone in Western Europe, Spanish women enjoyed significant property and inheritance rights long after the general shift to impartible inheritance and primogeniture.

8.

Peasants Before the Black Death:
1200-1347

The thirteenth century brought the expansion and prosperity of the high Middle Ages to its peak, in active commerce, expanding population, and agricultural improvements that brought beneficial change to all classes, high and low, urban and rural, including the great lower class that formed the universal majority, the peasants. By a fortunate coincidence the thirteenth century provides the first extensive documentation of the lives of peasant families, mainly in the form of two kinds of English records, the manorial custumals and the manorial court rolls. The custumals, like the polyptychs of the Carolingian era, list the tenants on a manor and the rents and services that they owe. The court rolls record not only breaches of the law and disputes between peasants or between peasant and lord, but also transfers of land and the legislation that the village community enacted to regulate farming practices. Together the two sets of records yield our first comprehensive picture of peasant life, much fuller than that of the Carolingian polyptychs, including information on economics, status, agricultural techniques, marriage and inheritance practices, crime, and social relationships.

Across northwest Europe and England, two different modes of cultivation produced two different patterns of family life.[1] "Champion" country (from the French *champagne*), occupying most of the plain of Northern Europe and a band of England running northeast from the Channel through the Midlands to the North Sea, consisted of open country with large stretches of land suitable for cultivation. "Woodland" country, including Brittany and Normandy and the west, northwest, and southeast of England, included patches of arable land along with pastoral areas suitable for grazing.

In champion country the prevalent pattern of cultivation was the "open field system," the technique which has usually been identified with medieval agriculture. By this arrangement, two, three, or more large unfenced fields were divided into strips for plowing, each cultivator working a number of strips scattered among the different fields. Meadow, wasteland, fallow, and the harvested stubble were used as common pasture. The peasants themselves decided what crops to plant and when, and when the fields were to lie fallow. Families lived in large "nucleated" (clustered) villages, manorial control was typically strong, and inheritance was impartible and patrilineal, land passing from father to a single son, usually the eldest.

In woodland country, by contrast, each peasant family worked its individual farm, whose compact fields were enclosed by hedges and ditches. Small hamlets and scattered farmhouses marked the landscape. Manorial control was weak, and inheritance was partible among sons and in some places daughters.

The dividing line between the two types of cultivation and settlement was often blurred. Isolated examples of separate farmsteads and small hamlets were found in champion country, and large villages and open fields (though not communally regulated) in woodland.

Peasant Families in Open Field Country

Some scholars trace the open field system to the Germanic tribes of the Great Migrations. Others believe that its mature development barely preceded its appearance in thirteenth-century records, and that it resulted from the fragmentation of inheritances through partibility, a hypothesis that does not account for the introduction of impartibility, communal control of cultivation, or communal grazing. The origins of the system remain stubbornly obscure.[2]

The first studies of villages in champion country dealt largely with economics: the peasants as tenants of the lord's manor, the rents they paid, the services they performed, and especially their status as free or unfree. However, among the peasants themselves the distinction between free and unfree was virtually meaningless. In the words of the great Victorian legist, Frederic Maitland, the serf was a free man "in relation to all men other than his lord."[3] But in relation to the lord, servile status was important enough for peasants to make strenuous efforts to rid themselves of it. Disputes over a peasant family's status sometimes led to violent confrontations between lord and tenant.

Three distinguishing characteristics marked the unfree peasant ("serf" on the Continent, "villein" in England). First, he was subject to an array of fees on a variety of occasions: when he succeeded to his father's holding; when his daughter married; when he died; and on certain others. Second, he was subject to the lord's manorial courts rather than to the royal courts, and he needed his lord's permission to quit the manor. Third, and most important, he owed the lord heavy labor service, which by the thirteenth century was beginning to be commuted to money payments but remained burdensome.

In England, all the land, from earldom to peasant holding, was governed by the conditional terms of feudalism, which had been imposed by the Norman Conquest. There was no "ownership," no allodial land owned outright. Peasant holdings, however, were normally transmitted from one generation to the next very much as if they were owned. Common (feudal) law did not recognize this right for villeins, but practice contradicted law, and was endorsed by the manorial courts.[4] A further complication: the land itself was classified as free or villein, that is, either money rents on the one hand or labor services on the other might be owed for it. The status of land had originally coincided with that of its tenants, but by the thirteenth century the vagaries of inheritance had uncoupled the two, so that a free man might hold some villein land, or a villein some free land. Land held by villein tenure was called "customary land," that is, held under the custom of the manor.

The manor (in French, *seigneurie*)—the lord's estate consisting of a "demesne" or "reserve" directly exploited by him, and of a collection of peasant holdings over which he enjoyed rights and assessed fees—had been imposed on rural England by the Norman Conquest and did not necessarily coincide with the village. Recent studies of peasants in open field country have focused on the social rather than the economic aspects, that is, on the peasants not as tenants of a manor but as members of a village community. From these studies emerges a picture of a village hierarchy only partly related to tenurial status. Typically, at the top and bottom were a few free families, in the middle a range of unfree families, some prosperous, some less so.

In 1279 the village of Cuxham, near Oxford, had essentially three classes of tenants. At the top were two free peasants, Robert Serviens and Robert ate Grene. When Robert Serviens died without heirs, part of his land reverted to villein status and was redistributed, while the rest, including his house and farmyard, was granted to Robert ate Grene. Over the next decades the ate Grenes acquired a number of scattered small holdings in parishes near Cuxham. In 1316 Robert's son, John ate Grene, who had married an heiress from the nearby village of Watlington, was assessed at the highest rate in the village.

Yet his taxes were only a third greater than those of the Heycrofts, Benyts, and Oldmans, the most affluent among the thirteen villein families that held a messuage (house and farmyard) with a half-virgate of land (about twelve acres). Below these thirteen families were the cottagers, who held parcels of land insufficient to support themselves and had to hire out as laborers to make ends meet.[5] In Cuxham, the cottagers were all villeins, but elsewhere many were free. In a study of southern Warwickshire in the thirteenth century, R. H. Hilton estimated that two thirds of the cottagers were free.[6]

In champion country sentiment still ran strongly against alienating—selling or giving away—land belonging to an established holding. Such a transaction ran contrary to the interest of both heir and lord. Villein land could be sold only with the permission of the lord, whose manorial court registered the transaction. The pressure of population and shifting family fortunes, however, inevitably created a land market, and sale and sublease of both villein and free land took place. In Cuxham, other villagers besides Robert ate Grene are recorded as purchasing land. In 1315 Robert Oldman, Alice Benyt, and William ate Heycroft were fined by the court for having bought land without permission and warned not to resell on pain of forfeiting their principal holdings. Such small purchases, of one to three acres, were probably for the purpose of providing dowries or gifts for daughters or younger sons.[7] But Robert Oldman also made more substantial purchases: six acres of free land in 1315, another six acres of villein land in 1323. One of the wealthier villagers, by his death he owned at least four horses, fifty-six sheep, eleven lambs, two cows, and three calves, and employed on his land at least two laborers in addition to two of his sons.[8]

The family was the basic labor unit, its tasks subdivided into a men's and a women's share. Men did the "outside" work—plowing, sowing, reaping, haying, winnowing, threshing—as they had always done. Women performed their traditional "inside" jobs, not all of which kept them indoors: cooking, milking, making

Women's tasks: a woman spins, while the dog raids the kettle. Misericord from Church of St. Mary, Fairford. (Batsford)

Woman preparing wool for spinning. (Bodleian Library, MS Douce 6, 101 v)

butter and cheese, spinning and weaving, feeding the poultry, cultivating the vegetable patch, foraging in the woods and fields for berries, nuts, and greens. Children assisted in these last duties, and also helped in gleaning, herding sheep, tending poultry, and baby-sitting for younger siblings. In the seasons of intensive labor, women and older children joined the men in the fields.[9]

Villages also contained some individuals with specialized skills, their number and variety depending on the size of the village and the nature of its economy. Two trades were indispensable: those of the miller and the blacksmith. The mill where the villagers' wheat was ground was usually the monopoly of the lord, who farmed it out to the miller in return for an annual payment. The blacksmith shoed the horses and made and mended the plow irons and other tools. Villages might also have carpenters, tailors, butchers, tanners, carters, and other tradesmen. A trade found in every English village was the brewing of ale, open to all but generally practiced by the affluent, who could afford the large iron cauldron and other equipment. In some communities brewing was monopolized by women; in others men also participated.[10]

An ale-wife. Misericord from the Church of St. Lawrence, Ludlow. (Batsford)

The open field village in its communal role has often been pictured as a kind of Eden of mutual aid, cooperation, and solidarity, as the peasants worked their strips in the fields side by side, shared pastureland, and lived in close communion. Village bylaws show a less idyllic, more competitive aspect. Framed by the villagers in meetings held at regular intervals, usually in conjunction with manorial courts, the bylaws dealt with a wide range of problems created by the communal system: trampling another tenant's grain; cutting hay in the meadow without waiting for lots to be drawn; allowing one's cows, pigs, or geese to damage another's crops; "stealing plow furrows," that is, plowing part of a neighbor's land. Bylaws ruled that "able-bodied" people should not be allowed to do the relatively easy work of gleaning reserved for "the young, the old, and those who are decrepit and unable to work," but should be employed to their capacity in reaping. Peas and beans, especially valuable in a protein-short diet, could be picked only at specified times when all villagers were present and could watch each other. All kinds of precautions were taken to prevent the theft of sheaves. Rules restricted carting and carrying to daylight hours, via specified entries and exits to the fields. The picture conveyed by the bylaws is that of a community aware of both the necessity for cooperation and the need for carefully policing cooperative tasks.[11]

Bylaw enforcement was entrusted to wardens elected by the villagers. Like other village offices, that of warden was filled mainly by peasants with substantial holdings. Studies of villages in the manorial system of Ramsey Abbey have revealed a kind of peasant aristocracy dominating village affairs. In Broughton, a third of the families held village offices on a regular basis.[12] In Holywell-cum-Needingworth, slightly more than half the families were involved in administration. Of these "official families," a little more than half were intensively involved.[13] Edward Britton found evidence in Broughton of "mergence," a practice employed by royalty and aristocracy by which an office was passed on to a son before his father's death to provide training and ensure the continuity of the office in the family. In fifteen of the forty-two "main" families of Broughton, sons held office while their fathers were still active in administration.[14]

A key office was that of juror, not to be confused in function with modern jurors. Where today jurors are selected partly for their ignorance of a case and consequent lack of prejudice, the jurors (*jurati*, "sworn men") of manorial courts were chosen for their acquaintance with the facts and with plaintiff and defendant, as well as with the law, that is, the "custom of the manor," the law of precedent. They not only rendered judgment but testified and conducted the investigation. They could be fined for falsifying or concealing charges, and their responsibilities continued between court sessions.[15] At Holywell over a period of 150 years, about half of the village families contributed jurors with varying frequency, one thirty-two times.[16] At Broughton, where Britton identified about a third of the families he studied as "important," he found that 80 percent of such families held the office for two generations.[17]

Other village offices were also largely monopolized by the leading families. One was that of reeve, always a villein (but a prosperous one), who managed the lord's demesne farm and was responsible for overseeing the labor services owed by the unfree villagers. That of ale taster, responsible for checking the quality of ale brewed in the village, was the only office occasionally held by women.[18]

Vanished from the society of thirteenth-century England were the old Germanic familial instruments of protection and justice of Anglo-Saxon times, feud and wergeld,* their functions usurped by new institutions. A hierarchy of courts from manorial to royal now settled disputes and meted out justice. A policing system known as frankpledge, which probably originated before the Norman Conquest, assigned all males over the age of twelve to groups called tithings, each numbering ten to a dozen and headed by a capital pledge or chief pledge. Collectively, the tithing was responsible for the behavior of its members. It presented minor local police matters in court.[19]

Another distinctive English village practice of the central Middle Ages was that of personal pledging, by which one person stood guarantee for another. If the pledgee reneged, the pledge paid a fine. Usually the action to be guaranteed was appearance in court,

---

*Recent discussion in legal circles of compensation for victims of crime suggests that the abolition of wergeld may have involved a historic social loss.

or fulfilling a neglected labor service, or repairing outbuildings; in one case a pledge guaranteed that a man would cease mistreating his wife. The person who needed the guarantee was obliged to "find" a pledge. With the exception of women fined for infractions of the ale-brewing standard, who often chose their husbands, pledgees rarely chose pledges from their own families, but rather from families prominent in the village, persons who were esteemed as responsible members of the village community.[20]

By the late thirteenth century, peasant families could be identified by fairly stable surnames. J. A. Raftis in his study of Warboys, a Ramsey Abbey village, found that a survey late in the twelfth century listing 116 tenants gave no surnames and identified only eight by their fathers' Christian names ("Walter, son of John"). Sixty years later, in 1251, a similar survey supplied surnames for many villagers, identifying most of the others by their fathers' first names. By 1290 surnames were firmly established. Most were derived from occupations, places, or Christian names.[21] In the first category were Fisher, Smyth, Shepperd, Coke (cook), Wright, Carter, Carpenter, Miller, Baker, Skinner, Taylor. In the manorial records these were at first entered in their Latin equivalents but later were translated, Bercar, Faber, and Molendinarius becoming Shepperd, Smyth, and Miller. The families might or might not still practice the trade named. Village officials also lent their titles: Reeve, Woodward, Hayward, Beadle. Some names indicated location in the village: Bovecheriche (above the church), Est (eastern end), ate Green (at the village green), ate Dam, ate Gate, ate Bridge, ate Wood, ate Well, ate Water. Some families bore names from their villages of origin, as the de Wendale and de Wistow families of Broughton. Surnames using fathers' Christian names gradually dropped the "son of" and became simply William Aleyn or William Roger.[22] Raftis notes that in Warboys in the latter half of the fourteenth century the "son" reappeared as a suffix, Robyn becoming Robynsson, Reeve Revisson, Thomas Thomisson.[23] In two cases in Cuxham, sons bore names derived from their mothers' Christian names.[24]

Some instability lingered. In Cuxham when Richard Oldman turned miller he became known alternately as Richard le Muleward (mill-keeper) or Richard Le Mouner (miller). When a man married a widow and took over her first husband's holding, he might assume the husband's surname; thus Gilbert Bourdoun of Cuxham married Sarah le Wyte and was thereafter called Gilbert le Wyte. Robert Waldrugge married Agnes Oldman and became Robert Oldman. Or both widow and second husband might keep their names, as did Alice Aumoner and John le Totere.[25]

A new tendency appeared at the end of the thirteenth century: instead of tenants' taking their names from their holdings, the holdings began to be named after the tenants. In one case a man named John ate Hethe took over a mill in Cuxham previously called Cutt Mill, which thereafter became Hethemill; he was then known as John ate Hethemill.[26]

Christian names were chosen from a limited list, the most popular for men being John, Robert, Richard, William, Godfrey, Hugh, and Thomas, and for women Joan, Margaret, Matilda, Alice, and Agnes. Some Adams, Rogers, Henrys, Simons, Stephens, and Walters also appear in the records, and Catherines, Christinas, Beatrices, Sarahs, Emmas, Julianas, and Mariotas. The name Mary was, surprisingly, rare to nonexistent (even, as Edwin De Windt points out in his study of Holywell, in the Christemesse family). First names were repeated from generation to generation in the same family.[27]

In Broughton first names of some members of leading families were taken from surnames of others, suggesting that a child had been given a mother's maiden name: Pelage John, Aspelon Aleyn.[28] Intermarriage was as natural between the better-off peasant families as among lords and barons. As with the nobility, marriage went with landholding; among the peasants this meant sons marrying when their fathers died or retired. Men consequently tended to marry in their twenties or early thirties, and to be sought after rather than seeking.

Fathers of brides not only supplied dowries but usually also paid the merchet, the fine exacted upon the marriage of a villein's daughter. Recent research by Eleanor Searle has illuminated the character of merchet (the etymology of the word has proved a stubborn mystery) as deriving from manorial property and inheritance rules rather than as a simple marriage license fee. It applied only to unfree peasants or unfree land held by free peasants and was in effect a charge against the alienation of manorial property as dowry. Apparently only a minority of villeins paid it, since for most a daughter's dowry would be nonexistent or trifling. "A foolish girl, or a poor one, might marry as she liked"—without property. But if she took part of the family inheritance, it had to be taxed.[29] If she married outside the manor, the merchet was usually slightly higher, though not always. In 1283 two merchets in the village of Newton Longville were each identified as "twelve cocks," paid by the bride, one for a marriage within the manor, the other for one to an outsider. In 1320 a merchet recorded in the village of Great Horwood was a quarter (eight bushels) of oats, for permission to marry a man apparently from outside the manor.[30]

A Berkshire widow in 1339 married her daughter to a free man outside the lord's jurisdiction; all her goods and chattels were ordered forfeit, but the widow appealed to the lord and, by marrying her daughter with no chattels, escaped with a fine of two shillings. Just as fathers of brides haggled with grooms' families over dowries, they bargained with lords' stewards over merchet. Where land formed part of a dowry, merchet could run as high as four pounds; where no land was involved, it was usually in the range of sixpence to two shillings.[31]

Dowries commonly included both money and chattels, the latter comprising animals, farm implements, utensils, grain, oil, jewels, silverware, or such trousseau items as furniture and furnishings, blankets, sheets, and tablecloths. That for which William Aleyn of Broughton sued his father-in-law in 1294 consisted (or should have consisted) of a dress, a two-gallon pot, a half-gallon vessel, two carpets, five shillings "to repair a cart with iron," and six shillings to be given to the church. The same year in Abbot's Ripton Agnes Hubert was sued for a dowry that included a horse, a pig, four bushels of wheat, and three goats.[32] These were contributions of considerable value, but were more than matched by the dowers that the bridegroom typically promised his bride, from a third to a half of his land, to be hers for life when he died.

Common law fixed one third to one half as the widow's portion of an estate, but often a peasant's widow did better than that. Manorial court records show that widows often took control of the entire holding without paying the entry fee of heirs, suggesting that they were recognized as co-tenants rather than inheritors.[33] Alice Benyt took over a Cuxham tenement on her husband's death in 1311 and on her own death thirty years later left it to her unmarried daughter Emma.[34] At Broughton, Cristina Neel and Agnes Kateline managed holdings after their husbands' deaths. Such widows had to hire laborers to work their lands and also to perform services owed the lord.[35] Consequently, though under no legal compulsion, they often found remarriage a convenience.

Among the peasants as among the nobles, the exclusion of younger sons from the family patrimony by primogeniture created problems. In his pioneering work, *English Villagers of the Thirteenth Century* (1941), George Homans postulated very limited choices for such young men: working as day laborers, entering the Church, enlisting as soldiers.[36] Britton's study of Broughton (1976) found that many younger sons, especially among the better-off peasants, were not so circumscribed. In twenty-one "main" families—almost half the village elite—two or more sons married and established themselves during the same period. Simon Crane's son Robert took over his father's jurorship as well as his land, but another son, Walter, succeeded in marrying and raising a family. Both of John de Broughton's sons became capital pledges and jurors, indicating that both had established themselves. Noninheriting children received part of their parents' money and movables, perhaps enough to allow them to buy land.

Among the other half of the leading families of Broughton, however, the younger sons evidently acquired no land, and in eleven of these only one son, presumably the eldest, remained in the village. Among the lesser families, the proportion able to provide land for younger sons was much smaller.[37]

For peasant daughters even more than for the daughters of the nobility, marriage was the universal objective. The convent, open to noblewomen, was closed to peasant girls, for whom the only practical alternatives to marriage were to remain on the family holding and work for the inheriting brother, to become a servant for another village family or in the lord's household, or to hire out as a casual laborer.

From the inheritance rules of champion country, Homans deduced a stem family of the type visualized by Frédéric Le Play, with husband, wife, children, grandparents, unmarried brothers and sisters, and servants.[38] In actual fact, late marriage, high infant mortality, low life expectancy, and the incapacity of most holdings to support large numbers probably created a majority of nuclear households, with those holding the most land tending to be larger and more complex. At Broughton the "main" families, about a third of the households, accounted for over half the population.[39]

They also accounted for a preponderance of the crime. The young men of Broughton, and especially those of the main families, appear frequently in the court rolls cited for disorderly or violent behavior. In 1297 three young men, all sons of capital pledges and jurors, attacked a neighbor's house; later one of these men and an accomplice damaged the houses of two other villagers. Assault was a common charge, sometimes bringing private domestic problems into court. In 1311 Sarra Henry was fined for assaulting her daughter; in 1314 Thomas de Broughton was fined for attacking his sister.[40] When young women appear in complaints it is usually for sexual misdemeanors: fornication or having children out of wedlock. In only two of thirty-four cases in Broughton in which women were cited were their male partners even named, and in those two the partners were married men. In twenty-six of the cases, the young women bore illegitimate children, in the other eight they did not, the proportion reflecting the relative ease of detection of the two misdemeanors rather than their actual incidence.[41] An illustration of the capricious character of fines for fornication comes from the records of Wakefield in the early fourteenth century. Very few court sessions in that village had levied such fines until suddenly in January 1316 a whole crowd of young women were rounded up and fined. One of the entries: "Juliana, daughter of John Sibbeson, a villein, was deflowered before she was married and has not yet paid lechewytt [legerwite, the fine for an unfree unmarried woman's fornication] nor merchet" [indicating that Juliana was now married]. The reason for the summary roundup was that Earl John needed money. He was in the process of abandoning his wife, who was a niece of the king, and seeking a divorce in order to marry his mistress, the mother of his children.[42]

In cases of adultery, men were charged equally with women. Though the crime fell within the jurisdiction of Church courts, the lord exacted a fine from a tenant who was found guilty. The court rolls of Broughton list twenty-four cases of adultery between 1294 and 1323. The names of both guilty parties are cited in ten of these, only the man's in eight, only the woman's in six. Some names recur with different partners, and almost two thirds of the culprits were from the leading families.[43]

Widows' dalliances were treated as cases of adultery, tried in the ecclesiastical court, and fined in the manor court, sometimes with a temporary forfeit of lands. At Girton in 1291, Matilda, widow of Robert Warewyk, was convicted of fornication with Robert Corebes "and lost some of the lord's chattels thereby." Her lover was apparently a thief. Matilda's land was "taken into the lord's hands," and she was fined three shillings. There may have been similar complications in the case of Agnes Faber, a widow of Warboys convicted of fornication with Richard Ingram. Her land was confiscated and it cost her twenty shillings to recover it.[44]

A case with a modern ring was recorded in 1288 in Broughton when Emma, daughter of Robert le Clerk, charged that when she was harrowing in Agnes Gylbert's fields, Agnes's son William Gylbert "threw her to the ground and by force and violence raped her and drew blood." William denied the force and violence and shedding of blood, deposing that "he did not rape the said Emma but that for the past three years he had known the same Emma by her own free will whenever he wished." William and Emma submitted the inquiry to the chief pledges and jurors, "who came and say that the said William did not rape the said Emma on the day specified nor did he know her against her will as she charged but in the way he was used to knowing her nor did he shed her blood." William was acquitted and Emma was fined. The court roll added: "She is poor" (indicating that the fine would be small or rescinded).[45]

In old age, a provident villager could take advantage of a maintenance contract, a medieval form of social security. Originally informal agreements between generations involving the exchange of land by the old for the labor of the young, these contracts were now often spelled out in the manorial courts. In the era before the Black Death, they were usually between family members, a son taking over a holding in return for lifetime maintenance of his parents. The son acquired land; the parents obtained his labor and a variety of benefits such as a room in the house, specified amounts of food, fuel, and clothing, clothes washed on a regular basis, bed linens, and the right to warm themselves at the fire. Details of the arrangements were carefully spelled out.[46] At Cranfield, one of the Ramsey Abbey manors, in 1294, John de Bretendon agreed to provide his father and mother with "suitable food and drink while they are alive" and residence in his house. If "trouble and discord" arose from the arrangement, John was to furnish them with a place where they could "decently reside," as well as certain quantities of grain and legumes. Such contracts were strictly enforceable in the manor courts, for example at Warboys in 1334: "And since Stephen the Smith did not keep his mother according to their agreement he is [fined] sixpence. . . ."[47] Some manors wrote general rules for the provision of widowed parents, including amounts of food and drink.[48]

Most old people showed a preference for remaining in their own houses, but some moved to a cottage. They might purchase from a monastery a kind of pension called a "corrody," originally a grant of charity to paupers, lepers, and other unfortunates. A typical corrody contract for a man and wife specified a number of loaves of bread, gallons of ale, amounts of tallow, salt, and oatmeal per year, plus meat and fish served daily from the monastery kitchen, and either a room "with a place by the fire" or a dwelling house supplied with firewood and hay. The corrody had great flexibility. In 1317 a woman purchased a lavish version for 140 marks, while the same year a servant of Worcester Cathedral Priory contracted for one for 10 marks. The first contract guaranteed three loaves of bread (one white) and two gallons of ale per day, and every year six pigs, two oxen, twelve cheeses, a hundred stockfish, a thousand herrings, and 24 shillings' worth of clothing. The 10-mark corrody bought four "servants' loaves" and six gallons of beer a week plus a daily "dish" from the monastery kitchen.[49]

Still another form of pension, employed by parish priests for their old age, involved hiring a "keeper" who in return for his services was remembered in the priest's will.

Elderly peasants also bargained with religious establishments for their well-being in the next world, some, like the nobles criticized in *Garin le Loherain*, mortgaging their family's future in this one by excessive bequests for prayers. Wills included provisions benefiting the local parish church and sometimes, with surprising practicality, serving the community by earmarking sums to repair roads and bridges. A widow who left sixpence to every village maiden exemplified a growing philanthropic form: contributions to poor girls' dowries.[50]

A late thirteenth-century Dominican preacher told a story about the deathbed confrontation of an avaricious parish priest and a "very rich peasant" whose stinginess both to the poor and the church had enabled him to fill a coffer with money and "other treasures," which he caused to be set before him as he lay dying. By the time the priest was summoned, the sick man was no longer able to speak. The priest suggested a means of dialogue: he would put questions to which a "Ha!" from the patient would indicate approval. He addressed the dying man:

"Do you wish to bequeath your soul to God and your body to Mother Church for burial?" The man managed a "Ha!"

"Do you wish to leave twenty shillings to the fabric of your church where you have chosen to be buried?" Silence. The priest gave the patient's ear a violent tug and the man cried, "Ha!"

"Write down twenty shillings for the church fabric," said the priest, "for see, he has granted it with his 'Ha!' "

Then the priest said to the sick man, "I have some books, but I have no chest to keep them in. That coffer over there would be most useful to me. Would you like me, therefore, to have that coffer to put my books in?" No answer. The priest pinched his ear so hard that he drew blood. The enfeebled old miser suddenly found his voice: "Oh, you greedy priest, by Christ's death, never shall you have from me as much as a farthing of the money which is in that chest!" Having thus spoken, he said a prayer and died. Accordingly, his wife and relatives divided the money between them.[51]

Much research, archeological as well as documentary, has been done in recent years on the physical environment of the thirteenth-century English peasant: the shape and pattern of the village in which he lived, the layout of his house. Villages clustered around a common green, or around the church. If village and manor coincided, the lord's manor house stood nearby; if they did not, the lord might dwell in a neighboring village. Paths, already worn and sunken with use, connected the houses and led to the fields. Other communities were "street villages," straggling along a road leading to other villages or to a market town.[52]

Each family occupied a messuage, a house surrounded by a close or yard where poultry scratched and outbuildings stood: a storage shed, a barn, a byre. Village animals often ran loose, roaming among the houses or even into them. The right of "free beast" belonged to the lord's own animals, his ram, bull, or boar roving, grazing, and mating at random, lending a metaphor to Chaucer: "[Corrupt] priests . . . think they are free and have no judge, any more than has a free bull that takes whatever cow pleases him."[53] A part of the yard was the croft, a small enclosed area cultivated by spade as a vegetable garden. In many cases, house, barn, and animal sheds were under the same roof, with barn and byre at the lower end, separated from the living space by a cross-passage, the animals helping to provide warmth in winter.[54]

Most of the houses were still built by the ancient technique of wattle and daub, a timber frame supporting interlaced wands coated with clay. A newer form was "cruck" construction, a truss consisting of two split halves of the trunk and main branch of a tree supporting roof and walls.[55] The roof was invariably thatched. Straw was cheap, and when thickly piled kept the house dry, though adding to the fire hazard, especially in the absence of a chimney.

The size of the house reflected the wealth and status of the family. The simplest, those of poor cottagers and laborers, were single rooms about twelve by sixteen feet. Even those of more prosperous peasants consisted of a single hall subdivided into two or three bays. An open hearth in the middle was vented through a hole in the roof. Some houses had a separate kitchen in a lean-to. Windows were few, and shuttered rather than glazed. For added illumination in daytime, the door was left open, allowing free access for children, poultry, and animals. Sometimes a loft at one end, reached by ladder, was used for sleeping.[56] Retirement arrangements for parents occasionally specified that the inheriting son was to build them a house. In 1281, Thomas Brid, taking over his widowed mother's holding in the village of Halesowen, promised to build her a house thirty feet long and fourteen feet wide, with three doors and two windows.[57]

Little information has survived about peasant furnishings in the thirteenth century. Lists of chattels that occasionally occur in court rolls mention wooden tables, benches, and chests and brass pots, cups, and dishes, but never beds. Adults and children slept on the floor, on straw pallets.[58]

Peasants in a Region of Partible Inheritance

In the period before the Black Death, society in champion country remained relatively stable. The family's concern with keeping the patrimony intact tended to limit the number of heirs and thereby the population. Economic inequality in the village was present but not pronounced. No one was very rich.

In woodland country, where partible inheritance was the rule, a different picture emerges.[59]

In Norfolk and Suffolk (eastern England), probably following the Norman Conquest, land had been granted to tenants in large holdings *(tenementa)*, each given the name of the individual tenant. By the thirteenth century these holdings no longer belonged to individuals or families but were retained as administrative units for the purpose of determining rents and services, for which the varying numbers of tenants had joint responsibility. During the thirteenth century the process of subdivision continued at an accelerated pace. The number of fields in each manor was much greater than the two, three, or four of champion country, and the pattern of landholding very irregular. No community control of cultivation existed, and if common grazing was practiced, it was by private arrangement.

Three elements operated in these areas to produce instability and change: partible inheritance; manorial policies favorable to alienation; and an active land market. The result was a society in which marked variations in social and economic status had developed, some families making fortunes in land, others losing their small holdings entirely.[60]

Just as he pictured impartible-inheritance regions peopled by the stem family of Frédéric Le Play, George Homans believed that partible inheritance created the joint family, one in which a man's sons and their descendants "would hold and work the land in common, and dwell together in one great house or in a small cluster of adjoining houses."[61] Information about the real constitution of households in woodland country remains scanty, but we do know that several different strategies were employed by co-inheriting brothers: partition of the holding, joint cultivation, or a combination of joint cultivation by some of the brothers while others worked their own inheritances. A father might distribute part of his land before he died, apportioning it as he saw fit; or one son might buy up another's share; or a son might die without heirs and his portion revert to his brothers.

A study of Redgrave, a manor in northern Suffolk comprising several hamlets and isolated farms, illustrates how partibility worked in practice. A peasant who held land that owed villein services typically passed his patrimony on to all his sons. A survey of 1289 listed fifty identifiable sets of brothers among the villeins, thirty-three of the sets (totaling seventy-seven individuals) holding land jointly in the same *tenementum*. Many of the fraternal holdings were of equal size, implying inheritance too recent for other arrangements to have been made. In Redgrave no prohibition barred the sale of villein land and evidently little sentiment existed for keeping land in the family. Partibility itself encouraged sale by creating small, easy-to-market parcels. In the thirty years that followed the 1289 survey, most of the sets of brothers were active in the land market. Thirteen of the sets gained land in their dealings, twenty-seven lost, and the apportionment within sets of brothers became unequal.[62]

That a set of brothers might all profit from land dealings is shown by the case of the sons of Adam Jop. In the 1289 survey Adam appears as an active and successful dealer in land, holding thirty-nine acres, two farmsteads, and part of another as a villein, plus a farmstead and nine acres freely. Sixteen of his thirty-nine customary acres had been recently acquired through no fewer than twenty-seven separate small purchases, to which over the ensuing years he added eight more acres. Adam had three sons, Richard, John Senior, and John Junior, and at least four daughters, Alice, Isabel, Cristina, and Basilia. In 1295 he gave John Senior a house and eight acres, and two years later another holding; in 1301 he gave John Junior two acres. Richard, the eldest son, had already purchased land of his own in the 1280s, possibly with his father's help. The marriages of three of the four daughters are signaled by the record of merchet paid in the manorial court. Alice and Isabel each received a gift of an acre from their father. When old Adam died in 1314, the three brothers shared the patrimony and purchased more land until among them they held over ninety acres. Acting independently rather than jointly, frequently buying from co-heirs of poorer tenant families, the Jops continued to expand their holdings in the early fourteenth century.[63]

Meantime, the families who provided most of the land bought by people like the Jops gravitated toward the other end of the economic scale. In 1289 Walter Chapman and his brother Ralph inherited from their father Richard identical parcels distributed over a number of *tenementa*. The total acreage is unknown, but in 1297 Ralph sold his share to Walter, who over the next few years sold more than twenty acres outside the family. When he died in 1304, he left only fourteen acres to his sons. Another peasant, Walter Beneyt, inherited nine and a half acres from his father in 1289, and in 1290 bought his brother John's share. Over the next ten years, Walter sold more than sixteen acres, and at his death in 1301 left his two sons jointly only three quarters of an acre.[64]

Thus in areas where partible inheritance was practiced, society was fluid, dynamic, and unstable, the fortunes of families shifting through the effects of industry, skill, shrewdness, perhaps sharp dealing, and luck, as opposed to sloth, improvidence, and ill fortune. The same factors doubtless operated in open field regions, albeit under more constraint, and so with less dramatic results. That the peasantry, in England as on the Continent, far from being a monolithic subclass, was divided into distinct social and economic strata, is well established; a study of taxes in 1327 in the Midlands village of Wigston, for example, showed that 70 percent of the total tax was paid by 10 families out of 120.[65]

Peasants of the Pyrenees

The village of Montaillou was an isolated mountain community in the foothills of the Pyrenees, whose peasants raised sheep and grew cereal crops for subsistence. A lingering pocket of the Cathar (Albigensian) heresy, it became in 1318 the object of an investigation by the Inquisition, which left an extensive written record of its interrogations. In 1975 Emmanuel Le Roy Ladurie published *Montaillou*, a study of the Inquisitorial record in which the peasants themselves, men and women, voice their ideas about love, marriage, death, and the family.[66] Despite the special geographical character of Montaillou and the special circumstances of the documentation, the Inquisition's record as analyzed by Ladurie provides an unequaled insight into the daily life of thirteenth-century peasants.

Physically, Montaillou was a Mediterranean type of village,[67] its hilltop houses clustered around a castle that was intermittently occupied by the castellan and his family, some houses abutting, some separated by gardens and yards. Many consisted of a single

View from Montaillou, in the foothills of the Pyrenees. (Authors' photograph)

room where the cooking was done over an open hearth in the middle and where the family ate, slept, and socialized. Some had a separate room or rooms for sleeping, either next to the kitchen or in a cellar, where beds shared space with barrels. Some even had a second-floor solar accessible by a ladder. In the larger dwellings, the central hearth room was built of stone, the solar and ground-floor adjuncts of wattle and daub. Pigs, sheep, and oxen were usually housed under the same roof as people.[68]

House and family were both comprised in the Provençal term *ostal*, rendered by the Inquisition's Latin record as *domus*: human beings related by blood, the walls and hearthfire, and the furnishings. When one peasant woman discussed giving information to the Inquisition, a Cathar reproached her: "If you confess all these things, you will lose all your possessions and put out the fire of your house *(domus)*. Your children, their hearts full of anger, will [have to] go and beg for alms. . . ."[69] One peasant's idea of space, in fact, was measured by the *domus:* "If you want to have an idea of heaven," he remarked, "imagine a huge *domus* stretching from the Merens Pass to the town of Toulouse."[70]

The centrality of the *domus* was present even in the consciousness of the itinerant shepherds, who formed a kind of separate nomad proletariat, victims of misfortune or poverty, or merely of status as noninheriting sons. Usually they did not marry. In summer, the season for shearing, milking, and cheesemaking, they shared a mountain *cabane*. After crossing the Pyrenees to Spain, they wintered in another *cabane*, through lambing time. Yet, although they were "without hearth or home," they remained linked to the paternal *domus* in Montaillou, and to parents, brothers, and sisters there.[71]

Families were aware of their ancestors up to as many as four generations. Identification of forebears by surname was well established, though the name was sometimes transmitted through the maternal rather than the paternal line. But the *domus* and the relatives outside it, including cousins, aunts, and uncles living in nearby villages, were more important than ancestry. In the tense atmosphere of the Inquisition investigation, groups of families related by blood and marriage confronted each other, often reinforced by neighbors.

In 1308 Pierre Clergue, a priest who had first embraced and then

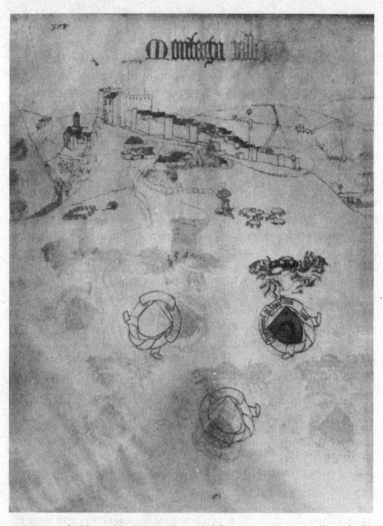

Montaigut-le-Blanc, like Montaillou a Mediterranean type of village, built around a castle. From the Armorial de Guillaume Revel. (Bibliothèque Nationale, MS Fr. 22297, p. 308)

abjured Catharism, denounced Pierre Maur and his sons Guillaume and Arnaud. All were arrested. Released while his father and brother remained in prison, Guillaume Maur angrily rebuked Clergue, who replied, "I will see that you all rot in Carcassonne prison—all the Maurs, you, your father, your brother, all that belong to your *domus.*" Guillaume exclaimed that he would be revenged, "so beware of me and all my supporters." Through the agency of his brother, the village bailiff, Pierre Clergue caused Guillaume's mother's tongue to be cut out for "false witness"—speaking ill of Pierre. Pursued by the Clergue family, Guillaume took refuge in nearby Ax-les-Thermes, where he was joined by his brother Raymond and a relation by marriage, Jean Benet. The three swore an oath on bread and wine to kill the priest, and pooled their resources to hire an assassin. Outlawed, Guillaume escaped to the mountains and became a shepherd. In the subsequent eight years, the conspirators made several unsuccessful attempts to murder their enemy. Eventually Guillaume was captured in Spain and sent back to Carcassonne prison.[72]

The households of Montaillou were mostly conjugal, though some families were extended by the addition of widowed parents, unmarried brothers and sisters, servants (who were sometimes illegitimate children), and an occasional lodger. The household of Bernard Maur, Guillaume's uncle and neighbor, contained his wife, two children, his widowed mother, and a hired shepherd and a plowboy. Bernard Clergue, the bailiff, employed an illegitimate daughter as a servant. The well-to-do Belot household consisted of Raymond Belot, his wife, their children, two unmarried brothers, a sister, his widowed mother, and a servant girl who was a poor relation from a neighboring village. Family structure, as everywhere, varied with wealth and with stage in the cycle.[73]

Even more than elsewhere, family authority in Montaillou centered in the male head of the house, who usually ruled with an iron hand. The Inquisition record mentions several cases of wives who were beaten and who were afraid of their husbands. "A man is worth nothing if he is not his wife's master," one peasant remarked.[74]

Partible inheritance was the rule in Montaillou, but the head of the family was endowed with the power of designating his heir. A son who did not inherit left with a *fratrisia* (fraternal portion).

A reversal: in this misericord from Carlisle Cathedral a wife is beating a husband. (National Monuments Record)

A daughter left with a dowry, which reverted to her on her husband's death. These provisions often strained the resources of the family. Cynical Pierre Clergue remarked to a mistress that things would have been much better if two of his brothers, Guillaume and Bernard, could have married his sisters Esclarmonde and Guillemette: "Our house would not have been ruined because of the wealth carried away by those sisters as dowry; our *ostal* would have remained intact, and with just one wife brought into our house for our brother Bernard, we would have had enough wives, and our *ostal* would have been richer than it is today."[75]

Women sometimes succeeded to a patrimony, and with it acquired authority. Sybille Baille, who inherited a house in Ax-les-Thermes, was an active Cathar who forced her husband, anti-Cathar Arnaud Sicre, to leave the house. Arnaud settled in Tarascon, becoming a notary; their sons alternated between using their mother's and their father's names. Widows also managed to establish themselves independently. Guillemette, the wife of Bernard Marty, fled from Montaillou with her husband and two sons in 1308 and after her husband's death settled in Spain, where she and her sons bought an *ostal* of their own and prospered. Guillemette reverted to her maiden name, Maury, which her sons adopted, and acted as head of the family, managing the property and negotiating her sons' marriages.[76]

The women of Montaillou all married sooner or later; the village had no old maids. Even more than in most rural communities, marriages were made at home. The shepherd Pierre Maury explained the incest taboo in terms of family intimacy. Mother and son, brother and sister, and first cousins were all people whose bodies in the ordinary course of affairs "touched," and who were consequently forbidden to marry. But in Montaillou, sex between second cousins, whose bodies were unlikely to touch, was permissible. Another peasant expressed the view that to sleep with one's mother, sister, or cousin was not a sin but was nonetheless shameful. He quoted a local proverb: "With a second cousin, give her the works."[77]

Marriages were arranged, sometimes by a number of go-betweens—parents, brothers, aunts and uncles, friends. Catharism preached that marriage was evil because it produced children and therefore imprisoned pure souls in corrupt flesh, but the Cathars of Montaillou nevertheless married. Guillaume Bélibaste, a Cathar "perfect" (holy man), justified marriage by saying that since the sin was the same whether with a wife or a mistress, "it is better for a man to attach himself to a definite woman than to fly from one to another like a bee among the flowers." He added a practical consideration: not only did a promiscuous man engender bastards, but his mistresses among them would despoil him and turn him into a pauper. "But when a man is attached to one woman, she helps him maintain a good *ostal.*"[78]

Cathar perfects recommended the most favorable phase of the moon for the wedding ceremony, at which they presided. The day was filled with the usual dancing and feasting, the bride wore a wedding dress, which she packed away after the ceremony to keep all her life.[79]

Economics ruled marriage, but love was not excluded. Bernard Clergue the bailiff testified that he fell "madly in love with Raymonde [Belot], who is now my wife," his infatuation causing his brother Pierre to make fun of him. Bernard was able to afford to marry for love.[80] The women in the Inquisition record, however, do not talk about love in marriage. They felt themselves essentially objects in a game played by the men. Courtship was perfunctory. Women married as early as fourteen, men not until they were established in life, sometimes in their thirties. The differential in age meant many young widows, and frequent second and even third marriages for women.[81]

Sexual morals in Montaillou were relaxed. Apart from Pierre Clergue, a dozen of whose love affairs are mentioned in the record, including one with his brother's wife and another with the widow of the castellan, five or six of the fifty couples in the village were openly "living in sin." Catharism at least provided an excuse; echoing Guillaume Bélibaste, but in a different sense, Pierre Clergue declared that it was no sin to sleep with a married woman: "One woman's just like another. The sin is the same, whether she is married or not. Which is as much as to say that there is no sin about it at all."[82] Grazide Lizier, an illegitimate cousin of the Clergues who became the mistress of the priest, justified her conduct by an innocent rationalization: "With Pierre Clergue I liked it. And so it could not displease God. It was not a sin." Later, when she tired of the affair, Grazide refused the priest. In the absence of desire, sex became a sin.[83]

The castellan's widow, Beatrice de Planissoles, at the beginning of her affair with Pierre Clergue, feared a possible pregnancy, but Pierre reassured her: he had a "certain herb" that would prevent conception by keeping his semen from curdling or solidifying to produce a fetus. Beatrice testified that Pierre wrapped the herb in a piece of linen and hung it around her neck at the end of a long cord so that it hung down "as far as the opening of my belly." He refused to leave the herb with Beatrice for fear she might use it with another man. Thanks to the talisman or not, Beatrice did not conceive.[84] Many others did. Montaillou's numerous bastards were consigned to the lower levels of society, the females often as household servants, the males in equally menial employment. Both, however, managed to marry into peasant families.[85]

The typical *ostal* provided little privacy for illicit sex, but lovers managed. Pierre Clergue seduced Grazide "in the barn in which we kept the straw" and after that made love to her in her mother's house, usually during the daytime, with the mother's compliance. When he married her off to Pierre Lizier, who seems to have been elderly, her husband allowed the relationship to continue, only warning Grazide not to "go having other men." They did not make love when her husband was at home, however, only "when he was out."[86] Pierre made love with Beatrice de Planissoles in the cellar of her house with a maid on guard at the door, and once perversely in the church. Later an aging Beatrice slept with a young priest, Barthelemy Amilhac, in her own house, but always when her daughters and the servant were away.[87]

A medieval tableau: Beatrice de Planissoles delousing her lover in bed while Pierre philosophized about Catharism and love.[88]

Morals were permissive for young girls, servants, and widows, but wives were expected to be virtuous. Honor, an external, family concept, more than conscience, an internal, individual one, influenced women's behavior. Husbands too were usually faithful. One peasant, Pierre Authie, remarked, "It's still within marriage that people make love most often."[89]

Divorce was unknown, but married couples occasionally separated. Pons Rives and his mother, both Cathars, drove his wife Fabrisse, who was not, from their house. Becoming the village wine seller, Fabrisse was another woman who maintained herself independently.[90]

Old age began in the fifties. Old people lived with their children, men generally yielding their position as head of the family to their sons, who sometimes tyrannized them. Old women, however, often outliving their husbands, might become matriarchs, heading families, respected and loved by both their own descendants and the other villagers, and acquiring the title "Na," from *domina,* mistress; such were Na Roqua, a Cathar leader, and Na Carminagua, head of a household in Montaillou.[91]

Death was immured in ritual, the laments of daughters and daughters-in-law commencing before the stricken peasant expired and continuing until burial, for which the women of the house prepared the body. Cathar rites included the administration by the perfect of the *consolamentum,* after which the dying person was encouraged to embark on the *endura,* a fast of purification. To the man or woman on the deathbed, whether Cathar or Catholic, two things were important: to be surrounded by one's family and, whatever the ritual, to achieve salvation.[92]

9.

The Aristocratic Lineage: Perils of Primogeniture

The system of primogeniture, buttressed by the adoption of estate names, genealogies, coats of arms, family mottos, and the impressive symbol of the family castle, gave the self-conscious aristocratic male lineages of the thirteenth century an appearance of invincible solidity. The earl of Lancaster, the earl of Leicester, the count of Champagne, the duke of Burgundy—such titles seemed to breathe a lofty perpetuity, a descent proceeding majestically through unbroken generations and centuries. The appearance was deceiving. "It is not generally realized," says Kenneth McFarlane in his study of the English nobility, "how near to extinction most [noble] families were; their survival was always in the balance and only a tiny handful managed to hang on in the male line from one century to another."[1] In England the upper nobility was explicitly identified at frequent intervals when the king summoned his "barons" to meet in what was turning into Parliament. Between 1300 and 1500 the number of heritable ranks was increased from one to five, but of the 136 baronial families favored with a summons at the end of the thirteenth century, 36 were extinct by 1325, 89 by 1400, and all but 16 by 1500.[2]

McFarlane supplies another striking set of figures: of seventeen earldoms in England in 1400, only three had belonged to the same family for more than a century, ten for less than half a century.

*The heir is born: birth of Richard Beauchamp, c. 1382. Only women are
present.* (British Library, MS Cotton Julius E IV, art. 6, f. 1)

"The turnover was always rapid, the eminence short-lived, the survivors invariably few."[3] One result was that fear of extinction—or of royal wardship, sure to be costly to the estate—caused parents to hasten children's marriages to the limit of legal decorum. Peter Lombard and Pope Alexander III had made consummation unnecessary for legality, and canon lawyers held that nine and a half was not too early an age to give acceptable consent. Many noble children were committed to marriage by their tenth birthdays, without, however, arresting the extinction of lineages.

In addition to continuity in the male line, primogeniture was designed to protect the integrity of the estate. This too presented a problem. Despite acceptance of primogeniture by law and custom, many parents wanted to give something to each of their children, even at the expense of the lineage's future. Two ancient principles still commanded loyalty in the thirteenth century. The first was that property inherited from one's father should be given to the eldest son, while that conquered or purchased might be disposed of at will. It was on the basis of this principle that William the Conqueror had bestowed his duchy of Normandy on his eldest son, Robert, and the kingdom of England on his second son, William Rufus. The second principle was that land of some kind, in some measure, should be given to every son. If primogeniture forbade its bequest, a father could nevertheless give away land while he still lived.[4]

A difficulty arose. A generous, dutiful father, wishing to provide for all rather than merely one of his sons, yet shrank from losing part of his own income. "Members of the medieval nobility did not often fall into King Lear's error," observes McFarlane.[5] A new property-law principle, that of entail, was therefore cleverly subverted to do the opposite of what it was intended to do, which was to fortify primogeniture in protecting the integrity of the estate. Entailing a piece of land made it heritable in perpetuity by the nearest male heir. But a father could entail a part of his estate upon a younger son and his issue while retaining it for his own lifetime. Since the father thus preserved all his revenues, he was tempted to greater generosity than he might have shown if he had had to give away land and income on the spot.[6]

Entail had one drawback: once done, it could not be undone. No matter how tempting the offer or how pressing the need, the inheritor of entailed land could not sell. Not, at least, until the lawyers figured out a way in the fifteenth century, as F. R. H. Du Boulay says, "a great age for lawyers." A technique invented for breaking an entail involved a collusive lawsuit on behalf of the person to whom the estate owner wanted to sell part of his estate. The customer claimed that the land in question was really his, and the two parties together blamed the muddle on a third party who did not even have to appear. The land was awarded, uncontested, to the customer—who then quietly paid the agreed-upon price.[7]

Another legal innovation provided the landowner with great flexibility in disposing of his estate. This was "use," by which a man could grant his lands, in whole or in part, to trustworthy friends, in law dubbed "feoffees," to hold for his use throughout his lifetime and to dispose of at his death in accordance with his last will. Through use, a father could change his mind, dealing with his children in accordance with their merits and behavior, including illegitimate sons. The invention of use facilitated the endowment of the noble bastard, so prominent in late medieval England.[8] It also facilitated the disappearance of peerages. An affectionate regard for all a father's children, legitimate or other, when expressed through use and entail, could "dis-ennoble" a lineage. Sir John Larchdeacon's father was summoned to Parliament as a baron in the 1320s. Sir John, blessed with eight sons, divided his inheritance into eight equal parts, all entailed, and none of his descendants ever received a summons to Parliament.[9]

Besides younger sons, there were daughters. The thirteenth century dealt more successfully with the daughters than with the sons. Instead of giving away land as dowry, fathers took to giving away money, along with jewels, furnishings, and other valuables, so that by the time the Statute of Westminster known as *De Donis* was enacted in 1285 it was virtually a dead letter as far as daughters were concerned. *De Donis* forbade alienation of land given to younger sons or daughters until their line had survived three generations. If the line failed, the land reverted to the main family stem. Even in respect to younger sons, however, the statute was ineffective and in time the three-generational rule was dropped.[10]

A more serious threat to the principal heir than a daughter's dowry was a daughter-in-law's dower. By ancient custom, sometimes infringed, but firmed up in 1215 by a guarantee in Magna

Carta, the bride was promised a one-third share of her husband's property in case of widowhood. Widowhood in fact usually materialized and in the context of early marriage for women was typically of long duration. Sometime before 1185, Maud, the ten-year-old daughter of Thomas Fitz Bernard, married John de Bidun and was quickly widowed. Maud then lived more than seventy years, remarrying and holding her dower throughout her life.[11] Such widowhoods deprived a family whose son had died of a third of the family estate for long periods. Some widows, remarrying, acquired more than one dower. In the early fourteenth century Agnes Beresford successively married John Argentine, John Narford, and John Mautravers within a period of fifteen years. The first two left her with dower lands in Cambridgeshire, Hertfordshire, and East Anglia, which she continued to administer from Mautravers's home in Dorset for the thirty-three years of their marriage (1331–1364), then for another eight years following Mautravers's death. When Agnes herself finally died in 1375, lands in eight different counties were redistributed to the various heirs of her three husbands. One heir, John Argentine's son, had been waiting for fifty-seven years.[12]

Dowered widowhoods contributed to a bewildering complexity that afflicted the management of great estates. While individual manors or groupings of manors could easily be supervised, the rents collected, the services exacted, the fines levied, a serious problem arose with the large aggregation of lands scattered about England (or France). Lest the local managers cheat the earl or the dowered widow, meticulous accountings had to be kept. A corps of estate bureaucrats, mostly lawyers, materialized, occupying positions of trust that encouraged rendering their offices unofficially hereditary. Petty bureaucratic dynasties served the great feudal ones: several generations of Hugfords and Throckmortons kept track of the immense properties and revenues of the earls of Warwick.[13]

Late in the thirteenth century a new form of marriage contract, very favorable to the bride, was introduced in England. "Jointure" pledged joint tenancy of land by husband and wife during their lifetime, and by the survivor alone after the death of one spouse. A jointured widow might acquire most or even all of her husband's estates instead of merely the dower third. The origin of jointure is unknown, but, according to McFarlane, "in most marriage contracts of the fourteenth and fifteenth centuries the wife was made sure of a jointure in part of her husband's lands."[14] Jointure contributed further to the prominence of the late medieval dowager, the widowed mother who controlled the family property and merely by surviving kept a son from his inheritance through most of his life. Some dowagers married handsome fortune hunters, some married men of equal wealth or greater nobility, and some simply enjoyed the freedom conferred by property.

Jointure also contributed to the shifting character of fiefs. How an estate might make a rapid progress through three different families via jointure and entail is illustrated by that of Bishop Burnell. The bishop accumulated his holdings as a minister of the appreciative Edward I, and left it, in an established episcopal tradition, to his nephew, from whom it soon passed to the nephew's sister Maud. Maud's first husband, John Lovel, did not live to enjoy his fortune, getting killed at the battle of Bannockburn (1314). A posthumous son, named for his father, stood to inherit, but Maud married again, and entailed most of her wealth on herself and her new husband, John Hadlow, in jointure. By Hadlow she had two more sons, and John Lovel lost most of his inheritance.[15]

Thus by a variety of means the purpose of primogeniture was frustrated and lordly lineages were robbed of their property bases. By far the commonest root cause of the extinction of noble lines, however, was mortality. A scholar has estimated that in a stationary population 20 percent of married men have no children when they die, and another 20 percent have only daughters. For the medieval lineage, infant mortality, disease, and war all accentuated the danger. Large families with a number of sons were no guarantee of a line's survival. Arnoul of Ardres's marriage to Beatrice, heiress to the castle of Bourbourg, was made possible by a typical chain of circumstances. Henry of Bourbourg sired twelve children, of whom seven were sons. Two of the sons were given to the Church; two died accidentally, one in adolescence, the other as a knight. A fifth son was blinded in a tournament, an affliction that prevented him from marrying. The eldest son, the designated heir, married twice but failed to produce a son. The seventh and youngest fathered a single son, who died in infancy. The inheritance consequently went to Beatrice, and through her marriage to Arnoul passed to the lords of Guines.[16]

Similarly, William Marshal, becoming earl of Pembroke in 1199, safeguarded his dynasty by siring ten children, including five boys. But the eldest died of a cause unknown to us, one was murdered in Ireland, one was mortally wounded in a tournament, and the last two died suddenly in 1245 within a week of each other. A surviving daughter, Maud, married a Bigod, the earl of Norfolk, and a new Pembroke dynasty was founded. Chronicler Matthew Paris regarded the event as the fulfillment of a curse on the Marshals for their litigation with the Church over disputed Irish property: " 'In one generation his name shall be destroyed' [in the words of the psalm] and his sons shall be without share in that benediction of the Lord, 'Increase and multiply!' "[17] The curse affected only the male line, including the family name. Maud's son, though named Bigod, succeeded as earl of Pembroke and by blood was as much William Marshal's grandson as if his father had been a Marshal. Nevertheless, Matthew Paris considered that the Marshals had been visited with a divine retribution.[18]

The "honor"—the title and estates—could survive indefinitely, but only by sidestepping over to a collateral branch or by jumping via an heiress-daughter to a different male line. The history of the great earldom of Leicester in the twelfth and thirteenth centuries illustrates the variety of changes that could be visited on an honor in the course of a few generations. Originally forming one of the princely grants entrusted to his chief lieutenants by William the Conqueror, the earldom of Leicester remained in the family of the Beaumonts throughout the twelfth century. The last Beaumont earl, a companion-in-arms of Richard Lionheart known as Robert FitzParnel, was invested with the honor of Leicester in 1191, while on the Third Crusade. When Robert died childless in 1204, the bulk of his estate passed to his two sisters, the elder of whom assumed the title of countess of Leicester.[19]

This lady married a younger son of a noble family of northern France, Simon de Montfort. They had six children, three sons and three daughters. The oldest son had already achieved the rank of earl by marrying the heiress of another earldom, that of Glouces-ter. On the death of his widowed mother, the second son, Simon de Montfort II, laid claim to Leicester, but encountered an obstacle. He had taken service under the king of France, enemy of England's King John, who therefore put the Leicester earldom in a sort of cold storage by entrusting its lands to a third party on the pretext of a debt owed the crown. Peace with France and the intervention of the pope brought a restoration of Leicester to the Montforts, in the form of an English relation, Ranulf, earl of Chester.[20] Simon II was at the moment occupied with command of the army sent to crush the Albigensian heretics in southern France, where he was killed at the siege of Toulouse (1218). New hostile relations between England and France postponed a reclamation of Leicester by his sons until 1231. By that time a change in atmosphere had set in for the Anglo-French nobility. Where for a hundred and fifty years French lords and knights had been equally at home on both sides of the Channel, they now found it necessary to choose which they wanted to be, French or English. Simon's eldest son, Amaury de Montfort, opted for France, where he enjoyed extensive possessions, and proposed his younger brother, still another Simon, for the earldom of Leicester. Rather surprisingly, twenty-eight-year-old Simon III persuaded both the king, Henry III, and his own cousin, the earl of Chester, to agree, and so transformed himself overnight from a penniless cadet into the wealthy earl of Leicester.[21]

Simon III then startled the whole English court and country by an even more unlikely coup, seducing and marrying the king's sister Eleanor. Nobility and clergy were equally upset, the nobles by the spectacle of a foreign adventurer capturing such a prize from under their noses, the clergy by the scandal of Eleanor, the young widow of William Marshal's eldest son, airily forgetting a solemn vow of chastity made to the archbishop of Canterbury. Simon bought off the leader of the barons, Eleanor's brother Richard of Cornwall, with suitable gifts, and, sailing to Rome, by similar means induced the Vatican to cancel Eleanor's vow.[22]

Unfortunately, to raise the cash necessary for his bribes, Simon had named King Henry as security without first consulting the king, whose reaction almost landed both Simon and Eleanor in the Tower of London. Once more, Simon succeeded in winning the king over, to such effect that he and Eleanor received as a residence Kenilworth Castle, a great brooding Norman keep in Warwickshire, half surrounded by an artificial lake.[23] An outstanding example of the military-residential architecture of the Conquest, Kenilworth was not by later standards very cozy quarters. It did not even have a fireplace, the novel invention that heated great halls in many more recently built castles. Henry had a new roof put on the drafty upper hall, repaired the latrine and some of the walls and outbuildings, and paneled the chapel, but Kenilworth remained stolidly a fortress-barracks rather than a country house.[24]

Simon soon entered on a political career that gave him a place in history but ultimately lost him his castle, his earldom, and his life. Starting as a lieutenant of King Henry, he passed to the role of mediator between the king and the disaffected English barons and then to that of leader of the barons. When the quarrel escalated to civil war, Simon led the baronial army first to victory at Lewes, then to disaster at Evesham, where he and his son Henry both fell. Another son, yet another Simon de Montfort, defended Kenilworth in a memorable siege, but in the end he, his brothers, and his mother had to take refuge in flight abroad.

The earldom of Leicester was confiscated by the king, who bestowed it on his son Edmund, known as Edmund Crouchback, who left it to his son Thomas. Thomas, like Simon de Montfort, dabbled dangerously in politics and lost his head, but his brother Henry stayed clear of trouble and managed to inherit Leicester (along with many other lands). His son Henry inherited everything but died without male heirs. The honor of Leicester then passed to Maud's sister Blanche, who was married to John of Gaunt, a younger son of Edward III.[25]

Thus in a space of little more than a century and a half the great earldom of Leicester, whose manors dotted twenty English counties, was held by four different noble lineages, changing lines twice on failure of male issue and once by royal confiscation. Only in the case of the royal confiscation was the biological descent group changed, but to the men and women of the thirteenth century, committed to the ideology of male descent, the difference between the two kinds of family extinction was slight.

The Leicester story was typical rather than unusual. During the same period the French branch of Simon de Montfort's family lost their own large estates piece by piece through the out-marriages of inheriting daughters.[26]

Primogeniture, arrogantly male in its pretensions, in its actual working gave women a crucial role in determining the fate of noble lineages. Not surprisingly, women with their dowers, jointures, and early marriages were very often parties to the property litigation so prevalent in the high Middle Ages. Eleanor de Montfort actually delayed a peace treaty between England and France for two years. As a sister of the king, she refused to acquiesce in the abandonment of her Plantagenet family's properties in France. Eleanor cared nothing for the English loss of Normandy, but seized the opportunity to press a long-standing claim to compensation for dower rights she had surrendered on the estates of her first husband, William Marshal II.[27]

The thirteenth century saw some improvements in women's legal rights in England, partly through Magna Carta, which, besides confirming the dower one third, forbade "disparagement"—selling of noble wards by the king to less noble suitors. It also gave widows greater freedom to remarry as they chose, which contributed to the continued shifting of the great estates among male lineages and also acted against their concentration in ever fewer hands.[28] So did the unpredictability of the mortality of heirs. A daughter, especially a second or third daughter, might be married off to a nobody to economize on her dowry and help preserve the estate for the male heir. A few years later, through the death of siblings, she might suddenly herself become an heiress, even the sole heiress, converting her nobody of a husband into a very wealthy baron.

As long as kings, in England and elsewhere, continued to create new lords and endow them with estates old or new, as a reward for service in war or in government, or merely for being born into the royal family, the upper nobility was certain to continue its existence. What was far less sure to continue was any particular male lineage included in it, primogeniture, family name, genealogy, and coat of arms notwithstanding.

10.

Children in
the High Middle Ages

Children have soft flesh and lithe and pliant bodies, nimble and light of movement, and are easily trained. They live without thought or care. . . . They are easily angered and easily pleased and forgive easily. . . .

Children often have bad habits, and think only of the present, ignoring the future. They love games and vain pursuits, disregarding what is profitable and useful. They consider important matters of no significance and unimportant matters important. They desire what is contrary and harmful, and appreciate pictures of children more than those of adults. They cry and weep more over the loss of an apple than over the loss of an inheritance. They forget favors done for them. They desire everything they see, and call and reach for it.

They love talking to other children and avoid the company of old men. They keep no secrets but repeat all that they see and hear. Suddenly they laugh, suddenly they weep, and are continuously yelling, chattering, and laughing. They are scarcely silent when they are asleep. When they have been washed, they dirty themselves again. While they are being bathed or combed by their mothers they kick and sprawl and move their feet and hands and resist with all their might. They think only about their stomachs, always wanting to eat and drink. Scarcely have they risen from bed than they desire food.[1]

Thus the thirteenth-century Franciscan monk known as Bartholomaeus Anglicus (Bartholomew the Englishman) voiced one medieval assessment of the child in his encyclopedia, *On the Properties of Things.* He also included observations about growth and development: "The upper part of the child's body is bigger and heavier than the other parts. Therefore the infant, in the beginning, walks on his hands and feet; he then raises his body up gradually because the anterior part is reduced and as a result becomes lighter, while the lower part increases in size and gets heavier."[2]

The medieval encyclopedias treated children separately from adults in their medical sections, as needing special care. Medieval law, whether feudal, Roman, canon, or customary, also placed the child in a special category, endowed with personal and property rights that had to be protected during minority. The very concept of minority implied vulnerability and need for special protection.

Philippe Ariès's theory of 1960 that medieval children were treated as small-sized adults derived partly from his observation that children in medieval art are dressed the same as adults. Even this is not quite true. In the illuminations of manuscripts, children's costumes are simpler and shorter than those of adults. Boys wear a shirt, hose, and jacket, girls a robe and tunic. More to the point, however, the illustrations show children playing ball, swinging, shooting arrows, manipulating puppets, enjoying puppet shows, a range of recreation typical of children of all centuries. In his history of the lords of Guines, Lambert of Ardres tells us that the count's young wife, perhaps fourteen years old, still liked to play with dolls.[3] The chronicler Gerald of Wales recalls that his brothers built castles in the sand (while Gerald, future monk, built sand monasteries and churches).[4]

The thirteenth-century *Nun's Rule* compares the nun's distress when God seems to have abandoned her to the pleasurable emotion of a child playing hide-and-seek with its mother: "She runs away from the child and hides, and leaves him on his own, and he looks around for her, calling, 'Mama! Mama!' and crying a little, and then she runs out to him quickly, her arms outspread, and she puts them round him, and kisses him, and dries his eyes." Thus when God seems to withdraw from the nun, she should "cry out and weep for him as the little baby does for his mother," and he will console her.[5]

In an account of London life written in the 1180s, William Fitzstephen describes the activities of the youth of London on the Shrove Tuesday holiday, who "go out into the fields to play at the well-known game of football." Each school had its own ball, as did the bands of apprentices of different trades. The citizens of London, including the boys' fathers, rode out on horseback to watch the game and thus "recapture their youth with the young." In the winter the boys played on frozen Smithfield marsh, some running and then "placing their feet apart, and turning their bodies sideways," sliding on the ice; others sat on large cakes of ice and were pulled along by their companions—"if at any time they slip . . . all fall down headlong together." Still others, using skates fashioned of bone, propelled themselves with iron-tipped poles and were "carried along with as great rapidity as a bird flying or a bolt discharged from a cross-bow." Sometimes the skaters hurled themselves at each other, striking with their poles. Usually one or both fell and "whatever part of their heads comes in contact with the ice is laid bare to the very skull." Frequently legs or arms were broken, but the boys were not deterred by the danger, youth being "an age eager for glory and desirous of victory."[6]

In the encyclopedias and in treatises such as that of the famous twelfth-century woman master Trotula, of the medical school at Salerno, careful treatment was prescribed for the newborn: instructions for tying the umbilical cord, bathing the child, clearing mucus from his lungs and throat. Births invariably took place at home (the hospital having been invented but not yet applied to childbirth) with a midwife in attendance. Midwives delivered the babies even of queens and noble ladies, since men were excluded from the lying-in chamber. Trotula recommended rubbing the palate with honey and cleansing the tongue with hot water "in order that he may speak more correctly," and protecting him from bright lights and loud noises during his first hours. The newborn's senses should be stimulated instead by "varied pictures, cloths of various colors, and pearls" and by "songs and gentle voices."

The infant's ears, the treatise warned, "must be pressed and shaped immediately and it must be done frequently." His limbs should also be "bound with a swaddling band" to straighten them.[7] Infants' flesh was regarded as pliable and in danger of deformity—"fluid and soft," in the words of Bartholomaeus An-

Bathing the newborn child: Tamar has given birth to twins. (British Library, MS Cotton Claudius BIV, f. 57)

glicus, in keeping with the "softness of the child's nature," susceptible of being distorted by improper handling.

Whether peasant children were swaddled is uncertain. In her study of coroners' inquests among English peasant and urban lower-class families, Barbara Hanawalt found many accidents involving infants but no mention of swaddling.[8] Gerald of Wales observed that the Irish did not follow the practice; their infants were "abandoned to ruthless nature. They are not put in cradles, or swathed; nor are their tender limbs helped by frequent baths or formed by any useful art. The midwives do not use hot water to raise the nose, or press down the face, or lengthen the legs. Unaided nature according to her own judgment arranges and disposes without the help of any art the limbs she has produced." To Gerald's amazement, in Ireland nature "forms and finishes [children] in their full strength with beautiful upright bodies and handsome and well-complexioned faces."[9]

In the English villages of the coroners' reports, babies were kept in a cradle by the fire. In Montaillou they seem to have been carried much of the time. "One holiday I was standing in the square at Montaillou with my little daughter in my arms," testified Guillemette Clergue. Another village woman described a wedding

Mother and swaddled child. (Corpus Christi College, Cambridge, MS 2, f. 147 v)

feast at which "I was standing by the hearth holding in my arms the baby daughter" of the bridegroom's sister.[10]

Peasant and artisan women nursed their own babies unless circumstances, mainly a mother's employment, prevented. When Raymonde Arsen of Montaillou went to work for a family in the town of Pamiers she put her illegitimate infant out to nurse in a nearby village. Later, when she worked as an agricultural laborer during harvest time, she took the child with her and left it to nurse in another village.[11] For well-to-do women, on the other hand, resort to wet nurses had become so widespread by the thirteenth century that manuals for parish priests advised them to oppose the practice as contrary to the wisdom of both Scripture and medical science.[12] Statues in the churches and illustrations in manuscripts showed Mary nursing Jesus, but sermons and examples were lost on the nobility, who continued to bring nurses into the household, not only to nurse infants but also to care for growing children. At Kenilworth Castle, each of the Montfort children had its own nurse.[13]

Statues in the churches and illustrations in manuscripts showed Mary nursing Jesus. Twelfth-century statue in the Eglise St. Genest, Flavigny-sur-Ozerain, near Dijon. (Authors' photograph)

In choosing a wet nurse, responsible parents sought a clean, healthy young woman of good character, and made sure that she adhered to a sound regimen. Trotula of Salerno recommended that she get plenty of rest and sleep, abstain from food that was "salt, sharp, acid, or styptic [astringent]," especially garlic, and avoid anxiety. As soon as the infant was able to eat solid food, Trotula advised that he be given bits of chicken, pheasant, or breast of partridge "the size and shape of an acorn. He can hold them in his hand and play with them and sucking from them he will swallow some of it."[14]

Illumination from the Amesbury Psalter, 1240–1250. (All Souls College, Oxford, MS 6, f. 4r)

The nurse, said Bartholomaeus Anglicus, took the place of the mother, and like a mother was happy when the child was happy and suffered when he suffered. She picked him up when he fell down, nursed him when he cried, kissed him when he was sick. She taught him to speak, repeating words, "practically breaking her tongue." She chewed meat for the toothless infant, whispered and sang to him, stroked him as he slept, bathed and anointed him.[15]

An irresistibly appealing picture of adult interaction with children is painted by the biographer of Bishop Hugh of Lincoln (1140–1200), with whom "children made friends . . . surprisingly quickly and . . . came to him more readily than to their parents." As the saintly bishop baptized a six-month-old, the infant

> expressed . . . great delight by the movement of its limbs. The tiny mouth and face relaxed in continuous chuckles. . . . It then bent and stretched out its little arms, as if it were trying to fly, and moved its head to and fro. . . . Next it took his hand in both its tiny ones and, exerting all its strength, raised it to its face. It then proceeded to lick it instead of kissing it. . . . Those present were amazed at the unusual spectacle of the bishop and the infant absolutely happy in each other's company. . . . What could the infant have seen in the bishop which gave it so much delight, unless it were God in him? What drew the bishop to the baby and made so important a person pay such attention to so small a being except the knowledge of the greatness concealed in such a tiny frame? . . . The bishop gave the boy an apple and several other things which children usually like, but he refused to be amused by any of them. He rejected them all and seemed completely absorbed and fascinated by the bishop. Disdainfully pushing away the hands of the nurse who was holding him, he gazed hard at the bishop and clapped his hands, smiling all the time.[16]

A child's father, according to Bartholomaeus, was an agent of generation whose aim was the multiplication of the species through his sons, who would "preserve him through his progeny." Such a father would deprive himself of food to nurture them. He took a strong interest in his sons' education, placing them under the care of tutors and, to discourage impudence, "did not show [them] a cheerful countenance," although he loved them like himself. He worked to acquire wealth to augment his sons' inheritance, and fed them in their youth so that they might feed him in old age. The more the father loved the son "the more diligently is [the son] instructed by him," a diligence that did not exclude correction by the rod. "When he is especially loved by his father, he does not appear to be loved, because he is even more stricken by scoldings and beatings, lest he become insolent."[17]

Though no longer the summary recourse of the ancient world, infanticide persisted. Church courts, which in England and most other places had jurisdiction, assessed penalties ranging from the traditional public penances and bread-and-water fasting to whipping. Severer penalties were applied in cases where the parents were unmarried, hence fornicators, while married parents were allowed to clear themselves by "compurgation," that is, swearing to innocence and finding witnesses to swear to the honesty of the accused.

In two ways medieval legal attitudes toward child killing differed from modern: infanticide was treated as "something less than homicide," and, in the other direction, as something worse than negligence leading to death. Thus the Church's concern was not limited to the sin of the parents, but extended to the welfare of the child. Parents should not only have good intentions but should also exercise care. Barbara Hanawalt found only two cases of possible infanticides among four thousand homicides on the coroners' rolls she examined. In one case, two women were accused of drowning a three-day-old baby in a river at the request of a mother and her son and daughter; all parties were acquitted. In the other a newborn baby girl, umbilical cord left untied, was found drowned in a river, mother and father unknown. The hypothesis that infanticide was sometimes concealed as accident is unsupported by evidence of the classical pattern of bias against female children: 63 percent of the accidental deaths recorded were of males.[18]

Neglect on the part of busy parents was indeed often fatal. In one case in the coroners' rolls, the father was in the fields and the mother had gone to the well when the straw with which the floor was strewn caught fire and the child in the cradle was burned. Such tragedies might be caused by chickens scratching close to the fire, picking up a burning twig or catching a spark in their feathers.

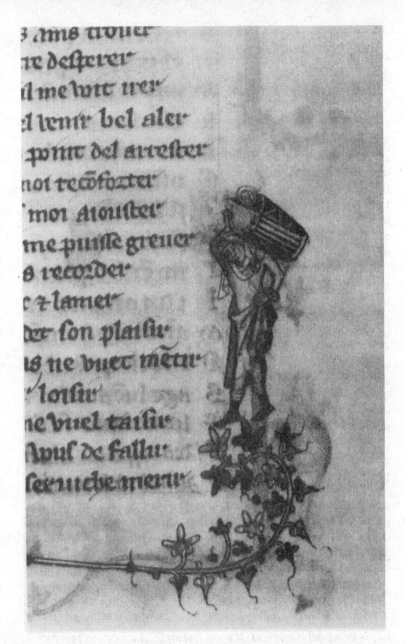

Peasant woman carries child in cradle. Voeux du Paon. (The Pierpont Morgan Library, Glazier Collection 24, f. 34)

Other livestock was also dangerous. Even in London, a sow wandered into the family shop and fatally bit a month-old infant.

Children out of the cradle were vulnerable to a new range of hazards: wells, ponds, ditches; boiling pots and kettles; knives, scythes, pitchforks. Accidents occurred when they were left alone by parents at work, when they were being watched by older siblings, or when the parents were present but occupied. While one father and mother were drinking in a tavern a burglar killed their two little girls. The inquest records reflect a censorious attitude by the jurors toward parental or sibling negligence. A child was "without anyone looking after him," or was "left without a caretaker." A five-year-old boy was described as a "bad custodian" of a younger child.[19]

Barbara Hanawalt's researches also reveal cases in which parents gave their lives for their children. One August night in 1298 in Oxford, a candle set fire to the straw on the floor of a shop. Husband and wife escaped, but, remembering her infant son, the wife "leapt back into the shop to seek him, and immediately when she entered she was overcome by the greatness of the fire and choked." In another case a father was killed defending his young daughter from rape.[20]

Parental feelings toward children are difficult to recover in the scarcity of the kind of sources that normally express sentiment: memoirs, personal letters, and biography. But the Inquisition investigation of Montaillou yields many pictures of parental attachment. A lady of Chateauverdun left her family to join the Cathars, but could scarcely bear saying goodbye to the baby in the cradle. "When she saw it she kissed it; then the child began to laugh. She had started to go out of the room where the infant lay so she came back to it again. The child began to laugh again, and so on, several times, so that she could not bear to tear herself away from the child. Seeing this she said to the maidservant: 'Take him out of the house.'" Only an overpowering religious conviction, for which she eventually died at the stake, could part the woman from her child.[21]

Loss of a child involved more than emotional considerations, but it involved those too. A good example of a father's feelings is the reaction of Guillaume Benet, a peasant of Montaillou, who told a friend comforting him, "I have lost all I had through the

Mother and children on the hearth. (Bodleian Library, MS Douce 6, f. 22)

death of my son Raymond. I have no one left to work for me."
And, weeping, Guillaume comforted himself with the thought
that his son had received the *consolamentum* before he died and
might be "in a better place than I am now."[22]

The Cathar religion consoled grieving parents with the belief
that the soul might be reincarnated in a later child, perhaps one
of their own. Pierre Austatz, the bailiff of Ornolac, comforted a
woman who had lost four sons by telling her that she would get
them back again, "for you are still young. You will be pregnant
again. The soul of one of your dead children will enter into the
new fetus." Another woman began to "weep and lament" when
she found her little son, who slept in her bed, dead beside her.
Pierre told her, "Do not weep. God will give the soul of your dead
son to the next child you conceive, male or female. Or else his soul
will find a good home somewhere else."[23]

One Cathar couple, Raymond and Sybille Pierre of the village
of Arques, whose infant daughter Jacotte fell seriously ill, decided
to have her receive the *consolamentum* usually reserved for persons
who had reached the age of understanding. Once it had been
administered, the father was content: "If Jacotte dies, she will be
an angel of God." But the mother had different feelings. The
perfect had instructed her not to give the baby milk or meat,
forbidden to the Cathar elect. But Sybille "could not bear it any
longer. I couldn't let my daughter die before my very eyes. So I
put her to the breast." Raymond was furious with her and for a
while "stopped loving the child, and he also stopped loving me for
a long while, until later, when he admitted that he had been
wrong." Raymond's admission coincided with the renunciation of
Catharism by all the inhabitants of Arques. The child survived for
a year and then died.[24]

Medieval children did not experience the prolonged stage of
formalized maturation that modern educational systems have imposed, and children were generally treated as responsible adults
from puberty, as indicated by the early ages at which boys and
girls were ruled competent to pronounce marriage vows, and the
still earlier ones at which betrothals were arranged. Such a contract
was often sealed by the transference of the bride-to-be or sometimes groom-to-be into the residence of her or his future in-laws.
Isabelle of Angoulême was betrothed to Hugh IX de Lusignan and

brought up in the Lusignans' castle southwest of Poitiers. But when she was twelve years old, King John of England induced her father to abduct her back to Angoulême so that John could marry her and take her home to England. John and Isabelle produced a daughter named Joan, who at ten was betrothed to the young son of Isabelle's former fiancé. Crossing the Channel, Joan in her turn took up residence at Lusignan. But a few years later, King John having died, Isabelle conceived the idea of marrying the younger Hugh de Lusignan herself. Daughter Joan was promised to the king of Scotland, and after a lengthy delay occasioned by an argument over the dowries of mother and daughter, both were married, Joan at the age of sixteen.[25]

Child marriage was confined to the aristocracy, peasant and artisan classes having no need for it. Neither did they thrust adult roles on their children. Barbara Hanawalt observes that between the ages of four and eight peasant children were occupied mainly with children's games, and usually only after the age of eight were given chores, most of them at home: the boys guarding the sheep or geese, pasturing or watering oxen and horses, gleaning after harvest; the girls picking wild fruit, fetching water, helping with the cooking. At adolescence, boys joined their fathers in the fields.[26]

Among all classes, noble, artisan, and peasant, some adolescents left home, to be educated, to learn a trade, or to become servants. The sons and daughters of the nobility were sent to other aristocratic households, often those of relatives, the sons to train as knights, the daughters to learn social graces. When twelve-year-old William Marshal departed for Normandy to become a squire, his biographer records, he wept at taking leave of his mother and brothers and sisters, like an adolescent going off to boarding school.[27]

A city boy might be boarded out as an apprentice to the master of a craft, his parents paying for his maintenance. Most guilds did not allow boys to be apprenticed to their own fathers, so apprenticeship normally meant leaving home at an early age. Even middle-class boys who went to school were commonly apprenticed when they had mastered their letters, education being a luxury whereas competence in business or a craft was life-sustaining. In 1248 a Marseilles lawyer apprenticed his son to a moneychanger for two years, paying a substantial fee in money and grain for William's "bread and wine and meat" and other necessities, and promising to reimburse the master if the lad should cause him any loss.[28] The master-apprentice relationship, according to Sylvia Thrupp, was "semi-paternal," with emphasis on the teaching of respect for authority. Apprentices were liable to corporal punishment, with the master's chastisement set out in the agreement "as if it was a duty rather than a right." The apprentice had to learn to restrain his temper and control himself before his superiors. If he felt mistreated, however, he could appeal to his master's guild.[29]

Illegitimate children were often given much the same consideration, including apprentice training, as legitimate children, and were sometimes even able to inherit property. A fourteenth-century Ghent tanner named Ghiselbrecht de Scouteete carried on a long-term liaison with a woman who presented him with six children. His wife having given him none, on his deathbed Ghiselbrecht left substantial bequests to all six, and apprenticed the eldest to a tanner so that he could follow in his father's profession, the tanners' guild being one of those that did not discriminate against bastards.[30]

Peasants, male and female, sometimes left home to become servants. A peasant might in effect sell his daughter to a master who paid him a modest lump sum, fed, clothed, and lodged her, and let her small wages accumulate for her dowry. When the girl was of marriageable age, the employer undertook to find her a match, or she might return home to marry. Boys also might go to work on the manorial farm or for other peasant families. From the evidence of the coroners' rolls, however, Barbara Hanawalt concluded that such a period of service "was not yet a well-established routine" for young people.[31]

Thirteenth-century schools taught their Latin book learning only to clerical trainees. A noble or peasant boy might board at a cathedral school such as that at Chartres, whose curriculum was described by John of Salisbury, secretary to Thomas Beckett. Devised in the early twelfth century by its famous chancellor, Bernard of Chartres, it included Latin grammar, the Latin classics, and philosophy. Masters devoted the morning to reading and interpreting Latin authors, the afternoon to grammar, and the evening to philosophical discussion, concluding with prayer. Every day, each student was required to recite part of what he had learned the day before, so "each succeeding day thus became the disciple of its predecessor." Students were then required to write compositions imitating the authors they had studied. To ensure that their reading was retained and not "precipitated to flight by spurs," each student daily had to memorize a poem or story and recite it. When they did poorly, they were beaten.[32]

Novice monks were trained in monastic schools. Although the discipline was severe, these schools had from the early years of the monastic movement practiced pedagogical methods that were a distinct improvement over those of Roman and barbarian society. According to French medievalist Pierre Riché, the monastic educator was instructed to use moderation and discretion in the treatment of children and to exert authority by good example rather than by raising his voice. The eighth-century Benedictine Paul the Deacon wrote that corporal punishment did more harm than good, and advised that brutal masters should themselves be punished. Children should be comfortably dressed, adequately fed, and warmly housed in winter. They should have an hour of recreation every day, and even, as a reward for good behavior, sweets at dinner.[33]

Monastic schools made allowance for children's physical as well as spiritual frailties. The monastic Rule composed by Lanfranc, William the Conqueror's archbishop, for the cathedral monastery at Canterbury appended to every duty for adults a modification for children. Adults were to eat only after vespers, but hungry children might eat earlier. Abstinence from food and drink was not to be inflicted on them as a penance. On the other hand, they were under strict surveillance, continuously watched by a master day and night, and were of course subject to beating.[34]

St. Anselm, who succeeded Lanfranc as abbot of Bec, in Normandy, surprised his contemporaries by not endorsing corporal punishment. The saint's biographer reported that another abbot complained to Anselm that the boys of the monastery were incorrigible and grew worse every day, although "we never give over beating them day and night."

"You never give over beating them?" Anselm asked. "And what are they like when they grow up?"

"Stupid brutes," the abbot replied.

Anselm rebuked him. "From men you have reared beasts. . . . Now tell me, my lord abbot, if you plant a tree-shoot in your garden, and straightway shut it in on every side so that it has no space to put out its branches, what kind of tree will you have in after years when you let it out of its confinement?"

"A useless one, certainly, with its branches all twisted and knotted."

"And whose fault would this be except your own for shutting it in so unnaturally? Without doubt, this is what you do with your boys. At their oblation they are planted in the garden of the Church, to grow and bring forth fruit for God. But you so terrify them and hem them in on all sides with threats and blows that they are utterly deprived of their liberty. And being thus injudiciously oppressed, they harbor and welcome and nurse within themselves evil and crooked thoughts like thorns, and cherish these thoughts so passionately that they doggedly reject everything which could minister to their correction. Hence, feeling no love or pity, good will or tenderness in your attitude towards them, they have in future no faith in your goodness but believe that all your actions proceed from hatred and malice against them. The deplorable result is that as they grow in body so their hatred increases, together with their apprehension of evil, and they are forward in all crookedness and vice."

Why, Anselm asked, was the abbot so incensed against the boys? Were they not flesh and blood like himself, and would he care to be treated as they were and to become what they were? Anselm compared the teacher's role to that of a goldsmith who shaped his leaves of precious metal with gentle, skillful pressure rather than blows. Thus he must apply encouragement, fatherly sympathy, and gentleness.

The abbot protested that "we do all we can to force them into sober and manly habits." Anselm explained that "bread and all kinds of solid food" were good for those who were mature enough to eat them, but that if you fed a suckling infant on such food and took away its milk he would be "strangled rather than strengthened by his diet." The weak soul needed milk: "gentleness from others, kindness, compassion, cheerful encouragement, loving forbearance, and much else of the same kind."[35]

Another churchman of the late eleventh century seems to have mingled Anselm's tolerant attitude toward children with churchly self-interest. Four boys of noble birth who were being educated at Ramsey Abbey were allowed to play outside the cloisters at specified times "lest they should be exhausted by the rigor of the Rule without the interpolation of recreation." During one recess they tried to toll one of the bells in the bell tower and broke its rim. The angry monks urged the abbot to punish them. But the abbot refused; the damage had been done by accident and not maliciously. He added sagely that since the boys were of noble birth, they would probably repay the abbey a hundredfold when they "arrived at the age of maturity."[36]

Until the late Middle Ages, the few records of childhood that were written were contained in the lives of saints and churchmen. One such is the biography of St. Peter Damian (1007–1072) by his disciple John of Lodi. Peter was born in Ravenna to a mother "worn out by child-bearing." His family was so numerous and so poor that his older brother bitterly reproached the mother for adding to the crowded household another heir to the meager inheritance. The despairing mother, declaring that she was utterly wretched and unworthy to live, "wholly rejected the baby," refusing to nurse, hold, or touch him. The child, abandoned "before he had learned to live," became so weak that he could hardly cry; "only the barest whisper came from his scarcely palpitating little chest." At that moment a woman who had been a servant in Peter's father's family intervened, reproaching the baby's mother for lacking even the maternal feeling of a lioness or tigress for its cubs. How could a Christian woman reject a child formed in the image of God and shaped in her own womb? Removing the baby's swaddling clothes, the woman warmed him at the fire and anointed his body so that "the tender little limbs, wrapped in poultices soaked in melted fat, [began] to grow rosy as their vital heat returned, and the beauty of infancy to flower again." Her maternal feelings restored, Peter's mother took the baby to nurse.

A few years later both parents died and Peter was adopted by the same elder brother who had protested at his birth. Both this brother and his wife, who played the role of a stepmother, treated him harshly, feeding him slops fit for the pigs, dressing him in rags, kicking and beating him, and finally turning him out to become a swineherd. But then a kinder brother took over his guardianship and lavished on him affection that "seemed to exceed a father's love." This brother, who became an archpriest of Ravenna, fostered Peter's career, first as a teacher and then as a prelate and leader in the Church reform movement of the eleventh century.[37]

A second account of a medieval childhood, one of the few intimate pictures that has come down to us, is the autobiography of Guibert, abbot of Nogent, written about 1115.[38] His father, a knight, came from a castellan family of Clermont, and Guibert was the youngest of several children. His parents' marriage was arranged when they were both very young, she "hardly of marriageable age," his father "a mere youth."[39] Although the mother seems to have been sexually frigid, Guibert asserts that she loved her husband and after his death kept his name "so constantly on her lips that her mind seemed to turn on no other subject."[40]

Guibert's mother almost died when he was born—she was in labor "almost the whole of Good Friday" and part of Holy Saturday—and his father and kinsfolk made a vow on an altar of the church of Clermont dedicated to the Virgin Mary that "should a male child be born, he should be given up to the religious life in the service of God and the Lady, and if one of the inferior sex, she should be handed over to the corresponding calling." The child was born immediately, "and at that timely birth there was rejoicing only for my mother's deliverance, the child being such a miserable object."[41]

Less than a year later, Guibert's father died. His mother never remarried, but dominated Guibert's childhood. He thought of her as the perfection of womanhood, a person that he could never live up to: beautiful, chaste, proud, strong, intelligent, virtuous. She was the "sole personal possession . . . I had in the world," the only human being in his whole life with whom he had a close relationship.[42] A sickly child, a "weak little being, almost an abortion," for his first six years Guibert monopolized his mother's attention. She provided him with nurses and "fine clothes for my little body, so that I seemed to equal the sons of kings and counts in indulgence."[43] When he was six and had learned "the shapes of the letters, but hardly yet to join them into syllables," she hired a tutor, stipulating that he should give up his other pupils and spend

Schoolboys being disciplined. (British Library, Burney MS 275, f. 94)

his time solely with Guibert. The schoolroom was "the dining hall of our house." Between this teacher and Guibert relations were ambivalent. On the one hand the man "loved me as well as he did himself" and devoted himself to the child with "watchful care," and the boy believed himself to return his feelings; on the other, Guibert recognized that he was an incompetent teacher who showered him "with a hail of blows and harsh words while he was forcing me to learn what he could not teach." While other children "wandered everywhere at will and were unchecked in the indulgence of such inclinations as were natural at their age," Guibert was permitted only to look on at their games.[44]

One evening when he went to see his mother "after a more severe beating than I had deserved," she asked him whether he had been whipped that day. The child, unwilling to be a tale-bearer, denied it. "Then against my will she threw off my inner garment . . . and saw my little arms blackened and the skin of my back everywhere puffed up with the cuts from the twigs." His mother, "grieved to the heart . . . troubled, agitated, and weeping with sorrow," declared that he should not become a priest "nor any more suffer so much to get an education." But the boy insisted that even if he died on the spot he would not give up his schooling.[45]

When Guibert was twelve, his mother suddenly decided to withdraw from life and become a kind of anchoress, retiring to a house near the monastery of Saint-Germer. Simultaneously, Guibert's tutor became a monk at the same monastery. Guibert was abandoned to relatives at the castle of Clermont. The separation was wrenching for both mother and son. "She knew that I should be utterly an orphan with no one at all on whom to depend, for great as was my wealth of kinsfolk and connections, yet there was no one to give me the loving care a little child needs at such an age. . . . I often suffered from the loss of that careful provision for the helplessness of tender years that only a woman can provide." He pictured his mother, passing "the stronghold where I remained" on her way to Saint-Germer, experiencing "intolerable anguish to her lacerated heart . . . [since] she knew for certain that she was a cruel and unnatural mother."[46]

Guibert went through a period of rebelliousness in which he indulged in "wanton pursuits" and imitated his young cousins, future knights, "in their juvenile rowdiness." His mother finally intervened, asking the monastery to take him in as a pupil. Inside the monastery, Guibert underwent a conversion and determined to become a monk. He remained at Saint-Germer for twenty years, leaving only to become abbot of Nogent.[47]

Guibert's memoirs yield a provocative picture of the childhood of one twelfth-century son of the nobility destined for the Church, but have only limited application to medieval childhood in general. A recent study of the early years of thirteenth-century saints revealed common elements, some of which are reminiscent of Guibert's experience: they all belonged to the landed nobility or to the urban patriciate; many had "emotionally deprived child-hoods" owing to parents' death, fathers' absence at war or on Crusade, their consignment to relatives or monasteries, or the fact that their families were so large that they suffered neglect. Reared by their mothers or by nurses, many may have found a substitute father in the Church.[48]

A purpose common to the education of medieval clergy and nobles, as it was to that of apprentices, was the inculcation of self-control and of respect for authority. During his novitiate at Saint-Germer, Guibert benefited from the advice and instruction of St. Anselm, who several times visited his monastery, and who "offered to teach me to manage the inner self, how to consult the laws of reason in the government of the body." In developing his own theories of pedagogy Guibert recommended that schoolmasters give their pupils time to relax, and that they season their instruction with variety. Self-control was a necessary attribute and must be taught. But children could not be expected to behave "like old men who are completely serious."[49]

Marriage and the Family
in the Year 1300

The economic surge of the high Middle Ages brought an enhancement in living standards to much of the European population, which also benefited from the broad improvement in public order. In this new environment the aristocratic family underwent a metamorphosis, freeing itself from its dependence on royal favor and assuming the characteristics of a hereditary titled nobility: the estate with family seat and family name, transmitted through the male line by primogeniture and memorialized in a written genealogy. Younger sons were losers; so in lesser degree were wives and daughters.

Peasant inheritance practices followed a different pattern of development, but by 1300 peasant families had also acquired names and some had acquired enough land to achieve modest affluence. Many peasants were free, and many of those who remained villeins had gained virtual ownership of land. Among the benefits of higher peasant living standards was the spread of maintenance contracts for old-age support.

The views of Gratian and Peter Lombard dominated the Church courts of the high Middle Ages. Consent of the two parties became the accepted basis of marriage, though parental consent remained important because the new household needed the economic support of the older generation: an estate for the noble couple, a piece of land and an animal or two for the peasant. The Fourth Lateran Council's retreat on the matter of consanguinity removed a cause of friction between Church and laity and an excuse for divorce. The Church courts now commanded jurisdiction in disputes over marriage. By a natural extension the parish priest had acquired an increased role in the marriage ceremony, as broadcaster of news of the nuptials, as participant in the ritual, as judge of possible impediments. To him was passing "the essential supporting role. . . . Representing neither family nor lord, [he] spoke for the larger religious community that had come to state the conditions in which a valid marriage could occur."[1]

Among peasants as well as nobles, primogeniture's purpose of ensuring male succession was frustrated by high mortality, causing estates to shift capriciously through marriage of daughters or remarriage of widows.

For children, whose lives we begin at last to discern in some detail, the high Middle Ages reveals a picture of a harsh environment with high mortality among parents as well as children, severe discipline, and early consignment to work, but one by no means bereft of parental concern and affection, or of a "concept of childhood."

IV.

The Late Middle Ages

II.

The Impact
of the Black Death

[My sons] Amerigo and Martino died the same day, in my arms, within a few hours. God knows what hopes I had for the eldest, already a companion to me, and, with me, a father to the others, and who was doing so well in Ardingo's bank . . . and God knows how for many years he never failed, night and morning, to say his prayers on his knees in his room. . . . And at the same time [my daughter] Antonia was in bed, sick to death, and the middle boy with her, and he died there. How my heart broke when the little ones cried, and their mother not well herself or strong, hearing the words of the elder boy. And now all three of them dead![1]

Ser Lapo Mazzei's letter to his friend Francesco Datini of Prato is one of the innumerable pathos-laden reports of the Europe-wide tragedy wrought by the Black Death, beginning with its arrival in Italy in 1347–1348. In Prato, after the original and several subsequent visitations, the number of hearths (households) was reduced from 4,000 in 1310 to 950 in 1427. In the *contado* (countryside) around Prato, the rate of extinction was lower, from 1,630 hearths in 1300 to 943 in the 1420s.[2] An outbreak in 1363–1364, labeled the "children's plague," extinguished few households but robbed a great many of infants and young chil-

Burial of plague victims at Tournai. (Bibliothèque Royale Albert Ier, MS 13076–77, f. 24 v)

dren. Still another outbreak, lingering through the turn of the century, had a similar effect. By the 1420s the surviving population of Prato was top-heavy with adults.[3]

Through 1347 and 1348 the original Black Death crept across Europe, reaching Britain in 1349. In the English countryside, recorded mortality in some districts ran as high as 65 percent. The records of a typical village in Leicestershire, Kibworth Harcourt, show a diminution in household size from an average of five persons to just under four.[4] Many families disappeared. In some cases whole villages were deserted.

From Sicily to Ireland, cities and hamlets witnessed repetitions of the scene depicted by Boccaccio (*Decameron*, First Day) in Florence: "They brought the bodies of those who had died forth from their houses and laid them before their doors, where, especially in the morning, those who went about might see corpses without number; then they fetched biers and some, in default thereof, they laid upon some board or other. Nor was it only one bier that carried two or three corpses, nor did this happen but once; nay, many might have been counted which contained husband and wife, two or three brothers, father and son, or the like."[5] A Sienese survivor wrote: "Father abandoned child, wife husband, one brother another; for the illness seemed to strike through the breath and sight. . . . Great pits were dug and piled deep with huge heaps of dead. . . . And I, Agnolo di Tura, buried my five children with my own hands, and so did many others likewise."[6]

The Prato merchant Francesco Datini lost father, mother, and one of his two brothers in the initial outbreak in 1348; in the severe recurrence in 1399 that killed Ser Lapo Mazzei's children, Francesco suffered the loss of one friend and business associate after another: his partner in a Bolognese bank, his two partners in Prato, his notary, his partners in Pisa, and the head of his firm's branch in Genoa.[7] Petrarch in Parma wrote his friend "Socrates" in Avignon:

How can I begin? Where shall I turn? Everywhere is woe, terror everywhere. . . . I am not mourning some slight distress but that dreadful year 1348, which not merely robbed us of our friends, but robbed the whole world of its peoples. And if that were not enough, now this following year reaps the remainder, and cuts down with its deadly scythe whatever survived the storm. . . . Posterity, will you believe what we who lived through it can hardly accept? We should think we were dreaming, had we not the testimony of our opened eyes. . . . Where now are those sweet friends, where are the loved faces, where the caressing words, the gay and gentle conversation?[8]

The Prato merchant Francesco Datini with four other citizens of Prato.
Detail of the Madonna del Ceppo, by Fra Lippo Lippi, Galleria Comunale,
Prato. (Alinari)

Throughout the intervening centuries, the Black Death has remained the foremost historic example of human calamity, a metaphor for disaster, and a first-class medical mystery. How could the original onslaught spread so far and so fast, and why the irregular pattern of its recurrences? ("Just when it seems to be over," wrote despairing Petrarch, "it returns and attacks once more those who were briefly happy."[9]) Modern scholarship, still baffled by many aspects of the plague, has made two significant additions to the total picture. The first is the qualification of the demographic impact through the discovery that at the moment when the plague struck, the population expansion of the twelfth and thirteenth centuries had in many places already been halted and even reversed. Overpopulation and adverse economic factors had created a negative demographic trend to which the plague brutally contributed.

The second discovery is that regardless of the demographic and economic factors at work in a region, the stunning shock did not bring the world to a halt. Rather, the mechanisms of marriage and child-bearing quickly adjusted to disaster. The resilience of the family as an institution did not lessen the tragedy, but it nevertheless performed a remarkable feat in limiting long-term consequences.

A study by David Herlihy of Impruneta, a rural commune of Florence, and studies of several Midland villages by a number of English scholars have done much to illuminate the process of recovery from the first great outbreak and its numerous, often local, recurrences. In Impruneta, Herlihy found a history of development before and after the Black Death that confirmed the hypothesis of a population already in decline.[10] The Tuscan countryside of which Impruneta was a part was one of Europe's more advanced regions in techniques of cultivation. On the farms belonging to the Church, a fifth of the total of the region, the three-field system prevailed. Tax rolls show returns of six to one on seed wheat, a very acceptable rate for the Middle Ages and long after. Yet notarial records reveal that before the Black Death many of the small farmers of Impruneta were forced to sell their wheat, oil, and wine in advance, even years in advance, and that the price concealed substantial usury on the part of the purchasers.[11]

A breakdown of the population engaged in agriculture in Impruneta shows three classes: tenants cultivating land owned by the Church or absentee landlords in Florence; the bulk, something over half, small independent farmers; and, the bottom fifth on the tax returns, the *mezzadri*, or sharecroppers.[12] Paradoxically, these last were often better off than the independent farmers, a situation intimately related to the population decline of the fourteenth century in northern Italy. The *mezzadri* were supplied by landowners with land, seed, tools, and animals, paid no rents or interest, and stood low on the tax rolls.[13] When the crop was good they were in a favorable position, which they were reputed to improve at their landlords' expense. "No account was ever kept with them in which they were the losers," wrote one Florentine observer. "If the crop is abundant, they keep the better two thirds" (instead of an equal one half).[14] The independent farmers, on the other hand, struggled with high rents and interest rates and by 1329, according to the tax commissioners, would be forced to "go begging through the world" unless they received relief in the form of lowered assessments. Ten years later the commissioners reported the impossibility of distributing the 200,000-lire assessment voted by the Signoria (city council) of Florence for the farmers of Impruneta, among whom poor families had "sold their goods and possessions to Florentine citizens and even clerics, and still they were burdened by various and diverse usurious debts."[15] That the Impruneta situation was not unique is shown by a study of the neighboring Florentine district of Passignano.[16]

The following year, 1340, brought famine and a minor epidemic to Impruneta, whose population, if not actually declining, had at least ceased expanding. Forced to grow their wheat on too small plots of hilly soil, with insufficient capital, and paying high rents, high interest rates, and high taxes, many of the independent farmers were already abandoning their farms when the Black Death swept through the district in 1348. Its impact here was only slightly greater than that of the famine and epidemic of 1340; the two together plus migration out of the commune for economic reasons brought a reduction in the number of households in Impruneta from 123 in 1330 to 101 in 1356. The decline continued through further visitations of the Black Death, a variety of local calamities, and the unremitting pressure of rents, interest, and taxes. In 1401 only 74 households remained in Impruneta. At this point the situation seems to have stabilized. The *catasto* (tax roll) of 1427 shows 72 households remaining, numbering 432 persons, and cites many dilapidated and abandoned farms for which no tenant could be found. A marked shift had taken place in the system of cultivation, with far fewer independent farmers and a substantial increase in the number of *mezzadri* sharecropping for wealthy urban families.[17] The *mezzadria* or crop-sharing farm had in fact become the cornerstone of agriculture. At the same time a rational shift in choice of crops had taken place, with less wheat and more wine and olive cultivation.[18]

Thus the plague, coming on top of an economic and demographic crisis, in the end had a positive effect on the economy of Impruneta and probably throughout northern Italy.

In England, the picture of recovery extracted by recent research also shows mixed results.[19] Halesowen, a Midlands manor that included a market town, twelve hamlets, and the lord's demesne farm, had like Impruneta been visited by famine in the years before the Black Death. Twenty-two peasants died in the famine year of 1317. The plague made its first appearance in May 1349, when 21 male deaths were signaled in the manorial records by the payment of heriots (death duties). It may be assumed that an approximately equal number of women died, and perhaps more children. In June the figure rose to 25 males, in July declined to 22, and in August fell to 3. The final toll was at least 88 male tenants out of 203 previously identified in the court records.[20]

Where famine pinched the poorest families most severely, the plague wrought its havoc even-handedly among rich and and poor, ragged cottagers and well-off virgaters. Indirect evidence suggests another difference, a higher mortality rate among children than among adults. Nearly every family had its victim or victims, and some households disappeared. Both Thomas Hyddeley and his wife are known to have died; that his children perished too is silently indicated by the award of his holding to his brother John. The deaths of Philip atte Lowe, his two sons, and one daughter were recorded, together with the bestowal of the holding on a new tenant. One boy in his late teens, Thomas Richard, lost his father and, along with his father's holding, was placed under the guardianship of another villager, Philip Thompkyns, who married the boy to his minor daughter Juliana. Shortly after, Thomas himself died of the plague, leaving a one-year-old son, Thomas II. Thomas's father-in-law and brother-in-law then perished, and the father-in-law's holding and his surviving minor son were turned over to the husband of another married daughter, who also probably provided a refuge for Juliana and Thomas II.[21]

Yet following the catastrophic summer of 1349, life at Halesowen returned almost uncannily to normal. No social turmoil followed. Zvi Razi in his study of Halesowen says: "The records of the court held between August 1349 and October 1350 show that the villagers harvested their crops and pastured their animals. They married and bore children in and out of wedlock. They brewed ale against the assize, trespassed against the lord and their neighbors, quarreled and shed each other's blood, lent money and stood surety for each other, and elected jurymen and other village officials."[22]

It is on the mechanics of recovery that Razi's study of Halesowen throws most valuable light. Of the holdings that fell vacant through the death of their tenants in 1349, four fifths were taken up within the following year, all but eighteen by sons and daughters, by wives or brothers, by other relations, or by guardians appointed for children of the tenant. With much higher casualties than Impruneta, Halesowen nevertheless continued on an almost business-as-usual basis. Not only were the vacant tenancies promptly filled, but they were worked. How, with the loss of two fifths of its labor force, did Halesowen succeed in not merely occupying all its holdings in a legal sense but in maintaining agricultural production? Two major responses in the realm of social and economic planning are known to have taken place: first, surviving villagers often compacted their scattered tenements into more coherent groupings, and second, hedges were now grown in what had been open pastureland to permit enclosure of cattle, saving the labor of herdsmen. Razi offers an additional hypothesis: if most of the survivors were young adults who could cope with extra work, especially the peak load of harvest time, they could manage, in light of the fewer mouths they had to feed.[23] One might postulate a medieval version of Parkinson's Law whereby the number of family members employed on a holding was irrelevant as long as a necessary minimum work force was available.[24]

Research on other English districts has turned up a slightly different pattern of recovery. In Kibworth Harcourt the first outbreak of plague in 1348–1349 killed forty-four male tenants. Nevertheless, by the end of 1349 only one fifth of the holdings remained tenantless. The rest had been taken up by sons, brothers, or nephews, without the need for recourse to daughters. Recurrences of plague in 1354, 1361, and 1376 brought more deaths and made heirs more difficult to find. One family after another became extinct in the male line, and land passed to sons-in-law and adopted heirs. The average size of holdings increased from twelve acres before the plague to twenty-four acres after it.[25] Surprisingly, new tenants who might have divided large holdings between two sons instead passed them on intact to the eldest son. The reason was evidently that previously inalienable customary land was now on the market and the new high wages provided a source of capital for the purchase of land by or for younger sons.

Was recovery from the catastrophe typically as smooth and free of social friction as these examples imply? Paris chronicler Jean de

Venette denies it: "The world was not changed for the better but for the worse. . . . For men were more avaricious and grasping than before, even though they had far greater possessions. They were more covetous and disturbed each other more frequently with suits, brawls, disputes, and pleas."[26] Some of the evidence from the English villages supports the French observer. J. A. Raftis found that in Warboys thirty-one families became extinct following the first outbreak of the plague, and several more families survived only for another generation.[27] Holdings were temporarily left vacant, but new family names soon began to appear on the court rolls, in fact outnumbering those that had disappeared. Raftis also noted an increase in cases of violence in the 1360s: assaults, "disobedience" to the lord's officials, "rebelliousness." In Holywell-cum-Needingworth no striking signs of disturbance in the village followed the plague, but a new taste for litigation in defending or claiming property rights affected all classes and sometimes led to minor acts of violence.[28] Another study by Raftis, of the village of Upwood, Huntingdonshire, showed a rise in cases of neglect of work on the lord's demesne, of trespass on the property of the lord and of fellow villagers, and of quarrels and assault, signs that "a disturbed atmosphere hangs over the village" in the decades following 1360.[29]

One long-standing institution of the English village vanished after the initial outbreak of the Black Death: the practice of personal pledging, of standing surety for a fellow villager. Though Zvi Razi found it continuing in Halesowen in the immediate aftermath of the plague, it was presently abandoned everywhere. Raftis comments: "Since the pledging of another person was customarily a free option of the individual, we must assume that villagers no longer wished to support one another in this fashion." In place of pledging, bylaws now multiplied, strictly enforced by village officials and imposing severe penalties for trespass and other violations.[30]

If the plague itself did not cause social turmoil, its after-effects may well have contributed to it. R. H. Hilton's study of Wat Tyler's Rebellion of 1381 indicates that behind the immediate provocation of the rising, a poll tax imposed by the costs of the Hundred Years War, lay the social pressures generated by depopulation. The expectations aroused in the peasants by the new conditions of land and labor collided with the determination of the lords to hold down wages, raise rents, and enforce labor services, in a word, to repeal the effects of the Black Death. The rebels were not the dregs of peasant society, as Hilton shows, but rather the "whole people below the ranks of those who exercised lordship in the countryside and established authority in the towns."[31] Many of the leaders were well-to-do peasants, such as the Suffolk rebel Thomas Sampson, who owned 200 acres of land, 300 sheep, and 100 cattle. The focus of the rising was the most developed region of England, East Anglia and the Home Counties, where free tenure was widespread, where a market economy prevailed, and where an active land market operated.[32]

The rebellion was suppressed and its leaders executed, but the economic tide set in motion by the plague could not be stemmed. In the context of labor shortage and land plenty, landless peasants were able to press not only for better pay but for two significant changes in its form: in place of the old annual stipend, a day wage, and in place of the old mixture of money, grain, and meals, all money. These reforms made it possible for a laborer to move about in search of optimum employment and lifted him permanently out of the status of serfdom. Armed with a little cash, a landless peasant might lease a field and plant a crop. The abbey of Halesowen, whose land had always been worked by hired labor, began leasing parts of it in the early 1350s, as did other lords with portions of their demesne farms.

In Halesowen before the plague, annual rents and labor services were light (partly owing to resistance against attempts to increase them): six shillings seven pence and a maximum of eighteen days' service per yardland per year. But elsewhere they ran much higher, up to thirteen shillings and fifty or even one hundred days' service.[33] With land now cheap and labor at a premium, the old servile commitment to the family holding rapidly weakened. At the same time intelligent lords and abbots discovered that reduced rents and services were preferable to untilled soil, and they even saw advantage in commuting servile duties for a cash payment or in selling a tenement outright.

The new labor conditions in England favored another change in agricultural practices, similar to that at Impruneta: a shift from the labor-intensive cultivation of cereals to land-intensive practices such as grazing of sheep and cattle and the production of hides, meat, butter, cheese, and legumes for sale as cash crops. The result was a more flexible and resilient agricultural economy, distinctly advantageous to the peasant family.[34]

As the Black Death repeated its visitations at roughly ten-year intervals, a response of the population everywhere became manifest in the records of marriage and childbirth. Jean de Venette wrote, with a chronicler's exaggeration: "After the cessation of the epidemic [of 1348] . . . the men and women who survived married each other. There was no sterility among the women but on the contrary fertility beyond the ordinary. Pregnant women were seen on every side. Many twins were born and even three children at once."[35] The ages of marrying couples dropped dramatically as aristocrats sought to ensure heirs and common people found economic opportunities improving. In Prato at the end of the thirteenth century men had married at close to forty, women at about twenty-five. In 1371 the average age of men at marriage had dropped to twenty-four, that of women to sixteen. With the stabilization of population in the fifteenth century, marriage ages began to rise, though not nearly to their old levels.[36]

Florentine merchant Giovanni Morelli recalled in his memoir that when his grandfather died in 1347, just before the first outbreak of the plague, none of his four sons was married, although the eldest was thirty-eight or thirty-nine. Two years later the first-born married "because he was the eldest [son]." Another visitation of the plague killed the eldest and two younger brothers, leaving only Morelli's father, Pagolo, who was the youngest. To ensure the survival of the family Pagolo was now obligated to marry, which he did in 1364. Each major epidemic in Florence, according to David Herlihy, similarly resulted in "a flurry of marriage arrangements."[37]

The birth rate was in turn stimulated by the reduced age at marriage, in addition to which high infant mortality may have lessened sexual restraint and use of contraceptive measures. Morelli reported that in the period before 1347 Florentine women bore an average of four to six children, while in the years from 1365 to 1389 the wife of Matteo di Niccolo Corsini bore twenty (of whom only five survived).[38] During an epidemic, baptisms fell by twelve percent, and the following year by even more, reflecting disrupted marriages and flight from the city, but in the second year after an epidemic they rebounded to their old levels or higher.[39]

To these data David Herlihy's study of Florentine records adds an intriguing mystery. Repeatedly, he found, births peaked in the year immediately *preceding* a fresh outbreak of the plague. This phenomenon occurred in the years before the return of the disease in 1457, in 1479, in 1495–1499, and in 1527. The plague cycle itself, he concludes, may actually have been influenced by the recurring cycle of marriage and reproduction.[40] The population surge appears to have acted as a stimulus on one or more components of the plague vector, creating a fateful ebb and flow of life and death. Whether the Florentine pattern was widely repeated elsewhere has not been established.

From one end of Europe to the other, the Black Death, often in combination with other factors, powerfully influenced the family, its size and shape, economic basis, social conditions, and inter- and intra-family relations in a variety of ways, some already determined, some yet to be discovered.

12.

The Late Medieval
Peasant Family: 1350-1500

In the fifteenth century two sources suddenly light up the changing village, its houses and their interiors, and the daily life of the family within. First, the inventories of chattels multiply, often not only listing items but telling in what room they were found. Second, a new international style of manuscript illustration, employed in "books of hours" (prayer books) and psalters (collections of psalms), celebrates both the castles of the aristocrats who commissioned the works and the countryside around the castles, with its fields, houses, and barns, alive with the seasonal activities of the peasants. The most striking impression derived from both sources is the marked improvement in material comfort.

The village now appears larger because of the proliferation of farm buildings and the increased size of many farmhouses. Wattle-and-daub construction has been supplemented by a stouter frame of finished square timbers filled in with plaster walls. Doorways are now sometimes framed with finished timber posts and crossbeams, while masonry blocks appear in foundations of houses, barns, and sheds. More houses have two distinct rooms, and even two floors, with sleeping quarters reached by ladder. In these better houses, the old open fire in the middle of the room has been replaced with a stone hearth, borrowed from the castle, built into the wall opposite the door and vented not through a hole in the roof but through a brick chimney. Slate and tile roofs are now common, their installation creating (in England) the professional surnames Slater and Tyler, but straw remains the most popular roofing material. Abundant, lightweight, requiring little support, it is easy to handle, yet a straw roof too can profit from the employment of an expert, inspiring another surname, Thatcher. To facilitate runoff, the thatched roof is steeply pitched, giving the house a characteristic profile. Straw also continues its role as floor covering, along with reeds and rushes, and as bedding for people and animals.[1]

In a manuscript illumination of the 1460s (from the *Book of Love of King René of Anjou*) a knight is depicted ducking his head under the crossbeam of a door while stepping over the raised threshold of a well-built rustic house. That the walls are plastered is evident from a few visible cracks. Inside, a woman sits before a fireplace whose chimney stack rises above the thatched roof. Three unglazed windows, one large, two smaller, pierce the walls.

In various illustrations, outside the typical new-style peasant's house are pictured cowbarn, sheepfold, stable, pigsty, dovecote, and kiln or drying oven, used in damp climates to dry grain, flax, hay, malt, and beans. Among peasant possessions may be an ox team with yoke and harness, a plow with iron share and coulter, a wooden harrow, a cart, an axe, a spade, a scythe, a flail, and a few other tools. The house interior now displays more furniture: chairs as well as stools and benches, cabinets, beds with mattresses sometimes supplanting pallets, cushions, bed curtains, and even wall hangings ("painted cloths"). Meals are still taken at a trestle table that can be dismantled and put out of the way.[2] An English accident report discloses a hazard in this universal piece of furniture: an angry or exhilarated guest banged his fist down and caused the loose table top to fly up and bruise his head.[3]

An illumination in the *Très Riches Heures* of the Duc de Berry shows peasants warming themselves by the fireplace in a tall room open to the ceiling rafters, in the background a large bed covered with a blue bedspread, and garments drying on a rack. Another book of hours, that of Catherine of Cleves, pictures the Holy Family as a youthful fifteenth-century household: Mary at a loom,

Mary nurses Jesus while Joseph sits in a barrel chair. Book of Hours of Catherine of Cleves. (The Pierpont Morgan Library, MS 917, p. 151)

Mary weaves and Joseph planes while the baby Jesus plays in a walker.
Book of Hours of Catherine of Cleves. (The Pierpont Morgan
Library, MS 917, p. 149)

carpenter Joseph smoothing a workpiece with a plane, baby Jesus playing in a walker. The house has stone walls (rare in England, but becoming more common in France, the Low Countries, and Italy), wooden window frames, and a wooden ceiling. The stone fireplace has a hook for hanging a kettle. Another illumination in the same book shows Mary nursing Jesus while Joseph sits in a barrel chair; nearby are a hand grill, shears, bellows, and a storage cabinet.

Documentary sources confirm the increased affluence. A York animal breeder in 1451 listed the contents of his cellar as including cloth, salt, silver spoons, and other items; his bedchamber as containing beds, blankets, sheets, chests, a coffer, and clothing; the kitchen, pewter dishes, trivets, and other equipment; and somewhere in the house, jewelry and silver objects.[4]

R. H. Hilton, surveying a number of late medieval regional studies, concluded that while only a few village households had servants, many communities had a large proportion of unattached laborers. In the villages of East Anglia, between 50 and 70 percent of the males were servants or laborers; in eighty Cotswold villages only about one household in eight had servants, but for every seventeen landholding households there were seven landless laborers. Surveys from other areas gave similar results. Surprisingly, a considerable number of the laborers were unattached women; also surprisingly, a large proportion of the landless of both sexes were well enough off to be assessed taxes at the maximum rate, that is, the same one twentieth of movable goods as the landed peasants who hired them, testimony to the change in the status of labor since the Black Death.[5]

In Leicestershire, women assisted with haymaking, weeding, mowing, grain transport, driving plow oxen, and even breaking stones for road mending. The court record of a robbery case in Ombersley in 1420 reports that the crime was committed while "Christina harrowed." According to Thorold Rogers, authority on medieval wages, women harvest workers of the fifteenth century were paid at the prevailing wage for men. Women reapers and binders at Minchinhampton in Gloucester in the late fourteenth century are known to have received men's wages, as did women thatchers at nearby Avening. Women who worked as manorial servants, however, were paid less than men.[6]

The new availability of wage-paying jobs helped even the lesser peasant families to acquire additional land, often by banding together to group-lease tracts of demesne. It was, however, the better-off family that most readily found the path of upward mobility. "Greatest increases of property," says J. A. Raftis of the changes in the village of Upwood, "were made by the already substantial tenants."[7] Their acquisitions were facilitated by their increased wealth and earning power, and also by their domination of manorial office. In Upwood as elsewhere, leading villagers exhibited a "readiness to perform official services for the rewards," that is, relief from rents and services owed the lord and the opportunity to buy or lease demesne land.[8] Chaucer's reeve, who "had grown rich and had a store of treasure," had such real-life counterparts as Walter Shayl, reeve on a manor of the bishop of Worcester, who cultivated a second yardland belonging to the demesne.[9]

After 1400, when commutation of rents and services had become widespread, village officials began to receive money wages. Edwin De Windt's study of Holywell over the period from 1252 to 1457 indicates that age as well as economic status was a factor in their selection.[10] Families tended to go through cycles, experiencing periods when none of their members were ripe enough for office. And while certain families "showed a remarkable ability to produce officials" for a certain period of time, these petty rustic aristocracies, like their great noble counterparts, were subject to extinction through failure of male heirs.[11] In Cuxham the sole free tenant and wealthiest man in the village in the early 1300s, John ate Grene, extended his holdings after the Black Death, taking over the half-virgates and farmsteads of two extinct families. Late in the fourteenth century his descendant, John Grene, moved to the town of Henley and failed to produce a male heir. His daughter Joan sold the Cuxham property in 1415, ending the Grenes' connection with the village and their history as a family.[12]

Some peasant lineages showed more endurance, lasting long enough to ascend out of the peasant class. In the Midlands village of Wigston a free peasant family first appeared in village records around 1200 when "Rannulf the clerk" was granted two virgates of land, which he divided between his two sons, John and Helias.

John bought up his brother's portion, and his descendants occupied the holding for more than two centuries, adding two more virgates with their farmsteads, some of it land taken over from victims of the Black Death. A John Randull died in the 1430s, and his son Richard moved to Leicester where he became a grocer—a small businessman of substance—and leased his property in Wigston. At this point the male line failed, but Richard had the satisfaction of providing handsomely for his daughter Elizabeth, who evidently married well; we know that her son, Thomas Kent, sold the land in Wigston to a wool merchant who used it to endow a hospital. And Richard just before his death was described in a cousin's will as "Richard Randolff, gentleman."[13]

Throughout the fifteenth century the better-off peasant families freed themselves from the encumbering vestiges of serfdom through their official posts or simply by defaulting on their services and paying a money fine. To describe the new status of such successful peasants, the word "yeoman" made its appearance in the English language. The yeoman was still subject to certain obligations to the lord and in addition to taxation by the state, but typically he had enough cash surplus to spend something on marriage feasts, baptismal gifts, and funeral masses. Often he found extra sources of income beyond sales of crops and animals. He could hire out his equipment—plow, cart, oxen—with or without his own or his sons' labor. His wife or other family member could brew ale. He might take in temporary lodgers, itinerant tinkers and carpenters, or pilgrims, since only the largest towns offered regular inns.[14]

But families at the middling as well as the affluent level made improvements in their condition. Besides acquiring land, they might renovate their dwelling, acquire additional animals and other chattels, marry sons and daughters profitably. Heiresses were almost as sought after on this level of society as on the higher one, while inheritance by indirect heirs in default of direct ones played the same role among the peasants as among barons. Long after the first visitation of the plague, entries continued to appear in manorial court rolls such as that in the Halesowen record of Agnes, widow of Philip Hypkis, who died in 1385 leaving a farmstead and other holdings. Following the payment of death duties (two oxen valued at sixteen shillings) there "came John le Warde the closest heir . . . namely son of her sister by blood, and claimed to succeed."[15]

Young peasants did not, however, leave their marriage arrangements to their parents as did noble youth. Instead, they actively courted, and in some places even organized their own village rituals. In Croscombe (Somerset), young men joined the Younglyngs' Guild, young women the Maidens' Guild. On a certain day the maidens blocked the village streets and permitted the young men to pass only on payment of a fine. Next day the Younglyngs blocked the streets and the maidens had to pay the fine, which in both cases went to the parish church. On May Day a king and queen were chosen, with dancing and games.[16]

Morality was more a concern of the preachers than of their parishioners, and virginity more valued by the former than by the latter. Premarital pregnancy was commonly a prelude and even a prerequisite to marriage, since a man wished to make certain that his wife would produce the children he needed to help on the land. Sex, love, and material interest interacted in familiar patterns. Joan Seustere in 1376 swore that she and Thomas Barbo had been married at Stourbridge Fair the Sunday after the Feast of Exaltations of the Holy Cross. Thomas admitted that he had promised to be true to her, but explained that he had only meant to have her as his mistress, not as his wife. The court pronounced a Solomon-like judgment. Thomas was ordered to say to Joan, "I accept you as my wife if, from now on, I have carnal knowledge of you." Joan acquiesced at once: "I accept you as my husband if, from now on, you have carnal knowledge of me." Twenty-five months later the court decided that the two were married.[17]

Whatever their courting freedom, young people on any level could not disregard the matchmaking concerns that preoccupied their elders. Few youths or maidens could be so empty-headed as to risk a marriage without land or chattels. Their elders, on the other hand, did not overlook nonmaterial considerations. In the fifteenth-century instructional poem "How the Wise Man Taught His Son," the father counsels against marriage for money but recommends that the son "wisely inquire" if the prospective bride is "meek, courteous, and wise," since it is better to eat homely fare in peace than to have "a hundred dishes" served with strife.[18]

Similarly, a companion poem, "How the Good Wife Taught Her Daughter," recommends that if only one man courts a girl she should "scorn him not, whatever he be." She should consult her friends on the choice of husband and, once married, keep domestic peace with "fair and meek words," managing the household tasks and the servants cheerfully and with order and firmness.[19]

The conventional marriage ceremony was now preceded by the reading of the banns as prescribed by the Fourth Lateran Council. In England the priest read the banns three times, with intervals of a few working days between. On the appointed date the bridal parties assembled at the church and the dower and dowry were announced. Merchet to the lord should have been paid by this time (by the bride's family) but often was not. The couple would probably already have enjoyed sex, might indeed already have a child, who was generally ruled legitimate if conceived between "trothplight" and marriage.[20]

Standing before the church door (the most public place in the village), the couple spoke vows that had changed little over the centuries: "I take thee, Agnes, to my wedded wife, to have and to hold, from this day forward, for better, for worse, for richer, for poorer, in sickness and in health, till death us depart, if holy church it will ordain, and thereto I plight thee my troth." The word "depart" had the sense of the verb "separate"; in later centuries it was altered to "do part." The rings were blessed and exchanged with the words "With this ring I thee wed and with my body I thee honor." If the couple wished, the wedding moved into the church and the priest said mass, but a common complaint among the country clergy was that the peasants preferred to economize on the ritual. A representative of the lord might be present to symbolize seigneurial interest.[21]

Most peasant marriages never found their way onto the docket of the Church court. But the troublesome clandestine marriage, without banns or public ceremony, still flourished, reluctantly blessed by Gratian, Peter Lombard, and Alexander III. A comparison of Church records indicates that in the late fourteenth century more words-of-the-present clandestine marriages took place in England than in France, where the Church courts treated such cases severely, with fines, orders to marry publicly, and excommunications. English courts generally dealt with the subject as a civil proceeding, usually with the woman as plaintiff.[22]

They dealt with it in extraordinary profusion. Examination by Michael M. Sheehan of a register for the Church court of Ely in the fourteenth century showed more than four fifths of the marriage cases to have involved clandestine unions.[23] Other English court records show vows exchanged in a variety of places: under an ash tree, in a bed, in a garden, in a blacksmith's shop, in a kitchen, at a tavern, and in the king's highway. Usually the woman claimed that marriage had taken place, the man denied it, and the principal mischief in the custom was perceived as the cloak it afforded to seduction.[24] In their retelling of the story of Dido and Aeneas, both Dante and Chaucer, in contrast to Vergil, sided with the woman, viewed as victim of an unacknowledged clandestine marriage.[25] However, many clandestine marriages were acted out before witnesses, whose public report of the event was regarded as a sort of substitute for banns and given credence by the Church courts (publica vox et fama). If the marriage had taken place but conflicted with a previous contract, or where the court's inquiry revealed an unsanctified menage, the couple were ordered to separate, or in appropriate cases, to marry. Sometimes the hearing was concluded by a marriage ceremony performed on the spot.[26]

In its practical application, Peter Lombard's "present consent" doctrine brought hairsplitting over wording. A distinction was drawn between "I will take you as my wife," ruled future (nonbinding) consent, and "I will have you as my wife," ruled present (firm) consent. Another legal conundrum was posed by conditional consent: "I will take you if my father consents," or if some other condition was fulfilled. First of all, when did such a condition have to be attached? John Sharp and Joan Broke entered into a contract in Rochester in 1442 "in a certain field near a ruined tower" by what the Church court recognized as words of present consent. As John and his friends sauntered off, Joan called, "Listen, if my master and friends are willing to agree, I will assent to that contract." John and his friends called back, "You are too late," meaning the contract was valid. But the court upheld Joan as having attached her condition soon enough for it to be honored.[27]

Authorities on canon law painstakingly identified and catalogued for the guidance of the courts a variety of future conditions:

If one party made the stipulation "If father consents," the condition was "effective" and had to be honored. But the condition "If you avoid offspring" was defined as "against the substance of marriage" and rendered invalid a marriage contracted under it. If one party stipulated an "impossible," that is, transparently frivolous, condition, such as "If you touch the sky with your finger," the court was instructed to disregard it.[28]

Among the peasants, divorce remained a rarity. Though consanguinity within the Church's forbidden degree might provide a pretext among the nobility, it did not work for peasants, who scarcely knew who their grandparents were, let alone their third and fourth cousins, and even if they did had no means, in the absence of written records, of proving such relationships. Furthermore, the very seriousness with which the laws of consanguinity were taken by both Church and people precluded their being put to cynical use. John Love had his eye on a good parcel of land that required three pounds for entry fee. Agnes Bentley promised to supply the fee if John would marry her daughter Alice. John was willing, but unfortunately had already had sex with a kinswoman of Alice and so was compelled to abandon the project.[29] In another case, John Tolle found Agnes Smith so desirable a match that he gave her twenty-four shillings to reserve herself for him. But this John also erred with a kinswoman of his intended bride, and found himself reduced to suing to recover his twenty-four shillings, which Agnes refused to hand over. John was left with neither wife nor shillings—and possibly a victim of collusion by two clever and unscrupulous women.[30]

In the rare cases in which annulment was granted, one English study showed the commonest ground to be bigamy, ahead of consanguinity or affinity. Nonconsummation after a reasonable period was sometimes accepted as grounds, following examination of the wife or even of the husband.[31] "Seven honest women" were appointed to confirm the wife's virginity and in most courts "seven honest men" deputed to verify the husband's impotence. In the York and Canterbury courts, however, this latter investigation was deemed more appropriately carried out by the seven honest women. In one recorded inspection at York, one honest woman "exposed her naked breasts, and with her hands warmed at the said fire, she held and rubbed the penis and testicles of the said John. And she embraced and frequently kissed the same John, and stirred him up in so far as she could to show his virility and potency, admonishing him that for shame he should then and there prove himself a man. And she says . . . that the whole time . . . the said penis was scarcely three inches long . . . remaining without any increase or decrease."[32]

If divorce was rare, separation was not. Informal separation, without benefit of court ruling, sometimes took place among both peasants and city craftsmen. Church courts also arranged formal separations, short of divorce—separations "from bed and board"—on grounds that included cruelty, adultery, impotence, and even mere incompatibility. In fourteenth-century Flanders a wife might leave home and then negotiate a property settlement with the aid of a Church court and the lay authorities.[33]

Most marriages endured, however, and even prospered. Peasant wills, which suddenly become abundant in the fifteenth century, testify to the affectionate regard of husbands for their wives, as well as for children, brothers and sisters, and godchildren. Wills began with stipulations about burial, followed by donations to the Church: the customary "mortuary" consisting of a cow or a horse, grain to be sold for "the upkeep of the torches" on the altar, wax for candles, money "for tithes forgotten," and provisions for the testator's "obit," a service to be said every year in his memory. Next were provisions for the widow, who was usually given the home tenement for life, or occasionally until the oldest son reached majority, or until she remarried. Other provisions for widows included their dower rights to a part of the property, return of the dowry, a separate house, money, and chattels, including pots and pans, livestock, and clothing.[34] The coroners' reports studied by Barbara Hanawalt confirm a variety of options actually accepted by peasant widows: use of the main house, use of a dower cottage, a room in the main house "and a place at the hearth," or a house and land separate from the home tenement.[35]

Children were also explicitly provided for in many fathers' wills, with guardianship entrusted to the widow (who paid a fee to the lord for the right) and property settled on the child. Bartholomew Atkyn, dying in Bedfordshire in 1500, wanted his eldest son John to become a priest, but if he did not he would receive the home farm, out of which he was to pay the legacies specified for the other children. And "if any child die, his portion to go to him who shall then have the greatest need."[36] Well-off and middling peasants perceived education as the key to opportunity for their children in the form of entry into the priesthood, the service of the lord, or a career in the law. Husbands enjoined wives to bring up children lovingly, and in the absence of a mother younger children were commended to the care of older ones, or to that of uncles, aunts, or grandparents.[37]

The maintenance contract continued to flourish, with its dual character as pension and transfer of holding. A study of contracts in East Anglia by Elaine Clark indicates that many retirement arrangements (one third to one half) were now made outside the family. Although informal, and therefore unrecorded, parent-child agreements were doubtless common, the increase in number of contracts with outsiders is significant, perhaps reflecting the severity of the plague among the very young. Aging parents might have no living children to take over their holding.[38]

When an elderly peasant could no longer perform his labor services, the manorial court intervened in the interest of the lord but also in that of the peasant himself, or herself. In 1382 at Hindolveston in Norfolk the jury reported that a "poor little woman" in the village, a widow with eighteen acres of land, was "feeble of body and simple of mind." The lord granted the land to her "nearest heir," ordering him to support her for life. In another Norfolk case in which a widow had no relations nearby, the lord assigned her holding to two villagers with the stipulation that they plow, sow, and harvest it and provide her with "all her necessities."[39]

More often, pensions were worked out voluntarily. Sometimes they were arranged by a third party. In 1407 John Whytyng of Wymondham (Norfolk) on his deathbed surrendered his farmstead and land to Simon Wellyng on condition that Simon provide John's widow with food and drink and sixteen bushels of malt a year, keep for her use six hens, a goose, and a cow, cultivate and sow an acre of land for her, and supply her with three shillings for clothing every Easter, plus a pair of shoes. She was also to have "freedom of entry" into her late husband's house, a place by the fire, and a bed.[40]

Most fifteenth-century pensions, however, were negotiated by the pensioners themselves, and involved bargaining that reflected the new affluence. Pensioners stipulated for payment of their debts, for their funeral expenses including masses, and for such extras as a horse to ride, a vat for brewing, an oven for baking, shears for cutting cloth, access to garden, well, and kitchen, storage space for grain, half the fruit on the farmstead, and again and again the right "to warm themselves at the fire." When a peasant named Henry Pekke died in South Elmham in 1408, his grandson and his widow worked out a settlement whereby she kept one ground-floor room and one upper room and a parcel of land "with free entry and exit for herself and her friends for life," plus a yearly ration of firewood and a stipend of eight shillings paid in quarterly installments. Her grandson was to keep her rooms in repair and to provide her "with the same food and drink that he himself has." If these did not suit her, she was to have an additional twelve pence yearly "on account of her displeasure."[41]

Poor cottagers had to make concessions. One old couple in Wymondham gave up not only their farmstead and their one acre of land but also all their bedding, carpets, napkins, utensils, and furnishings except two pots, two bowls, and two wooden chests; in another contract at Hindolveston, an elderly couple agreed to work for their new tenants as long as they were physically able, in return for lodgings in their former house and the food and drink that would normally be allotted to a servant.[42]

Though even poor people sometimes managed maintenance contracts, and though religious houses and private philanthropies tried to assist the old and impecunious, mainly by permitting them to beg at the church door, many peasants had nothing to offer a caretaker and ended up in the coroners' reports as dead of exposure or accident.[43] For these, old age was, in the words of the thirteenth-century preacher Humbert de Romans, "bitterer than winter with all its cold."[44]

In the classic story "The Divided Horsecloth," a father who has retired in his son's favor is about to be turned out of the house by the son, whose own little boy then indicates that he will do the same when the time comes. A fifteenth-century preacher told his congregation a similar story in one of the *exempla* (examples) with which medieval sermons were illustrated:*

There once was a rich man who, when he had had enough of the world and grew old and feeble and powerless, had a fair daughter and married her to a young man. And along with her he gave this young man his goods, his house, and all his land, in return for supporting him for the rest of his life. And the first year the young man fed him his own food and clothed him in his own clothing. And the second year he seated him at the end of the table and allowed him to fare somewhat worse than himself; both in meat and clothing. And the third year he seated him with the children on the floor at the end of the hearth, and the son-in-law said that he must move out of the chamber that he slept in, for his wife must lie there when she was delivered of her child. And on this pretext he put the old man out of his chamber and made him sleep in a little house at the utmost gate.

And when the man saw what he had been brought to, he sighed and sorrowed and searched for the best remedy. Then one day the old man came in to borrow a bushel basket. And when he had taken the basket to his house, he shut the door firmly and made a loud noise in the basket with old metal counters, as if he were counting money. And one of the children of the house followed him to see what he would do with the basket. And as he stood outside the door, he heard a great noise and thought that the old man had put his gold and silver in it, and went and told his father.

And when the son-in-law heard this, he went to him and said, "Father, you are old, and it would be good if you have any gold or silver that you entrust it to some good man to keep for your soul's sake." Then the old man answered, "I have a little money here in a coffer, some of which I will bequeath for my soul. And I want you to dispose of it when I am dead." And when he gave them back the basket, he left a [silver] penny inside, in a crack of the basket, for them to find.

And when they saw this, they brought the old man back to his chamber and to the table and to his clothing, and he lived as

*Rendered into modern English

before. Then when he was dead, they looked in the coffer and found nothing else but a little small mallet (such as was used to break up clods during plowing), on which was written that it should be used to smite anyone who was foolish enough to follow the example of the writer,

> *So that all the world well knows*
> *That whosoever gives up all his things*
> *Will go himself a-begging.*[45]

13.

A Family of the English Landed Gentry

In the final century of the Middle Ages, the shifting membership of the European aristocracy divided essentially into three tiers: the thin upper crust of the great regional lords, half royal and sovereign in their own territories; the larger castellan class of local lords; and the mass of knights and other free holders of lands sufficiently productive to support a noble life-style. In England the three classes were reduced to two, the barons who were the king's chief vassals, and the knights and gentry. The dividing line between these two as far as property was concerned was not rigid; some knights accumulated fortunes surpassing those of some barons. The real difference was that the lower tier was fairly easy to get into. The economic adjustments after the Black Death may have accelerated the process by which successful peasant and merchant families ascended, usually by degrees, to the lower aristocracy, through acquisition of property, fortunate marriage, or service to the king or great lord in peace or war.

One family that rose from the ranks of the prosperous Norfolk peasantry at the beginning of the fifteenth century was that of the Pastons.[1] A circumstantial account of their forebears written by a hostile contemporary named as their immediate antecedent one Clement Paston, a "good plain husband[man]," who lived in the Norfolk village of Paston and plowed his own land, took his own grain to the mill "on bare horseback" and brought back his own flour, carted his products to the market town of Winterton to sell, and who held "five score or six score acres of land" in Paston "with a little poor water mill running by a little river there." Evidently Clement was a well-to-do free peasant with sizable holdings in Paston, where his family had lived for at least two centuries. The Pastons were later constrained to prove before a royal council that their ancestors had not been villeins on either side of the family, in order to substantiate their claims on estates, and managed to satisfy the inquiry.[2]

Clement married Beatrix, the sister of Geoffrey of Somerton, a self-made lawyer. Clement borrowed to send his son William (born in 1378) to school, and with Geoffrey's help sent him to London to study law in the Inns of Court. William proved a capable lawyer, and was appointed in 1415 steward of the bishop of Norwich, in 1421 an officer of the Court of Common Pleas, and in 1429 a justice.

Meanwhile he bought enough land in Paston to become the largest landholder there and in 1420 married Agnes Berry, who was not only the daughter of a knight but an heiress. As dowry, she brought him one manor, and she stood to inherit three more; in return, William dowered her with a recently purchased manor at Oxnead. The couple had nine children, and by the time William died in 1444 were in possession of substantial estates.[3]

William's eldest son, John, born in 1421, attended Cambridge, studied law in London, and married an heiress of his own, Margaret Mauteby, through her acquiring still more property.[4] He soon had his hands full defending his holdings. The political disorders in the wake of English defeat in the Hundred Years War had begun, and local lords were employing armed retinues in private feuds reminiscent of those long fought by the Italian urban nobility. At the same time litigation, making liberal use of bribery and corruption, flourished in the courts. John and Margaret were soon embattled on both fronts. In London John fought a legal claim against his mother's dower lands at Oxnead. Margaret was besieged in their manor at Gresham by an armed band belonging to a certain Lord Molynes. The enemy battered down a wall and carried Margaret out bodily, but in the end the Pastons recovered Gresham and retained Oxnead.[5]

They presently experienced a dazzling turn of fortune that did not, however, spell the end of their troubles. Sir John Fastolf, a veteran captain and Knight of the Garter, had returned from the war to his native Norfolk enriched by rewards, spoils, and wise investments. Though his extensive properties in France were lost in the defeat, his estates in England brought him over a thousand pounds a year, permitting him to build himself a castle at Caister, on the site of the manor where he was born.[6]

Caister's architecture paid perfunctory tribute to its owner's military background in its moats and 98-foot tower, but aimed principally at comfort, and secondarily at show. Stone brought from France embellished the façade, while the interior was constructed from timber brought from Suffolk. Fastolf's coat of arms was carved on the wall of the Great Hall.[7]

In retirement, Fastolf proved a match for the age, quarrelsome and litigious, perpetually embroiled in troubles with his estate agents and his Norfolk neighbors. Apparently through a distant kinship with Margaret Paston, the old knight made the acquaintance of John Paston, who soon became not only his lawyer but his trusted friend and counselor. Fastolf's wife died in 1446 and he did not remarry; his only child, an illegitimate son who had become a monk, predeceased him, and he had no use for his only other relation, his wife's son by her first marriage. When the old soldier died in 1459, John Paston proved to be his sole heir.[8]

Outraged rival claimants at once forced the lawyer to employ all his skill to defend his vast inheritance: Caister Castle, ninety-four manors, houses in Yarmouth, Norwich, and Southwark, and a fortune in cash, jewels, plate, and furnishings. John Paston spent the rest of his life in fierce litigation, alternating with illegal seizures, assaults by hired ruffians, and even three brief terms in Fleet Prison in London. He finally died in London in 1466, worn out at the age of forty-five.[9]

A condition of the married life of John and Margaret Paston common to other couples of their period and class, and the one to which we owe their immense surviving correspondence, was that they spent much of it apart. While John fought the family's legal battles in London, Margaret remained in the country, managing and defending the estates, collecting the rents, selling products of the manors, ordering supplies from Norwich and Yarmouth, and running the household, while bearing an uncertain but large number of children, seven or possibly eight of whom survived to adulthood.[10]

Although John's and Margaret's letters are earnestly and ceaselessly occupied with business, they also express much reciprocal affection, on Margaret's side tinged with deference. Learning of an illness of his, she wrote: "By my troth, I had never so heavy a season as I had from the time that I knew of your sickness till I knew of your amending, and yet my heart is in no great ease, nor shall be, till I know that you be really well. . . . I pray you heartily that you will vouchsafe to send me a letter as hastily as you may, if writing be no inconvenience to you. . . . If I might have had my will, I should have been with you ere this time. . . . Almighty God have you in his keeping, and send you health."*[11]

When he failed to write, she worried: "If I had known that you should not have been at home before this time, I should have sent some man to you, for I think it right long till I have some good tidings from you."[12] And again: "I thank you heartily for your letter, for it was to me a great comfort to hear from you."[13] And: "Be not strange of writing letters to me betwixt this and the time that you come home. If I might, I would have one every day from you."[14] Once when he was angry with her, she wrote him from Norwich: "Right worshipful husband, I recommend me to you, beseeching you that you be not displeased with me, though my simpleness caused you for to be displeased. . . . By my troth, it is not my will neither to do nor say that should cause you for to be displeased; and if I have done, I am sorry thereof, and will amend it. Wherefore I beseech you to forgive me, and that you bear no heaviness in your heart against me, for your displeasure should be too heavy for me to endure with."[15] In his turn, John was concerned about Margaret's health: "John Hobbs tells me that you are sickly, which I do not like to hear. Praying you heartily that you take what may do you ease and spare not; and in anywise, take no thought nor too much labor for these matters [of business] nor set it not so to your heart that you fare the worse for it."[16]

The education of the two oldest of the Paston boys, both con-

---

*The Paston letters are quoted here in "translation," which consists mainly of modernizing the spelling.

fusingly named John, remains undocumented. The eldest was attached to the king's household at the age of nineteen and was knighted at twenty-one (although his father had himself paid a fine to be excused from the expensive and burdensome honor). Apparently not aggressive enough to make an impression at court, the young man made few useful connections and returned home to live.[17] His brother John II, similarly dispatched to the duke of Norfolk's household, remained in the duke's service and contracted valuable friendships.[18] The three younger sons, Walter, Edmund, and William, like their father and uncles, were university-educated. Institutions of higher learning now catered to the nobility and gentry as well as to the Church. The forms of clerical education, including "first tonsure," lingered, but no longer committed the student to the priestly calling. Fifteenth-century university graduates might seek posts as secretaries or other officials in great households, or might simply flaunt their polish at court or at home on their own estates.[19]

Pedagogical discipline remained rigorous, with the cordial approval of parents. The elder John Paston's brother Clement, as a student at Cambridge, was the subject of a letter from his mother Agnes inquiring about his progress, offering his master ten marks for giving the boy special attention, and stipulating, "If he has not done well, nor will not amend, pray [his master] that he will truly belash him till he will amend. So did the last master, and the best that he ever had, at Cambridge."[20] The learning that was so conscientiously instilled remained Latin: reading, writing, speaking. The new aristocracy's glibness with Ovid and Cicero would have startled their illiterate forebears.

Girls did not share in the advanced education open to boys, but they usually acquired literacy in English. Margaret Paston's numerous letters in many different hands show that normally she had recourse to amanuenses, though sometimes, perhaps in the interest of privacy, performing the labor herself. The multiplicity of hands shows that many of those around her could write.[21] The Paston daughters, Margery and Anne, were probably taught their letters at home; we know, however, that Anne was sent to live for a time with some cousins, Sir William and Lady Calthorpe, who wrote Margaret Paston in 1470 declaring that they were temporarily short of money and therefore needed to reduce their household; furthermore, Anne was "growing tall, and it were time to purvey her a marriage." Margaret worried that Anne might have somehow displeased Sir William, and urged John to talk to her cousin Robert Clere in London to see if he would take the girl. Otherwise "I shall have to send for her, and with me she will but waste her time"; London was a better marriage market than Norfolk.[22]

It is above all in the realm of courtship and marriage that the Paston correspondence provides a unique picture: fifteenth-century life: marriage strategies and clashes between parental wishes and children's consent.

For the male members of the family, consent was not a problem; they arranged their own marriages, or asked friends and relatives to find suitable matches, or were free not to marry at all, as they wished. Sir John, as the eldest son, was heir to the greater part of the family estates, including Caister Castle, yet no marriage arrangements were made for him and in fact he never married, though he left an illegitimate child.[23]

In 1468, twenty-six-year-old Sir John and his younger brother John II traveled to Flanders, in the company of a courtier friend, Thomas Lord Scales, to attend the wedding of the king's sister Margaret to the duke of Burgundy. In Calais, Sir John met a relative of Lord Scales, a lady named Mistress Anne Haute, who was also a kinswoman of the queen. The couple exchanged what they thought were binding words, though even the principals seemed unsure whether they were "words of the future" or "words of the present."

Sir John's interest in the lady was largely practical: he hoped that her influential friends would help him in his litigation over Fastolf's legacy. Shortly after the exchange of vows, Lord Scales wrote the duke of Norfolk, who had bought a claim from one of the trustees of Fastolf's will, intervening in Sir John's behalf, with the explanation that "a marriage is fully concluded between Sir John Paston and my right near kinswoman Haute." Since he and Sir John were now kinsmen, "nature must compel me to show my good will, assistance, and favour in such things as concern his inheritance."[24]

Lord Scales spoke of the transaction as a marriage, but Margaret Paston referred to it as a betrothal. She wrote her son: "I have not much knowledge of your ensurance [engagement], but if you are ensured, I pray God send you joy and worship together, and so I trust you shall have it if it be as is reported of her; and as concerns God you are as greatly bound to her as if you were married, and therefore I charge you . . . that you be as true to her as if she were married to you in all degrees. . . ." But, she reminded him, he should not be "too hasty to be married till you were more sure of your livelihood [income]," in a word, until he had "more surety" of Fastolf's estate.[25] Margaret proved a shrewd assessor of marriage-market stocks; Sir John's "surety" of his estate was slow to mature, and his marriage project faltered.

Though Sir John and Mistress Haute continued to move in the same court circles, they lived apart and rarely saw each other, and the match remained in limbo.[26] Three years after the first meeting, he had difficulty in even obtaining an interview with her. In September of 1471 he wrote, optimistically, "I had almost spoken with Mistress Anne Haute, but I did not; nevertheless this next term I hope to take one way with her or other; she is agreed to speak with me, and hopes to do me ease, as she says."[27] The following February he managed to arrange a meeting "at a pretty leisure," and reported to John II that "blessed be God, we be as far forth as we were heretofore . . . and I promised her that at the next leisure that I could find thereto I would come again and see her."[28]

The slow-motion courtship at last discouraged him and he decided to break off the affair. Now, despite her lack of enthusiasm for the match, Mistress Haute became concerned about its ambiguous status. They had never completed the marriage, had not lived together, and had rarely even seen each other in private, but "Mistress Haute's conscience" required an annulment from Rome.[29] Sir John made inquiry of his proctor, a Church official who was in touch with the Curia. An annulment, he was told, could be had—for a thousand ducats. Another "Rome runner," however, assured him that it could be done for a hundred or two hundred at the most. "He wrote to me also that the pope does this nowadays very frequently."[30] Four years later his mother was still wishing he were "well-delivered of Mistress Haute, and then I would trust that you should do the better [make a better match],"[31] but only in 1477, when Sir John was thirty-five years old, was the dispensation granted and the imperfect marriage finally "at a perfect end." What the dispensation cost Sir John is uncertain, but evidently it was closer to the thousand ducats than the hundred. "As God help me," he wrote, "I know not where to borrow." The whole matrimonial enterprise had lasted nine years.[32]

In 1478 Sir John was presented with another marriage prospect, a woman "right nigh to the Queen's blood." Margaret Paston hoped this match too would help them with the rearguard battles they were still fighting over Fastolf's estate, but Sir John died in 1479 before arrangements could be concluded.[33]

Concurrently with his own marital misadventures Sir John participated as matchmaker and go-between in those of his younger brother. The Paston correspondence records no fewer than eight unsuccessful undertakings by John II, most with decided economic motives, ending unexpectedly enough with a love match. The mother of one young gentlewoman, Alice Boleyn, disapproved. Sir John could "in no wise find her agreeable that you should have her daughter, for all the privy means that I could make." Alice had another suitor, a man named Crosby, but "there is no marriage concluded between them," and John still had a chance, since he was "personable." Sir John advised: "Bear yourself as lowly to the mother as you know how, but to the maid not too lowly, neither that you be too eager to speed matters, nor too sorry to fail." In the end he did fail.[34]

Another lady, Katherine Dudley, was "nothing displeased" with Sir John's proposals on his brother's behalf, but was beset with suitors. Sir John reported: "She does not know how many gentlemen love her; she is full of love. . . . She says she will have no one for this two year, and I believe her; for I think she is content with her life as it is."[35] A third young lady was offended in some way by John II's behavior—Sir John told him that he had "a little chafed it, but I cannot tell how."[36] In the case of the fourth prospect, the daughter of a London draper named Eberton, Sir John told the lady's mother that his brother had been offered a marriage with a dowry of more than six hundred marks, but that his passion for her daughter was such that he would marry her with less. Despite the alleged ardor, the project fell through.[37] Concurrently with the courting of Elizabeth Eberton, John II was investigating the possibilities of a rich widow of Blackfriars. He asked Sir John to speak with her husband's executor, an apothecary, to ask "what

[she] is worth, and what her husband's name was."[38] Next came a Lady Walgrave, whom Sir John tried to persuade to accept his brother's ring, but who replied that she intended to stick to the refusal she had given the suitor himself. Sir John rather fancied the lady and indulged in a bit of flirtatious byplay with her, stealing a muskball (perfume ball) to send to John and then telling her what he had done. "She was not displeased, nor forbade it not but that you should have the keeping of her muskball, wherefore do with it as you like." The ring, however, was returned to the sender.[39]

At this point John II declared to his brother that he was desperate and would marry anyone with a decent fortune, even "some old thrifty draff wife [ale wife]."[40] A friend named Fitzwalter had a marriageable sister, and Sir John was asked to "entreat him, [that] she might come into Christian men's hands."[41] Early in 1477 a Mistress Barley was suggested, and Sir John was delegated to investigate. He reported that the undertaking was "but a bare thing. I saw her for your sake. She is a little one; she may be a woman hereafter, if she be not old now. Her person seems thirteen years of age; her years men say be full eighteen."[42]

While Sir John was sounding out Mistress Barley, John II was making overtures to a young lady named Margery Brews, of whom he had heard through a friend,[43] and who, when they met, made an impression powerful enough to permit John, at least, to overlook the smallness of her dowry. Margery was promised 100 pounds by her father, Sir Thomas Brews, and her grandfather would contribute another 50 marks (33 1/3 pounds) as a wedding gift.

Margery's mother, Elizabeth Brews, extolled her daughter's personal qualities: "I shall give you . . . a witty gentlewoman, and if I say it, both good and virtuous; for if I should take money for her, I would not give her for a thousand pounds. But I trust you so much that I would think her well bestowed on you."[44] John agreed, for a little later Elizabeth wrote thanking him for "the great cheer you made me and all my folk the last time that I was in Norwich. . . . You have made [Margery] such an advocate for you that I may never have rest night nor day for [her] calling and crying upon [me] to bring the said matter to effect."[45] She reminded him that the following Friday was "Saint Valentine's Day,

A fifteenth-century wedding. (The Pierpont Morgan Library, MS 394, f. 9v)

and every bird chooses him a mate; and if you will come on Thursday at night and arrange it so that you may stay till Monday, I trust to God that you shall so speak to my husband . . . that we shall bring the matter to a conclusion. For 'It is but a simple oak/ That is cut down at the first stroke.' "[46]

Still, the dowry problem had to be settled. Letters followed from Margery to John. Addressing him as her "right well-beloved Valentine," she wrote that her mother had worked "full diligently" to persuade her father to increase the dowry, but without success, "for which I am full sorry. But if you love me, as I trust verily that you do, you will not leave me therefore; for if you had not half the livelihood that you have . . . I would not forsake you. . . . Wherefore, if you could be content with that [dowry] and my poor person, I would be the merriest maiden on earth."[47]

John himself was apparently willing, but his mother and brother resisted. Sir John even had some lingering thoughts about Lady Walgrave. "Bickerton tells me that [Margery] loves you well," he wrote John. ". . . Nevertheless [Lady Walgrave] sings well with the harp."[48]

Sir Thomas Brews now raised his dowry offer to two hundred marks, and added a trousseau of one hundred marks ("for her chamber and raiment"), plus board and room for the couple for three years after the marriage.[49] John arranged a meeting of the two families at Norwich on March 8, urging his mother to lend her "good help," for the "matter was in a reasonably good way" and he hoped it would work out. "I believe there is not a kinder woman living than I shall have for mother-in-law, if the matter takes, nor yet a kinder father-in-law than I shall have, though he be hard to me as yet."[50]

Sir Thomas sweetened the offer further, writing Sir John that he would lend the prospective bridegroom one hundred pounds that he had earmarked for the marriage of a younger daughter, with an added twenty pounds, the whole to be repaid "by such easy days as the contract, which I send you herewith, specifies." He was, however, "right loath to bestow so much upon one daughter that her other sisters should fare the worse."[51]

Sir Thomas, however, was also concerned about Margery's jointure. Margaret Paston named the income from the manor of Sweynsthorpe and ten marks a year from the manor of Sparham.

In response, Sir Thomas repeated his offer of two hundred marks, plus two or three years' free board, or three hundred marks without the board, the sum payable in yearly installments of fifty marks. Or, he would give four hundred marks, payable in yearly installments, if Margaret would endow Margery and John with the entire profits of both manors for life.[52]

Margaret apparently favored the proposal, but Sir John demurred. "I would be as glad as any man . . . that he should have her . . . considering her person, her youth, and the stock that she comes from, the love on both sides, the tender favour that she is in with her father and mother," and also the parents' evident affection for John and their own good character, "which predicts that it is likely the maid should be virtuous and good." But the Sparham manor was entailed; what if they had daughters, and Margery died and John remarried and produced a son by his second wife? "That son should have no land, though he was his father's heir." He knew of a similar case in Kent where there had been litigation between a gentleman and his sister. For these and "other causes," Sir John could not "ratify, grant, or confirm the said gift to my brother."[53]

Things were at a standstill. In June a meeting between the two families was cancelled because of Elizabeth Brews's illness. At John II's instruction, Margaret Paston wrote Elizabeth telling her that Sir John had refused to ratify the grant of Sparham. "Madam, he is my son, and I cannot find it in my heart to become a daily petitioner of his. . . . Madam, you are a mother as well as I, whereby I pray you will take it no other wise than well that I may not do by John Paston as you will have me do; for, madam . . . I have to purvey for more of my children than him, some of whom are old enough to tell me that I am not treating them fairly to give John Paston so much and them so little."[54]

Just when affairs looked darkest, an agreement was reached. The details disappointingly do not appear in the letters, but on August 7 Sir John wrote Margaret that he had "granted [John II] as much as I may," indicating a last-minute concession.[55] Late in August the marriage took place, and it proved happy and durable. In December Margery wrote John, in London on business: "I pray you that you will wear the ring with the image of Saint Margaret that I sent you for a remembrance till you come home; you have left me such a remembrance that makes me think about you both day and night when I would sleep."[56] Four years later her sentiments were unchanged, and given freer expression: "Sir, I pray you, if you tarry long at London that it will please you to send for me, for I think it long since I lay in your arms."[57]

The other Paston brothers underwent similar trials and errors. In 1478, the year after his own marriage, John II was looking for a wife for Edmund. He wrote his mother from Sweynesthorpe, "I heard while I was in London where there was a goodly young woman to marry, which was daughter to one Seff, a mercer, and she shall have £200 in money to her marriage, and twenty marks a year of land after the decease of a stepmother of hers, who is about fifty years of age; and before I left London, I spoke with some of the maid's friends and have gotten their good will to have her married to my brother Edmund."[58] This plan failed, but in 1479 Edmund was negotiating with the family of Katherine, widow of William Clippesby, whom he married the following year, going to live at her house in Oby.[59]

Margaret Paston's favorite son, Walter, went off to Oxford in 1472. "I were loath to lose him," she wrote, "for I trust to have more joy of him that I have of them that are older,"[60] but the young man died shortly after graduation. The youngest Paston son, William, while still at Eton, fell in love with the sister of the bride at the wedding of a classmate. The girl, Margaret Alborow, was "eighteen or nineteen at the farthest"; her father was dead, and her only sibling was the sister who had just married. "Her mother commanded her to make me good cheer, and so in good faith she did." Edmund urged John II to call on the family when they returned to London and inquire about their wealth. The dowry—"the money and plate"—he wrote, was "ready whensoever she were wedded," but her income would not begin until her mother died. "And as for her beauty, judge you that when you see her, if so be that you take the trouble, and especially behold her hands, for if it be as it is told me, she is disposed to get fat." Whether owing to this consideration or not, nothing more is heard of Mistress Alborow.[61]

Two years later Edmund was recommending another prospect to William, "a widow in worsted, which was wife to one Bolt, a worsted merchant, and [he was] worth £1000, and gave to his wife

100 marks in money, stuff of household, and plate to the value of 100 marks, and £10 a year in land. . . . She is called a fair gentle-woman. . . . She . . . is about 30 years old and has only two children."[62] This venture also failed, and whether William ever married is unknown.

The role of the women of the Paston family in their own mar-riage arrangements was passive, and their freedom limited. The story of Elizabeth, sister of John Paston, Senior, shows the mar-riage game in a harsher light. Elizabeth was offered Stephen Scrope, Sir John Fastolf's stepson, who was wealthy but fifty years old to her twenty and disfigured by smallpox. Elizabeth resisted, but Agnes Paston, her strong-willed mother, continued the negotiations. A cousin suggested a "goodly man" in the Inner Temple in London whose father had just died, but cautioned that John should "give Scrope a goodly answer . . . till you be sure of a better [prospect]."

Elizabeth remaining intractable, Agnes locked her in her room and by way of persuasion beat her once or twice a week, "some-times twice in one day, and her head broken in two or three places." To these arguments Elizabeth at last surrendered, stipulat-ing only that "her children and her may inherit, and she have reasonable jointure."[63] But now Sir John Fastolf decided to cancel the project.

Others blossomed. In 1453 Margaret Paston wrote her husband: "Knyvet the heir is for to marry; both his wife and child be dead." John should inquire "what his livelihood is."[64] Negotiations were opened with a Sir William Oldhall,[65] then with a country squire named John Clopton, who apparently proved not rich enough.[66] Next Lord Grey of Hastings wrote John saying that he knew of "a gentleman of 400 marks of livelihood, who is a great gentleman born and of good blood."[67] The "great gentleman" proved to be Lord Grey's own ward, Harry Grey, whose marriage he was eager to arrange in order to lay his hands on Elizabeth's dowry. When young Harry insisted that he "would have his marriage money himself," his greedy uncle dropped the matter.[68]

In 1457 Elizabeth was sent to London to live with Lady Pole, and the following year she married Robert Poynings, second son of Lord Poynings, a man of her own choice. She reported to her mother after her marriage that "my master, my best beloved as

you call him, and I must needs call him so now, for I find no cause
to do other and trust to Jesus I shall not . . . is full kind to me, and
is as busy as he can to make me sure of my jointure," for which,
in fact, he had given a bond of one thousand pounds to her mother
and brothers. Elizabeth begged Agnes to show her appreciation of
his assiduity about the jointure by being prompt with the payment
of one hundred marks of the dowry due "at the beginning of this
term," along with "the remnant of the money of father's will," so
that her husband could pay off his sureties for the bond. Elizabeth
also urged her "tender and good mother" to pay Lady Pole "for
all the costs [incurred by] me before my marriage."[69]

The daughters of John and Margaret caused their parents even
more concern. Anne, the younger, alarmed them by falling in love
with a family servant named John Pampyng. While they sought
an appropriate husband for her, John II wrote, "Among all things,
I pray you beware that the old love of Pampyng renew not."[70]
William Yelverton, son of a judge who had been a co-executor of
Fastolf's will, was proposed as a candidate, and John II reported
that "he said but late that he would have her if she had her money,
and else not; wherefore I think that they be not very sure."[71] Three
years later, "Skipwith's son and heir of Lincolnshire, a man with
five or six marks a year," was suggested.[72] Eventually Anne was
wed to Yelverton in the summer of 1477.

Margery Paston, some five years older than Anne, actually committed the transgression that Anne had threatened. At seventeen,
following several projects that had misfired, she suddenly announced that she had plighted herself to the Pastons' bailiff, Richard Calle. The family was aghast. A rich mercer's widow was one
matter, but a servant, even a high-ranking servant, was something
else. Mother and grandmother stormed and threatened and kept
Margery incommunicado. Calle managed to smuggle a letter to her
in which he addressed her "with heart full sorrowful . . . for this
life that we lead now is neither pleasure to God nor to the world,
considering the great bond of matrimony that is made between us,
and also the great love that hath been, and as I trust yet is betwixt
us, and as on my part never greater. . . . Meseems it is a thousand
years ago since I spoke with you. I had liever than all the goods
in the world [that] I might be with you. . . . I understand, lady, you
have had as much sorrow for me as any gentlewoman has had in

the world. . . . This is a painful life that we lead." He urged Margery to tell her family the truth, for if they knew that he and Margery had taken vows and were therefore "bound by the law of God," they "would not damn their souls for us." He closed by warning her to burn the letter, "for I would that no man should see it."[73]

After three years of impasse, apparently Calle or his friends requested the intervention of the bishop of Norwich. The bishop's procedure was firm, judicious, and effective, and was carried out over Margaret Paston's protest, as she reported in an angry letter to Sir John. "On pain of cursing," the bishop commanded her to have Margery brought before him the next day. "I said plainly that I would neither bring her nor send her; and then he said that he would send for her himself and charged that she should be at her liberty to come."

The following day, he began the interview by reminding Margery "how she was born, what kin and friends she had, and [that she] should have more if she were ruled and guided by them; and if she did not, what rebuke, and shame, and loss it should be to her." Then he asked her what words she had said to Calle. "And she rehearsed what she had said, and . . . if those words made it not sure, she said boldly that she would make sure ere she went thence, for she said she thought in her conscience she was bound, whatsoever the words were. These lewd words grieve me and her granddam," Margaret wrote, "as much as all the remnant." Calle was examined separately to see if his account agreed with Margery's. The bishop then announced that he would pronounce judgment on the Wednesday or Thursday after Michaelmas (September 29).

Margaret reported: "When I heard say what [Margery's] demeanor was, I charged my servants that she should not be received in my house." The threat was carried out. When Margery was brought back to the Pastons' Norwich house, the family chaplain stood in the door and turned her away. The bishop had to find lodging for her until the judgment was pronounced.

Margaret concluded her long communiqué to Sir John: "I pray you and require you that you take it not pensily [sadly], for I know well it goes right near your heart, and so does it to mine and to others; but remember you, and so do I, that we have lost of her but a brethel [worthless person], and set it the less to heart, for if she had been good, whatsoever she had been, it should not have been as it was, for if [Calle] were dead at this hour, she should never be at my heart as she was."

In reply to a previous mention by Sir John of the possibility of seeking a divorce, Margaret appended an admonition "that you do not, nor cause another to do, that which should offend God and your conscience, for if you do, or cause for to be done, God will take vengeance thereupon, and you should put yourself and others in great jeopardy; for know well, she shall full sore repent her lewdness hereafter, and I pray God she might so."[74]

The bishop's decision was in the young couple's favor, and Margery and Calle were formally married the following year. Strangely enough, Calle retained his post as bailiff and continued to oversee the family properties, but the Pastons treated Margery as if she were dead, and their business correspondence with Calle remained coldly impersonal, devoid of the normal terms recognizing kinship. When Margaret died in 1484, she left only twenty pounds to Margery's eldest child, the same amount that she bequeathed to Sir John's illegitimate offspring. This was the only recognition of the Calles in her will.[75]

All these endless marriage projects, negotiations, misfires, disappointments, successes, and calamities were played out against the continuous background of warfare, legal and actual, over the great Fastolf inheritance. In 1469, in the midst of the confrontation over Richard Calle, the duke of Norfolk sent an armed force to besiege Caister Castle. John II, commanding the small garrison, was forced to capitulate, to the distress of Margaret Paston, who felt that Sir John had not adequately supported his brother with supplies.[76] Loss of the castle's dependent manors brought a severe impairment of the Paston family's revenues, but when Margaret wrote Sir John in London proposing that he reduce his scale of living, he responded with counterproposals for advance collection of rents, sale of manors, and pawn of silver.[77] In the end Sir John's unheroic and thriftless posture was rewarded. Outliving the duke of Norfolk and profiting from the passivity of the dowager duchess, he legally and peacefully reoccupied Caister.[78] It was the end, at long last, of the Pastons' private war.

Through all their vicissitudes, however, like the rest of the aristocracy high and low, the Pastons managed to live comfortably. "The greater part of the earnings of the [late medieval] nobility," according to Kenneth McFarlane, "was used to achieve a higher standard of luxury."[79] At Caister Castle, Sir John Paston spent his late years in rooms warmed by blazing fires, their stone walls softened by woven tapestries. Beds were canopied and curtained and outfitted with mattresses, featherbeds, and silk coverlets. A scattering of chairs were added to the benches and stools, now padded with cushions. Expensive clothes and fine linens were stored in chests. John Paston II asked his mother to send him certain deeds locked in a box inside the coffer in his bedroom. Other letters mention chests containing money, books, clothes, and account books. The kitchen at Caister was equipped with a profusion of brass pots, utensils, spits, and knives; the buttery with bottles, tankards, and silver dishes, salt cellars, and basins. In the buttery of their manor house at Hellesdon the Pastons kept a store of silver spoons, knives, tablecloths, towels, napkins, candlesticks, and vinegar barrels.[80]

Besides comfort and luxury, the dwellings of the rich now also provided a substantial measure of privacy. Where the lord of Guines's twelfth-century stronghold (and many thirteenth-century castles) had a chamber for the lord and lady and dormitories for everyone else, private bedrooms were now the rule. Despite Sir John Fastolf's childlessness, Caister Castle had twenty-six. Where formerly the entire household had dined and socialized in the great hall, now the family slept, ate, and relaxed in state apartments, away from servants, tenants, and other inferiors. The new privacy brought a new separation between lords and dependents, a new distance between rich and poor. In *Piers Plowman*, William Langland expressed regret: "Now every rich man eats by himself/ In a private parlor to be rid of poor men . . . and leaves the great hall."[81]

Like others of the new aristocracy, Sir John Paston had a taste for literature. Gutenberg's technology not yet having replaced the hand copyist, he employed professional scribes and illuminators to copy books for him. One copyist charged one or two pence per page, a rate that made books expensive but left the copyist in penury. Pressing his patron for an overdue bill and at the same time begging him to send any cast-off gowns, he wrote, "I have great need. . . . God knows, whom I beseech preserve you from all adversity, I am somewhat acquainted with it."[82] Among the manuscripts that he copied for Sir John were a little book on medicine and a Great Book containing several different works: a 26-page treatise on the duties of knighthood, a 120-page treatise on war in four books, an 86-page work on wisdom, a 28-page Rules of Chivalry, and finally 90 pages comprising the poet John Lydgate's *Falls of Princes*. Other volumes also contained assortments from several authors. Some manuscripts remained unbound or were stitched in paper covers.[83]

The new nobility enjoyed display. The liveried retinues of the great lords served largely to show off wealth, as did their often numerous chapel personnel. Among the lesser nobility a funeral was a useful occasion for conspicuous employment. On John Paston's death in 1466, his body was accompanied from London to Norfolk by "twelve poor men," six on either side of the bier, carrying torches. At St. Peter's Hungate in Norwich a dirge was sung by an assemblage of friars, priests, boys in surplices, and clerks, with nuns from Norman's Hospital, hired bell ringers, and watchers swelling the audience. The funeral repast included poultry, fish, eggs, bread, and eighteen barrels of beer.[84]

The Paston family waxed under the Tudors and Stuarts, went into temporary eclipse during the Civil War, and under the Restoration rose to new heights of status as earls of Yarmouth. At this tardy date it imitated its noble precursors of the twelfth century by having its genealogy recorded. Exactly like his twelfth-century predecessors, the Paston genealogist traced the lineage to a fabled adventurer, "Wulstan de Paston," whom he unblushingly presented as one of the Norman conquerors. The more it changed, the more it was the same thing.[85]

Sir John Fastolf had raised himself to the nobility by training for war. John Paston had achieved the same rise by training for law. Sir John Paston was content to inherit his nobility and use it for his vanity and self-indulgence. Caister Castle had thus witnessed a three-generation revolution that neatly reflected the larger change going on in England and, with variations, throughout Europe. The new noble family, higher or lower, lived a better material life than had the old one, gave its children a superior education, and even began to cultivate literary and artistic tastes (tapestries, windows, architecture) at the expense of its former preoccupation with violence. It continued to negotiate its marriages with an overpowering emphasis on money and status (but now and again accidentally fell in love), and it continued jealously to guard and aggressively to pursue its property interests, with lawsuits and bribes largely, but not entirely, substituted for raids and sieges. Primogeniture was solidly established, in England fortified by entail. Wives remained subordinate to husbands, and in some ways suffered a diminution of status. On the other hand, they gained the protection of jointure and continued to exercise major responsibility in estate and household management.

14.

A Merchant's Family in Fifteenth-Century Florence

The Black Death and accompanying lesser calamities slowed but did not halt the economic resurgence of Europe, which regained momentum in the fifteenth century. Among the wealthy, the dramatic growth in commerce, especially long-distance commerce in luxury goods, contributed to the creation of a true merchant class with its own family customs, attitudes, and ideology. This class was especially prominent in Italy, Europe's vanguard country, and nowhere more so than in Florence, which by the same token is among the best documented of medieval cities and regions. A large new trove of information was recently provided by a systematic examination of the *catasto,* or tax-information roll, of 1427. An international team of scholars headed by David Herlihy and Christiane Klapisch-Zuber has subjected this immense archive to a computer-assisted analysis whose results have been reported in a number of scholarly works, notably *Tuscans and Their Families,* by the two principal investigators.

In addition to the *catasto,* Florence provides many other sources of information, one valuable form of which is the "book of the affairs of the [business] house" kept by many merchant heads-of-family. Such a book was compiled by Lapo di Giovanni Niccolini dei Sirigatti, a prosperous wool merchant. Covering the years 1379 to 1421, his account illuminates family life among the

wealthy city dwellers of the time, and may be qualified and supplemented by information from the *catasto* and elsewhere.

Lapo's elaborate name derives from that of his father, Giovanni
Niccolini dei Sirigatti: he is Lapo di Giovanni, or "Giovanni's
Lapo." As he gives his name in the introduction to his book, in
fact, it is a veritable genealogy in the male line: "This is the book
of Lapo di Giovanni di Lapo di Niccholino de' Ruzza d'Arigho di
Luchese di Bonavia di Luchese de' Sirigatti."[1] His father was Giovanni, his grandfather Lapo. His great-grandfather Niccolino, a
silk merchant, had founded the branch of the family that bore his
name, splitting off from the older Sirigatti lineage when it moved
to Florence from nearby Passignano early in the fourteenth century. From Niccolino, Lapo then traces his ancestry back to Luchese de' Sirigatti, a thirteenth-century forebear who is the
remotest ancestor that he knows.[2]

Wealthy Florentines, whose kinship connections were freighted
with such importance, had long used family names. Among the
urban masses and in the rural countryside, here as in England, such
names made slower progress. By the time of the *catasto*, 37 percent
of Florentine taxpayers are listed by "apparent family name." In
Prato only 19 percent are so listed, and in Montepulciano only 7
percent. Others are identified for the tax collector only by append-
ing the individual father's given name, and sometimes that of the
grandfather or great-grandfather. As everywhere, names of
professions or occupations, places of residence or origin, and nicknames supply additional identification.

First names, especially of firstborn children, commonly repro-
duced the name of a grandfather or other forebear, a custom
known as "remaking the name." If the first child died in infancy
the same name was often given to a later infant. Sometimes even
if the first child lived, the same name was given to a second (a
custom not limited to Tuscany, as shown by the Paston nomenclature).[3]

At the time of his death in 1381, Lapo's father Giovanni had
headed a household consisting of a wife, two unmarried sons, and
one married (elder) son with his wife and children.[4] Such a three-
generational household was not uncommon among the wealthy.
In 1427 one out of eight Florentine families contained three gener-

House in Prato of Francesco Datini, a contemporary of Lapo di Niccolini. (Azienda Autonoma di Turismo, Prato)

ations, with the figure rising to nearly one in three in the country.[5] The Florentine custom by which the paterfamilias retained his position till death was an obvious factor in creating such households, with earlier marriage ages for rural men increasing the proportion.

At the time of his father's death, two of Lapo's sisters were married and living elsewhere and a third was already widowed. In distribution as well as size and structure, the family was typical of upper-class Florence. Following Giovanni's death, when the estate was divided, the two younger sons, Lapo and Filippo, remained with their mother in the main house in the Via del Palagio del Podestà, Santo Spirito quarter, while the eldest son, Niccolaio, received the house next door. In 1384 both the younger sons married, Lapo staying on in the main house while Filippo found another, doubtless nearby.[6] The settlement was typical. Though partible male inheritance was the Florentine rule, most heirs came to an agreement whereby one eventually succeeded, with his family, to the ancestral home.[7]

Lapo's book does not describe his house, but it must have corresponded to the general type of patrician house built in the fourteenth century: tall and square, with a narrow street frontage, its façade perhaps ornamented with a religious fresco. The ground floor contained loggia or parlor, kitchen, perhaps a guest room, and the business offices. The second floor probably contained a "great room" or salon in front, a master bedroom, and other family bedrooms. The upper floor or floors contained servants' quarters and perhaps a summer loggia or penthouse for retreat in hot weather. Every important room had a fireplace. Lighting was by tallow candles, horn lanterns, and brass oil lamps. Furniture included trestle tables, wooden chairs as well as benches, curtained beds, and chests, similar to the comforts of Caister Castle. Whether Lapo indulged in paintings and sculpture by way of interior decoration he does not say, but Renaissance art was already moving out of churches and cathedrals into private residences. In the rear of the house a kitchen garden probably grew, and perhaps a flower garden as well.[8]

Next door was a house also belonging to Lapo that included a barber shop and public bath. The two barbers paid a rent of six gold florins, against which they charged Lapo three florins nineteen solidi for shaving him, cutting his own and his children's hair, and allowing his family to bathe.[9]

Lapo also owned more than one house in the country, on his several inherited or purchased properties. His principal country seat included a large garden and vineyard, a house for the "Signori" and one for the tenant who worked the land. Lapo's father had paid 775 gold florins for the property, but had had the contract made out for 700, "in order," as Lapo blandly records, "to pay a lower tax."[10]

Lapo felt an affinity not only for his own but for all the houses belonging to the family, writing, "Although [some] houses were left to many institutions and to many persons and given by some as a dowry, they have finally returned to us, and may it please God that it be so for long years to come."[11] He did not, however, succeed in his apparent aim of grouping the city properties into a united stronghold. Such concentrations of allied families, pioneered in twelfth-century Genoa, had become traditional in cities, and by now were even a little archaic in Italy. Their exact character, and even a proper nomenclature to distinguish their varying types, awaits further study. In Ghent, David Nicholas found such kinship groupings (which he alternately calls clans and kindreds) actively functioning in the fourteenth century, allocating property among heirs, helping to arrange marriages, pursuing blood feuds, and collecting blood price for murders.[12] In Genoa the fifteenth-century grouping were called *alberghi*, had the main characteristics of clans, and numbered as many as six hundred members.[13] In Florence they were termed *consorterie* and were patrilineages—male descent lines—which, however, dominated their districts by attracting to themselves numbers of lesser families, either poor relations or clients, cemented into a coalition by nepotism and charity. As in Genoa, the Florentine kinship group remained strictly an instrument of the wealthy class.[14]

Lapo di Giovanni Niccolini married twice. By his first wife he had seven children, one of whom died in infancy, by his second six.[15] His mother was still alive at eighty, and, following a second widowhood, his sister Monna exercised the traditional right of *tornato* (return) and joined Lapo with her daughter Lena. For a time the house on the Via del Palagio contained Lapo's first cousin Lena Aghinetti, a non-cloistered nun whose presence was deemed auspicious as a sort of good-luck charm. In about 1418, Lapo's roof sheltered fifteen persons, not counting servants.[16]

The return of the plague in 1417 robbed Lapo of a son and a daughter living at home, and also of a married daughter and son-in-law whose three orphaned daughters he now took in. Niccolaio, the dead son, who had drawn his father's criticism as "too big a spender of his own money and that of others," was thirty-one but still unmarried at the time of his death.[17] The second son, Giovanni, married after Niccolaio's death and departed the house. Biagio, Lapo's third son, studied law in Bologna and set up for himself. A fourth son took orders and became abbot of the monastery of San Salvi.[18] At the time of the *catasto* of 1427, the household was reduced to eight family members: Lapo, his second wife, their five children, and a grandnephew. The three orphaned granddaughters, for whose care Lapo had been reimbursed by their father's family, had evidently married and departed. Among the servants was a woman slave.[19] The servant shortage created by the Black Death and its high-wage aftermath had brought a revival of the slave trade, but on a limited scale. At one time slaves had been imported in considerable numbers from eastern Europe (Slavs giving their name to the word "slaves"), a commerce ended by the conversion of that region to Christianity, the Church forbidding enslavement of Christians. Those imported in the fourteenth century, chiefly women, were for the most part Tatars and Circassians. The *catasto* listed only 300 slaves in Florence's population of nearly 40,000.[20]

Of forty-six blood relatives mentioned by Lapo in his book, twenty-three at one period or another enjoyed his hospitality in the Via del Palagio.[21] Lapo's open-house policy was shared by Florence's wealthy, who alone had houses commodious enough to practice it. Slightly fewer than 4 percent of city homes in 1427 contained more than 10 persons, including servants, while the average household counted only 3.8 persons. Those of the Florentine countryside averaged 4.7 persons and sometimes consisted of more than one family "sharing bread and wine," in the tax collector's words. Such occupation was usually by related families, especially those of brothers, in other words, the "joint family" model.[22]

Lapo's enlarged household was also strictly familial. Christiane Klapisch-Zuber points out that in contrast to his forty-six blood relatives and fifty or more affines (in-laws) his book mentions only a handful of friends.[23] David Herlihy believes that the late medieval urban household suffered psychologically from its loss of members to the plague and other mortality and so tended to emphasize membership in the larger kinship group.[24]

Household management was in the hands of Lapo's wife, who may have profited from the advice given by Leon Battista Alberti's remarkable *Books of the Family (I Libri della Famiglia)*. Alberti emphasized orderly arrangements: "Everything should be set where it is absolutely safe, yet accessible and ready to hand, while encumbering the house as little as possible. . . . Be sure that when something has been used it is immediately put back in its place."[25] All keys should be kept in the hands of the mistress except those used daily for the pantry and storeroom, which should be entrusted to a reliable servant. Purchases should be made by the husband from the wife's checklist, which should be foresighted enough to permit buying commodities "at the lowest cost and of the highest quality. Things bought . . . out of season [are often] unclean, about to spoil, and expensive." True thrift, according to Alberti, meant always buying quality, in food or clothing.[26]

Alberti's work, highly popular in the fifteenth century and a permanent Italian classic, has been described as painting the Florentine merchant class to which Lapo di Giovanni belonged "in the fullness of its good sense and sober ostentation."[27] Marriage for this class remained as relentlessly purposeful as ever, but Alberti did not overlook personal attributes in a wife. He laid stress on "an honorable manner," pointing out that "a wild, prodigal, greasy, drunken woman may be beautiful of feature, but no one would call her a beautiful wife," and concluding, "In a bride, therefore, a man must first seek beauty of mind, that is, good conduct and virtue." He considered that a woman should be neither too fat nor too thin, but of "a joyful nature, fresh and lively." Much to the point was the likelihood that she would become a mother. "Loveliness, grace, and charm" were all very well, but a man should "choose a woman who is well made for bearing children, with the kind of constitution that promises to make them strong and big. There's an old proverb, 'When you pick your wife, you choose your children.' "[28]

Of paramount importance in merchant-class marriage was the formation of family alliances. Lapo's father chose spouses for his children in keeping with either of two principles, to marry them out and upward, gaining alliances with better situated families, or to marry them within the neighborhood and so strengthen local ties. One of Lapo's sisters received a dowry of 975 florins, reflecting a movement upward socially in the form of alliance with a prestigious landed family. Lapo's brother Niccolaio was married to a young woman of the Bardi lineage, the greatest in Florence, memorialized in the Via dei Bardi where their numerous households and enterprises clustered. Lapo and his brother Filippo married within their own Santo Spirito quarter, gaining dowries of 700 and 800 florins.[29]

Lapo's second marriage, contracted by himself, was to Caterina, a Milanese lady, the widowed daughter of another wool merchant.[30] It brought him a dowry of 1,000 florins, reflecting Lapo's prestige at this point in his career, when he had achieved substantial business success and had held city office. His two daughters received dowries of 700 and 1,000 florins, representing a calculation of the difference in social status of the Altovita and Albizzi families into which they were entering.[31] On the subject of dowry, the sage Alberti argued for one "middling in size, certain and prompt rather than large, vague, or promised for an indefinite future," and pictured the too frequent scene in which the new wife reinforced with her tears the pleas of her family for more time to pay the dowry in light of various debts, setbacks, and losses. The counsel accorded with a general premise favored by Alberti of marrying neither too far above nor too far below one's station. Not only might superior in-laws overshadow a man but the ever-present hazard of a business collapse might drag him down with them. So "let them be equals . . . modest and respectable people." And on the whole, since one couldn't have everything, better a good wife than a large dowry, and better also good kinsmen.[32]

Commonly the calculation of the dowry included the value of the trousseau. As with all nonmoney gifts, donor and recipient might not arrive at identical figures. Gregorio Dati, a silk merchant and neighbor of Lapo di Giovanni in the Santo Spirito quarter, was promised by his bride's two cousins a dowry of 900 gold florins. Four days after the wedding he received from the bank of Giacomino and Company the sum of 800 gold florins and a trousseau which the cousins valued at 106 florins, "in the light of which they deducted six florins from another account, leaving me the equivalent of one hundred gold florins. But from what I heard from her and what I saw myself, they had overestimated it by thirty florins or more. However, from politeness, I said nothing about this."[33]

Besides the in-laws, a marriage brought further social and business alliances in the form of *compari,* or godparent relations, typically neighbors of equal or if possible greater affluence. Some of Lapo's children's godparents acted gratis, *"per l'amore di Dio,"* while others were recruited with gifts. All were "good men . . . of substance and power," as recommended by merchant-author Giovanni Morelli.[34] The number of godparents had long been fixed at three, two of the same sex as the infant. Close kin were excluded, as were potential marriage partners, since godparenthood created "spiritual kinship" and activated the incest taboo.[35] It also involved gift giving in the opposite direction. Recruited as a sponsor, Francesco Datini jestingly asked a friend, "How much does it cost to make a child a Christian?" The friend answered in the same vein, "According to how much you want to do yourself honor!" Cakes were customary, but Datini on at least one occasion made a gift of three ells of fine cloth.[36]

Among the Florentine elite the revived dowry had long since grown to notorious size. Dante in *Paradiso* (1315–1321) had harked all the way back to the days of his great-great-grandfather, "when the birth of a daughter did not yet appall/The father, for the marrying age and dowry/Were not immoderate. . . ."[37] In a family with several daughters the plainest were thriftily earmarked for the convent. In 1425 the city government of Florence, casting about for quick revenue, took cognizance of the dowry problem by establishing the *Monte delle Doti*, a savings-bond institution in which a father could invest for a girl child's future. After some experimentation with terms and interest rates, the *Monte delle Doti* became extremely popular.[38] Payoff was made to the new husband upon consummation of the marriage. Typically he was eager to collect. Consequently it often happened that days or even weeks before she was scheduled to move into her new home the act was carried out at the bride's house, to permit the groom to hasten first thing in the morning to the *Monte delle Doti*.

If marriage expenses oppressed the bride's father, they also weighed on the groom and his family. The old *donatio propter nuptias* (bride gift) had been limited by Florentine law to fifty lire, but a husband of high status was expected to lavish on his beloved a stream of jewels, furs, clothing, and furnishings to "make the chamber" where they were to sleep. This counter-trousseau had by the fifteenth century grown so extravagant that a coterie of professional trousseau lenders had sprung up.

Marriage economics helped preserve the traditional Florentine age differential. The plague had reduced marriage ages since a century earlier, when three of Lapo's male forebears had passed their fortieth birthdays before their nuptials,[39] but in 1427 the average male of all classes still did not wed for the first time before he was thirty. Young peasant grooms of the countryside, needing wives to help run the farm, averaged only twenty-five years, but a Florentine businessman was typically in his mid-thirties. He chose a bride half his age; the average city bride of all classes was only eighteen, and rich girls married younger than poor girls.[40] The situation may have had a character of self-fulfilling prophecy.

In Florence, where as in Genoa partible inheritance among males reigned, young men received their share of the estate—money, house, movables—on emancipation, usually just before marriage, which also involved no trifling direct expenditure. Families pressed to supply dowries for daughters might be inclined to postpone emancipating sons. Lapo di Giovanni recorded the act by which he emancipated his son Giovanni:

"I made a deed of arrangement with Giovanni my son on the seventh of November, 1418. . . . My reason for making the settlement was that, Giovanni being about twenty-six years of age, I wanted to give him a wife. My family being very large, I decided to separate from him and to give him his rightful share of my property, and much more as well. This I did because he was the eldest of my surviving sons. The deed was drawn up by Ser Antonio, a Florentine notary."[41] Lapo had already emancipated his other sons by his first marriage. His sons by his second marriage had not yet reached majority at his death.

Few fathers could afford Lapo's liberality. The streets of Florence were filled with young bachelors of good family, a gilded youth prone to dissipation and violence, a crowd of Tybalts and Mercutios. Meantime the poorer girls, handicapped in the dowry competition, in the long run overtook their wealthy sisters by working as servants until they had accumulated savings for a modest trousseau and cash sufficient to attract an apprentice coppersmith or a fishmonger's son.

Among wealthy Florentines, the marriage enterprise was deliberate, time-consuming, and ceremonious, at an opposite extreme from the clandestine peasant marriages whose casual vows so often vexed the Church courts. When the union of two Florentine merchant families was complete, there could be no doubt that a marriage had indeed taken place. In the metaphor of Christiane Klapisch-Zuber, the event consisted of a triptych, whose predella, or base, was formed by the inaugural conference of the two parties, commonly initiated by a *sensale* or marriage broker, or by a friend of both families. Agreement reached on the fundamental points—desirability of the alliance, size of dowry—the two sets of parents, accompanied by close kinsmen but not by the principals to the marriage, met again to put the treaty in writing and seal it with an exchange of handclasps, the *impalmamento*. Bride and groom now met, the young man calling on his betrothed with gifts of rings or jewels, and usually being invited to stay for dinner.[42]

The machinery of betrothal obviously worked against the possibility of a bride's exercising choice, and yet it would not be safe to conclude that all Florentine brides tamely accepted whatever was served them. The popular preacher Fra Bernardino of Siena encouraged the girls' independence with the story of the "very short young man" who, taken to meet his intended, found her a "fine tall young woman." To his brother's query, "Well, does she please you?" he answered, "Indeed she does." But the girl, examining his small stature, cried, "But you do not please me!" To which the preacher added with satisfaction, "Served him right!"[43]

The first panel of the triptych was a solemn public gathering, usually in church, of friends and relatives that included only the male members of the immediate families. The groom was present but not the bride; instead, her father or whatever man had authority over her made the official pledge of betrothal to her future husband. The groom in turn promised to accept his bride within the specified time and on the conditions agreed to. A notary recorded the terms in a paper *(sponsalia)* that stopped short of legal compulsion, but that was highly binding on both parties, with a feud likely to result if either sought to break off.[44]

In the second panel of the triptych, women members of the family and friends joined the men at the bride's house for "ring day."[45] The notary now posed the formal questions prescribed by the Church to assure free consent, then drew the bride's right hand toward the bridegroom, who placed the nuptial ring on her finger. (Elsewhere the priest blessed the ring and handed it to the groom.) Gifts were presented by the groom and his family and friends, and a repast was offered by the bride's family while the notary completed his composition of the *instrumentum matrimonii*.[46]

The bride did not immediately move into her new home, but her trousseau was delivered thither with a flourish of publicity. The husband's reciprocal gifts extended over a long period, and might still later be returned, presumably with the bride's acquiescence, to the relative or professional lender who had supplied them. Strictly temporary were the rings that Florentine custom exacted

Wedding of Lucrezia Malavolti and Conte Roberto Sanseverino, by Sano di Pietro, Siena, Archivio di Stato. (Alinari)

from the husband's women relatives by way of welcoming the bride into her new family and that she, in her turn, gave to subsequent new brides. Gifts of food at the wedding feast represented a similar continuity, for the bride later joined in the preparations of wedding confections for others.

The third panel of the triptych was the *nozze:* To make the marriage *perfetto,* meaning primarily to publicize it thoroughly, the bride was transported to the house of her husband, crowned and costumed, by torchlight, riding a white palfrey and escorted by a troop of her husband's friends. In Rome a part of the *nozze* was a stop at the church, where the couple heard mass and received a blessing; in Florence the church service was optional.[47]

If the union had not already been consummated, it was now, amid feasting and entertainment that might continue for several days. The lengthy sequence was subject to variations, including the telescoping of two of the panels into one. The less affluent classes were more likely to include a religious element, which outside Italy now existed nearly everywhere, if only in the form of speaking the vows at the church door.

A final ritual, a sort of community postscript to the formalities, widely popular throughout Europe, was known in France and England as the *charivari*, in Italy as the *mattinata*. In France, masked revelers serenaded the bridal couple with noisy improvised instruments. In Italy the masks were omitted but the music was even rowdier, the *rumore* (racket) provoking numerous statutes as well as the Church's condemnation. Remarrying widows and widowers were especially favored with the *charivari*, which often concluded with a brawl. In Avignon, fines levied on participants were used to finance street cleaning. In Modena the *mattinata* was tamed into a civilized arrangement whereby the noise makers were bought off with a bribe sufficient to permit a celebration at the inn while real musicians were dispatched to serenade the conjugal couple.[48]

The age differential between husbands and wives created early widowhoods and consequent remarriages in which, paradoxically, the differential was likely to be even larger, older men, widowers or not, showing a distinct preference for younger women. An older widow, perhaps like Lapo's sister Monna a woman twice widowed, usually had to go home to her family, where she might not receive an enthusiastic welcome, especially if she brought little with her. In some cases a widow might be impelled to leave her husband's house because it contained one or more of his brothers, to whom she was forbidden marriage or sex by the incest prohibition. If she was left in solitude, she ran another risk, that to her reputation. The pleasures of sex, once tasted, were thought dangerously addictive. The clergy were suspect companions, especially the mendicant orders, who, according to Boccaccio, were "great consolers of widows."[49] Fra Bernardino, who had a story for every occasion, warned the widows in his congregation to "take care" with the tale of the priest who had rescued a woman from a brothel. To keep herself from temptation, she had him wall her up in a "hermitage" with only a small hole to speak through. But while the two were communicating via the hole, "each of them had those thoughts that sometimes come to one," she invited him in, and "let us not drag it out, soon she was with child. And what did all this come from? From not taking enough care."[50]

A fifteenth-century Florentine widow normally enjoyed financial security, based on the recovery of her dowry. Although freely utilized by the husband during his lifetime, the dowry never

Fra Bernardino preaching to his congregation (separated by sex), by Neroccio di Bartolomeo, Palazzo Comunale, Siena. (Alinari)

ceased to be the wife's property, and, to defend her interests, the law accorded her rights ahead of her husband's creditors and even her husband if his profligacy or mismanagement threatened to dissipate it.[51]

The remarrying young widow (or the girl marrying a widower) frequently found herself confronted with another problem: stepchildren. Fra Bernardino asserted that the young bride of an older husband moving into her new home might find "stepsons and love them so little that she grudges them even their food . . . or if she finds a daughter-in-law . . . peace lasts a very short time. And oh, oh, oh, if there is a mother-in-law—I will say nothing; you know it for yourselves. Little peace; the happy time is soon over."[52] Stepchildren sometimes sued stepparents over rights to property, though wills often show even-handed treatment of all children.

Stepchildren aside, the pattern of young bride and older husband gave the fifteenth-century wife an especially sensitive role in the family, in a first marriage roughly midway in age between father and children. Child-rearing was done mainly by her, and, since the middle-aged husband was unlikely to survive to his children's adulthood, she did much of it alone. Moralists suspected the overmaternal upbringing of children of contributing to the turbulence of Florentine youth. "Mothers say 'no' to no request," according to poet Maffeo Vegio. "They let [the children] have their way; they take their side when they complain about the hurts of their playmates or the blows of their teachers, just as if . . . they themselves were injured. Finally, they allow them complete license for whatever they may want. . . . What could be called more monstrous than this easy and permissive education, which mothers in particular are wont to follow?" Fathers should share in the responsibility of raising the children.[53]

One important function that was usually performed by the father was that of choosing a wet nurse (balia). Widely employed among the late medieval aristocracy, in Florence wet-nursing had by this time descended to the middle class. Wet nurses were, in the words of a carnival song, "young married women well-experienced in our art, we can swaddle the baby in a flash."[54] Some wives of Florentine craftsmen nursed the infants of merchants and bankers while putting their own babies out to nurse with peasant women at a lower rate; the fee paid by the wealthy non-nursing mother gave both the nursing mothers an equal profit.

The wet nurse sometimes moved into the house of the infant, but much more commonly (four times out of five in one study) she took the baby to her own home, often at a distance outside the city. Transported in a basket aboard a donkey led by a servant, such infants remained entirely separated from their families for eighteen months or more.[55] The practice was viewed unfavorably by the preachers, not on spiritual but on practical grounds: "You give your child to be suckled by a sow," Fra Bernardino told his parishioners, "where he picks up the habits of his nurse. . . . And when he comes home you cry, 'I know not whom you are like; this is no son of ours!' "[56] As for the milk of animals—goat, sheep, cow—it was regarded as at best useful in a pinch. The child "nourished on animal milk doesn't have perfect wits," according to Paolo da Certaldo in an advice book. All agreed that a baby resembled a plant that required nurturing by proper soil. Michelangelo, who was put out to nurse to the wife of a stonecutter in 1475, jokingly claimed that with his nurse's milk he had imbibed "the hammer and chisels I use for my statues."[57] Fathers were at pains to find nurses of sound physical and moral character, and in the contract specified "good and healthy milk."[58]

The baby's return home from the nursing sojourn was evidently a signal for rejoicing, giving the father the opportunity to express his affection, often in a way already time-honored. Alberti is at pains to criticize the paternal practice of tossing offspring in the air. Babies, according to Alberti, needed to be handled with the utmost gentleness, and in fact were best consigned exclusively to the arms of their mothers. "The age which follows," however, is "full of delight" for both parents and toddlers, "accompanied by general laughter. The child begins to make known his wishes and partly to express them in words. The whole family listens and the whole neighborhood repeats his sayings, not without joyful and merry discussion. . . . On his ways, infinite hopes are founded, wonderful evidence is seen of subtle intelligence and keen memory, and so everyone says that small children are the comfort and delight of their fathers and of the old people of the family."[59]

Education, in Alberti's view, was indispensable "for any person who must manage and govern things," an attitude unmistakably shared by the Florentine elite. According to the fourteenth-century chronicler Giovanni Villani, 60 percent of Florentine children even at that early date attended school.[60] Learning began even before formal schooling. A letter from eight-year-old Piero de' Medici to his father, Lorenzo, in 1479 reports: "We are all well and studying. Giovanni is beginning to spell. Lucrezia sews, sings, and reads. . . . Luisa begins to say a few little words. Contessina fills the house with her noise." In the fifteenth century most middle-class and wealthy children began formal instruction at about seven in the schools of the commune. Their education came in three stages: first, learning to read and write; second, learning to do accounting, by this time using the Arabic numerals taught to Europe by Leonardo Fibonacci; third, entering on active apprenticeship in a bank or mercantile house.[61]

"If there is anything which combines handsomely with nobility or is a worthy adornment in human life," wrote Alberti, "or gives grace, authority, and reputation to a family, certainly it is the cultivation of letters. . . . A father should make sure that his sons devote themselves seriously to their studies. He should teach his children to read and write correctly. . . . They must learn the abacus . . . make the acquaintance of geometry . . . the poets, orators, philosophers . . . good morals may be gained as well as a knowledge of literature." Contemporary textbooks in "barbarous" Latin drew the scorn of Alberti, who insisted on the pure Latin of Cicero, Livy, and Sallust.[62]

Though Florentine girls sometimes attended school, their educational requirements were relaxed, compared with those of boys. They might be enrolled in a religious establishment, to remain either until they married or permanently, but might or might not learn their letters. Margherita Datini, wife of Francesco Datini of Prato, acquired literacy only as a mature woman, in order to correspond in privacy with her often absent husband.[63] Even for patrician women, training in household duties took precedence over book learning. Fra Bernardino admonished parents to teach their daughters "to sew, to cut out, to spin, to sweep, to cook, to wash their own heads and their brothers', to do the household washing, and to serve at table. Let them not be like the girl who, when she went to her husband, could not cook an egg!"[64]

Discipline was par excellence the domain of the father, who in the eyes of Alberti should exercise it with measured restraint and unlimited vigilance: "The duty of the father is not only, as they say, to stock the cupboard and the cradle. He ought, far more, to watch over and guard the family from all sides, to check over and consider the whole company [including the servants], to examine all the practices of every member, inside and outside the house, and to correct and improve every bad habit. He ought preferably to use reasonable rather than indignant words, authority rather than power."[65]

Especially to be curbed were the grown-up young men of the household. The good father "knows how to . . . restrain the spirits of the young men. . . . He must never allow them to try something irresponsible and wild, either for revenge or to satisfy some youthful and frivolous optimism."[66] A father, Alberti summed up, "must always act like a father, not odious but dignified, not overly familiar, but kind. Every father and elder should remember always that power sustained by force has always, inevitably, proved less stable than authority maintained by love. No fear can last very long; love lasts much longer."[67]

Alberti's humanistic rationalism was the voice of the future. That of the past continued to be heard. Fra Giovanni Domenici recommended a parent-child relationship that would have accorded with the views of a Roman *paterfamilias:* "At least twice a day" children should be made to "kneel down reverently at their father's and mother's knee and ask their blessing . . . and on rising, bend their head and kiss their father's hand. . . . They should not presume to speak in their father's and mother's presence, even when they are bearded men, but only to listen and answer."[68] And further: "A son is his father's and mother's thing and may therefore be beaten as much as they wish." A widowed mother must take on the father's role and deal the "slaps and floggings." To teach both justice and patience, discipline should be imposed even on a son of twenty-five.[69]

Girls, everyone agreed, required the most vigilant supervision. "Keep your eye upon [your daughter]," warned Fra Bernardino. "If she does not stay quietly at home spinning and weaving, but runs to the window at every sound—then, if you don't chastise her, you will see her bring you to shame. . . . Beware how you let [young girls] go to feasts or weddings. . . . Let them have nothing to do with servants. Let them not have too much converse even with their relations; for if you then find them pregnant, you need not ask how such a thing came about. Do not trust them in your kinsmen's houses. . . . And never, never, never let them sleep with their own brothers, as they begin to grow bigger; for the Devil is subtle. . . . Hardly trust [your daughter] even to her father. . . ."[70] Despite such ceaseless preoccupation with the sin of incest, surviving records show few actual cases. As far as ordinary chastity went, however, Fra Bernardino's warnings to parents seem well founded. A popular book of etiquette and dress offered instructions for a bride on how to appear a virgin if she was not.[71]

Illegitimate children now came for the first time to be recognized as a social problem requiring government attention. In the 1420s Florence instituted the world's first foundling asylum, the famous *Ospedale degli Innocenti*, whose revolutionary design by Brunelleschi is credited with the inauguration of Renaissance architecture.[72] Like its successors in all countries, it hardly sufficed to cope with the problem, augmented as it was by numerous orphans with no relatives to take them in. Christiane Klapisch-Zuber's study of

Florentine records reveals the sad childhoods of small vagabonds and beggars, of older children who supported siblings, of girls sold by their parents, of babies left at church doors. Adoption, a solution of considerable effectiveness in later times, and well known to ancient Rome, was little practiced in the Middle Ages.[73]

Despite the numbers of unwanted children, the Church hardened its attitude toward contraception. The biblical story of the sin of Onan was advanced as an explicit condemnation of the widely used technique of coitus interruptus. Another technique, sodomy, was denounced as a degrading sin. Dante alluded to it, and in the next century Benvenuto Cellini was accused in Paris of relations with a girl "in the Italian fashion."[74] Material means, physical obstructions of the vagina, as well as such nostrums as Pierre Clergue's herb and other magical or semimagical practices, were widely used, the popularity of their purpose suggested by a proverb in Latin that descended to modern times: *"Si non caste, tamen caute,"* "If not chaste, then cautious," or "If you can't be good, be careful."[75] David Herlihy believes that contraceptive practices in sum may have had demographic effects, though age at marriage and other nondeliberate factors were doubtless far more significant.[76] The practice of wet-nursing had the effect of reducing the interval between pregnancies for mothers who did not nurse and increasing it for those who did. Florentine statistics show that among two categories of women who typically nursed infants, peasant mothers had more babies than poor city mothers.[77] Rich city mothers, who put their babies out to nurse, were more fertile than the poor, and better able to protect infants from illness and hazard. Their households were "overflowing with young people and children."[78]

Old age brought its hardships even for wealthy Florentines, but a Lapo di Giovanni Niccolini could call on more material comforts than could his forebears. He also benefited from the Tuscan regional custom of keeping the *capo di famiglia* enthroned as long as he drew breath. The obedience and respect inculcated in children were explicitly extended to their parents' advanced age, for which the preachers prescribed kindness and forbearance. "Men are not like oxen, which grow tougher as they grow older," observed Fra Bernardino. "If [your father] is ill, irascible in speech, and stormy in temper, strew his path with roses."[79] Given the continuing power of the *capo di famiglia*, the adjuration was as prudent as it was humane.

Lapo di Giovanni lived till 1430, after serving in several important public offices. At the time of his death he was governor *(vicario)* of the castle of Vico Pisano.[80] His son Paolo recorded his death and burial with a reverence through which can be glimpsed more than a trace of self-satisfaction with the cost of the obsequies:

> Almighty God called to himself the blessed soul of Lapo, my father, son of Giovanni Niccolini. May God of his pity and mercy have given his soul true pardon, and this was on the twenty-fourth of December, 1430, at the tenth hour. . . . And we had the body of the said Lapo brought from Vico Pisano to Florence in a sealed coffin on the twenty-sixth of December, 1430, and we deposited the said coffin in San Jacopo tra le Fosse on the same day at the hour of vespers. And then we had him buried on the twenty-seventh of December in the evening in the Church of Santa Croce of Florence in the tomb of Giovanni, his father, at the foot of the high altar, where the others of our family are buried, and the marble slab is there with the name of the said Giovanni inscribed on it and our arms are in the middle. . . . And then on the fourth of January we celebrated the funeral service and the commemoration of the said Lapo my father, as it was our duty and according to our wish, because he had been a man of great worth and much honored in all the principal offices of our country both at home and abroad. Though it was a very unpleasant time of war and pestilence, and though we had the heaviest taxes and little substance, we considered his honor and ours above our interest, as good sons should do. We spent a great deal, as appears in the book of the heirs of the said Lapo, written by the hand of Bernardo Niccolini.

The funeral included banners, coats of arms, and flags, borne on foot and on horseback, signifying Lapo's many distinctions, business and political, and numerous clergy: ". . . It was a great expense, and we four younger sons, Paolo, Lorenzo, Bernardo, and Otto, paid everything, also the expenses of the vigil. . . . For all these things may God be praised and thanked, because I spent my fourth part with good will, and so I hope did the other three."[81]

Marriage and the Family
After the Black Death

The plague that crept across Europe in 1347–1349 in many places devastated a region already suffering from economic and demographic decline. Despite the unparalleled ferocity of the epidemic and its several recurrences, the medieval family demonstrated remarkable resilience in recovery, partly compensating for its losses through earlier marriage and production of more children. Tenantless holdings were peaceably transferred, usually to relatives, and despite some increases in social friction, large-scale turmoil was generally avoided.

Depopulation even had certain positive effects. As wages rose and land prices fell, serfdom gave way to free tenure and hired labor. Fifteenth-century houses expanded in size and improved in construction and furnishing, especially for the urban affluent. Surviving peasant families increased their holdings and made better deals with their landlords. Profiting from newly available educational facilities, some of these families, such as the Pastons of England, waxed sufficiently prosperous to rise from the lower classes into the gentry.

Marriage remained an economic enterprise, the dowry growing larger and more important than ever. Marriage negotiations among wealthy families of both country and city were deliberate and ceremonious, and more often involved religious ritual. Yet affection was possible in arranged marriages, as the Paston letters prove, and determined young people married even in the face of their parents' objections.

V.

The End of the Middle Ages

15.

Legacy

By the last decade of the fifteenth century the completion of the Reconquest had created a new political power in the kingdom of Spain, formed from the union of Castile and Aragon, whose sovereigns sponsored the voyage of a sailor-entrepreneur from Genoa, city of businessmen, that inadvertently discovered the New World. The opening of the age of European exploration and colonization, coming on top of the technological revolutions of printing and firearms, and soon followed by the Protestant Reformation, provided later historians with a convenient stopping point for the Middle Ages.

The Reformation brought a fresh perspective to questions relating to marriage and the family, while the new economic environment had profound long-term impact on both. Viewed over the thousand years of the Middle Ages, the two institutions appear in some respects almost static by comparison with the changes that have shaped and shaken them since. Yet the Middle Ages brought large transformations, essential to preparing the way for the modern family. Both Romans and barbarians would have found marriage and the family in 1500 radically different from what they had known.

The single most important change in the European family between Roman times and the Reformation was the reduction in its functions. Religion was now the property of the Christian Church, justice had passed into the hands of lay and ecclesiastical courts.

Feudal custom, craft guilds, national governments and armed forces, schools and universities had further impinged on the family's economic, social, and educational roles.

Nevertheless, the household-family's place as society's fundamental building block remained unchallenged, and in one direction had been enhanced. The larger kinship group—clan, lineage, or kindred—had lost relative importance. What had happened was not, as once imagined, a "progressive nuclearization" of the family but something more complicated. It included such dramatic resurgences of the supra-family as the rise of the patrilineage among the landed nobility in the eleventh and twelfth centuries and the rise of the great patrician clans or lineages of the Italian cities at approximately the same time. The power of clan or kindred waxed and waned with the power of the State; when government was weak, the supra-family was strong, and as government acquired durable vitality, the clan withered. To the vertical descent group, the Middle Ages on the contrary gave a permanent significance through the adoption of surnames, history reversing the order in which the individual acquires names in life by bestowing first names first and last names last.

In size and shape the household through the medieval millennium presented every conceivable permutation but underwent no progressive development. At the end as at the beginning, there were differences among different kinds of families: peasant families differed from aristocratic, poor from rich (contrary to the modern proverb, the rich had more children), city from country (for one thing, money was easier to divide among children than was land). At the end as at the beginning, at any given moment most families were "imperfect," that is, exhibited either subtractions or additions or both to the conventional image of conjugal pair plus children.

And at the end of the period as at the beginning, it may be that people lived only fleetingly in the family environment they really preferred. Richard Ring's hypothesis about the ninth-century peasants of the Farfa polyptych has a haunting quality. If the people of Farfa longed for the security and companionship of a large circle of close relatives, they could hardly have been alone in their preference. In fifteenth-century Florence, Leon Battista Alberti wrote: "I would want all my family to live under one roof, to warm themselves at one hearth, and to seat themselves at one table."[1] The stem and joint families conceived by Frédéric Le Play, and identified respectively with the peasants of open-field and woodland country by George Homans, may indeed represent natural ideals, frustrated by merciless reality. The history of the family, here as in other aspects, seems to call for new psychological and emotional tools and approaches.

The danger of reaching conclusions on the basis of insufficient information has been demonstrated. The hypothesis advanced in the 1960s and 1970s by Philippe Ariès, Lawrence Stone, and Edward Shorter to the effect that medieval families led impoverished emotional lives has not survived subsequent research. Evidence for marital and parental sentiment does not abound, especially in the earlier centuries where all documentation is scarce. But sufficient information has been found to demonstrate that familial affection was present among Romans, Franks, Anglo-Saxons, thirteenth-century English peasants, fifteenth-century Italian merchants, and other members of the large cast of medieval people. In David Herlihy's words, "The medieval family was never dead to sentiment; it is only poor in sources."[2] In light of recent scholarship, controversy on this point no longer really exists.

Certainly the family environment was austere and often harsh. The economic function that ensured the family's survival tended to take precedence over other considerations. Marriage partners were chosen to help perpetuate the estate, the farm, or the business; children were an element in the enterprise. In some places— late Rome, ninth-century Farfa, fifteenth-century Tuscany are three that we know about—the father exercised to his final breath the authoritarian role that society imposed. In others, his place was taken in his late years by a successor capable of exercising power more vigorously.

Children, in the family, in apprenticeship, and in school, were taught to honor authority. Sylvia Thrupp, speaking of the London apprentice, says that he had to learn to "comprehend his own role as member of a governing and employing class," depending chiefly on "the necessity of restraining the temper, especially before inferiors or superiors," a restraint that gave him "a personal dignity . . . fitting to his station."[3] The same applied to the clergy. Guibert of Nogent sought the help of St. Anselm in learning "to manage the inner self" (though deploring the means his own tutor had employed to the same end). Aristocrats and peasants alike had to practice self-discipline. Overindulgence of children was consequently condemned. "What could be called more monstrous than this . . . permissive education?" wrote Maffeo Vegio, criticizing fifteenth-century mothers with an indignation echoed long after.

Inheritance customs, modified or transformed by outside pressures, came to favor some family members against others, often making older sons rich and younger sons poor, marrying off some daughters and consigning others to the convent. But on their deathbeds countless parents bestowed their last thoughts on their children. Ralph Sneuth entreated "that my wife have a tender and a faithful love and favour in bringing up her children and mine, as she will answer to God and me."[4] Older children were enjoined to care for younger; grandparents, uncles, and aunts were called on.

Among peasants and craftsmen the demands of field and shop forced children into work roles and imposed parental neglect that sometimes led to tragedy. Nevertheless, people felt toward children the same mixture of tenderness, amusement, and wonder that they feel today. To the picture of Gregory of Tours brushing away a tear, of Bishop Hugh of Lincoln playing happily with a baby at the baptismal font, of the neighbors in Alberti's book delighting over a child's first words, many more could be added. An irresistible one: Cosimo de' Medici interrupting his conference with a visiting embassy because his little grandson wanted him to make a toy whistle. Taking knife in hand, Grandfather Cosimo told his visitors, "My lords, know you not the love of children and grandchildren? It is as well that he didn't ask me to play it, because I would have done that too!"[5]

What is true of parental sentiment is no less true of marital affection, the quality that Gratian ruled indispensable to legality. Nor was Gratian's formulation left to gather dust in the ecclesiastical library. A twelfth-century missal of Cahors instructs the priest to "firmly inquire as to the relationship of the couple and whether they love each other. . . . If . . . they are in love [and no impediment is found], let them be married."[6] The Church's spokesmen frequently criticized the emphasis given material considerations. Sharp-tongued Paris preacher Jacques de Vitry sarcastically observed that in some cases one should lead to church not the affianced lady but her money or her cows.[7] Marriage was a privilege, and had to be paid for, even by those free of the lord's merchet. The assigns contributed by both sides fluctuated in relation to each other as the marriage market shifted. The Germanic groom paying the *Morgengabe* to his bride the morning after consummation of the marriage was succeeded centuries later by the Florentine groom hastening to the *Monte delle Doti* to collect her dowry. The dowry still had a lengthy historic course to run, its enduring importance attested by its frequent service as a plot mechanism, as in Shakespeare's *Measure for Measure*. The significant shift in marriage assigns had, however, been completed, in the intergenerational transfer of wealth. Where the Germanic husband of Caesar's time paid the bride's parents, medieval parents on one side or the other or both contributed to underwriting the new conjugal household.

But amid dowries and dowers, morning gifts and jointures, trousseaus and counter-trousseaus, affection, romance, and even passion managed to flourish. Bernard Clergue of Montaillou fell "madly in love" with Raymonde, his future bride. The Frisian wife who welcomed her sailor husband's return in the *Exeter Book* "washes his sea-stained raiment" and "grants him on the land what his love requires." The lord of Guines whose historian credited him (admiringly) with twenty-three illegitimate children nevertheless conceived such an affection for his legitimate spouse that upon her death in childbirth he fell ill, took to his bed, and bolted his door "for days on end." "My heart languishes with this desire [to see her husband and son]," wrote the lady Dhuoda in the ninth century, and six hundred years later Margery Brews Paston echoed the sentiment: "Sir, I pray you, if you tarry long at London . . . to send for me, for I think it long since I lay in your arms."

Among peasant youth, ardor was less inhibited by economics, though land and chattels were if anything more important to them than silks and jewels to their betters. That the couple standing before the door of the village church felt genuine affection is shown by the wills they made after long years of living together. Clandestine marriage, whatever its defects, itself carried a suggestion of romantic impetuosity. If the Church courts reasonably frowned on marriage vows sworn "under an ash tree, in a bed, in a garden, in a blacksmith's shop, in a kitchen, at a tavern, and in the king's highway," such locations imply spontaneity.

The tendency for young people to make their own marriage decisions caused friction that did not cease with the close of the Middle Ages. A complaint to the city council of Avignon in 1546 alleged that "the young women of Avignon . . . give themselves in marriage without the endorsement or consent of their fathers and mothers and other kinsfolk, which is a thing most wonderfully scandalous and injurious to the public well-being."[8] The linking of parental with kin consent is significant. Parental consent was always in part the voice of the supra-family, while consent of the principals was that of the newly created conjugal family. Gratian's clear-cut emphasis on the consent of the principals, even in the teeth of parental wishes, was a radical break with the past. Clandestine marriage, the extreme expression of principal consent over parental consent, became an obvious target for Protestant criticism, which focused on its convenience for seducers. An ordinance of Zwingli's Zurich in 1525 stipulated the presence of two respectable witnesses for a legal wedding,[9] and the Catholic Church's Council of Trent in 1563 repudiated Gratian to the extent of doing away with clandestine marriage. The trend toward public and in fact church weddings with full participation of the priest was accentuated, putting an end to the long-standing ambiguity about whether or not marriage had taken place. Sir John Paston's uncertain status with Mistress Haute, either betrothed or married, was replaced with a situation in which marriage was an event that transpired in a definite way at a definite moment; in Philippe Ariès's words, "At five to eleven, one is not married, at five past, one is."[10] Clandestine marriage never again prevailed against priest, church, banns, rings, witnessed vows, and wedding feasts.

Was the change an improvement? In many ways, it certainly was, but James A. Brundage suggests a reservation: "The inflexible rigidity of the Tridentine [Council of Trent] marriage law has created endless tragedies. This may have been too high a price to pay for an illusory certainty." The rule that a couple were "either married or not married" allowed "no legally acceptable intermediate situation."[11] Thus the emergence in the late twentieth century of informal conjugal living arrangements as a prelude or substitute for marriage may be seen historically as a long-delayed response to a problem created by the Reformation and Counter-Reformation.

In the sixteenth century the effect of hardening the definition of marriage was to swing the pendulum toward parental influence. In the longer run, the decline in importance of income derived from land made free choice by the principals the wave of the future. Juan de Torquemada proved an eloquent prophet in his proclamation of 1457: "Marriage . . . signifies the conjunction of Christ and the Church which is made through the liberty of love. Therefore, it cannot be made by coerced consent."[12]

Marriage formation had created problems on the lower levels of lay society and ecclesiastical courts. On the upper levels, it was rather the dissolution of marriage that had created problems that troubled the deliberations of bishops and popes. The free-spirited kings and nobles of the new barbarian states had been hectored and coaxed into giving up their surplus wives and at least half-concealing their concubines, but had clung to their old custom of unilateral divorce, enjoying sanction in public opinion on the grounds of the need for heirs. The heroic battles waged by Hinc-mar of Reims and other bishops and popes had brought succor to queens and other women oppressed by male divorce power, but bequeathed several new dilemmas to later authorities. Royal couples had seized on the Church's consanguinity rules to win annulments (in the medieval vocabulary synonymous with divorce), despite living together many years and producing children, as in the case of Louis VII and Eleanor of Aquitaine. Even after the Fourth Lateran Council undercut this device by abandoning the extreme seventh-degree taboo, divorce seekers (or betrothal-breaking seekers like Sir John Paston) exploited and contributed to Vatican corruption, supplying the Protestants with a double critical thrust, against corruption and toward orderly divorce. Luther and Calvin, reinterpreting St. Paul, found a wife's adultery sufficient grounds for divorce, though it was some time before adultery by the husband was given equal recognition even by the Protestants, who eventually added desertion and severe cruelty by either spouse to the list of justifications.

Formulated in the context of male license, the medieval

Church's posture on divorce may be seen as a liberating rather than an oppressive doctrine. Nor was it ever so inflexible in operation as sometimes pictured. Throughout the Middle Ages, couples were separated under a variety of conditions by Church courts, by lay authorities, or by the two in combination. Notarial acts in Avignon record many mutually agreed-on separations that "served as a substitute for divorce."[13] The town council of Ghent dealt routinely with marital breakups, attempting reconciliation where possible: Kateline Cant was ordered to reunite with Jan Cant in 1377 but Jan must mend his ways; if he "gambled or drank immoderately or took . . . jewels from the house or mismanaged any property," he had to go to the episcopal court at Tournai and arrange at his own expense the formal separation previously agreed on.[14]

Luther also attacked the consanguinity restrictions that remained after the Fourth Lateran Council, especially those relating to "spiritual" relatives, in respect to which some of the clergy had come to do a thriving business in dispensations. "Take as your spouse whomsoever you please, whether it be godparent, godchild, or the daughter or sister of a sponsor," Luther bade his followers, "and disregard those artificial, money-seeking impediments."[15] It proved easier to criticize the existing rules than to redefine them. Luther himself read Leviticus 18 as barring only twelve kinds of relationships, but his follower Andreas Osiander thought several more were implied, and that the law of Moses and other considerations multiplied still further the network of forbidden marital or sexual connections. Osiander was also troubled by the spectacle in his native Nuremberg of people abusing the new liberty by carrying on notoriously incestuous relationships.[16] Eventually the Christian world, Catholic and Protestant, settled into a fairly stable though by no means uniformly consistent set of consanguinity rules, but the basic rationale of the incest taboo has never yet been confronted. Anthropology, history, and psychology remain as baffled as theology. Society in general has tended to follow the Montaillou peasant who tempered superstition with common sense, finding it shameful rather than sinful to sleep with a sister, mother, or first cousin, while with a second cousin, "give her the works!"

The Reformation also took issue with the medieval Church's

preference for chastity over marriage. Family life was superior to celibacy, Luther declared; marriage created healthy bodies and consciences and protected property and honor. It laid the foundation of the household that created the values by which society was governed.[17] Many of the virtues Luther attributed to marriage might have been borrowed from Hincmar of Reims, who seven centuries before had pointed out the function of marriage in bringing order to social relations. Like Luther, Hincmar valued marriage, but like St. Paul he believed celibacy even better.

Popular perceptions of the Middle Ages have always included sex, thanks to Boccaccio, the fabliaux, the troubadours, and Andreas Capellanus. Literary sex, however, focuses overwhelmingly on the extramarital. Modern research confirms the extramarital sex but also throws light on sex within marriage, and in the Middle Ages, as another Montaillou deponent observes, "It's still within marriage that people make love most often." That the Church was never blind to the sexual needs of husbands and wives is indicated by its first gingerly pronouncements about the "marital debt" mutually owed by spouses. Sex as a subject for consideration was even more important to the Church than to the laity, who regarded it more casually. From the Penitentials it is clear that the Church held a narrow view of bedroom propriety, and was doubly opposed to practices that had a contraceptive significance. "The couple were not alone in the marriage bed," says Jean-Louis Flandrin; "the shadow of the confessor loomed over their frolics."[18] The confessor was in fact educated by Church manuals in a variety of usages that were labeled sinful, but how effective he was in curbing them may be doubted from the prudent warning he was given that in interrogating his parishioners he must take care not to be too specific lest he put ideas in their heads.

Medieval theologians in general followed St. Jerome rather than St. Augustine in condemning sex for pleasure alone. The sin, however, was not easy to detect, and perhaps not even very clearly identifiable by its practitioners. The sixteenth-century Spanish theologian Thomas Sanchez was the first authority of weight to go so far as to endorse sex in marriage with no procreative intent as long as there was no procreative impediment.[19] Given medieval notions about reproduction, however, Sanchez's liberalism may not have been very necessary. It was widely believed that at the moment of orgasm the woman emitted her own semen, which at least according to Galen was essential to conception. Therefore the question was raised in theological circles, should not the husband prolong copulation until his wife's climax? Antonius Guainerius, early fifteenth-century professor of medicine at the University of Pavia, in his *Tractatus de matricibus (Treatise on the Womb),* went so far as to assert that the pleasure of both partners contributed to conception. Therefore Guainerius spelled out meticulous instructions to the husband on how to arouse the wife, by kisses and caresses, till her eyes shone and she spoke with shortened words, to a full state of readiness. Guainerius recommended certain substances to heighten pleasure for the lady, for whom he appended precise details on the optimum supine posture.[20]

Guainerius agreed with the Church in defining procreation as the aim of marriage. Contraception and abortion were not in fact terribly controversial subjects in the Middle Ages; their history as controversy belongs to the modern period. Infanticide, on the other hand, ceased to be controversial. The accepted means of population control in the classical world was outlawed by the untiring efforts of the Christian Church. The acceptance of the Church's humane ideology, unfortunately, did not solve the problem. A study by R. H. Helmholz of the Canterbury records of the late fifteenth century shows "good evidence" of the continued existence of infanticide and, while providing no index of its incidence, suggests that it was "common enough."[21] Its secularization as a crime by later centuries proved so little of a solution that Disraeli maintained it to be hardly less prevalent in Victorian England than in notorious India. It is difficult to argue with William L. Langer's conclusion that only the twentieth century's contraceptive technology and legalization of abortion—over the Church's opposition—have "removed all valid excuses for unwanted pregnancy or infanticide."[22]

A category in which family life visibly improved, especially in the later Middle Ages, was that of physical environment. By the fifteenth century, both ends of the social scale had gained in comfort, space, and privacy. The peasants had turned one-room huts into three-room houses and created the milieu for a village middle class. The landed aristocracy had exchanged its bleak twelfth-century donjons for cozier Caister Castles. Most conspicuously of

A fourteenth-century Italian city, by Ambrogio Lorenzetti, Pinacoteca, Siena. (Alinari)

all, the merchant-and-banking aristocracy of the city, whose stately home-and-office residences lined patrician quarters from Flanders to Sicily, had augmented comfort not only with opulence but with aesthetics, two conceptions related to each other as well as to a third: family pride. A Genoese businessman, Francesco Sassetti, overwhelmed by debts, hoped to save his palazzo because it had "given great renown to our family" and was "highly praised in Italy and elsewhere because it is so beautiful and cost so much money."[23]

As the old fortified enclave, the towered city-within-a-city, lost its function along with the decay of the supra-family, its place was usurped, first of all in Florence and Venice, by the vast Renaissance palazzo, whose three tall and generously proportioned stories, sometimes rising as high as a modern seven-story building, supplied a new world of privacy and luxury. Its façade decorated with frescos, carvings, moldings, coats-of-arms, cornices, and pilasters concealed vaulted staircases, arcaded courts, and private gardens. To look out, one mounted steps in the bay to attain a lofty window; to look in from outside was impossible. The works of

Ucello, Fra Angelico, and other masters flaunted both the tastes and pretensions of their owners.[24] Benozzo Gozzoli adorned the chapel walls of the Medici palace with a splendid Procession of the Magi, a panorama in whose faces are preserved portraits of several members of Cosimo de' Medici's family.[25]

In the course of the Middle Ages, monogamous marriage triumphed over polygamy and male divorce power, and gradually shifted its focus away from parental and kinship concerns to the advantage of the conjugal couple. The family they were founding, despite losses of important functions to Church, state, and society, consolidated its position as the basic cell of Western society. The ancient clan lost its authority and faded from sight. Though perpetually altering its composition through its life cycle, the family household dominated the social landscape at all levels as the Middle Ages moved imperceptibly across the threshold of modern times.

Notes

Chapter 1. Historians Discover the Family

1. Donald R. Bender, "A Refinement of the Concept of Household: Families, Co-Residence, and Domestic Function," *American Anthropologist* 69 (1967), pp. 495–504.

2. Michael Mitterauer and Reinhard Sieder, *The European Family: Patriarchy to Partnership from the Middle Ages to the Present*, trans. Karla Oosterveen and Manfred Hörzinger, Chicago, 1982, pp. 6–7.

3. Frédéric Le Play, *L'Organisation de la famille selon le vrai modèle signalé par l'histoire de toutes les races et tous les temps*, Paris, 1871.

4. Philippe Ariès, *Centuries of Childhood: A Social History of Family Life*, trans. Robert Baldick, London, 1962.

5. Peter Laslett and Richard Wall, eds., *Household and Family in Past Time*, Cambridge, 1972; Peter Laslett, "The Comparative History of Household and Family," *Journal of Social History* 4 (1970), pp. 75–87; Peter Laslett, "La Famille et le ménage: approches historiques," *Annales: Economies, Sociétés, Civilisations* 27 (1972), pp. 847–872; E. A. Hammell and Peter Laslett, "Comparing Household Structure over Time and Between Cultures," *Comparative Studies in Society and History* 16 (1974), pp. 73–109.

6. Mitterauer and Sieder, *The European Family;* Jean-Louis Flandrin, *Families in Former Times: Kinship, Household, and Sexuality*, trans. Richard Southern, Cambridge, 1979; Robert Wheaton and Tamara K. Hareven, eds., *Family and Sexuality in French History*, Philadelphia, 1980.

7. David Herlihy, *Medieval Households*, Cambridge, Mass., 1985.

8. Georges Duby and Jacques le Goff, eds., *Famille et parenté dans l'Occident médiéval*, Rome, 1977.

9. Georges Duby, *Medieval Marriage: Two Models from Twelfth-Century France*, trans. Elborg Foster, Baltimore, 1978; and *The Knight, the Lady, and the Priest: The Making of Modern Marriage in Medieval France*, trans. Barbara Bray, New York, 1983.

10. Heath Dillard, *Daughters of the Reconquest: Women in Castilian Town Society, 1100–1300*, Cambridge, 1985; Christiane Klapisch-Zuber, *Women, Family, and Ritual in Renaissance Italy*, Chicago, 1985; Christine Fell, *Women in Anglo-Saxon England and the Impact of 1066*, Bloomington, Ind., 1984; Suzanne Fonay Wemple, *Women in Frankish Society: Marriage and the Cloister, 500 to 900*, Philadelphia, 1981; Barbara Kenner, ed., *The Women of England from Anglo-Saxon Times to the Present*, Hamden, Conn., 1979; Frances and Joseph Gies, *Women in the Middle Ages*, New York, 1978.

11. David Herlihy and Christiane Klapisch-Zuber, *Tuscans and Their Families: A Study of the Florentine Catasto of 1427*, New Haven, 1985.

12. David Nicholas, *The Domestic Life of a Medieval City: Women, Children, and the Family in Fourteenth-Century Ghent*, Lincoln, Nebr., 1985.

13. Barbara A. Hanawalt, *The Ties That Bound: Peasant Families in Medieval England*, Oxford, 1986.

14. Lawrence Stone, *The Family, Sex and Marriage in England, 1500–1800*, New York, 1977.

15. Laslett, "Comparative History of Household and Family."

16. Robert Wheaton, "Family and Kinship in Western Europe: The Problem of the Joint Family Household," *Journal of Interdisciplinary History* 5 (1975), pp. 601–628. Also Tamara K. Hareven, "The Family as Process: The Historical Study of the Family Cycle," *Journal of Social History* 7 (1974), pp. 322–329.

17. Marion J. Levy, Jr., "Aspects of the Analysis of Family Structure," in Ansley J. Coale et al., eds., *Aspects of the Analysis of Family Structure*, Princeton, 1965, pp. 1–63.

18. For a discussion of the problem: Robin Fox, *Kinship and Marriage: An Anthropological Perspective*, Cambridge, 1983, pp. 54–76.

19. Diane Owen Hughes, "From Brideprice to Dowry in Mediterranean Europe," *Journal of Family History* 3 (1978), pp. 262–296.

20. Ariès, *Centuries of Childhood*, pp. 128, 38–40.

21. Edward Shorter, *The Making of the Modern Family*, New York, 1975, pp. 168–204. Shorter bases his conclusions mainly on the practice of wet nursing in nineteenth-century France. His thesis is contradicted by George D. Sussman, "The End of the Wet-Nursing Business in France, 1874–1914," in Wheaton and Hareven, *Family and Sexuality in French History*, pp. 224–252.

22. Lloyd DeMause, "The Evolution of Childhood," in Lloyd De-

Mause, ed., *The History of Childhood*, London, 1976, pp. 1–74.

23. Linda A. Pollock, *Forgotten Children: Parent-Child Relations from 1500 to 1900*, Cambridge, 1983, p. 12.

24. Peter and Carol Stearns, "Emotionology: Clarifying the History of Emotions and Emotional Standards," *American Historical Review* 90 (1985), pp. 813–836.

25. Shorter, *Making of the Modern Family*, pp. 79–119.

26. Jean-Louis Flandrin, "Repression and Change in the Sexual Life of Young People in Medieval and Early Modern Times," in Wheaton and Hareven, *Family and Sexuality in French History*, pp. 27–48.

27. Philippe Ariès, *Western Attitudes Toward Death from the Middle Ages to the Present*, trans. Patricia M. Ranum, Baltimore, 1974.

Chapter 2. Roots: Roman, German, Christian

1. William F. Kenkel, *The Family in Perspective: A Fourfold Analysis*, New York, 1960, pp. 65–66.

2. Robert A. Nisbet, "Kinship and Political Power in First-Century Rome," in W. J. Cahnman and A. Bostoff, eds., *Sociology and History*, New York, 1964, p. 261.

3. Numa Denis Fustel de Coulanges, *The Ancient City*, trans. Willard Small, Garden City, 1956, p. 24.

4. Martin Heinzelmann, "Les Changements de la dénomination latine à la fin de l'antiquité," in Duby and Le Goff, *Famille et parenté*, pp. 19–20.

5. Judith P. Hallett, *Fathers and Daughters in Roman Society*, Princeton, 1984, p. 78.

6. Joseph Declareuil, *Rome the Law Giver*, New York, 1926, pp. 37–39.

7. Nisbet, "Kinship," p. 261.

8. Kenkel, *Family*, p. 69.

9. Ibid., p. 74; Nisbet, "Kinship," p. 266.

10. Frank Cowell, *Everyday Life in Ancient Rome*, London, 1961, pp. 61, 148–150.

11. Kenkel, *Family*, p. 76.

12. Kenkel, *Family*, p. 69; Ugo Enrico Paoli, *Rome: Its People, Life, and Customs*, New York, 1963 (first published 1940), trans. R. D. Macnaghtan, p. 115; Declareuil, *Rome the Lawgiver*, p. 101.

13. Jérôme Carcopino, *Daily Life in Ancient Rome*, trans. E. O. Lorimer, New York, 1941, p. 94.

14. Herlihy, *Medieval Households*, pp. 15–16, citing L. Anné, *Les Rites des fiançailles et la donation pour cause de mariage dans le Bas-Empire*, Louvain, 1941, pp. 450ff.

15. Kenkel, *Family*, p. 70.

16. Suetonius, *Lives of the Twelve Caesars*, ed. Joseph Gavorse, New York, 1931, p. 227.

17. Kenkel, *Family*, p. 70.

18. J. P. V. D. Balsdon, *Roman Women: Their History and Habits*, New York, 1962. p. 183.

19. Carcopino, *Daily Life*, p. 107.

20. Balsdon, *Roman Women*, p. 231.

21. Carcopino, *Daily Life*, p. 108.

22. Ibid., p. 111.

23. Ibid., p. 108.

24. Ibid., p. 109.

25. Ibid., p. 111.

26. Ibid., p. 113.

27. Ludwig Friedlander, *Roman Life and Manners Under the Early Empire*, trans. Leonard Magnus, New York, 1965 (first printed 1907), vol. 1, p. 243.

28. Ibid., p. 265.

29. John T. Noonan, Jr., *Contraception: A History of Its Treatment by the Catholic Theologists and Canonists*, Cambridge, Mass., 1965, pp. 12–29.

30. Soranus, *Gynaecology*, I, 19–20, trans. O. Temkin, in Mary R. Lefkowitz and Maureen B. Fant, eds., *Women's Life in Greece and Rome*, Baltimore, 1982, p. 178.

31. Declareuil, *Rome the Law Giver*, pp. 126–127.

32. Cowell, *Everyday Life*, p. 56.

33. Ibid., p. 56.

34. Ibid., p. 56.

35. Balsdon, *Roman Women*, pp. 77, 218–219.

36. Friedlander, *Roman Life*, vol. 1, p. 241.

37. Juvenal, *Satires*, 6, trans. M. R. Lefkowitz, in Lefkowitz and Fant, *Women's Life*, p. 152.

38. Paul Veyne, "Homosexuality in Ancient Rome," in Philippe Ariès and André Béjin, eds., *Western Sexuality: Practice and Precept in Past and Present Times*, London, 1985, pp. 27–35.

39. Cowell, *Everyday Life*, p. 133.

40. Tacitus, *Germania*, in *The Agricola and the Germania*, trans. H. Mattingly, revised by S. A. Handford, Harmondsworth, 1948, p. 117.

41. Malcolm Todd, *Everyday Life of the Barbarians, Goths, Franks, and Vandals*, London, 1972 (Todd does not identify the source), p. 18.

42. Todd, *Everyday Life*, pp. 10–11, 116–117.

43. Lucien Musset, *The Germanic Invasions: The Making of Europe A.D. 400–600*, trans. Edward and Columba James, London, 1975, pp. 173–

174; Herlihy, *Medieval Households,* p. 47.

44. *The Lombard Laws,* trans. and ed. Katherine Fischer Drew, Philadelphia, 1973, pp. 101, 110, 121.

45. Todd, *Everyday Life,* pp. 73–77.

46. Katherine Fischer Drew, "The Germanic Family of the *Leges Burgundionum,"* *Medievalia et Humanistica* 15 (1963), p. 7.

47. Ibid., p. 13.

48. Tacitus, *Germania,* p. 116.

49. Drew, "Germanic Family," p. 8.

50. Adhémar Esmein, *Le Mariage en droit canonique,* ed. R. Génestal, Paris, 1929–1935, vol. 1, p. 47.

51. Tacitus, *Germania,* p. 117.

52. Drew, *Lombard Laws,* Title 213, p. 93.

53. Todd, *Everyday Life,* pp. 74, 86, 87, 174; Herlihy, *Medieval Households,* p. 51.

54. Tacitus, *Germania,* p. 118.

55. Ibid., p. 118.

56. Todd, *Everyday Life,* p. 86.

57. Ibid., pp. 77–78.

58. Ibid., pp. 65–66.

59. Ibid., p. 66.

60. Ibid., pp. 71–72.

61. Noonan, *Contraception,* pp. 30–34.

62. Ibid., pp. 37–40.

63. Ibid., pp. 46–55.

64. Herlihy, *Medieval Households,* p. 24, citing St. Augustine, *Treatises on Marriage and Other Subjects,* trans. Charles T. Wilcox et al., New York, 1955, pp. 21–22.

65. Noonan, *Contraception,* p. 121.

66. Herlihy, *Medieval Households,* p. 22, citing M. Humbert, *Le Remariage à Rome,* Milan, 1972, p. 321; Noonan, *Contraception,* pp. 83–85.

67. Herlihy, *Medieval Households,* p. 11; Noonan, *Contraception,* pp. 126–127.

68. Charles Galy, *La Famille à l'époque Mérovingienne, étude faite principalement d'après les récits de Grégoire de Tours,* Paris, 1901, p. 85.

69. Esmein, *Mariage.* vol. 1, p. 50.

70. Ibid., vol. 1, p. 53.

71. W. J. Dooley, *Marriage According to St. Ambrose,* Washington, D.C., 1948, p. 95.

72. Esmein, *Mariage,* vol. 1, p. 384.

73. Pierre Riché, *Education and Culture in the Barbarian West, Sixth Through Eighth Centuries,* trans. John J. Contreni, Columbia, S.C., 1976, p. 10.

Chapter 3. The European Family: 500–700

1. Georges Duby, *Rural Economy and Country Life in the Medieval West*, trans. Cynthia Postan, Columbia, S.C., 1968, p. 3.

2. Herlihy, *Medieval Households*, pp. 56–61.

3. David Herlihy, "The Carolingian Mansus," *Economic History Review* 13 (1960), pp. 79–89; Marc Bloch, *Slavery and Serfdom in the Middle Ages*, trans. William R. Beer, Berkeley, 1975, pp. 1–31.

4. Marc Bloch, *Feudal Society*, trans. L. A. Manyon, Chicago, 1964, vol. 1, pp. 255–274; Duby, *Rural Economy*, p. 53; Emily Coleman, "Medieval Marriage Characteristics, a Neglected Factor in the History of Medieval Serfdom," *Journal of Interdisciplinary History* 2 (1971), p. 207.

5. J. T. McNeill and H. M. Gamer, *Medieval Handbooks of Penance*, New York, 1938; Raoul Manselli, "Vie familiale et éthique sexuelle dans les pénitentiels," in Duby and Le Goff, *Famille et parenté*, pp. 363–382.

6. Gregory of Tours, *The History of the Franks*, trans. Lewis Thorpe, Harmondsworth, 1974.

7. Galy, *La Famille à l'époque Mérovingienne*, pp. 391–401.

8. Gregory of Tours, *History*, pp. 586–587.

9. Ibid., pp. 294–295.

10. Ibid., pp. 366–367.

11. Ibid., p. 321.

12. Ibid., p. 158.

13. Wemple, *Women in Frankish Society*, pp. 52–63; Herlihy, *Medieval Households*, p. 47.

14. Gregory of Tours, *History*, p. 170.

15. Ibid., pp. 519–520.

16. Martin Heinzelmann, "Les changements de la dénomination latine à la fin de l'antiquité," and Karl Ferdinand Werner, "Liens de parenté et noms de personne: un problème historique et méthodologique," in Duby and Le Goff, *Famille et parenté*, pp. 19–34.

17. Galy, *La Famille à l'époque Mérovingienne*, pp. 290–291; Wemple, *Women in Frankish Society*, pp. 44–50. On the legal status of women: François-Louis Ganshof, "Le Statut de la femme dans la monarchie franque," *Recueils de la Société Jean Bodin* 12 (1962), pp. 5–58.

18. Galy, *La Famille à l'époque Mérovingienne*, p. 52.

19. *Bede's Ecclesiastical History of the English Nation*, trans. J. Stevens, revised by J. A. Giles, London, 1963, p. 40.

20. Gregory of Tours, *History*, pp. 167, 198, 253, 255.

21. Jo Ann McNamara and Suzanne F. Wemple, "Marriage and Divorce in the Frankish Kingdom," in Susan Mosher Stuard, ed., *Women in*

Medieval Society, Philadelphia, 1976, p. 99.

22. Galy, *La Famille à l'époque Mérovingienne,* pp. 51–52.

23. *Bede's Ecclesiastical History,* p. 40.

24. McNeill and Gamer, *Medieval Handbooks of Penance,* pp. 210–211.

25. Pauline Stafford, *Queens, Concubines, and Dowagers: The King's Wife in the Early Middle Ages,* Athens, Ga., 1983, pp. 73–74.

26. Ibid., p. 55.

27. Gregory of Tours, *History,* pp. 219–220.

28. Ibid., p. 222.

29. Wemple, *Women in Frankish Society,* p. 39.

30. Cited in John T. Noonan, "Power to Choose," *Viator* 4 (1973), p. 419. See also Michael M. Sheehan, "Choice of Marriage Partner in the Middle Ages: Development and Mode of Application of a Theory of Marriage," *Studies in Medieval and Renaissance History* 11 (1978), pp. 9–10.

31. Katherine Fischer Drew, trans. and ed., *The Lombard Laws,* Philadelphia, 1973, p. 89 (no. 195).

32. McNeill and Gamer, *Medieval Handbooks of Penance,* p. 85.

33. Ibid., p. 211.

34. Galy, *La Famille à l'époque Mérovingienne,* p. 40.

35. Ibid., p. 47.

36. Ibid., pp. 46–49.

37. Ibid., pp. 73–74.

38. Hughes, "From Brideprice to Dowry," pp. 266–269.

39. Ibid., pp. 275–276.

40. Drew, *Lombard Laws,* p. 87 (no. 188).

41. Gregory of Tours, *History,* pp. 378–379.

42. Galy, *La Famille à l'époque Mérovingienne,* pp. 83–84.

43. Ibid., p. 107.

44. Wemple, *Women in Frankish Society,* pp. 42–43.

45. Esmein, *Le Mariage en droit canonique,* vol. 2, p. 68.

46. McNeill and Gamer, *Medieval Handbooks of Penance,* pp. 95–96.

47. Ibid., pp. 208–209.

48. Ibid., p. 211.

49. Ibid., p. 210.

50. Ibid., p. 209.

51. Ibid., pp. 195–196.

52. Galy, *La Famille à l'époque Mérovingienne,* p. 63; Wemple, *Women in Frankish Society,* p. 130.

53. Ibid., pp. 62–63.

54. Gregory of Tours, *History,* p. 199.

55. Ibid., pp. 93–94.

56. Ibid., p. 198.

57. Ibid., p. 219.

58. Ibid., p. 222.

59. Ibid., p. 296.

60. Ibid., pp. 297–298.

61. Ibid., pp. 365–366.

62. McNeill and Gamer, *Medieval Handbooks of Penance*, pp. 246–247.

63. Ibid., p. 197.

64. Ibid., pp. 254–255.

65. Wemple, *Women in Frankish Society*, p. 59.

66. McNeill and Gamer, *Medieval Handbooks of Penance*, p. 96.

67. *Bede's Ecclesiastical History*, p. 44.

68. Gregory of Tours, *History*, pp. 95–97.

69. McNeill and Gamer, *Medieval Handbooks of Penance*, p. 96.

70. Ibid., p. 211.

71. Ibid., pp. 197, 186.

72. Ibid., p. 254.

73. Ibid., pp. 89–90.

74. Ibid., p. 185.

75. Fox, *Kinship and Marriage*, pp. 71–72.

76. McNeill and Gamer, *Medieval Handbooks of Penance*, p. 103.

77. Ibid., p. 186.

78. Gregory of Tours, *History*, p. 156.

79. Ibid., p. 243.

80. Ibid., p. 389.

81. Ibid., p. 258.

82. Ibid., p. 466.

83. Ibid., p. 587.

84. Ibid., p. 523.

85. Ibid., p. 436.

86. Ibid., p. 514.

87. Jean Chapelot and Robert Fossier, *The Village and House in the Middle Ages*, trans. Henry Cleere, Berkeley, 1985, pp. 41–71.

88. Ibid., pp. 72–128.

Chapter 4. The Carolingian Age

1. Herlihy, "The Carolingian Mansus."

2. Dhuoda, *Manuel pour mon fils*, ed. and trans. Pierre Riché, Paris, 1975.

3. *Il Chronicon Farfense di Gregorio di Catino*, ed. Ugo Balzani, in *Fonti per la storia d'Italia*, Rome, 1903, vol. 33, pp. 243–277.

4. Ibid., p. 274.

5. Richard Ring, "Early Medieval Peasant Households in Central

Italy," *Journal of Family History* 4 (1979), pp. 2–21.

6. Ibid., p. 11.

7. *Chronicon Farfense*, pp. 271, 270.

8. Ibid., p. 263.

9. Ring, "Early Medieval Peasant Households," p. 11.

10. Ibid., p. 13; *Chronicon Farfense*, pp. 275, 267.

11. Ring, "Early Medieval Peasant Households," pp. 13–15.

12. *Chronicon Farfense*, pp. 274, 272.

13. Ibid., pp. 265, 273.

14. Ibid., p. 271.

15. Ring, "Early Medieval Peasant Households," p. 14.

16. Ibid., p. 19; *Chronicon Farfense*, p. 265.

17. *Chronicon Farfense*, pp. 267–268.

18. Ring, "Early Medieval Peasant Households," pp. 18–19; *Chronicon Farfense*, pp. 264, 267.

19. Ring, "Early Medieval Peasant Households," pp. 8–9.

20. Ibid., pp. 15–19.

21. Ibid., pp. 15–20.

22. *Polyptych de l'abbaye de Saint Germain-des-Prés*, ed. A. Longnon, Paris, 1886–1895.

23. Emily Coleman, "Infanticide in the Early Middle Ages," in Stuard, *Women in Medieval Society*, pp. 48–50.

24. Herlihy, *Medieval Households*, pp. 62–72.

25. "Descriptio mancipiorum ecclesie massiliensis," in *Cartulaire de l'abbaye de Saint Victor de Marseilles*, ed. Benjamin Guérard, Paris, 1857, vol. 2, pp. 633–654.

26. Stephen Weinberger, "Peasant Households in Provence, c. 800–1000," *Speculum* 48 (1973), pp. 247–257.

27. Ibid., pp. 253–255.

28. Carl I. Hammer, Jr., "Family and *Familia* in Early Medieval Bavaria," in Richard Wall, ed., *Family Forms in Historic Europe*, Cambridge, 1983, pp. 217–248.

29. Coleman, "Infanticide."

30. Ring, "Early Medieval Peasant Households, pp. 5–8.

31. David Herlihy, "Life Expectancies for Women in Medieval Society," in Rosemarie Thee Morewedge, ed., *The Role of Woman in the Middle Ages*, Albany, 1975, pp. 5–6.

32. For an analysis of Dhuoda's *Manual*: Joachim Wollasch, "Eine adlige Familie des frühen Mittelalters, Ihr Selbstverständnis und ihre Wirklichkeit," *Archiv für Kulturgeschichte* 39 (1957), pp. 150–188.

33. Pierre Riché, *Daily Life in the World of Charlemagne*, trans. Jo Ann MacNamara, Philadelphia, 1978, pp. 42–46.

34. Einhard and Notker the Stammerer, *Two Lives of Charlemagne*, trans. Lewis Thorpe, Harmondsworth, 1969, p. 79.

35. Ibid., p. 127.

36. Ibid., p. 77.

37. Riché, *Daily Life*, pp. 162–163.

38. Dhuoda, *Manuel*, p. 85.

39. *Nithard's Histories*, in *Carolingian Chronicles*, trans. Bernhard Walter Scholz with Barbara Rogers, Ann Arbor, 1970, p. 131.

40. Dhuoda, *Manuel*, pp. 350–353.

41. *Nithard's Histories*, p. 135.

42. Ibid., p. 135.

43. Ibid., p. 131.

44. Dhuoda, *Manuel*, p. 84.

45. Ibid., p. 86.

46. *Nithard's Histories*, p. 156.

47. Dhuoda, *Manuel*, p. 81.

48. Ibid., p. 79.

49. Ibid., pp. 20–21; Lina Malbos, "La capture de Bernard de Septimanie," *Le Moyen Age* (1970), pp. 5–13; A. R. Lewis, *The Development of Southern French and Catalan Society, 718–1050*, Austin, 1965, p. 107.

50. Dhuoda, *Manuel*, pp. 86–87.

51. Ibid., pp. 116–117.

52. Ibid., pp. 134–135.

53. Ibid., pp. 138–141.

54. Ibid., pp. 354–355.

55. Karl Leyser, "Maternal Kin in Early Medieval Germany, a Reply," *Past and Present* 49 (1970), p. 126.

56. D. A. Bullough, "Early Medieval Social Groupings: The Terminology of Kinship," *Past and Present* 45 (1969), pp. 3–18; Karl Leyser, "The German Aristocracy from the Ninth to the Early Twelfth Century," *Past and Present* 41 (1968). Also three essays in Timothy Reuter, ed. and trans., *The Medieval Nobility: Studies on the Ruling Classes of France and Germany from the Sixth to the Twelfth Century*, Amsterdam, 1978: Léopold Génicot, "Recent Research on the Medieval Nobility"; Karl Schmid, "The Structure of the Nobility in the Earlier Middle Ages"; Karl Ferdinand Werner, "Important Noble Families in the Kingdom of Charlemagne—a Prosopographical Study of the Relationship Between King and Nobility in the Early Middle Ages."

57. Dhuoda, *Manuel*, pp. 78–79.

58. Jack Goody, *The Development of the Family and Marriage in Europe*, Cambridge, 1983, pp. 34–47, 123–125, 134–146.

59. Herlihy, *Medieval Households*, pp. 11–13, 61–62.

60. Wemple, *Women in Frankish Society*, pp. 76–77.

61. E. Emerton, trans., *Letters of Saint Boniface*, New York, 1940, pp. 61–64.

62. Constance B. Bouchard, "Consanguinity and Noble Marriages in the Tenth and Eleventh Centuries," *Speculum* 56 (1981), pp. 268–271.

63. Esmein, *Le Mariage en droit canonique*, vol. 1, pp. 344–345.

64. Wemple, *Women in Frankish Society*, p. 81.

65. Ibid., pp. 78–81.

66. For Lothair's divorce case: Jane Bishop, "Bishops as Marital Advisors in the Ninth Century," in Julius Kirshner and Suzanne F. Wemple, eds., *Women of the Medieval World: Essays in Honor of John H. Mundy*, London, 1985, pp. 53–84; Jean Devisse, *Hincmar, Archevêque de Reims, 845–882*, Geneva, 1975, Vol. 1, pp. 367–466; Wemple, *Women in Frankish Society*, pp. 85–87.

67. Hincmar of Reims, *De Divortio Lotharii Regis et Tetbergae Reginae*, in J. P. Migne, ed., *Patrologia Latina*, Paris, 1857–1866, vol. 125, cols. 637–638.

68. Ibid., col. 761

69. Ibid., cols. 659, 677.

70. Ibid., cols. 659–677.

71. Ibid., cols. 689, 694–695.

72. Ibid., col. 695.

73. Ibid., cols. 686–687, 697.

74. Ibid., cols. 636–640.

75. Ibid., cols. 641–645.

76. Ibid., cols. 655, 740–742, 690, 705.

77. Ibid., cols. 732–733.

78. Ibid., col. 569.

79. Bishop, "Bishops as Marital Advisors," p. 62.

80. Wemple, *Women in Frankish Society*, pp. 85–88; Bishop, "Bishops as Marital Advisors," pp. 61–62, 68–69.

81. Bishop, "Bishops as Marital Advisors," pp. 66, 71–72.

82. Ibid., p. 74; Wemple, *Women in Frankish Society*, p. 86.

83. Bishop, "Bishops as Marital Advisors," pp. 72, 74–75.

84. Ibid., p. 63.

85. Wemple, *Women in Frankish Society*, pp. 94, 104.

86. Ibid., p. 86.

87. Bishop, "Bishops as Marital Advisors," pp. 60–61, 73–74; Devisse, *Hincmar*, pp. 429–432; Wemple, *Women in Frankish Society*, pp. 86–87.

88. Bishop, "Bishops as Marital Advisors," pp. 55–56, 59–60, 70; Wemple, *Women in Frankish Society*, pp. 93–94; Devisse, *Hincmar*, pp. 432–435.

89. Hincmar, *De Divortio*, col. 642.

90. Ibid., cols. 655–656.

91. Ibid., cols. 657–658.

92. Ibid., cols. 644–645; Devisse, *Hincmar*, p. 388.

93. Hincmar, *De Divortio*, cols. 650, 708.

94. Ibid., cols. 648–650.

95. Devisse, *Hincmar*, pp. 397, 401–402.

96. Hincmar, *De Divortio*, col. 642.

97. Ibid., col. 732.

98. Devisse, *Hincmar*, p. 405.

Chapter 5. Anglo-Saxon England

1. Fell, *Women in Anglo-Saxon England*, pp. 22–24.

2. Lorraine Lancaster, "Kinship in Anglo-Saxon Society," *British Journal of Sociology* 9 (1958), pp. 230–232.

3. H. R. Loyn, "Kinship in Anglo-Saxon England," *Anglo-Saxon England* 3 (1974), pp. 197–209.

4. *Beowulf*, trans. William Alfred, in *Medieval Epics*, New York, 1963, p. 21, line 407.

5. *The Wanderer*, trans. Edwin Morgan, in Angel Flores, ed., *Medieval Age*, New York, 1963, pp. 130–131, lines 19–21, 26–29.

6. Lancaster, "Kinship," pp. 232–239; Loyn, "Kinship," pp. 204–206.

7. Loyn, "Kinship," p. 206.

8. *Beowulf*, pp. 36–38, lines 1071–1159.

9. *Bede's Ecclesiastical History*, pp. 199–200, 282.

10. Loyn, "Kinship," pp. 201–202.

11. Dorothy Whitelock, ed. and trans., *English Historical Documents*, New York, 1968, vol. 1, p. 359. Also Marc A. Meyer, "Land Charters and the Legal Position of Anglo-Saxon Women," in Barbara Kenner, ed., *The Women of England from Anglo-Saxon Times to the Present*, Hamden, Conn., 1979, pp. 57–81.

12. Whitelock, *English Historical Documents*, vol. 1, p. 379.

13. Ibid., p. 428.

14. Lancaster, "Kinship," pp. 362–366.

15. Whitelock, *English Historical Documents*, vol. 1, pp. 492–495.

16. Ibid., pp. 495–496.

17. Kenneth Sisam, "Anglo-Saxon Royal Genealogies," *Proceedings of the British Academy* 39 (1953), pp. 287–346; *The Anglo-Saxon Chronicle*, trans. G. N. Garmonsway, London, 1953, p. 66.

18. Peter Hunter Blair, *An Introduction to Anglo-Saxon England*, Cambridge, 1966, pp. 198–204.

19. Craig Williamson, ed. and trans., *A Feast of Creatures: Anglo-Saxon*

Riddle-Songs, Philadelphia, 1982, p. 192.

20. Ibid., p. 106 (riddle 44).

21. *Bede's Ecclesiastical History,* pp. 40–41.

22. Rosalind Hill, "Marriage in Seventh-Century England," in *Saints, Scholars, and Heroes,* ed. M. H. King and W. M. Stevens, Minneapolis, 1979, p. 71.

23. Stafford, *Queens,* pp. 43–44.

24. *Bede's Ecclesiastical History,* p. 73.

25. Lancaster, "Kinship," p. 241.

26. Ibid., p. 246; Stafford, *Queens,* pp. 70–71.

27. Stafford, *Queens,* pp. 70, 74.

28. Whitelock, *English Historical Documents,* vol. 1, p. 359.

29. Fell, *Women in Anglo-Saxon England,* pp. 56–57.

30. Whitelock, *English Historical Documents,* vol. 1, p. 431.

31. Ibid., p. 429.

32. Ibid., p. 524.

33. Fell, *Women in Anglo-Saxon England,* pp. 44–45.

34. A. J. Robertson, *Anglo-Saxon Charters,* Cambridge, 1956, pp. 148–151.

35. Whitelock, *English Historical Documents,* vol. 1, pp. 359, 348.

36. *Bede's Ecclesiastical History,* pp. 194–195.

37. Whitelock, *English Historical Documents,* p. 430.

38. I. Gollancz and W. S. Mackie, eds., and trans., *The Exeter Book,* Oxford, 1895 (reprinted 1934 and 1975), pt. 2, p. 39, lines 84–92.

39. *Bede's Ecclesiastical History,* pp. 228–229.

40. *Beowulf,* p. 26, lines 617–631; p. 38, lines 1161–1176.

41. *Exeter Book,* pt. 2, p. 37, lines 63–65.

42. Fell, *Women in Anglo-Saxon England,* p. 59.

43. Whitelock, *English Historical Documents,* p. 430.

44. Ibid., p. 368.

45. Ibid., p. 360.

46. Fell, *Women in Anglo-Saxon England,* pp. 61–62.

47. *Bede's Ecclesiastical History,* p. 203.

48. Ibid., p. 307.

49. Ibid., pp. 80–81.

50. *Exeter Book,* pt. 2, p. 39, lines 94–99.

51. *Beowulf,* pp. 66–67, lines 2421–2472.

52. *Exeter Book,* pt. 2, p. 27, lines 1–14; p. 29, lines 43–47.

53. *Bede's Ecclesiastical History,* pp. 288–289.

54. Whitelock, *English Historical Documents,* vol. 1., p. 358.

55. Ibid., pp. 376–378.

56. Ibid., p. 426.

57. Williamson, *Feast of Creatures*, p. 78 (riddle 18).

58. *Exeter Book*, pt. 2, pp. 115–116 (riddle 25).

59. Williamson, *Feast of Creatures*, p. 114 (riddle 52).

60. Ibid., p. 105 (riddle 43).

61. Chapelot and Fossier, *Village and House*, pp. 96–100, 104–124, 127–128.

62. *Bede's Ecclesiastical History*, pp. 305–306.

63. *Beowulf*, p. 13, lines 922–924; p. 34, lines 996–1000; p. 35, lines 1034–1035.

64. Blair, *Anglo-Saxon England*, p. 211.

Chapter 6. The Family Revolution of the Eleventh Century

1. *Li Romans de Garin le Loherain*, Paris, 1832–1838, reprinted Geneva, 1969; Joel H. Grisward, "Individualisme et 'Esprit de famille' dans 'Garin le Loherain," in Duby and Le Goff, *Famille et parenté*, pp. 385–396.

2. *Garin le Loherain*, vol. 1, p. 2.

3. Ibid., pp. 3–7.

4. Ibid., pp. 7–49.

5. For a summary of historians' views: John B. Freed, *The Counts of Falkenstein: Noble Self-Consciousness in Twelfth-Century Germany*, Philadelphia, 1984, pp. 1–13. Also Karl Schmid, "Structures of the Nobility," in Reuter, *The Medieval Nobility*; Schmid, "Zur Problematik von Familie, Sippe und Geschlecht, Haus und Dynastie beim mittelalterlichen Adel, Vorfrage zum Thema," *Zeitschrift für die Geschichte des Oberrheins* 106 (1957), pp. 1–62; Schmid, "Neue Quellen zum Verständnis des Adels im 10. Jahrhundert, *Zeitschrift für die Geschichte des Oberrheins* 108 (1960), pp. 185–232; Karl Leyser, *Rule and Conflict in an Early Medieval Society: Ottonian Saxony*, Bloomington, Ind., 1979, pp. 50–51; Georges Duby, "Lineage, Nobility, and Knighthood, the Mâconnais in the Twelfth Century—a Revision," "The Nobility in Medieval France," "The Structure of Kinship and Nobility, Northern France in the Eleventh and Twelfth Centuries," and "French Genealogical Literature, the Eleventh and Twelfth Centuries," all in *The Chivalrous Society*, trans. Cynthia Postan, Berkeley, 1977, pp. 59–80, 94–111, 134–148, 149–157; Duby, *La Société aux xie et xiie siècles dans la région Mâconnaise*, Paris, 1955, pp. 7–87; Herlihy, *Medieval Households*, pp. 82–98.

6. Duby, "Lineage," pp. 62–67; Duby, *Société*, pp. 39–47.

7. Duby, *Société*, p. 54.

8. Ibid., pp. 50–52.

9. Ibid., pp. 53–54.

10. Ibid., p. 48.

11. Ibid., pp. 59–60.

12. Ibid., p. 61.

13. Duby, "Lineage," pp. 64–67.

14. Duby, *Société*, pp. 269–270; Duby, "Lineage," pp. 69–73.

15. Duby, *Société*, pp. 89–94.

16. Joseph and Frances Gies, *Life in a Medieval Castle*, New York, 1974, pp. 9–12.

17. Duby, *Société*, pp. 106–109; Duby, "Structure of Kinship," pp. 147–148.

18. Duby, *Société*, pp. 277–281.

19. Duby, "Nobility," p. 101.

20. Constance Bouchard, "The Structure of a Twelfth-Century French Family: The Lords of Seignelay," *Viator* 10 (1979), pp. 47–49.

21. Duby, "Lineage," pp. 60–62.

22. Ibid., pp. 62–63.

23. Werner, "Liens de parenté," pp. 26–27.

24. Bouchard, "Lords of Seignelay," pp. 44–47.

25. Freed, *Counts of Falkenstein*, p. 8.

26. Hughes, "From Brideprice to Dowry," pp. 276–277; Duby, *Société*, pp. 268–269.

27. Duby, *Société*, pp. 272–275.

28. Duby, "Lineage," p. 69.

29. Duby, *Société*, pp. 264–265.

30. Bouchard, "Lords of Seignelay," p. 55.

31. Duby, "French Genealogical Literature," p. 154.

32. Ibid., pp. 152–156.

33. *Genealogiae Comitum Flandrae*, in Migne, *Patrologia Latina*, vol. 209, cols. 929–932.

34. René Poupardin, "Généalogies angevines du xie siècle," in *Mélanges d'archéologie et d'histoire de l'école française de Rome* 20 (1900), pp. 199–208.

35. *Chroniques des comtes d'Anjou*, ed. Paul Marchegay and Alexandre Salmon, Paris, 1856–1871, pp. 375–379.

36. Herlihy, *Medieval Households*, p. 83.

37. *Garin le Loherain*, pp. 50–51.

Chapter 7. The Twelfth Century: New Family Models

1. Duby, *The Knight, the Lady, and the Priest*, p. 9; Duby, *Medieval Marriage*, p. 32.

2. Duby, *The Knight, the Lady, and the Priest*, p. 10; Duby, *Medieval Marriage*, pp. 30, 119.

3. John T. Noonan, "Marriage in the Middle Ages: Power to Choose," *Viator* 4 (1973), pp. 419–420.

4. James A. Brundage, "Concubinage and Marriage in Medieval Canon Law," *Journal of Medieval History* 1 (1975), pp. 1–17.

5. Duby, *The Knight, the Lady, and the Priest*, p. 6.

6. Noonan, "Power to Choose," p. 420.

7. Beatrice Gottlieb, "The Meaning of Clandestine Marriage," in Wheaton and Hareven, *Family and Sexuality in French History*, p. 50.

8. Noonan, "Power to Choose," p. 425; Sheehan, "Choice of Marriage Partner," p. 12.

9. Noonan, "Power to Choose," pp. 424–425.

10. Brundage, "Concubinage and Marriage," pp. 3–4.

11. Esmein, *Le Mariage en droit canonique*, vol. 1, p. 118; Dillard, *Daughters of the Reconquest*, pp. 37–38; Brundage, "Concubinage and Marriage," pp. 6–7; R. H. Helmholz, *Marriage Litigation in Medieval England*, Cambridge, 1974, p. 26; Herlihy, *Medieval Households*, pp. 80–81.

12. Duby, *The Knight, the Lady, and the Priest*, pp. 183–184; Helmholz, *Marriage Litigation*, pp. 26–27.

13. Charles Donahue, "The Canon Law on the Formation of Marriage and Social Practice in the Later Middle Ages," *Journal of Family History* 8 (1983), pp. 143–146; Esmein, *Le Mariage en droit canonique*, vol. 1, p. 124.

14. Michael M. Sheehan, "The Formation and Stability of Marriage in Fourteenth-Century England: Evidence of an Ely Register," *Medieval Studies* 32 (1971), p. 230.

15. Duby, *The Knight, the Lady, and the Priest*, pp. 189–198.

16. Ibid., pp. 203–206.

17. Ibid., pp. 208–209; Sheehan, "Choice of Marriage Partner," p. 15; Esmein, *Le Mariage en droit canonique*, vol. 1, p. 355.

18. Freed, *Counts of Falkenstein*, p. 35.

19. Constance Bouchard, "The Origins of the French Nobility," *American Historical Review* 86 (1981), pp. 508–509; Duby, "Structures of Kinship and Nobility," pp. 146–147.

20. Bouchard, "Origins of the French Nobility," pp. 513–532.

21. Duby, "French Genealogical Literature," p. 153.

22. Georges Duby, "Youth in Aristocratic Society," in *The Chivalrous Society*, p. 121; Duby, "French Genealogical Literature," pp. 156–157.

23. T. H. White, trans., *The Book of Beasts*, New York, 1960, p. 142.

24. Duby, *The Knight, the Lady, and the Priest*, pp. 255–256.

25. Lambert of Ardres, *Historia comitum Ghisnensium*, in *Monumenta Germaniae Historica, Scriptores*, ed. G. H. Pertz et al., Hanover, 1826–1913, vol. 24, ch. 127, p. 624.

26. Duby, "Youth in Aristocratic Society," pp. 119–120.

27. Fernand Vercauteren, "A Kindred in Northern France in the Eleventh and Twelfth Centuries," in Reuter, *The Medieval Nobility*, pp. 94–95.

28. Duby, "Youth in Aristocratic Society," pp. 114–117.

29. Ibid., p. 113.

30. Frances Gies, *The Knight in History*, New York, 1984, pp. 84–97.

31. Vercauteren, "A Kindred in Northern France," p. 94. Vercauteren speculates that the battle might have been that of Cassel (February 22, 1071) but believes that a private feud is more likely.

32. Gies, *Women in the Middle Ages*, pp. 91–92.

33. Diane Owen Hughes, "Urban Growth and Family Structure in Medieval Genoa," *Past and Present* 66 (1975), pp. 5–10; Hughes, "Kinsmen and Neighbors in Medieval Genoa," in Harry A. Miskimin, David Herlihy, and A. L. Udovitch, eds., *The Medieval City*, New Haven, 1977, p. 100; Jacques Heers, "Urbanisme et structure sociale à Gênes au Moyen Age," in *Studi in onore di Amintore Fanfani*, Milan, 1962, vol. 1, pp. 386–387.

34. Diane Owen Hughes, "Domestic Ideals and Social Behavior: Evidence from Medieval Genoa," in Charles E. Rosenberg, ed., *The Family in History*, Philadelphia, 1975, pp. 118–121.

35. Ibid., p. 121.

36. Hughes, "Urban Growth," pp. 10–11, 19–20.

37. Ibid., p. 20.

38. Ibid., p. 10.

39. Ibid., pp. 13–15.

40. Hughes, "Domestic Ideals," pp. 124–125.

41. Ibid., p. 126.

42. Ibid., pp. 129–130.

43. Ibid., p. 131.

44. Ibid., pp. 132–133.

45. Ibid., pp. 139–140.

46. Ibid., pp. 141–142.

47. Ibid., p. 143.

48. Dillard, *Daughters of the Reconquest*, pp. 12–18.

49. Ibid., p. 26.

50. Ibid., p. 75.

51. Ibid., p. 41.

52. Ibid., pp. 46–49.

53. Ibid., pp. 49–50.

54. Ibid., pp. 51–55.

55. Ibid., pp. 61–64.

56. Ibid., pp. 136–139.

57. Ibid., p. 136.

58. Esmein, *Le Mariage en droit canonique*, vol. 1, p. 131.

59. Dillard, *Daughters of the Reconquest*, pp. 127–133.

60. Ibid., pp. 57–58.

61. Ibid., p. 68.

62. Ibid., p. 79.

63. Ibid., p. 137.

Chapter 8. Peasants Before the Black Death: 1200–1347

1. George C. Homans, *English Villagers of the Thirteenth Century*, New York, 1975 (first published 1941), pp. 12–28. See also Rosamond Jane Faith, "Peasant Families and Inheritance Customs in Medieval England," *Agricultural History Review* 14 (1966), pp. 77–95.

2. Warren O. Ault, *Open-Field Husbandry and the Village Community: A Study of Agrarian By-Laws in Medieval England*, Philadelphia, 1965; Ault, *Open-Field Farming in Medieval England: A Study of Village By-Laws*, New York, 1972; Joan Thirsk, "The Common Fields" and "The Origin of the Common Fields," and J. Z. Titow, "Medieval England and the Open-Field System" in R. H. Hilton, ed., *Peasants, Knights, and Heretics*, Cambridge, 1976, pp. 10–32, 51–56, 33–50. Also Bruce M. S. Campbell, "Population Change and the Genesis of Commonfields on a Norfolk Manor," *Economic History Review*, 2nd ser. 33 (1980), pp. 174–192.

3. F. Pollock and F. W. Maitland, *The History of English Law Before the Time of Edward I*, Cambridge, 1968, vol. 1, p. 419. On freedom, see also F. W. Maitland, *Domesday Book and Beyond*, New York, 1966, pp. 23–61.

4. Cecily Howell, "Peasant Inheritance Customs in the Midlands, 1280–1700," in Jack Goody, ed., *Family and Inheritance: Rural Society in Western Europe*, Cambridge, 1976, p. 119.

5. P. D. A. Harvey, *A Medieval Oxfordshire Village, Cuxham, 1240 to 1400*, Oxford, 1965, pp. 113–119, 133–135.

6. R. H. Hilton, *A Medieval Society: The West Midlands at the End of the Thirteenth Century*, New York, 1966, p. 131.

7. Harvey, *Cuxham*, p. 133.

8. Ibid., pp. 71–72.

9. Barbara Hanawalt, *The Ties That Bound: Peasant Families in Medieval England*, Oxford, 1986, pp. 146–151, 158–160.

10. Homans, *English Villagers*, pp. 285–288, 312–313; Edward Britton, *The Community of the Vill: A Study in the History of the Family and Village Life in Fourteenth-Century England*, Toronto, 1977, pp. 25–26; Harvey, *Cuxham*, p. 145; J. A. Raftis, "Social Structures in Five East Midland Villages, a Study of the Possibilities in the Use of Court Roll Data," *Economic History Review*, 2nd ser. 18 (1965), pp. 91–92; Hanawalt, *Ties That Bound*, p. 132; R. H. Hilton, *The English Peasantry in the Later Middle Ages*, Oxford, 1975, pp. 104–105.

11. Ault, *Open-Field Farming*; Ault, *Open-Field Husbandry*.

12. Britton, *Community of the Vill*, pp. 12–14.

13. Edwin De Windt, *Land and People in Holywell-cum-Needingworth: Structures of Tenure and Patterns of Social Organization in an East Midlands Village, 1252–1457*, Toronto, 1972, pp. 208–210.

14. Britton, *Community of the Vill*, pp. 44–49.

15. Homans, *English Villagers*, pp. 311–312, 318.

16. De Windt, *Holywell*, p. 211.

17. Britton, *Community of the Vill*, p. 46.

18. Hilton, *Peasantry in the Later Middle Ages*, pp. 105–106.

19. Homans, *English Villagers*, pp. 324–325.

20. Britton, *Community of the Vill*, pp. 25–32; De Windt, *Holywell*, pp. 245–250; Martin Pimsler, "Solidarity in the Medieval Village? The Evidence of Personal Pledging at Elton, Huntingdonshire," *Journal of British Studies* 17 (1977), pp. 1–11.

21. J. A. Raftis, *Warboys: Two Hundred Years in the Life of an English Medieval Village*, Toronto, 1974, pp. 3–6, 8, 64.

22. Britton, *Community of the Vill*, pp. 11–12; Harvey, *Cuxham*, pp. 126–128.

23. Raftis, *Warboys*, pp. 67–68.

24. Harvey, *Cuxham*, p. 127.

25. Ibid., pp. 127–128.

26. Ibid., pp. 126–127.

27. Raftis, *Warboys*, pp. 64–65; De Windt, *Holywell*, pp. 184–185.

28. Britton, *Community of the Vill*, p. 18.

29. Eleanor Searle, "Seigneurial Control of Women's Marriage: The Antecedents and Functions of Merchet in England," *Past and Present* 82 (1979), pp. 3–43; also R. H. Hilton, "Freedom and Villeinage in England," in Hilton, *Peasants, Knights, and Heretics*, pp. 180–181, 189–190; Jean Scammell, "Freedom and Marriage in Medieval England," *Economic History Review*, 2nd ser. 27 (1974), pp. 523–537.

30. Ault, *Open-Field Farming*, pp. 145, 163.

31. Searle, "Merchet," p. 21.

32. Homans, *English Villagers*, p. 140; J. A. Raftis, *Tenure and Mobility: Studies in the Social History of the Mediaeval English Village*, Toronto, 1964, p. 46.

33. Raftis, *Tenure and Mobility*, pp. 36–42; Harvey, *Cuxham*, pp. 123–125; Britton, *Community of the Vill*, pp. 20–24.

34. Harvey, *Cuxham*, p. 124.

35. Britton, *Community of the Vill*, pp. 21–22.

36. Homans, *English Villagers*, pp. 133–143.

37. Britton, *Community of the Vill*, pp. 59–64.

38. Homans, *English Villagers*, pp. 212–215.

39. Britton, *Community of the Vill*, pp. 14, 64–67.

40. Ibid., pp. 39–44.

41. Ibid., pp. 51–54.

42. Searle, "Merchet," pp. 28–29.

43. Britton, *Community of the Vill*, pp. 34–37.

44. Raftis, *Tenure and Mobility*, p. 38.

45. Ault, *Open-Field Farming*, p. 158.

46. Elaine Clark, "Some Aspects of Social Security in Medieval England," *Journal of Family History* 7 (1982), pp. 307–320; Homans, *English Villagers*, pp. 144–148; Raftis, *Tenure and Mobility*, pp. 42–46; Hilton, *A Medieval Society*, p. 52.

47. Raftis, *Tenure and Mobility*, pp. 44–45.

48. Hilton, *A Medieval Society*, p. 111.

49. Howard Morris Stuckert, *Corrodies in English Monasteries: A Study in English Social History of the Middle Ages*, Philadelphia, 1923; Hilton, *A Medieval Society*, pp. 111–113.

50. Hanawalt, *Ties That Bound*, p. 235.

51. G. R. Owst, *Literature and Pulpit in Medieval England*, Oxford, 1961, pp. 164–165.

52. Chapelot and Fossier, *Village and House*, p. 185; Hilton, *A Medieval Society*, pp. 93–95; Harvey, *Cuxham*, provides a map of fourteenth-century Cuxham, p. 122.

53. Chaucer, "The Parson's Tale," *The Canterbury Tales*, in *The Complete Works of Geoffrey Chaucer*, ed. F. N. Robinson, Boston, 1933, p. 306, lines 897–899.

54. Hilton, *A Medieval Society*, pp. 94–95; Homans, *English Villagers*, pp. 208–209; Chapelot and Fossier, *Village and House*, pp. 243–244.

55. Chapelot and Fossier, *Village and House*, pp. 296–302; Hilton, *A Medieval Society*, p. 95.

56. Hilton, *A Medieval Society*, pp. 95–100.

57. J. Amphlett, S. G. Hamilton, and R. A. Wilson, eds., *Court Rolls of the Manor of Hales*, Oxford, 1910–1933, vol. 1, p. 167.

58. Hilton, *A Medieval Society*, pp. 100–101.

59. For inheritance and landholding practices in areas of partible inheritance: Richard M. Smith, "Families and Their Land in an Area of Partible Inheritance: Redgrave, Suffolk, 1280–1360," in Richard M. Smith, ed., *Land, Kinship, and Life Cycle*, Cambridge, 1986, pp. 135–195; Barbara Dodwell, "Holdings and Inheritance in Medieval East Anglia," *Economic History Review*, 2nd ser. 20 (1967), pp. 53–66; Alan R. H. Baker, "Open Fields and Partible Inheritance on a Kent Manor," *Economic History Review*, 2nd ser. 17 (1964), pp. 1–23; Baker, "Some Fields and Farms in Medieval Kent," *Archeologia Cantiana* 80 (1965), pp. 152–174; Campbell, "Population Change"; F. R. H. DuBoulay, *The Lordship of Canterbury*, London, 1966.

60. Campbell, "Population Change."

61. Homans, *English Villagers*, pp. 113–120.

62. Smith "Redgrave," pp. 145–149, 175–177.

63. Ibid. pp. 165–170, 174–175.

64. Ibid., pp. 171–172.

65. W. G. Hoskins, *The Midland Peasant: The Economic and Social History of a Lancashire Village*, London, 1957, p. 73.

66. Emmanuel Le Roy Ladurie, *Montaillou, the Promised Land of Error*, trans. Barbara Bray, New York, 1978; originally published as *Montaillou, village occitan de 1294 à 1324*, Paris, 1975. The text of the Inquisition record has been published in French translation (from the original Latin) as *Le Régistre d'Inquisition de Jacques Fournier, evêque de Pamiers (1318–1324)*, trans. and ed. Jean Duvernoy, Toulouse, 1978. A commentary by Leonard E. Boyle of the Pontifical Institute of Mediaeval Studies in Toronto, "Montaillou Revisited: *Mentalité* and Methodology," was published in J. A. Raftis, ed., *Pathways to Medieval Peasants*, Toronto, 1981.

67. Chapelot and Fossier, *Village and House*, pp. 133–134, 182–184.

68. Le Roy Ladurie, *Montaillou* (references are to the English translation), pp. 3–4, 37–41.

69. Ibid., p. 25.

70. Ibid., p. 283.

71. Ibid., pp. 103–114.

72. Ibid., pp. 48–52.

73. Ibid., pp. 41–48.

74. Ibid., pp. 192–194.

75. Ibid., p. 36.

76. Ibid., pp. 195–196.

77. Ibid., p. 185. Barbara Bray's English rendition of the phrase perhaps loses a little of its pungency. The Inquisitorial Register departs from Latin to give the original Provençal, *A cosina secunda, tot le li afonia!* which Jean Duvernoy, in his modern French version of the Register, makes *A cousine seconde, enfonce-le-lui tout!* or "With a second cousin, plunge it in her all the way!"

78. Ibid., pp. 179–180.

79. Ibid., pp. 181–182.

80. Ibid., pp. 187–188.

81. Ibid., pp. 189–190.

82. Ibid., pp. 157, 169–172.

83. Ibid., p. 159.

84. Ibid., pp. 172–173.

85. Ibid., pp. 174–176.

86. Ibid., p. 158.

87. Ibid., pp. 39, 164, 167.

88. Ibid., p. 165.

89. Ibid., pp. 176–178.

90. Ibid., p. 34.

91. Ibid., pp. 196, 216–217.

92. Ibid., pp. 223–230.

Chapter 9. The Aristocratic Lineage: Perils of Primogeniture

1. Kenneth B. McFarlane, *The Nobility of Later Medieval England*, Oxford, 1973, p. 78.

2. Ibid., pp. 123, 173.

3. Ibid., p. 143.

4. Ibid., pp. 71–72.

5. Ibid., p. 63.

6. Ibid., pp. 62–63.

7. F. R. H. DuBoulay, *The Age of Ambition: English Society in the Late Middle Ages*, New York, 1970.

8. McFarlane, *Nobility of Later Medieval England*, pp. 68–70.

9. Ibid., p. 277.

10. Ibid., pp. 71–72.

11. Janet S. Loengard, " 'Of the Gift of Her Husband': English Dower and Its Consequences in the Year 1200," in Kirshner and Wemple, *Women of the Medieval World*, p. 238.

12. McFarlane, *Nobility of Later Medieval England*, pp. 64–67, 137–138.

13. Ibid., pp. 139–140.

14. Ibid., p. 65.

15. Ibid., p. 67.

16. Duby, "Nobility in Medieval France," p. 109.

17. Matthew Paris, *English History from the Year 1235 to 1273 (Chronica Majora)*, trans. J. A. Giles, London, 1854, pp. 119–122.

18. Gies, *Life in a Medieval Castle*, pp. 36–38.

19. Levi Fox, "The Honor and Earldom of Leicester: Origin and Descent, 1066–1399," *English Historical Review* 215 (1939), pp. 385–391.

20. G. W. Prothero, *The Life of Simon de Montfort, Earl of Leicester*, London, 1877, pp. 34–37; Fox, "Honor and Earldom of Leicester," pp. 392–395.

21. Fox, "Honor and Earldom of Leicester," pp. 395–396.

22. Prothero, *Simon de Montfort*, pp. 42–46.

23. Ibid., pp. 47–52.

24. Mary Ann Everett Green, *Lives of the Princesses of England*, London, 1849, vol. 2, p. 82.

25. Fox, "Honor and Earldom of Leicester," pp. 396–399.

26. F. M. Powicke, "Guy de Montfort (1265–1271)," *Transactions of the Royal Historical Society*, ser. 4, 18 (1935), pp. 7–9.

27. Gies, *Women in the Middle Ages*, p. 135.

28. Loengard, "English Dower," pp. 216–235.

Chapter 10. Children in the High Middle Ages

1. Bartholomaeus Anglicus, *De proprietatibus rerum*, published as *Medieval Lore from Bartholomew Anglicus*, edited by Robert Steele from an early English translation by John of Trevisa (1326–1402), London, 1924, here rendered into modern English, pp. 51–52.

2. Michael Goodich, "Bartholomaeus Anglicus on Childrearing," *History of Childhood Quarterly* 3 (1975), p. 78.

For discussions of medieval attitudes toward children: David Herlihy, "Medieval Children," in *Essays on Medieval Civilization: The Walter Prescott Webb Memorial Lectures*, edited by B. K. Lackner and K. R. Philip, London, 1978, pp. 109–142; Urban Tigner Holmes, "Medieval Children," *Journal of Social History* 2 (1968), pp. 164–172; Antonia Gransden, "Childhood and Youth in Medieval England," *Nottingham Medieval Studies* 16 (1972), pp. 3–19; Jerome Kroll, "The Concept of Childhood in the Middle Ages," *Journal of the History of Behavioural Sciences* 13 (1977), pp. 384–393; Richard B. Lyman, Jr., "Barbarism and Religion: Late Roman and Early Medieval Childhood" and Mary McLaughlin, "Survivors and Surrogates: Children and Parents from the Ninth to the Thirteenth Centuries," both in De-Mause, *History of Childhood*, pp. 75–181 (interestingly, these two essays in no way bear out DeMause's theory of mistreatment of children). An exhaustive study of the medieval iconography of childhood by art historian Ilene H. Forsyth is "Children in Early Medieval Art: Ninth Through Twelfth Centuries," *Journal of Psychohistory* 4 (1976), pp. 31–70.

3. *Monumenta Germaniae Historica*, vol. 24, p. 629.

4. *Giraldi Cambrensis Opera*, ed. J. S. Brewer, London, 1961, vol. 1, p. 21.

5. M. B. Salu, trans., *The Ancrene Riwle (The Corpus MS: Ancrene Wisse)*, London, 1955, pp. 102–103.

6. "Fitzstephen's Description of London," in John Stow, *Survey of London*, ed. H. B. Wheatley, London, 1956, pp. 507–509.

7. Trotula of Salerno, *The Diseases of Women (Passionibus mulierum curandorum)*, trans. Elizabeth Mason-Holt, Los Angeles, 1940, pp. 25–26.

8. Barbara A. Hanawalt, "Childrearing among the Lower Classes of Late Medieval England," *Journal of Interdisciplinary History* 8 (1977), pp. 14–15.

9. Giraldus Cambrensis, *The First Version of the Topography of Ireland*, trans. John J. O'Meara, Dundalk, 1951, p. 84.

10. Le Roy Ladurie, *Montaillou*, pp. 213–214.

11. Ibid., pp. 207–208.

12. W. A. Pantin, *The English Church in the Fourteenth Century*, Cambridge, 1955, p. 197.

13. Margaret Wade LaBarge, *A Baronial Household of the Thirteenth Century*, New York, 1966, pp. 45–47.

14. Trotula, *Diseases of Women*, p. 26.

15. Bartholomaeus Anglicus, *De proprietatibus rerum*, pp. 53–54.

16. *Magna Vita Sancti Hugonis (The Life of St. Hugh of Lincoln)*, ed. and trans. Decima L. Dowie and Dom Hugh Farmer, London, 1961–1962, vol. 1, pp. 128–130.

17. Bartholomaeus Anglicus, *De proprietatibus rerum*, pp. 58–59.

18. Richard Helmholz, "Infanticide in the Province of Canterbury during the Fifteenth Century," *History of Childhood Quarterly* 2 (1975), pp. 379–390. Hanawalt, "Medieval Childrearing," pp. 9–14.

19. Ibid., pp. 14–17.

20. Ibid., pp. 20–21.

21. Le Roy Ladurie, *Montaillou*, p. 210.

22. Ibid., pp. 210–211.

23. Ibid., pp. 206, 210.

24. Ibid., pp. 211–212.

25. Kate Norgate, *The Minority of Henry III*, London, 1912, pp. 132–143, 175–177; Sue Sheridan Walker, "Widow and Ward: The Feudal Law of Child Custody in Medieval England," in Stuard, *Women in Medieval Society*, pp. 161–162.

26. Hanawalt, "Childrearing," pp. 18, 19; Hanawalt, *Ties That Bound*, pp. 156–162.

27. *L'Histoire de Guillaume Maréchal*, ed. Paul Meyer, Paris, 1901, vol. 1, p. 28.

28. Roy C. Cave and Herbert H. Coulson, eds., *A Source Book for Medieval Economic History*, New York, 1936, pp. 144–145.

29. Sylvia Thrupp, *The Merchant Class of Medieval London, 1300–1500*, Ann Arbor, 1948, pp. 164–166, 192–193, 213–219.

30. Nicholas, *Domestic Life of a Medieval City*, p. 167.

31. Hanawalt, *Ties That Bound*, pp. 166–167.

32. *The Metalogicon of John of Salisbury, a Twelfth-Century Defense of the Verbal and Logical Arts of the Trivium*, trans. Daniel D. McGarry, Berkeley, 1955, pp. 65–71.

33. Riché, *Education and Culture*, pp. 451–454.

34. *The Monastic Constitutions of Lanfranc*, trans. David Knowles, New York, 1951, pp. 115–117.

35. *The Life of St. Anselm, Archbishop of Canterbury (Eadmeri monachi cantuariensis Vita Sancti Anselmi archiepiscopi cantuariensis)*, trans. R. W. Southern, London, 1962, pp. 36–39.

36. *Chronicon abbatiae Ramesiensis*, ed. W. Dunn Macray, London, 1886, pp. 112–114.

37. McLaughlin, "Survivors and Surrogates," pp. 103–105; *Vita B. Petri Damiani per Joannem monachem eius discipulum*, in Migne, *Patrologia Latina*, vol. 144, cols. 113–117.

38. *Self and Society in Medieval France: The Memoirs of Abbot Guibert of Nogent*, ed. John F. Benton, New York, 1970.

39. Ibid., pp. 63–64.

40. Ibid., p. 72.

41. Ibid., pp. 40–42.

42. Ibid., p. 132.

43. Ibid., p. 68.

44. Ibid., pp. 45–48.

45. Ibid., pp. 49–50.

46. Ibid., pp. 72–74.

47. Ibid., pp. 76–78.

48. Michael Goodich, "Childhood and Adolescence Among the Thirteenth-Century Saints," *History of Childhood Quarterly* 1 (1973), pp. 285–309.

49. *Self and Society*, pp. 89, 47–48.

Marriage and the Family in the Year 1300

1. Sheehan, "Choice of Marriage Partner," p. 32.

Chapter 11. The Impact of the Black Death

1. Cesare Guasti, *Ser Lapo Mazzei: Lettere di un notaro a un mercante del secolo XIV con altre lettere e documenti*, Florence, 1880, letter 18.

2. Christiane Klapisch, "Déclin démographique et structure du ménage: l'exemple de Prato, fin XIVe–fin XVe," in Duby and Le Goff, *Famille et parenté*, p. 258.

3. Ibid., pp. 258–259.

4. Howell, "Peasant Inheritance Customs," p. 125.

5. Boccaccio, *The Decameron*, trans. John Payne, New York, 1931, p. 6.

6. Agnolo di Tura, "Cronica Senese di Agnolo di Tura del Grasso," in L. A. Muratori, *Rerum Italicarum Scriptores*, Bologna, 1934, vol. 15, pt. 6, p. 555.

7. Iris Origo, *The Merchant of Prato: Francesco di Marco Datini, 1335–1410*, Boston, 1986 (reprint of 1957 edition), pp. 371–372.

8. *Letters from Petrarch,* trans. Morris Bishop, Bloomington, Ind., 1966, pp. 73–74.

9. Renée Neu Watkins, "Petrarch and the Black Death: From Fear to Monuments," *Studies in the Renaissance* 19–20 (1972–1973), pp. 19–20.

10. David Herlihy, "Santa Maria Impruneta: A Rural Commune in the Late Middle Ages," in David Herlihy, *Cities and Society in Medieval Italy,* London, 1980, pp. 242–276.

11. Ibid., pp. 249–266.

12. Ibid., pp. 258–264.

13. Ibid., pp. 263–264.

14. Renée Neu Watkins, trans., *The Family in Renaissance Florence* (Leon Battista Alberti's *I Libri della famiglia),* Columbia, S.C., 1969, p. 189; Ginevra Niccolini da Camugliano, "A Medieval Florentine, His Family and His Possessions," *American Historical Review* 31 (1925), p. 18.

15. Herlihy, "Impruneta," p. 266.

16. Ibid., p. 268.

17. Ibid., p. 272.

18. Ibid., pp. 273–274.

19. Zvi Razi, *Life, Marriage, and Death in a Medieval Parish: Economy, Society and Demography in Halesowen, 1270–1400,* Cambridge, 1980, pp. 99–113.

20. Ibid., pp. 101–104.

21. Ibid., pp. 104–105.

22. Ibid., p. 110.

23. Ibid., pp. 112–113.

24. A. R. Bridbury, "The Black Death," *Economic History Review,* 2nd ser., 26 (1973), pp. 590–591, cites W. A. Lewis's "classic exposition" in "Economic Development with Unlimited Supplies of Labor," *The Manchester School* 22 (1954): ". . . the phenomenon of an economy in which labour is so plentiful that its marginal productivity is negligible, or nil, or even negative; an economy in fact which has nothing to lose in productive power if its surplus manpower is removed, and indeed, something, perhaps much, to gain."

25. Howell, "Peasant Inheritance Customs," pp. 124–126.

26. *The Chronicle of Jean de Venette,* trans. Jean Birdsall and R. A. Newhall, New York, 1953, p. 51.

27. Raftis, *Warboys,* p. 219.

28. De Windt, *Holywell,* pp. 263–275.

29. J. A. Raftis, "Changes in an English Village after the Black Death," *Medieval Studies* 29 (1967), p. 165.

30. Raftis, *Warboys,* pp. 216–217.

31. R. H. Hilton, *Bond Men Made Free: Medieval Peasant Movements and the English Rising of 1381,* New York, 1973, p. 184.

32. Ibid., p. 180.

33. Christopher Dyer, "Families and Land in the West Midlands," in Smith, *Land, Kinship, and Life Cycle*, p. 306; Homans, *English Villagers*, pp. 276–284.

34. Harry A. Miskimin, *The Economy of Early Renaissance Europe, 1300–1460*, Englewood Cliffs, N.J., 1969, pp. 32–43, 57–61, 70–72.

35. Jean de Venette, *Chronicle*, pp. 50–51.

36. Klapisch, "Déclin démographique," pp. 259–260.

37. David Herlihy, "Deaths, Marriages, Births, and the Tuscan Economy (ca. 1300–1550)," in Herlihy, *Cities and Society*, p. 150.

38. Ibid., pp. 152–153.

39. Ibid., p. 154.

40. Ibid., p. 157.

Chapter 12. The Late Medieval Peasant Family: 1350–1500

1. Hoskins, *Midland Peasant*, pp. 284–294; Sarah McKinnon, "The Peasant House: Evidence of Manuscript Illumination," in Raftis, *Pathways to Medieval Peasants*, pp. 301–309.

2. McKinnon, "The Peasant House," pp. 305–307.

3. Hanawalt, *Ties That Bound*, p. 48.

4. Ibid., p. 49; Hoskins, *Midland Peasant*, pp. 295–297.

5. Hilton, *English Peasantry in the Later Middle Ages*, pp. 31–34.

6. Ibid., pp. 101–102.

7. Raftis, "Changes in the English Village," p. 173.

8. Ibid., p. 176.

9. Hanawalt, *Ties That Bound*, p. 121.

10. De Windt, *Holywell*, pp. 216–217.

11. Raftis, *Warboys*, p. 230.

12. Harvey, *Cuxham*, pp. 136–137, 118.

13. Hoskins, *Midland Peasant*, pp. 41–42.

14. Hanawalt, *Ties That Bound*, pp. 132–134.

15. Zvi Razi, "The Erosion of the Family Land Bond in the Late Fourteenth and Fifteenth Centuries, a Methodological Note," in Smith, *Land, Kinship, and Life Cycle*, p. 301.

16. *Church-Wardens' Accounts of Coscombe, Pilton, Latton, Tintinhull, Morebath, and St. Michael's Bath*, ed. Edmund Hobhouse, Somerset Record Society 4 (1890), p. 1, cited in Hanawalt, *Ties That Bound*, p. 193.

17. Sheehan, "Formation and Stability of Marriage," pp. 254–255.

18. Frederick Furnivall, ed., *The Babees Book*, New York, 1969 (first printed in London, 1868), p. 48.

19. Ibid., p. 36.

20. Searle, "Seigneurial Control," p. 26.

21. Kenneth Stevenson, *Nuptial Blessings: A Study of Christian Marriage Rites*, New York, 1983, pp. 76–80.

22. Donahue, "Canon Law on the Formation of Marriage," pp. 146–150.

23. Sheehan, "Formation and Stability of Marriage," p. 250.

24. Helmholz, *Marriage Litigation*, p. 29.

25. Henry Ansgar Kelly, "Clandestine Marriage and Chaucer's 'Troilus,'" *Viator* 4 (1973), pp. 435–437.

26. Sheehan, "Formation and Stability of Marriage," p. 249.

27. Helmholz, *Marriage Litigation*, pp. 49–50.

28. Ibid., pp. 50–51.

29. Hilton, *English Peasantry in the Later Middle Ages*, p. 59.

30. Searle, "Seigneurial Control," pp. 31–32.

31. Sheehan, "Formation and Stability of Marriage," pp. 261–263.

32. Helmholz, *Marriage Litigation*, pp. 88–89.

33. Nicholas, *Domestic Life of a Medieval City*, p. 36.

34. *Bedfordshire Wills 1480–1519*, trans. Patricia Bell, *Bedfordshire Historical Record Society* 45 (1966).

35. Hanawalt, *Ties That Bound*, pp. 221–222.

36. *Bedfordshire Wills*, pp. 11–12.

37. Hanawalt, *Ties That Bound*, pp. 76–78.

38. Clark, "Aspects of Social Security," pp. 308–309, 316.

39. Ibid., p. 310.

40. Ibid., p. 311.

41. Ibid., pp. 311–312, 318.

42. Ibid., p. 312.

43. Hanawalt, *Ties That Bound*, pp. 236–237.

44. Alexander Murray, "Religion Among the Poor in Thirteenth-Century France, the Testimony of Humbert de Romans," *Traditio* XXX (1974), p. 295.

45. *Middle English Sermons*, ed. Woodburn O. Ross, London, 1940, pp. 89–90.

Chapter 13. A Family of the English Landed Gentry

1. H. S. Bennett, *The Pastons and Their England: Studies in an Age of Transition*, Cambridge, 1970 (first published 1922). James Gairdner, ed., *The Paston Letters, A.D. 1422–1509*, 6 vols., New York, 1965 (first published London, 1900, revised 1904). Norman Davis, ed., *The Paston Letters*, 2 vols, Oxford, 1971.

2. Davis, *Paston Letters*, pp. xli–xliii; also Gairdner, *Paston Letters*, no. 643 (IV, pp. 247–249).

3. Bennett, *The Pastons and Their England*, pp. 2–3.

4. Ibid., pp. 3–4.

5. Gairdner, *Paston Letters*, no. 702 (II, pp. 127–130).

6. Gies, *The Knight in History*, pp. 206–207.

7. H. D. Barnes and W. D. Simpson, "The Building Accounts of Caister Castle, A.D. 1432–1435," *Norfolk Archaeology* 30 (1952), pp. 178–188.

8. Gies, *Knight in History*, pp. 188–190.

9. Bennett, *The Pastons and Their England*, pp. 11–17; Gairdner, *Paston Letters*, nos. 488 (IV, pp. 1–4), 568 (IV, pp. 107–108), 569 (IV, pp. 109–110), 572 (IV, pp. 116–117).

10. Ann S. Haskell, "The Paston Women on Marriage in Fifteenth-Century England," *Viator* 4 (1973), pp. 463–465.

11. Gairdner, *Paston Letters*, no. 47 (II, pp. 55–56).

12. Ibid., no. 497 (IV, p. 15).

13. Ibid., no. 489 (IV, pp. 4–5).

14. Ibid., no. 224 (II, p. 282).

15. Ibid., no. 183 (II, pp. 228–229).

16. Ibid., no. 595 (IV, p. 164).

17. Bennett, *The Pastons and Their England*, pp. 12–13, 83–84. Davis, *Paston Letters*, p. xlvi.

18. Bennett, *The Pastons and Their England*, p. 13; Davis, *Paston Letters*, pp. xlvi–xlvii.

19. Bennett, *The Pastons and Their England*, pp. 102–108.

20. Gairdner, *Paston Letters*, no. 362 (III, p. 123).

21. Davis, *Paston Letters*, pp. xxxvii–xxxviii.

22. Gairdner, *Paston Letters*, no. 766 (V, p. 93).

23. Ibid., no. 978 (VI, p. 52).

24. Ibid., nos. 706, 707 (V, pp. 18–19).

25. Ibid., no. 704 (V, pp. 14–16).

26. Ibid., no. 742 (V, p. 69).

27. Ibid., no. 781 (V, p. 111).

28. Ibid., no. 798 (V, p. 135).

29. Ibid., no. 831 (V, p. 181).

30. Ibid., no. 842 (V, p. 198).

31. Ibid., no. 863 (V, pp. 220–221).

32. Ibid., nos. 900, 916 (V, pp. 293–294).

33. Ibid., no. 933 (V, pp. 323–324).

34. Ibid., no. 662 (IV, pp. 270–271).

35. Ibid., no. 742 (V, pp. 68–70).

36. Ibid., no. 781 (V, p. 109).

37. Ibid., nos. 850, 858 (V, pp. 206–208).

38. Ibid., no. 850 (V, p. 207).

39. Ibid., no. 860 (V, pp. 216–218).

40. Ibid., no. 885 (V, pp. 251–252).

41. Ibid., no. 890 (V, p. 259).

42. Ibid., no. 903 (V, pp. 273–274).

43. Ibid., no. 887 (V, pp. 255–256).

44. Ibid., no. 895 (V, p. 265).

45. Ibid., no. 896 (V, p. 266).

46. Ibid., no. 896 (V, p. 266).

47. Ibid., nos. 897, 898 (V. pp. 267–268).

48. Ibid., no. 903 (V, p. 274).

49. Ibid., no. 899 (V, p. 269).

50. Ibid., no. 901 (V, pp. 271–272).

51. Ibid., no. 902 (V, pp. 272–273).

52. Ibid., no. 905 (V, pp. 275–276).

53. Ibid., no. 911 (V, pp. 285–286).

54. Ibid., no. 915 (V, pp. 290–292).

55. Ibid., no. 916 (V, p. 294).

56. Ibid., no. 923 (V, pp. 307–308).

57. Ibid., no. 982 (VI, p. 58).

58. Ibid., no. 926 (V, p. 312).

59. Davis, *Paston Letters*, p. 11.

60. Gairdner, *Paston Letters*, no. 825 (V, p. 173).

61. Ibid., no. 942 (VI, pp. 7–8).

62. Ibid., no. 974 (VI, pp. 43–44).

63. Ibid., no. 94 (II, pp. 109–111).

64. Ibid., no. 224 (II, pp. 281–282).

65. Ibid., no. 237 (II, p. 301).

66. Ibid., nos. 242, 243 (II, pp. 314–316).

67. Ibid., nos. 250, 252 (II, pp. 325–328).

68. Ibid., no. 260 (III, pp. 1–3).

69. Ibid., no. 374 (III, pp. 233–234).

70. Ibid., no. 843 (V, p. 200). Bennett believed that Anne was the elder of the two daughters; Norman Davis concluded that Anne was born about 1455, Margery before 1450 (*Paston Letters*, p. lxii).

71. Ibid., no. 842 (V, p. 199).

72. Ibid., no. 884 (V, p. 250).

73. Ibid., no. 713 (V, pp. 25–28).

74. Ibid., no. 721 (V, pp. 37–40).

75. Ibid., no. 978 (VI, p. 52).

76. Ibid., no. 733 (V, pp. 57–58).

77. Ibid., I, pp. 292–294; nos. 856, 857, 862, 863, 875, 916, 917 (V, pp. 211–214, 220–222, 293–296).

78. Bennett, *The Pastons and Their England*, pp. 25–26.

79. McFarlane, *Nobility of Later Medieval England*, p. 97.

80. Bennett, *The Pastons and Their England*, pp. 90–100.

81. William Langland, *The Vision and Creed of Piers Plowman*, ed. Thomas Wright, London, 1887, vol. 1, p. 179 (Passus 10, lines 5795–5808).

82. Gairdner, *Paston Letters*, no. 695 (V, pp. 1–4).

83. Bennett, *The Pastons and Their England*, pp. 111–113.

84. Gairdner, *Paston Letters*, no. 637 (IV, pp. 226–231).

85. Francis Worship, "Account of a MS. Genealogy of the Paston Family," *Norfolk Archaeology* 4 (1855), pp. 1–55.

Chapter 14. A Merchant's Family in Fifteenth-Century Florence

1. *Il Libro degli affari proprii di casa di Lapo di Giovanni Niccolini de' Sirigatti*, ed. Christian Bec, Paris, 1969, p. 55.

2. Ibid., pp. 55–56.

3. Herlihy and Klapisch-Zuber, *Tuscans and Their Families*, p. 349.

4. Klapisch-Zuber, *Women, Family, and Ritual*, p. 71.

5. David Herlihy, "Mapping Households in Medieval Italy," *Catholic History Review* 58 (1972), pp. 1–19.

6. Klapisch-Zuber, *Women, Family, and Ritual*, pp. 70–72.

7. R. A. Goldthwaite, "The Florentine Palace as Domestic Architecture," *American Historical Review* 77 (1972), p. 1002.

8. Origo, *Merchant of Prato*, pp. 245–263.

9. Niccolini, "A Medieval Florentine," pp. 5–6.

10. Ibid., p. 10.

11. Klapisch-Zuber, *Women, Family, and Ritual*, p. 79.

12. Nicholas, *Domestic Life of a Medieval City*, pp. 175–206.

13. Heers, "Urbanisme et structure sociale a Gênes au Moyen-Age," pp. 384–389.

14. Herlihy, *Medieval Households*, pp. 88–92.

15. Niccolini, "A Medieval Florentine," p. 2.

16. Klapisch-Zuber, *Women, Family, and Ritual*, p. 72.

17. Ibid., pp. 72–73.

18. Niccolini, "A Medieval Florentine," pp. 4–5.

19. Klapisch-Zuber, *Women, Family, and Ritual*, pp. 72–73.

20. Herlihy, "Mapping Households," p. 80; Herlihy, "The Tuscan Town in the Quattrocento," in *Cities and Society*, p. 87. See also Iris Origo, "The Domestic Enemy: The Eastern Slaves in Tuscany in the Fourteenth

and Fifteenth Centuries," *Speculum* 30 (1955), pp. 321–366.

21. Klapisch-Zuber, *Women, Family, and Ritual*, p. 75.

22. Herlihy and Klapisch-Zuber, *Tuscans and Their Families*, p. 283.

23. Klapisch-Zuber, *Women, Family, and Ritual*, p. 88.

24. Herlihy, "Mapping Households," p. 19.

25. Watkins, *The Family in Renaissance Florence*, trans. of Leon Battista Alberti, *I Libri della famiglia* (henceforth referred to as Alberti, *I Libri della famiglia*), p. 222.

26. Ibid., p. 224.

27. Ibid., Introduction (R. R. Bolgar), pp. 1–2.

28. Ibid., pp. 115–116.

29. Klapisch-Zuber, *Women, Family, and Ritual*, pp. 81–83.

30. Niccolini, "A Medieval Florentine," p. 2.

31. Klapisch-Zuber, *Women, Family, and Ritual*, pp. 83–84.

32. Alberti, *I Libri della famiglia*, p. 117.

33. Gregorio Dati, *Diary*, in *Two Memoirs of Renaissance Florence: The Diaries of Buonaccorso Pitti and Gregorio Dati*, trans. Julia Martines, New York, 1967, p. 114.

34. Klapisch-Zuber, *Women, Family, and Ritual*, p. 90.

35. Joseph H. Lynch, "Hugh I of Cluny's Sponsorship of Henry IV, Its Context and Consequences," *Speculum* 60 (1985), pp. 806–807.

36. James Bruce Ross, "The Middle Class Child in Urban Italy, Fourteenth to Early Sixteenth Century," in DeMause, *History of Childhood*, p. 189.

37. Dante, *Divine Comedy*, trans. Louis Biancolli, New York, 1966, vol. 1, p. 59.

38. Julius Kirshner and Anthony Molho, "The Dowry Fund and the Marriage Market in Early Quattrocento Florence," *Journal of Modern History* 50 (1978), pp. 403–438.

39. Herlihy and Klapisch-Zuber, *Tuscans and Their Families*, p. 86.

40. Herlihy, "The Tuscan Town in the Quattrocento," pp. 91–92.

41. Niccolini, "A Medieval Florentine," p. 4.

42. Klapisch-Zuber, *Women, Family, and Ritual*, p. 183.

43. Iris Origo, *The World of San Bernardino*, New York, 1962, p. 55.

44. Klapisch-Zuber, *Women, Family, and Ritual*, p. 185.

45. Ibid., p. 194.

46. Ibid., p. 185; Sheehan, "Choice of Marriage Partner," pp. 31–32.

47. Klapisch-Zuber, *Women, Family, and Ritual*, pp. 186–187.

48. Ibid., pp. 262–266; René Girard, "Marriage in Avignon in the Second Half of the Fifteenth Century," *Speculum* 28 (1953), p. 492.

49. Giovanni Boccaccio, *Corbaccio*, ed. P. G. Ricci, Turin, 1977, pp. 71–72, cited in Christiane Klapisch, "La 'Mère cruelle,' maternité, veuvage,

et dot dans la Florence des XIVe–XVe siècles," *Annales: Economies, Sociétés, Civilisations* 38 (1983), p. 1107.

50. Origo, *World of San Bernardino*, p. 71.

51. Julius Kirshner, "Wives' Claims Against Insolvent Husbands," in Kirshner and Wemple, *Women of the Medieval World*, p. 257.

52. Origo, *World of San Bernardino*, p. 59.

53. David Herlihy, "Some Social and Psychological Roots of Violence in the Tuscan Cities," in Herlihy, *Cities and Society*, pp. 129–154.

54. Ross, "The Middle Class Child," p. 194.

55. Klapisch-Zuber, *Women, Family, and Ritual*, pp. 137–138.

56. Origo, *World of San Bernardino*, p. 60.

57. Ross, "Middle Class Child," p. 187.

58. Klapisch-Zuber, *Women, Family, and Ritual*, p. 144.

59. Alberti, *I Libri della famiglia*, p. 50.

60. Klapisch-Zuber, *Women, Family, and Ritual*, p. 108.

61. Ross, "Middle Class Child," pp. 204, 212; Joseph and Frances Gies, *Leonard of Pisa and the New Mathematics of the Middle Ages*, New York, 1969, p. 98.

62. Alberti, *I Libri della famiglia*, p. 82.

63. Origo, *Merchant of Prato*, pp. 227–228.

64. Origo, *World of San Bernardino*, p. 65.

65. Alberti, *I Libri della famiglia*, pp. 36–37.

66. Ibid., p. 37.

67. Ibid., p. 88.

68. Origo, *World of San Bernardino*, p. 62.

69. Ibid., p. 63.

70. Ibid., pp. 65–66.

71. Ibid., p. 269.

72. Goldthwaite, "The Florentine Palace," p. 1010.

73. Klapisch-Zuber, *Women, Family, and Ritual*, p. 112.

74. Herlihy, "The Tuscan Town in the Quattrocento," p. 97.

75. P. P. A. Biller, "Birth Control in the West," *Past and Present* 94 (1982), p. 17.

76. Herlihy and Klapisch-Zuber, *Tuscans and Their Families*, p. 253; Herlihy, "The Tuscan Town in the Quattrocento," p. 97.

77. Herlihy, "Mapping Households in Medieval Italy," pp. 14–15; Herlihy and Klapisch-Zuber, *Tuscans and Their Families*, pp. 250–251.

78. Klapisch-Zuber, *Women, Family, and Ritual*, p. 17; Herlihy and Klapisch-Zuber, *Tuscans and Their Families*, p. 245.

79. Origo, *World of San Bernardino*, p. 63.

80. Niccolini, "A Medieval Florentine," p. 8.

81. Ibid., pp. 8–9.

Chapter 15. Legacy

1. Alberti, *I Libri della famiglia*, p. 80.

2. Herlihy, *Medieval Households*, p. 158.

3. Thrupp, *Merchant Class of Medieval London*, pp. 164–165.

4. Hanawalt, *Ties That Bound*, p. 248.

5. Curt S. Gutkind, *Cosimo de' Medici, Pater Patriae, 1389–1464*, Oxford, 1938, pp. 216–217.

6. Sheehan, "Choice of Marriage Partner," p. 29.

7. A. Lecoy de la Marche, *La Chaire française au moyen âge*, Paris, 1886, p. 431.

8. Jacques Rossiaud, "Prostitution, Sex, and Society in French Towns in the Fifteenth Century," in Ariès and Béjin, *Western Sexuality*, p. 93.

9. Steven Ozment, *When Fathers Ruled: Family Life in Reformation Europe*, Cambridge, Mass., 1983, p. 36.

10. Philippe Ariès, "The Indissoluble Marriage," in Ariès and Béjin, *Western Sexuality*, p. 155.

11. Brundage, "Concubinage and Marriage," p. 11.

12. Noonan, "Power to Choose," p. 434.

13. P. Ourliac, *Le Droit privé avignonais aux XIVe et XVe siècles*, Paris, 1936, cited in René Girard, "Marriage in Avignon," p. 493.

14. Nicholas, *Domestic Life of a Medieval City*, pp. 36–37.

15. Ozment, *When Fathers Ruled*, p. 46.

16. Ibid., p. 48.

17. Ibid., p. 8.

18. Jean-Louis Flandrin, "Sex in Married Life in the Early Middle Ages: The Church's Teaching and Behavioural Reality," in Ariès and Béjin, *Western Sexuality*, p. 126.

19. Ibid., p. 115.

20. Helen R. Lemay, "Antonius Guainerius and Medieval Gynecology," in Kirshner and Wemple, *Women in the Medieval World*, pp. 331–333.

21. Helmholz, "Infanticide," p. 395.

22. William L. Langer, "Infanticide: A Historical Review," *History of Childhood Quarterly* 1 (1974), p. 362.

23. J. Heers, *Le Clan familial au moyen âge*, Paris, 1974, p. 112.

24. Goldthwaite, "The Florentine Palace," pp. 977–1012.

25. Ferdinand Schevill, *The Medici*, New York, 1949, p. 108; Gutkind, *Cosimo de' Medici*, pp. 235–236.

Bibliography

Amphlett, J., S. G. Hamilton, and R. A. Wilson, eds. *Court Rolls of the Manor of Hales.* Oxford, 1910–1933.

The Anglo-Saxon Chronicle. Translated by G. N. Garmonsway. London, 1953.

Ariès, Philippe. *Centuries of Childhood: A Social History of Family Life.* Translated by Robert Baldick. New York, 1962.

———. "The Indissoluble Marriage." In *Western Sexuality: Practice and Precept in Past and Present Times,* edited by Philippe Ariès and André Béjin, 140–157. London, 1985.

———. *Western Attitudes Toward Death, from the Middle Ages to the Present.* Translated by Patricia M. Ranum. Baltimore, 1974.

Ault, Warren O. *Open-Field Farming in Medieval England: A Study of Village By-Laws.* New York, 1972.

———. *Open-Field Husbandry and the Village Community: A Study of Agrarian By-Laws in Medieval England.* Philadelphia, 1965.

Baker, A. R. H. "Open Fields and Partible Inheritance on a Kent Manor." *Economic History Review,* 2nd ser., 17 (1964–1965): 1–22.

———. "Some Fields and Farms in Medieval Kent." *Archeologia Cantiana* 80 (1965): 152–174.

Baker, Derek, ed. *Medieval Women.* Oxford, 1978.

Balsdon, J. P. V. D. *Life and Leisure in Ancient Rome.* London, 1969.

———. *Roman Women: Their History and Habits.* New York, 1963.

Barnes, H. D., and W. D. Simpson. "The Building Accounts of Caister Castle, A.D. 1432–1435." *Norfolk Archaeology* 30 (1952): 178–188.

Bartholomaeus Anglicus. *De proprietatibus rerum.* Published as *Medieval Lore from Bartholomew Anglicus,* edited by Robert Steele. London, 1924.

Baum, Paull F., trans. *Anglo-Saxon Riddles of the Exeter Book*. Durham, N.C., 1963.

Becker, Marvin. "Individualism in the Early Italian Renaissance: Burden and Blessing." *Studies in the Renaissance* 19 (1972): 273–297.

Bede's Ecclesiastical History of the English Nation. Translated by J. Stevens, revised by J. A. Giles. London, 1963.

Bedfordshire Wills, 1480–1519. Translated by Patricia Bell. *Bedfordshire Historical Record Society* 45 (1966).

Bemont, Charles. *Simon de Montfort, Earl of Leicester, 1208–1265*. Translated by E. F. Jacob. Oxford, 1930.

Bender, Donald. "A Refinement of the Concept of the Household: Families, Co-Residence, and Domestic Function." *American Anthropologist* 69 (1967): 493–504.

Bennett, H. S. *The Pastons and Their England*. Cambridge, 1970 (reprint of 1922 edition).

Beowulf. Translated by William Alfred. In *Medieval Epics*. New York, 1963.

Berkner, Lutz K. "Recent Research on the History of the Family in Western Europe." *Journal of Marriage and the Family* 35 (1973): 395–405.

———. "Rural Family Organization in Europe: A Problem in Comparative History." *Peasant Studies Newsletter* 1, no. 4 (1972): 145–156.

———. "The Stem Family and the Developmental Cycle of the Peasant Household: An Eighteenth-Century Austrian Example." *American Historical Review* 77 (1972): 398–418.

———. "The Use and Misuse of Census Data for the Historical Analysis of Family Structure." *Journal of Interdisciplinary History* 5 (1975): 721–738.

Biller, P. P. A. "Birth Control in the West in the Thirteenth and Fourteenth Centuries." *Past and Present* 94 (1982): 3–26.

Bishop, Jane. "Bishops as Marital Advisors in the Ninth Century." In *Women of the Medieval World: Essays in Honor of John H. Mundy*, edited by Julius Kirshner and Suzanne F. Wemple, 53–84. London, 1985.

Blair, Peter Hunter. *An Introduction to Anglo-Saxon England*. Cambridge, 1966.

Bloch, Marc. *Feudal Society*. Translated by L. A. Manyon. 2 vols. Chicago, 1964.

———. *Slavery and Serfdom in the Middle Ages*. Translated by William R. Beer. Berkeley, 1975.

Bondurand, E. *L'Éducation Carolingienne: le Manuel de Dhuoda*. Paris, 1887.

Bouchard, Constance B. "Consanguinity and Noble Marriages in the Tenth and Eleventh Centuries." *Speculum* 56 (1981): 268–287.

———. "The Origins of the French Nobility: A Reassessment." *American Historical Review* 86 (1981): 501–532.

_____. "The Structure of a Twelfth-Century French Family: The Lords of Seignelay." *Viator* 10 (1979): 39–56.

Boussard, Jacques. *The Civilization of Charlemagne.* New York, 1968.

Boyle, Leonard. "Montaillou Revisited." In *Pathways to Medieval Peasants,* edited by J. A. Raftis, 119–140. Toronto, 1981.

_____. "The *Oculus sacerdotis* and Some Other Works of William of Pagula." *Transactions of the Royal Historical Society,* 5th ser., 5 (1955): 81–110.

Bridbury, A. R. "The Black Death." *Economic History Review,* 2nd ser., 26 (1973): 577–591.

Britton, Edward. *The Community of the Vill: A Study in the History of the Family and Village Life in Fourteenth-Century England.* Toronto, 1977.

_____. "The Peasant Family in Fourteenth-Century England." *Peasant Studies* 5 (1976): 2–7.

Brooke, Christopher. "Marriage and Society in the Central Middle Ages." In *Marriage and Society,* edited by R. B. Outhwaite, 17–34. Baltimore, 1983.

Brundage, James A. "Concubinage and Marriage in Medieval Canon Law." *Journal of Medieval History* 1 (1975): 1–17.

Bullough, D. A. "Early Medieval Social Groupings: The Terminology of Kinship." *Past and Present* 45 (1969): 3–18.

Cammarosano, Paolo. "Les Structures familiales dans les villes de l'Italie communale (XIIe–XIVe siècles)." In *Famille et parenté dans l'Occident médiéval,* edited by Georges Duby and Jacques Le Goff, 181–194. Rome, 1977.

Campbell, B. M. S. "Population Change and the Genesis of Common Fields on a Norfolk Manor." *Economic History Review,* 2nd ser., 33 (1980): 174–192.

Cantor, Leonard, ed. *The English Medieval Landscape.* Philadelphia, 1982.

Carcopino, Jérôme. *Daily Life in Ancient Rome.* Translated by E. O. Lorimer. New York, 1971 (reprint of 1940 edition).

Carolingian Chronicles: Royal Frankish Annals and Nithard's Histories. Translated by Bernhard Walter Scholz and Barbara Rogers. Ann Arbor, 1970.

Chapelot, Jean, and Robert Fossier. *The Village and House in the Middle Ages.* Translated by Henry Cleere. Berkeley, 1985.

The Chronicle of Jean de Venette. Translated by Jean Birdsall and R. A. Newhall. New York, 1953.

Chronicon Abbatiae Ramesiensis. Edited by W. Dunn Macray. London, 1886.

Il Chronicon Farfense di Gregorio di Catino. Edited by Ugo Balzani. Vols. 33–34 of *Fonti per la Storia d'Italia.* Rome, 1903.

Chroniques des comtes d'Anjou. Edited by Paul Marchegay and Alexandre Salmon. Paris, 1856–1871.

Church-Wardens' Accounts of Croscombe, Pilton, Latton, Tintinhull, Morebath, and St. Michael's Bath. Edited by Edmund Hobhouse. *Somerset Record Society* 4 (1890).

Clark, Elaine. "Some Aspects of Social Security in Medieval England." *Journal of Family History* 7 (1982): 307–320.

Coleman, Emily. "L'Infanticide dans le Haut Moyen Age." *Annales: Economies, Sociétés, Civilisations* 29 (1974): 315–335 (reprinted as "Infanticide in the Early Middle Ages," in Susan Mosher Stuard, ed., *Women in Medieval Society,* Philadelphia, 1976).

————. "Medieval Marriage Characteristics: A Neglected Factor in the History of Medieval Serfdom." *Journal of Interdisciplinary History* 2 (1971): 205–217.

Court Roll of Chalgrave Manor. Edited by Marian K. Dale. *Bedfordshire Historical Record Society* 28 (1950).

Cowell, Frank. R. *Everyday Life in Ancient Rome.* London, 1961.

Cronica Senese di Agnolo di Tura del Grasso. Vol. 15, part 6 of *Rerum Italicarum Scriptores,* edited by L. A. Muratori. Bologna, 1934.

Dati, Gregorio. *Diary.* In *Two Memoirs of Renaissance Florence: The Diaries of Buonaccorso Pitti and Gregorio Dati.* Translated by Julia Martines. New York, 1967.

Davis, Norman, ed. *The Paston Letters.* 2 vols. Oxford, 1971.

Declareuil, Joseph. *Rome the Law Giver.* New York, 1926.

DeMause, Lloyd. "The Evolution of Childhood." In *The History of Childhood,* edited by Lloyd DeMause, 1–74. London, 1976. Also published in *History of Childhood Quarterly* 1 (1974): 503–606.

Devisse, Jean. *Hincmar, Archevêque de Reims, 845–882.* 2 vols. Geneva, 1975.

De Windt, Anne. "A Peasant Land Market and Its Participants, King's Ripton (1280–1400)." *Midland History* 4 (1978): 142–159.

De Windt, Edwin. *Land and People in Holywell-cum-Needingworth: Structures of Tenure and Patterns of Social Organization in an East Midlands Village, 1253–1457.* Toronto, 1972.

Dhuoda. *Manuel pour mon fils.* Edited and translated by Pierre Riché. Paris, 1975.

Dillard, Heath. *Daughters of the Reconquest: Women in Castilian Town Society, 1100–1300.* Cambridge, 1985.

Dodwell, Barbara. "Holdings and Inheritance in Medieval East Anglia." *Economic History Review,* 2nd ser., 20 (1967): 53–66.

Donahue, Charles, Jr. "The Canon Law on the Formation of Marriage and Social Practice in the Later Middle Ages." *Journal of Family History* 8 (1983): 144–158.

Dooley, W. J. *Marriage According to St. Ambrose.* Washington, D.C., 1948.

Drew, Katherine Fischer. "The Germanic Family of the *Leges Burgundionum.*" *Medievalia et Humanistica* 15 (1963): 5–14.

———, trans. and ed. *The Burgundian Code.* Philadelphia, 1972.

———, trans. and ed. *The Lombard Laws.* Philadelphia, 1973.

Du Boulay, F. R. H. *An Age of Ambition: English Society in the Late Middle Ages.* New York, 1970.

———. *The Lordship of Canterbury.* London, 1966.

Duby, Georges. *The Chivalrous Society.* Translated by Cynthia Postan. Berkeley, 1977. Articles cited in text:

"French Genealogical Literature, the Eleventh and Twelfth Centuries": 149–157.

"Lineage, Nobility, and Knighthood, the Mâconnais in the Twelfth Century—a Revision": 59–80.

"The Nobility in Medieval France": 94–111.

"The Structure of Kinship and Nobility, Northern France in the Eleventh and Twelfth Centuries": 134–148.

"Youth in Aristocratic Society": 112–122.

———. *The Early Growth of the European Economy: Warriors and Peasants from the Seventh to the Twelfth Century.* Translated by Howard B. Clarke. Ithaca, New York, 1973.

———. "Histoire des mentalités." In *L'Histoire et ses méthodes*, edited by C. Samaran, 937–966. Paris, 1961.

———. *The Knight, the Lady, and the Priest: The Making of Modern Marriage in Medieval France.* Translated by Barbara Bray. New York, 1983.

———. *Medieval Marriage: Two Models from Twelfth-Century France.* Translated by Elborg Forster. Baltimore, 1978.

———. *Rural Economy and Country Life in the Medieval West.* Translated by Cynthia Postan. Columbia, S.C., 1968.

———. *La Société aux xie et xiie siècles dans la région Mâconnaise.* Paris, 1955.

Duby, Georges, and Jacques Le Goff, eds. *Famille et parenté dans l'Occident médiéval.* Rome, 1977.

Duvernoy, Jean, ed. *Le Régistre d'Inquisition de Jacques Fournier, evêque de Pamiers (1318–1325).* 3 vols. Toulouse, 1965.

Dyer, Christopher. "Families and Land in the West Midlands." In *Land, Kinship, and Life Cycle*, edited by R. M. Smith, 305–311. Cambridge, 1986.

Easton, Stewart C., and Helene Wieruszowski. *The Era of Charlemagne.* Princeton, 1961.

Einhard and Notker the Stammerer. *Two Lives of Charlemagne.* Translated by Lewis Thorpe. Harmondsworth, 1969.

Emerton, E., trans. *The Letters of Saint Boniface.* New York, 1940.

Erickson, Carolly, and Kathleen Casey. "Women in the Middle Ages, a Working Bibliography." *Medieval Studies* 37 (1975): 340–359.

Esmein, Adhémar. *Le Mariage en droit canonique.* Edited by R. Génestal. 2 vols. Paris, 1929–1935.

Faith, Rosamond J. "Peasant Families and Inheritance Customs in Medieval England." *Agricultural History Review* 4 (1966): 77–95.

Faulkner, P. A. "Domestic Planning from the Twelfth to the Fourteenth Centuries." *Archaeological Journal* 115 (1958): 150–183.

Fell, Christine. *Women in Anglo-Saxon England and the Impact of 1066.* Bloomington, Ind., 1984.

"Fitzstephen's Description of London." In John Stow, *Survey of London,* edited by H. B. Wheatley. London, 1956.

Flandrin, Jean-Louis. *Families in Former Times: Kinship, Household, and Sexuality.* Translated by Richard Southern. Cambridge, 1979.

———. "Mariage tardif et vie sexuelle: discussions et hypothèses de recherche." *Annales d'Histoire Economique et Sociale* 27 (1972): 1351–1378.

———. "Repression and Change in the Sexual Life of Young People in Medieval and Early Modern Times." In *Family and Sexuality in French History,* edited by Robert Wheaton and Tamara K. Hareven, 27–48. Philadelphia, 1980.

———. "Sex in Married Life in the Early Middle Ages: The Church's Teaching and Behavioural Reality." In *Western Sexuality: Practice and Precept in Past and Present Times,* edited by Philippe Ariès and André Béjin, 114–129. London, 1985.

Forster, Robert, and Orest Ranum, eds. *Family and Society: Selections from the Annales.* Baltimore, 1976.

Forsyth, Ilene H. "Children in Early Medieval Art: Ninth Through Twelfth Centuries." *Journal of Psychohistory* 4 (1976): 31–70.

Fox, Levi. "The Honour and Earldom of Leicester." *English History Review* 54 (1939): 385–399.

Fox, Robin. *Kinship and Marriage: An Anthropological Perspective.* Cambridge, 1983.

Freed, John B. *The Counts of Falkenstein: Noble Self-Consciousness in Twelfth-Century Germany.* Philadelphia, 1984.

Freeman, J. D. "On the Concept of the Kindred." *Journal of the Royal Anthropological Institute* 91 (1961): 192–219.

Friedlander, Ludwig. *Roman Life and Manners under the Early Empire.* Translated by Leonard A. Magnus. 4 vols. New York, 1965 (reprint of 1907 edition).

Furnivall, Frederick, ed. *The Babees Book.* New York, 1969 (first published London, 1868).

Fustel de Coulanges, Numa Denis. *The Ancient City.* Translated by Willard Small. New York, 1956.

Gairdner, James, ed. *The Paston Letters,* A.D. *1422–1509.* 6 vols. New

York, 1965 (first published London, 1900, revised 1904).

Galy, Charles. *La Famille à l'époque Mérovingienne, étude faite principalement d'après les récits de Grégoire de Tours*. Paris, 1901.

Ganshof, François. "Le Statut de la femme dans la monarchie franque." *Recueils de la Société Jean Bodin* 12 (1962): 5–58.

Garin le Loherain. Edited by A. Paulin. Paris, 1862.

Genealogiae Comitum Flandriae. In *Patrologia Latina*, edited by J. P. Migne, 209, cols. 929–990. Paris, 1857–1866.

Génicot, Léopold. "Recent Research on the Medieval Nobility." In *The Medieval Nobility: Studies on the Ruling Classes of France and Germany from the Sixth to the Twelfth Century*, edited by Timothy Reuter. 17–35. Amsterdam, 1978.

Gies, Frances. *The Knight in History*. New York, 1984.

Gies, Frances and Joseph. *Women in the Middle Ages*. New York, 1978.

Gies, Joseph and Frances. *Leonard of Pisa and the New Mathematics of the Middle Ages*. New York, 1969.

———. *Life in a Medieval Castle*. New York, 1974.

Giraldus Cambrensis. *Autobiography*. Translated by H. E. Butler. London, 1937.

Girard, René. "Marriage in Avignon in the Second Half of the Fifteenth Century." *Speculum* 28 (1953): 485–498.

Goffart, Walter. *Barbarians and Romans, A.D. 481–584: The Techniques of Accommodation*. Princeton, 1980.

Goldthwaite, Richard. "The Florentine Palace as Domestic Architecture." *American Historical Review* 77 (1972): 977–1012.

Gollancz, Israel, and W. S. Mackie, eds. and trans. *The Exeter Book*. 2 vols. Oxford, 1895 and 1934 (reprinted 1975).

Goodich, Michael. "Bartholomaeus Anglicus on Child Rearing." *History of Childhood Quarterly* 3 (1975): 75–84.

———. "Childhood and Adolescence Among the Thirteenth-Century Saints." *History of Childhood Quarterly* 1 (1973): 285–309.

Goody, Jack, ed. *The Character of Kinship*. London, 1973.

———. *The Development of the Family and Marriage in Europe*. Cambridge, 1983.

———, ed. *Family and Inheritance: Rural Society in Western Europe*. Cambridge, 1976.

Gottfried, Robert S. *The Black Death: Natural and Human Disaster in Medieval Europe*. New York, 1983.

Gottlieb, Beatrice. "The Meaning of Clandestine Marriage." In *Family and Sexuality in French History*, edited by Robert Wheaton and Tamara K. Hareven, 49–83. Philadelphia, 1980.

Gransden, Antonia. "Childhood and Youth in Medieval England." *Nottingham Medieval Studies* 16 (1972): 3–19.

Grant, Michael. *The World of Rome.* New York, 1960.

Green, Mary Ann Everett. *Lives of the Princesses of England.* Vol. 2. London, 1849.

Gregory of Tours. *The History of the Franks.* Translated by Lewis Thorpe. Harmondsworth, 1974.

Guérard, Benjamin, ed. *Cartulaire de l'Abbaye de Saint-Victor de Marseilles.* 2 vols. Paris, 1857.

Gutkind, Curt S. *Cosimo de' Medici, Pater Patriae, 1389–1464.* Oxford, 1938.

Hallett, Judith P. *Fathers and Daughters in Roman Society.* Princeton, 1984.

Halphen, Louis. *Le Comté d'Anjou au XIe siècle.* Paris, 1906.

———. *Etude sur les chroniques des comtes d'Anjou.* Paris, 1906.

———. *Recueil d'annales angevines et vendômoises.* Paris, 1903.

Hammell, Eugene A., and Peter Laslett. "Comparing Household Structure over Time and Between Cultures." *Comparative Studies in Society and History* 16 (1974): 73–109.

Hammer, Carl I., Jr. "Family and *Familia* in Early Medieval Bavaria." In *Family Forms in Historic Europe,* edited by Richard Wall, with Jean Robin and Peter Laslett, 217–248. Cambridge, 1983.

Hanawalt, Barbara A. "Childrearing Among the Lower Classes of Late Medieval England." *Journal of Interdisciplinary History* 8 (1972): 1–22.

———. *The Ties That Bound: Peasant Families in Medieval England.* Oxford, 1986.

Hanham, Alison. *The Celys and Their World.* Cambridge, 1985.

Hareven, Tamara K. "The Family as Process: The Historical Study of the Family Cycle." *Journal of Social History* 7 (1974): 322–329.

———. "The History of the Family as an Interdisciplinary Field." *Journal of Interdisciplinary History* 2 (1971): 399–414.

Harvey, P. D. A. *A Medieval Oxfordshire Village: Cuxham, 1240 to 1400.* Oxford, 1965.

Haskell, Ann S. "The Paston Women on Marriage in Fifteenth-Century England." *Viator* 8 (1973): 459–471.

Heers, J. *Le Clan familial au Moyen Age.* Paris, 1974.

———. "Urbanisme et structure sociale à Gênes au Moyen Age." In *Studi in onore di Amintore Fanfani,* vol. 1, 369–412. Milan, 1962.

Heinzelmann, Martin. "Les Changements de la dénomination latine à la fin de l'antiquité." In *Famille et parenté dans l'Occident médiéval,* edited by Georges Duby and Jacques Le Goff, 19–24. Rome, 1977.

Helmholz, Richard H. "Infanticide in the Province of Canterbury During the Fifteenth Century." *History of Childhood Quarterly* 2 (1975): 379–390.

———. *Marriage Litigation in Medieval England.* Cambridge, 1974.

Herlihy, David. "The Carolingian Mansus." *Economic History Review* 13 (1960): 79–89.

———. *Cities and Society in Medieval Italy*. London, 1980. Articles cited in text:

"Deaths, Marriages, Births, and the Tuscan Economy ca. 1300–1550": 135–163.

"Family and Property in Renaissance Florence": 3–24.

"Some Social and Psychological Roots of Violence in the Tuscan Cities": 129–154.

"Santa Maria Impruneta: a Rural Commune in the Late Middle Ages": 242–276.

"The Tuscan Town in the Quattrocento: a Demographic Profile": 68–81.

———. "Land, Family, and Women in Continental Europe, 701–1200." In *Women in Medieval Society*, edited by Susan Mosher Stuard, 13–45. Philadelphia, 1976.

———. "Life Expectancies for Women in Medieval Society." In *The Role of Woman in the Middle Ages*, edited by Rosemarie Thee Morewedge, 1–22. Albany, New York, 1975.

———. "The Making of the Medieval Family: Symmetry, Structure, and Sentiment." *Journal of Family History* 8 (1983): 116–130.

———. "Mapping Households in Medieval Italy." *Catholic Historical Review* 58 (1972): 1–19.

———. "Medieval Children." In *Essays on Medieval Civilization: The Walter Prescott Webb Memorial Lectures*, edited by B. K. Lackner and K. R. Philip, 109–142. London, 1978.

———. *Medieval Households*. Cambridge, Mass., 1985.

———. "Vieillir à Florence au Quattrocento." *Annales: Economies, Sociétés, Civilisations* 24 (1969): 1338–1354.

———. "Women in Medieval Society." The Smith History Lecture. Houston, Texas, 1971.

Herlihy, David, and Christiane Klapisch-Zuber. *Tuscans and Their Families*. New Haven, 1985.

Hill, Rosalind. "Marriage in Seventh-Century England." In *Saints, Scholars, and Heroes*, edited by M. H. King and W. M. Stevens, 67–75. Minneapolis, 1979.

Hilton, Rodney H. *Bond Men Made Free, Medieval Peasant Movements and the English Rising of 1381*. New York, 1973.

———. *The English Peasantry in the Later Middle Ages*. Oxford, 1975.

———. *A Medieval Society: The West Midlands at the End of the Thirteenth Century*. New York, 1966.

———, ed. *Peasants, Knights, and Heretics: Studies in Medieval English Social History*. Cambridge, 1981.

Hincmar of Reims. *De Divortio Lotharii Regis et Tetbergae Reginae*. In *Patrologia Latina*, edited by J. P. Migne, vol. 125, cols. 619–772. Paris, 1857–1866.

L'Histoire de Guillaume Maréchal. Edited by Paul Meyer. 3 vols. Paris, 1901.

Holmes, George Andrew. *The Estates of the Higher Nobility in Fourteenth-Century England.* Cambridge, 1957.

Holmes, Urban Tigner. "Medieval Children: *L'enfant et la vie familiale sous l'ancien régime* by Philippe Ariès." *Journal of Social History* 2 (1968): 164–172.

Homans, George C. *English Villagers of the Thirteenth Century.* New York, 1975 (reprint of 1941 edition).

Hopkins, Keith. *Conquerors and Slaves: Sociological Studies in Roman History.* Cambridge, 1978.

Hoskins, W. G. *The Midland Peasant: The Economic and Social History of a Leicestershire Village.* London, 1957.

Howell, Cecily. "Peasant Inheritance Customs in the Midlands, 1280–1700." In *Family and Inheritance: Rural Society in Western Europe,* edited by Jack Goody, 112–155. Cambridge, 1976.

Hughes, Diane Owen. "Domestic Ideals and Social Behavior, Evidence from Medieval Genoa," In *The Family in History,* edited by Charles E. Rosenberg, Philadelphia, 1975: 115–143.

———. "From Brideprice to Dowry in Mediterranean Europe." *Journal of Family History* 3 (1978): 262–296.

———. "Kinsmen and Neighbors in Medieval Genoa." In *The Medieval City,* edited by Harry Miskimin, David Herlihy, and A. L. Udovitch, 95–111. New Haven, 1977.

———. "Toward Historical Ethnography: Notarial Records and Family History in the Middle Ages." *Historical Methods Newsletter* 7 (1974): 61–71.

———. "Urban Growth and Family Structure in Medieval Genoa." *Past and Present* 66 (1975): 3–28.

Jones, Philip. "Florentine Families and Florentine Diaries in the Fourteenth Century." *Papers of the British School at Rome* 24 (1956): 183–205.

Karsten, T. E. *Les Anciens Germains.* Paris, 1931.

Kelly, Henry Ansgar. "Clandestine Marriage and Chaucer's 'Troilus.' " *Viator* 4 (1973): 435–457.

Kenkel, William F. "The Ancient Roman Family." In *The Family in Perspective: A Fourfold Analysis.* New York, 1960.

Kenner, Barbara, ed. *The Women of England from Anglo-Saxon Times to the Present.* Hamden, Conn., 1979.

Kent, Francis William. "A la recherche du clan perdu: Jacques Heers and the 'family clans' in the Middle Ages." *Journal of Family History* 2 (1977): 77–86.

Kirshner, Julius. "Wives' Claims Against Insolvent Husbands." In *Women of the Medieval World: Essays in Honor of John H. Mundy,* edited by Julius

Kirshner and Suzanne F. Wemple, 256–303. London, 1985.

Kirshner, Julius, and Anthony Molho. "The Dowry Fund and the Marriage Market in Early Quattrocento Florence." *Journal of Modern History* 50 (1978): 405–438.

Klapisch, Christiane. "Déclin démographique et structure du ménage: l'exemple de Prato, fin XIVe fin XVe." In *Fàmille et parenté dans l'Occident médiéval,* edited by Georges Duby and Jacques Le Goff, 255–268. Rome, 1977.

———. "L'Enfance en Toscane au début du XVe siècle." *Annales de démographie historique,* 1973: 99–127.

———. "La 'mère cruelle': maternité, veuvage, et dot dans la Florence des XIVe–XVe siècles." *Annales: Economies, Sociétés, Civilisations* 38 (1983): 1097–1107.

Klapisch-Zuber, Christiane. *Women, Family, and Ritual in Renaissance Italy.* Chicago, 1985.

Krause, John. "The Medieval Household: Large or Small?" *Economic History Review* 9 (1957): 420–432.

Kroll, Jerome. "The Concept of Childhood in the Middle Ages." *Journal of the History of Behavioural Sciences* 13 (1977): 384–393.

Labarge, Margaret Wade. *A Baronial Household of the Thirteenth Century.* New York, 1966.

———. *Simon de Montfort.* London, 1962.

Lambert of Ardres. *Historia comitum Ghisnensium.* In *Monumenta Germaniae Historica, Scriptores,* edited by G. H. Pertz et al., vol. 24, chap. 127. Hanover, 1826–1913.

Lancaster, Lorraine. "Kinship in Anglo-Saxon Society." *British Journal of Sociology* 9 (1958): 230–250, 359–377.

Langer, William L. "Infanticide: A Historical Survey." *History of Childhood Quarterly* 1 (1974): 353–365.

Langland, William. *The Vision and Creed of Piers Plowman.* Edited by Thomas Wright. London, 1887.

Laslett, Peter. "The Comparative History of Household and Family." *Journal of Social History* 4 (1970): 75–87.

———. "La Famille et le ménage: approches historiques." *Annales: Economies, Sociétés, Civilisations* 27 (1972): 847–872.

———. *Family Life and Illicit Love in Earlier Generations: Essays in Historical Sociology.* Cambridge, 1977.

———. *The World We Have Lost: England Before the Industrial Age.* New York, 1971 (revision of 1965 edition).

Laslett, Peter, and Richard Wall, eds. *Household and Family in Past Time.* Cambridge, 1972.

Latouche, Robert. *Caesar to Charlemagne: The Beginnings of France.* Translated by Jennifer Nicholson. London, 1965.

_____. *Les Grandes invasions et la crise de l'Occident au Ve siècle*. Paris, 1946.

Lautmann, Françoise. "Differences or Changes in Family Organization." In *Family and Society: Selections from the Annales*, edited by Robert Forster and Orest Ranum, 251–261. Baltimore, 1976.

Lecoy de la Marche, A. *La Chaire française au moyen âge*. Paris, 1886.

Lefkowitz, Mary R., and Maureen B. Fant. *Women's Life in Greece and Rome: A Source Book in Translation*. Baltimore, 1982.

Lemay, Helen R. "Antonius Guainerius and Medieval Gynecology." In *Women of the Medieval World: Essays in Honor of John H. Mundy*, edited by Julius Kirshner and Suzanne F. Wemple, 317–336. London, 1985.

Le Play, Frédéric. *L'Organisation de la famille selon le vrai modèle signalé par l'histoire de toutes les races et tous les temps*. Paris, 1871.

Le Roy Ladurie, Emmanuel. *Montaillou, the Promised Land of Error*. Translated by Barbara Bray. New York, 1978.

Letters from Petrarch. Translated by Morris Bishop. Bloomington, Ind., 1966.

Levy, Marion, Jr. "Aspects of the Analysis of Family Structure." In *Aspects of the Analysis of Family Structure*, edited by Ansley J. Coale et al., 1–63. Princeton, 1965.

Lewis, A. R. *The Development of Southern French and Catalan Society, 718–1050*. Austin, 1965.

Leyser, K. T. "The German Aristocracy from the Ninth to the Early Twelfth Century." *Past and Present* 41 (1968): 25–53.

_____. "Maternal Kin in Early Medieval Germany, a Reply." *Past and Present* 49 (1970), pp. 126–134.

_____. *Rule and Conflict in an Early Medieval Society, Ottonian Saxony*. London, 1979.

Il Libro degli affari proprii di casa di Lapo di Giovanni Niccolini de' Sirigatti. Edited by Christian Bec. Paris, 1969.

The Life of St. Anselm, Archbishop of Canterbury (Eadmeri monachi cantuarensis Vita Sancti Anselmi archiepiscopi cantuarensis). Edited and translated by R. W. Southern. London, 1962.

Loengard, Janet S. " 'Of the Gift of Her Husband': English Dower and Its Consequences in the Year 1200." In *Women of the Medieval World: Essays in Honor of John H. Mundy*, edited by Julius Kirshner and Suzanne F. Wemple, 215–255. London 1985.

Lopez, Manuel D. "A Guide to the Interdisciplinary Literature of the History of Childhood." *History of Childhood Quarterly* 1 (1974): 463–494.

Loyn, H. R. "Kinship in Anglo-Saxon England." *Anglo-Saxon England* 3 (1973): 197–209.

Lyman, Richard B., Jr. "Barbarism and Religion: Late Roman and Early

Medieval Childhood." In *History of Childhood,* edited by Lloyd DeMause, 75–99. London, 1976.

Lynch, Joseph H. "Hugh I of Cluny's Sponsorship of Henry IV: Its Context and Consequences." *Speculum* 60 (1985): 800–826.

McFarlane, Kenneth B. *The Nobility of Late Medieval England.* Oxford, 1973.

McLaughlin, Mary Martin. "Survivors and Surrogates: Children and Parents from the Ninth to the Thirteenth Centuries." In *History of Childhood,* edited by Lloyd DeMause, 101–181. London, 1976.

McNamara, Jo Ann, and Suzanne F. Wemple. "Marriage and Divorce in the Frankish Kingdom." In *Women in Medieval Society,* edited by Susan Mosher Stuard, 95–124. Philadelphia, 1976.

———. "The Power of Women Through the Family in Medieval Europe, 500–1100." In *Clio's Consciousness Raised: New Perspectives in the History of Women,* edited by Mary Hartman and Lois W. Banner, 103–118. New York, 1974.

McNeill, J. T., and H. M. Gamer, *Medieval Handbooks of Penance.* New York, 1965.

Magna Vita Sancti Hugonis. Edited by D. L. Dowie and Hugh Farmer. 2 vols. London, 1961–1962.

Maitland, Frederic William. *Domesday Book and Beyond: Three Essays in the Early History of England.* New York, 1966 (reprint of 1897 edition).

Manselli, Raoul. "Vie familiale et éthique sexuelle dans les pénitentiels." In *Famille et parenté dans l'Occident médiéval,* edited by Georges Duby and Jacques Le Goff, 363–382. Rome, 1977.

Martindale, Jane. "The French Aristocracy in the Early Middle Ages: A Reappraisal." *Past and Present* 75 (1977): 5–45.

The Metalogicon of John of Salisbury: A Twelfth-Century Defense of the Verbal and Logical Arts of the Trivium. Translated by Daniel D. McGarry. Berkeley, 1955.

Middle English Sermons. Edited by Woodburn O. Ross. London, 1940.

Milden, James Wallace. *The Family in Past Time: A Guide to the Literature.* New York, 1977.

Miskimin, Harry A. *The Economy of Early Renaissance Europe, 1300–1460.* Englewood Cliffs, N.J., 1969.

Mitterauer, Michael, and Reinhard Sieder. *The European Family: Patriarchy to Partnership from the Middle Ages to the Present.* Translated by Karla Oosterveen and Manfred Horzinger. Chicago, 1982.

Mogey, J. M. "Residence, Family, Kinship: Some Recent Research." *Journal of Family History* 1 (1976): 95–109.

The Monastic Constitutions of Lanfranc. Edited and translated by David Knowles. New York, 1951.

Murray, A. V. "Religion Among the Poor in Thirteenth-Century

France: The Testimony of Humbert de Romans." *Traditio* 30 (1974): 285–324.

Musset, Lucien. *The Germanic Invasions: The Making of Europe* A.D. *400–600.* Translated by Edward and Columba James. London, 1975.

Niccolini da Camugliano, G. "A Medieval Florentine, His Family and His Possessions." *American Historical Review* 31 (1925): 1–19.

Nicholas, David. *The Domestic Life of a Medieval City: Women, Children, and the Family in Fourteenth-Century Ghent.* Lincoln, Nebr., 1985.

Nisbet, R. A. "Kinship and Political Power in First-Century Rome." In *Sociology and History,* edited by W. J. Cahnman and A. Bostoff, 257–271. New York, 1964.

Noonan, John T., Jr. *Contraception: A History of Its Treatment by the Catholic Theologians and Canonists.* Cambridge, Mass., 1965.

———. "Power to Choose." *Viator* 4 (1973): 419–434.

Norgate, Kate. *The Minority of Henry III.* London, 1912.

Opler, Marvin K. "History of the Family as a Social and Cultural Institution." In *The Family in Contemporary Society,* edited by Iago Galdston, 23–38. New York, 1958.

Origo, Iris. "The Domestic Enemy: The Eastern Slaves in Tuscany in the Fourteenth and Fifteenth Centuries." *Speculum* 30 (1955): 321–366.

———. *The Merchant of Prato: Francesco di Marco Datini, 1335–1410.* Boston, 1986 (reprint of 1957 edition).

———. *The World of San Bernardino.* New York, 1962.

Owst, G. R. *Literature and Pulpit in Medieval England.* Oxford, 1961.

Ozment, Steven. *When Fathers Ruled: Family Life in Reformation Europe.* Cambridge, Mass., 1983.

Pantin, W. A. *The English Church in the Fourteenth Century.* Cambridge, 1955.

Paris, Matthew. *English History from the Year 1235 to 1273 (Chronica Majora).* Translated by J. A. Giles. London, 1854.

Pimsler, Martin. "Solidarity in the Medieval Village? The Evidence of Personal Pledging at Elton, Huntingdonshire." *Journal of British Studies* 17 (1977): 1–11.

Pollock, F., and F. W. Maitland. *The History of English Law Before the Time of Edward I.* 2nd. ed. 2 vols. Cambridge, 1968.

Pollock, Linda A. *Forgotten Children: Parent-Child Relations from 1500 to 1900.* Cambridge, 1983.

Pomeroy, Sarah. *Goddesses, Whores, Wives, and Slaves: Women in Classical Antiquity.* New York, 1975.

Poupardin, René. "Généalogies angevines du xie siècle." *Mélanges d'archéologie et d'histoire de l'école française de Rome* 20 (1900): 199–208.

Powicke, F. M. "Guy de Montfort (1265–71)." *Transactions of the Royal*

Historical Society, ser. 4, 18 (1935): 1–23.

Prothero, George Walter. *The Life of Simon de Montfort, Earl of Leicester*. London, 1877.

Raftis, J. A. "Changes in an English Village after the Black Death." *Medieval Studies* 29 (1967): 158–177.

———. "Social Structures in Five East Midland Villages: A Study of Possibilities in the Use of Court Roll Data." *Economic History Review*, 2nd ser., 18 (1965): 83–100.

———. *Tenure and Mobility: Studies in the Social History of the Mediaeval English Village*. Toronto, 1964.

———. *Warboys: Two Hundred Years in the Life of an English Mediaeval Village*. Toronto, 1974.

———, ed. *Pathways to Medieval Peasants*. Toronto, 1981.

Razi, Zvi. "The Erosion of the Family Land Bond in the Late Fourteenth and Fifteenth Centuries: A Methodological Note." In *Land, Kinship, and Life Cycle*, edited by R. M. Smith, 295–304. Cambridge, 1986.

———. *Life, Death, and Marriage in a Medieval Parish: Economy, Society, and Demography in Halesowen, 1270–1400*. Cambridge, 1980.

Reuter, Timothy, ed. and trans. *The Medieval Nobility: Studies on the Ruling Classes of France and Germany from the Sixth to the Twelfth Century*. Amsterdam, 1978.

Riché, Pierre. *Daily Life in the World of Charlemagne*. Translated by Jo Ann McNamara. Philadelphia, 1978.

———. *Education and Culture in the Barbarian West, Sixth Through Eighth Centuries*. Translated by John J. Contreni. Columbia, S.C., 1976.

Ring, Richard R. "Early Medieval Peasant Households in Central Italy." *Journal of Family History* 4 (1979): 2–21.

Robertson, A. J. *Anglo-Saxon Charters*. Cambridge, 1956.

Li Romans de Garin le Loherain. 2 vols. Paris, 1832–1848 (reprinted Geneva, 1969).

Roncière, Charles M. de la. "Une famille florentine au XIVe siècle: les Velluti." In *Famille et parenté dans l'Occident médiéval*, edited by Georges Duby and Jacques Le Goff, 227–248. Rome, 1977.

Rosenberg, Charles E., ed. *The Family in History*. Philadelphia, 1975.

Rosenthal, Joel T. "Marriage and the Blood Feud in 'Heroic' Europe." *British Journal of Sociology* 17 (1966): 133–144.

Ross, James Bruce. "The Middle Class Child in Urban Italy, Fourteenth to Early Sixteenth Century." In *The History of Childhood*, edited by Lloyd DeMause, 183–228. London, 1976.

Rossiaud, Jacques. "Prostitution, Sex, and Society in French Towns in the Fifteenth Century." In *Western Sexuality: Practice and Precept in Past and Present Times*, edited by Philippe Ariès and André Béjin, 76–94. London, 1985.

Rostovtzeff, Michael. *The Social and Economic History of the Roman Empire.* 2 vols. Oxford, 1957.

Russell, Josiah Cox. *Late Ancient and Medieval Population Control.* Philadelphia, 1985.

Salu, M. B., ed. and trans. *The Ancrene Riwle (The Corpus MS: Ancrene Wisse).* London, 1955.

Sawyer, P. H. *Anglo-Saxon Charters.* London, 1968.

Scammell, Jean. "Freedom and Marriage in Medieval England." *Economic History Review* 27 (1974): 523–537.

Schevill, Ferdinand. *The Medici.* New York, 1949.

Schmid, Karl. "Neue Quellen zum Verständnis des Adels im 10. Jahrhundert." *Zeitschrift für die Geschichte des Oberrheins* 108 (1960): 185–232.

_____. "The Structure of the Nobility in the Earlier Middle Ages." In *The Medieval Nobility*, edited and translated by Timothy Reuter, 37–59. Amsterdam, 1978.

_____. "Zur Problematik von Familie, Sippe und Geschlecht, Haus und Dynastie beim mittelalterlichen Adel, Vorfragen zum Thema." *Zeitschrift für die Geschichte des Oberrheins* 105 (1957): 1–62.

Searle, Eleanor. "Seigneurial Control of Women's Marriage: The Antecedents and Function of Merchet in England." *Past and Present* 82 (1979): 3–43.

Self and Society in Medieval France: The Memoirs of Abbot Guibert of Nogent. Edited by John F. Benton. New York, 1970.

Sheehan, Michael M. "Choice of Marriage Partner in the Middle Ages: Development and Mode of Application of a Theory of Marriage." *Studies in Medieval and Renaissance History* 11 (1978): 4–15.

_____. "The Formation and Stability of Marriage in Fourteenth-Century England: Evidence of an Ely Register." *Medieval Studies* 32 (1971): 228–263.

Sheehan, Michael, and Kathy Scardellato. *Family and Marriage in Medieval Europe: A Working Bibliography.* Vancouver, 1976.

Shore, Miles F. "The Child and Historiography." *Journal of Interdisciplinary History* 6 (1976): 495–505.

Shorter, Edward. *The Making of the Modern Family.* New York, 1975.

Sisam, Kenneth. "Anglo-Saxon Royal Genealogies." *Proceedings of the British Academy* 39 (1953): 287–346.

Smith, R. M. "Families and Their Land in an Area of Partible Inheritance: Redgrave, Suffolk, 1260–1320." In *Land, Kinship, and Life Cycle*, edited by R. M. Smith, 135–195. Cambridge, 1986.

_____. "Kin and Neighbours in a Thirteenth-Century Suffolk Community." *Journal of Family History* 4 (1979): 219–256.

———, ed. *Land, Kinship, and Life Cycle*. Cambridge, 1986.

Somerville, C. John. "Toward a History of Childhood and Youth." *Journal of Interdisciplinary History* 3 (1972): 439–447.

Stafford, Pauline. *Queens, Concubines, and Dowagers: The King's Wife in the Early Middle Ages*. Athens, Ga., 1983.

———. "Sons and Mothers: Family Politics in the Early Middle Ages." In *Medieval Women*, edited by Derek Baker, 79–100. Oxford, 1978.

Stearns, Peter N. and Carol Z. "Emotionology: Clarifying the History of Emotions and Emotional Standards." *American Historical Review* 90 (1985): 813–836.

Stevenson, Kenneth. *Nuptial Blessings: A Study of Christian Marriage Rites*. New York, 1983.

Stone, Lawrence. *The Family, Sex, and Marriage in England, 1500–1800*. New York, 1979.

Stuard, Susan Mosher, ed. *Women in Medieval Society*. Philadelphia, 1976.

Stuckert, Howard M. *Corrodies in the English Monasteries: A Study in English Social History of the Middle Ages*. Philadelphia, 1923.

Suetonius. *The Lives of the Twelve Caesars*. Edited by Joseph Gavorse. New York, 1931.

Tacitus. *The Agricola and the Germania*. Translated by H. Mattingly, revised by S. A. Handford. Harmondsworth, 1948.

Tavard, George H. *Women in Christian Tradition*. Notre Dame, Ind., 1973.

Thirsk, Joan. "The Common Fields." *Past and Present* 29 (1964): 11–14.

———. "The Family." *Past and Present* 27 (1964): 116–122.

Thompson, Edward Arthur. *The Visigoths in the Time of Ulfila*. Oxford, 1966.

Thompson, E. P. "Happy Families: Review of Lawrence Stone, *The Family, Sex, and Marriage in England, 1500–1800*." *New Society* 1977: 499–501.

Thrupp, Sylvia L., ed. *Early Medieval Society*. New York, 1967.

———. *The Merchant Class of Medieval London*. Ann Arbor, 1948.

Todd, Malcolm. *Everyday Life of the Barbarians: Goths, Franks, and Vandals*. London, 1972.

Trexler, Richard C. "The Foundlings of Florence, 1395–1455." *History of Childhood Quarterly* 1 (1973): 259–284.

———. "Infanticide in Florence: New Sources and First Results." *History of Childhood Quarterly* 1 (1973): 98–116.

Trumbach, Randolf. "Europe and Its Families: A Review Essay of Lawrence Stone, *The Family, Sex, and Marriage in England, 1500–1800*." *Journal of Social History* 13 (1976): 136–143.

Vercauteren, Ferdinand. "A Kindred in Northern France in the Eleventh and Twelfth Centuries." In *The Medieval Nobility*, edited and translated by Timothy Reuter, 87–103. Amsterdam, 1978.

Veyne, Paul. "Homosexuality in Ancient Rome." In *Western Sexuality: Practice and Precept in Past and Present Times,* edited by Philippe Ariès and André Béjin, 26–35. London, 1985.

Walker, Sue Sheridan. "Widow and Ward: The Feudal Law of Child Custody in Medieval England." In *Women in Medieval Society,* edited by Susan Mosher Stuard, 159–172. Philadelphia, 1976.

Watkins, Renée Neu. *The Family in Renaissance Florence* (translation of Leon Battista Alberti, *I Libri della Famiglia*). Columbia, S. C., 1969.

————. "Petrarch and the Black Death: From Fear to Monuments." *Studies in the Renaissance* 19–20 (1972–1973): 196–220.

Wemple, Suzanne Fonay. *Women in Frankish Society: Marriage and the Cloister, 500 to 900.* Philadelphia, 1981.

Weinberger, Stephen. "Peasant Households in Provence: c. 800–1100." *Speculum* 48 (1973): 247–257.

Werner, Karl Ferdinand. "Important Noble Families in the Kingdom of Charlemagne—A Prosopographical Study of the Relationship Between King and Nobility in the Early Middle Ages." In *The Medieval Nobility,* edited and translated by Timothy Reuter, 137–185. Amsterdam, 1978.

————. "Liens de parenté et noms de personne: un problème historique et méthodologique." In *Famille et parenté dans l'Occident médiéval,* edited by Georges Duby and Jacques Le Goff, 24–34. Rome, 1977.

Wheaton, Robert. "Family and Kinship in Western Europe: The Problem of the Joint Family Household." *Journal of Interdisciplinary History* 5 (1975): 601–628.

Wheaton, Robert, and Tamara K. Hareven, eds. *Family and Sexuality in French History.* Philadelphia, 1980.

White, T. H., trans. *The Book of Beasts.* New York, 1960.

Whitelock, Dorothy. *The Beginnings of English Society.* London, 1952.

————, ed. *English Historical Documents,* vol. 1, c. 500–1042. New York, 1968.

Williamson, Craig, trans. and ed. *A Feast of Creatures: Anglo-Saxon Riddle-Songs.* Philadelphia, 1982.

Wollasch, Joachim. "Eine adlige Familie des frühen Mittelalters." *Archiv für Kulturgeschichte* 39 (1957): 150–188.

Worship, Francis. "Account of a MS Genealogy of the Paston Family." *Norfolk Archaeology* 4 (1855): 1–55.

Ziegler, Philip. *The Black Death.* London, 1969.

Index

References to illustrations are in italics.

371

Insights,
Interviews
& More . . .

Meet Joseph and Frances Gies

JOSEPH GIES (1916–2006) and FRANCES GIES (1915–2013) were writers and medieval historians. They both graduated from the University of Michigan, Frances in 1937 and Joseph in 1939. In 1940 they married, and following careers spent in the film and magazine industries, respectively, they found their calling as historians in 1969 when they published *Life in a Medieval City*. Over the coming decades, the Gieses together and separately wrote eleven books on medieval history for both scholarly and popular audiences, including *Life in a Medieval Castle*, *Life in a Medieval Village*, and *The Knight in History*. Known for their collaborative writing process and cogent synthesis of vast swaths of historical material, the Gieses' books appear on numerous university syllabi. Their work has also had broad popular and cultural appeal and its influence continues to this day—both *Life in a Medieval Castle* and *Life in a Medieval City*, for instance, were identified by George R. R. Martin as primary sources for his Song of Ice and Fire series, the basis of the *Game of Thrones* television series. ～

Disasters
An Excerpt from *Life in a Medieval City*

Medieval cities were ill prepared for a variety of natural disasters. This excerpt from Life in a Medieval City *by Joseph and Frances Gies describes three catastrophes that hit Troyes in a single decade in the twelfth century: the worst flood in city history to date, a dreadful crop failure, and a fire that destroyed much of downtown.*

FEW TROYENS ALIVE in 1250 remember the decade of the 1180s, but everybody has heard tales of it. In a space of eight years three of the five major disasters that commonly befall medieval cities struck Troyes. In 1180 the Seine overflowed its banks in the worst flood recorded in the city's annals, inundating streets and houses and taking a heavy toll of people and animals. Four years later a crop failure in Champagne resulted in one of the worst famines the city has ever experienced. Finally, one night in 1188 fire broke out in the fair quarter near the Abbey of Notre-Dame-aux-Nonnains, crossed the canal to the old *cité*, gutted the cathedral and the new church of St.-Etienne, damaged the count's palace, razed the public baths, destroyed hundreds of houses, and consumed thousands of pounds' worth of fair merchandise.

Precautions against these recurring disasters are totally inadequate. Crop ▶

Disasters *(continued)*

surpluses are never enough to make possible a rational system of storage. Even great lords cannot put aside enough grain to carry them through a famine. The Lord of Brienne, scion of a famous Crusading family, was reduced by the famine of 1184 to robbing the Abbey of St.-Loup, something, he confessed later, "which I ought not to have done, but it was to provision my castle."

The first effects of a food shortage are rumors, hoarding, and black-marketing. The prices of both grain and bread are regulated in ordinary times, and even the size and weight of the round loaf. But bakers have many tricks for reducing the actual content of the standard loaf, and when grain is in short supply they are not slow to use them. Worse than the bakers are the speculators, who evade laws limiting the amount of grain a single individual can purchase, and who illegally buy up from farmers before the grain reaches the city market. The council and the provost may take extraordinary measures, and if the shortage is severe and prolonged, speculators dangle from the gallows. During a famine the clergy parade the relics of the cathedral. The knot of beggars at the church door grows into a crowd, and churchgoers must force their way through the whining, hand-stretching throng of men, women and children.

Famine is often accompanied by its sister, pestilence. Even a merely severe winter often leaves a city population prey to mysterious maladies, such as the scurvy that decimated St.-Louis' Crusading army in Egypt. Epidemic afflictions of skin, mouth, lungs, and other organs, such as that chronicled by Sigebert de Gembloux in Champagne and Flanders in 1089, recur unpredictably. The fourteenth century will experience a visitation of the Black Plague beside which all previous contagions will seem mild.

As for floods, inland Troyes is lucky in comparison with cities situated on larger rivers or in exposed coastal regions. The cities of the medieval Netherlands undergo repeated devastation despite their dikes. Once a storm finds a weak or low dike, the reciprocal flow of the tides through the hole swiftly widens the gap. The death toll for one thirteenth-century Dutch flood is more than fifty thousand.

4

Open-flame illumination and heating make fire a year-round hazard in every section of town. The cheek-by-jowl timber-frame dwellings and shops, sometimes sharing party walls, form a perfect avenue for the flames. Householders are theoretically forbidden to have straw roofs or wooden chimneys, but even these elementary precautions are hard to enforce. An effective measure, stone party walls, has been thought of, but only the rich can afford to build in stone. Buckets of sand and tubs of water quench many fires in early stages, but once furnishings, floors, and partitions take flame little can be done except to pray, and form a bucket brigade—measures about equally effective. If the season is wet and the wind from the right direction, damage may be limited to a few houses or a single street. If the season is dry and the wind fresh and contrary, a large part of a city may be doomed.

The chronicle that records the fire of 1188 gives few details except for the fact that the Devil made an appearance in Troyes shortly beforehand, and was exorcised by a priest with a vial of holy water. But a vivid account of a fire of the same era is that of Gervaise, a monk of Canterbury, in 1174:

At about the ninth hour, during an extraordinarily violent south wind, a fire broke out . . . by which three houses were half-destroyed. While the citizens were assembling and bringing the fire under control, cinders and sparks carried aloft by the wind were deposited upon the church, and being driven between the joints of the lead roof, remained there among the old timber rafters, to which they soon set fire; from these the fire was communicated to the larger beams and braces, no one yet perceiving. . . .

But beams and braces burning, the flames rose to the slopes of the roof; and the sheets of lead yielded to the increasing heat and began to melt. Thus the raging wind, finding a freer entrance, increased the fury of the fire; and the flames beginning to show themselves, a cry arose in the churchyard: "The church is on fire!"

Then the people and the monks assemble in haste, they draw water, they brandish their hatchets, they run up the ▶

stairs, full of eagerness to save the church, already, alas, beyond help. When they reach the roof and perceive the black smoke and scorching flames that pervade it throughout, they abandon the attempt in despair, and thinking only of their own safety, make all haste to descend.

And now that the fire had loosened the beams from the pegs that bound them together, the half-burnt timbers fell into the choir below upon the seats of the monks; the seats, consisting of a great mass of woodwork, caught fire, and thus the mischief grew worse and worse. . . .

And now the people ran to the ornaments of the church, and began to tear down the *pallia* and curtains, some that they might save, some to steal them. The reliquary chests were thrown down from the high beam and thus broken, and their contents scattered; but the monks collected them and carefully preserved them against the fire. . . .

Not only was the choir consumed in the fire, but also the infirmary, with the chapel of St. Mary, and several other offices in the court; moreover many ornaments and goods of the church were reduced to ashes.

Besides these peacetime calamities, there is always the possibility of war. Here at least people in the city enjoy an advantage over the peasants in the villages. When the feudal army rides, it sets fire to everything it cannot carry off, but the walls of a city like Troyes are nearly always proof against such depredations. The besieging army of Hugo of La Marche and Peter of Brittany was easily held at bay outside Troyes in 1230. Even an enemy armed with a formidable array of siege engines and missile weapons has a difficult time breaking into a walled city. A feudal army can rarely be kept in the field longer than a month or two. The military obligation of vassals does not extend further, and mercenary troops are too expensive for any but a very wealthy prince bent on a highly important objective, such as a Crusade. Ordinarily, the attacker must within the limits of a short campaign muster either an overwhelming assault force to scale the walls at many points simultaneously, or a powerful enough battery of siege engines to knock down walls or gates. He has a third alternative, if the ground is favorable, and if the defense is insufficiently alert: mining.

The overwhelming assault force may prevail when the stronghold under attack is a castle with a weak garrison. A tightly packed city of ten thousand citizens, like Troyes, is unlikely to succumb even to a very large storming party, because there are enough men night and day to keep an alert guard at every point of the two-thousand-yard rampart. When the assault force approaches, under cover of a "castle," or movable wooden platform, to fill in the ditch around the walls and plant scaling ladders, the garrison can quickly concentrate at the threatened point or points. Lofty walls, and especially round towers, give the defenders all the advantage in the contest of arrows, bolts, and missiles. Combustibles can be flung down on the attackers' castle, and even if some of the storming party gain a foothold on the wall, they can be isolated by the fire from the neighboring towers, for the space in front of the wall is always kept clear of any cover. The towers project, so that they can bring flanking fire to bear on attackers scaling the wall.

The old-fashioned Roman siege engines have been much improved. The Romans employed only tension and torsion as motive power. Medieval military engineers have added the counterweight, which provides both more power and greater accuracy. A trebuchet, or counterweight engine, consists of a long firing pole balanced on a pivot, or cross-pole, in turn mounted on a pair of uprights. The firing pole is not set on its midpoint, but on a point about a quarter from its butt end, which is faced toward the enemy. The long end is pulled down, the missile placed in a cavity or sling, and secured by a wooden catch worked by a winch, while the butt end is loaded with wedge-shaped weights of iron or stone. When the catch is released, the counterweight drops, sending the missile flying. On more sophisticated models, the counterweight can be moved closer or farther from the pivot, increasing or decreasing the range. A couple of zeroing-in shots permit a good engineer to fire with considerable accuracy. The missile is ordinarily a heavy stone, though variants include combustible materials and ▶

Disasters *(continued)*

occasionally the heads of enemies. Some military experts prefer a simpler model of counterweight engine, worked by ropes pulled down by men. This is inferior in range and accuracy, but it has the advantage of being highly maneuverable, so that several may be quickly brought to bear on a single weak point in the enemy's defenses.

Artillery, however, is no monopoly of the attackers. In the crypts of the towers of Troyes' ramparts, a great number of dismantled engines stand ready for assembly, together with a supply of stone ammunition.

How effective catapult artillery is against a stone wall depends on the wall. Some old walls, made of a thin shell of rough-cut stone covering an earth core, can be battered to pieces. But a good modern wall, laid in even courses locked into a rubble core, can defy all the engines an enemy can bring to bear, as has been repeatedly demonstrated by the redoubtable though weakly garrisoned Crusader forts in Syria.

The attackers' third alternative, mining, is the most promising, provided soft ground can be found. Against a castle it is particularly effective, because the mine can be driven under either a section of the wall or under the main keep. No explosive is involved—the mine is "discharged" simply by setting fire to the timbering which supports the mine roof. As the timbers burn, the ground above collapses. At one siege in Syria the Saracen engineers first undermined and collapsed a tower in the curtain wall. But the garrison, composed of Knights of St. John, successfully fought off the subsequent assault and reestablished the barricade in the rubble of the tower. The Saracens then dug a mine into the interior of the castle, directly under the keep, and invited the Franks to send their own engineers to inspect it. When the Frankish engineers reported back that the discharge of the mine would cause the certain collapse of the keep, the Knights agreed to surrender on terms—marching out and abandoning the castle to the Saracens.

The proper defense against the mine is the countermine. Ten years ago a memorable duel of mine and countermine took place between defending and attacking engineers at Carcassonne. The seneschal of the city, William des Ormes, reported that the Albigensian rebels, under Raymond Trencavel, viscount of Béziers, found their siege artillery of little avail and so switched to mining.

The rebels began a mine against the barbican [fortified tower] of the gate of Narbonne [wrote the seneschal]. And forthwith we, having heard the noise of their work underground, made a countermine, and constructed in the inside of the barbican a great and strong wall of stones . . . so that we retained full half the barbican when they set fire to the hole so that when the wood burned a portion of the front of the barbican fell.

They then began to mine against another turret. . . . We countermined, and got possession of the hole which they had excavated. They began therefore to run a mine between us and a certain wall and destroyed two embrasures. . . . But we set up there a good and strong palisade between us and them.

They also started a mine at the angle of the town wall, near the bishop's palace, and by dint of digging from a great way off they arrived at a certain wall . . . but when we detected it we made a good and strong palisade between them and us, higher up, and countermined. Thereupon they fired their mine and flung down some ten fathoms of our embrasured front. But we made hastily another good palisade with a brattice and loopholes, so none among them dared to come near us in that quarter.

They began also a mine against the barbican of the Rodez gate, and kept below ground, wishing to arrive at our walls, making a marvelous great tunnel. But when we perceived it we forthwith made a palisade on one side and the other of it. We countermined also, and having fallen in with them, carried the chamber of their mine.

Altogether the assailants drove seven different mines, starting from the cellars of houses in the suburb outside. A ▶

Disasters *(continued)*

final attempt to storm the barbican failed, and the approach of a
royal relieving army forced Trencavel to raise the siege.

This was an exceptionally determined effort. In the
skirmishing warfare more normal in the thirteenth century,
a walled city can usually assure its safety merely by closing its
gates on the approach of an enemy force. ⟋∿

*Siege of a City. Sketch by Viollet-le-Duc, who restored the fortified
medieval city of Carcassonne, shows how the assailant succeeded in
collapsing the outer wall of the city by digging a "mine" under it, then
setting fire to the timbering. The defenders countered by hastily erecting
a timber fortification inside the breach.*

Have You Read?
More by Joseph and Frances Gies

LIFE IN A MEDIEVAL CASTLE
by Joseph and Frances Gies

A widely respected academic work and a source for George R. R. Martin's *A Game of Thrones*, Joseph and Frances Gies's *Life in a Medieval Castle* was a bestseller in its day and remains a timeless work of popular medieval scholarship. Focusing on Chepstow, an English castle that survived a turbulent period with a relative lack of violence, the book offers an exquisite portrait of what day-to-day life was actually like in the Middle Ages and of the key role the castle played during the era. The Gieses take us through the full cycle of a medieval year, dictated by the rhythms of the harvest. We learn what lords and serfs alike would have worn, eaten, and done for leisure, and of the outside threats the castle always hoped to keep at bay. This reissue of the Gieses' classic remains the definitive work on this subject.

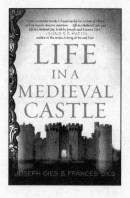

"The authors allow medieval man and woman to speak for themselves through selections from past journals, songs, even account books."   *—Time*

"The Gieses succeed in making a remote and unfamiliar world accessible."
                                        —Kirkus Reviews

Have You Read? *(continued)*

LIFE IN A MEDIEVAL CITY
by Joseph and Frances Gies
....

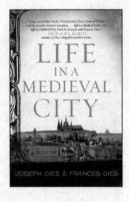

Life in a Medieval City evokes every aspect of city life in the Middle Ages by detailing what it was like to live in a prosperous city of Northwest Europe in the twelfth and thirteenth centuries. The time is AD 1250 and the city is Troyes, capital of the county of Champagne and site of two of the cycle of Champagne Fairs—the "Hot Fair" in August and the "Cold Fair" in December. European civilization has emerged from the Dark Ages and is in the midst of the Commercial Revolution. Merchants and moneymen from all over Europe gather at Troyes to buy, sell, borrow, and lend, creating a bustling market center typical of the feudal era.

"An excellently written account of what is known of the life of medieval burghers. . . . A delightful introduction to the subject."   —*Library Journal*

"A pleasing narrative about life and death, midwives and funerals, business, books, and authors, and town government."   —*Choice*

LIFE IN A MEDIEVAL VILLAGE
by Frances and Joseph Gies

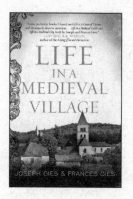

In this lively, detailed picture of village life in the Middle Ages, Frances and Joseph Gies have combined the recent discoveries of archaeology with information from contemporary documents to create an enjoyable and convincing portrait of rural people at work and at play seven hundred years ago. Focusing on the village of Elton, in the English East Midlands, the authors show medieval peasants not merely as tenants and elements in the manorial system, but as members of a village community, who plant their own fields and those of their lord, administer village affairs, and relate to one another in ways that surprisingly transcend their status as "free" or "villain." The authors describe the peasants' food, housing, and family life; the threatening tensions between them and the lord of the manor; and the place of the church in their lives. Though the main focus is on Elton, c. 1300, the Gieses supply enlightening historical context in an account of the origin, development, and decline of the European village, itself an invention of the Middle Ages

"A precisely drawn study of the vigorous character of a thirteenth-century English village." —*Kirkus Reviews*

Have You Read? *(continued)*

THE KNIGHT IN HISTORY
by Frances Gies

Born out of the chaos of the early
Middle Ages, the armored and highly
mobile knight revolutionized warfare
and quickly became a mythic figure
in history. From the Knights Templars
and English knighthood to the Crusades
and chivalry, *The Knight in History*
paints a remarkable true picture of
knighthood—exploring the knight's
earliest appearance as an agent of lawless
violence, his reemergence as a dynamic
social entity, his eventual disappearance
from the European stage, and his
transformation into Western culture's
most iconic hero.

"Splendid. . . . This detailed look,
focusing as it often does on individual
men, shows the knight in a new and
more interesting light, whether Roland
or Galahad."   —*Washington Post*

"Gies's writing is fresh and direct, her
scholarship is exact, and she approaches
her subject with excitement."
                                —*The New Yorker*

CATHEDRAL, FORGE, AND WATERWHEEL
by Frances and Joseph Gies

In this account of Europe's rise to world leadership in technology, Frances and Joseph Gies make use of recent scholarship to show how early modern technology and experimental science were direct outgrowths of the decisive innovations of medieval Europe, in the tools and techniques of agriculture, craft industry, metallurgy, building construction, navigation, and war. The Gieses report that many of Europe's most important inventions—the horse harness, the stirrup, the magnetic compass, cotton and silk cultivation and manufacture, papermaking, firearms, and "Arabic" numerals—had their origins outside Europe, in China, India, and Middle East. Europe synthesized its own innovations—the three-field system, water power in industry, the full-rigged ship, the putting-out system—into a powerful new combination of technology, economics, and politics. *Cathedral, Forge, and Waterwheel* is illustrated with more than ninety photographs and drawings.

"Explodes the myth of the Dark Ages, showing that the Fall of Rome did not plunge Europe into stagnation and lethargy."
                                                    —*Booklist*